CITIZENSHIP AND THE LAW
SERIES

General Editor
ROBERT BLACKBURN
Professor of Constitutional Law
King's College, University of London

Other titles in this series

JUDICIAL REVIEW AND SOCIAL WELFARE

Edited by

TREVOR BUCK

PINTER
London and Washington

First published 1998 by
Pinter, A Cassell Imprint
Wellington House, 125 Strand, London WC2R 0BB, England
PO Box 605, Herndon, Virginia 20172, USA

British Library Cataloguing in Publication Data
A catalogue record for this book is available from the British Library.

ISBN 1-85567-422-X

Library of Congress Cataloguing-in-Publication Data
Judicial review and social welfare / edited by Trevor Buck.
    p.   cm. − (Citizenship and the law)
Includes bibliographical references and index.
ISBN 1-85567-422-X (hardcover)
    1. Judicial review of administrative acts − Great Britain.
2. Social legislation − Great Britain.   3. Political questions and
judicial power − Great Britain.   I. Buck, Trevor.   II. Series.
Citizenship and the law series.
KD4902.A75J833   1988
344.41'03 − dc21   97-40766
                                                                                  CIP

Typeset by BookEns Ltd., Royston, Herts.
Printed and bound in Great Britain by Bookcraft (Bath) Ltd,
Midsomer Norton, Somerset

Contents

CONTENTS

Contributors

Trevor Buck is a Lecturer in Law at the University of Leicester and former Legal Adviser to the Social Fund Commissioner in the UK (1993–96). He teaches public law and family law. He is an advisory editor for the *Journal of Social Security Law* and a member of the Social Security Appeal Tribunal and Child Support Appeal Tribunal. He has published widely in the field of social welfare law and is author of *The Social Fund: Law and Practice* (1996).

Simon Creighton is the solicitor for the Prisoners' Advice Service. He studied sociology at the University of Essex and trained as a solicitor at the College of Law. He was appointed by the Prisoners' Advice Service in 1993 and is the only solicitor in the country who deals solely with prisoners' rights. He is the co-author of *Prisoners and the Law* (1996) and has contributed to the *Prisoners' Handbook* (1995, 1997) and *Liberty's Guide to Your Rights* (1997). He writes regular articles on prison law and is a member of the management committee for INQUEST, which campaigns on deaths in custody.

Phil Fennell is a Reader in Law at Cardiff Law School where he teaches medical law and EU law. From 1983 to 1989 he was a member of the Mental Health Act Commission. He is currently a member of the Law Society's Mental Health and Disability Committee. He has written widely on the subject of mental health law, and his book *Treatment Without Consent: Law, Psychiatry and the Treatment of Mentally Disordered People Since 1845* was published by Routledge in 1996.

Neville Harris is Professor of Law and Chair of Research in the School of Law and Applied Social Studies at Liverpool John Moores University. He researches in education law and social security law and is Senior Editor of *Education Law Reports*, Joint General Editor of the *Journal of Social Security Law* and a section editor in *Cross on Local Government Law*. He is the author of a number of books, including *Special Educational Needs and Access to Justice* (1997), *Law and Education* (1993) and *Social Security for Young People* (1989); and he edited *Children, Sex Education and the Law* (1996).

Chris Himsworth is a Reader in the Department of Public Law at the University of Edinburgh. His interests extend across constitutional and administrative law as well as housing law and environmental law. His publications include *Housing Law in Scotland* (4th edn, 1994) and *Local Government Law in Scotland* (1995).

John F. Larkin was called to the bar of Northern Ireland in 1986 and to the bar of Ireland in 1996. Between 1989 and 1992 he was Reid Professor in the Law School, Trinity College Dublin. Although in full-time public law/human rights practice at the bar, he maintains research interests in, *inter alia*, the development of proportionality doctrine, and comparative public law.

Bob Lee is Professor of Law at and Head of Cardiff Law School. He teaches on the Master's programme in Legal Aspects of Medical Practice at Cardiff, and researches in the area of health and environment. His principal publications include (with Derek Morgan); *Birthrights* (1990), *A Guide to the Human Fertilisation and Embryology Act* (1991), *Deathrites* (1995).

Dr Werner Menski is Senior Lecturer in Hindu and Modern South Asian Laws at the School of Oriental and African Studies (SOAS), University of London. He is a founder of the Group for Ethnic Minority Studies at SOAS set up to encourage research and the dissemination of information on immigration and ethnic minority issues. He has contributed to many books and journals on Hindu law, on Indian marriage and divorce laws and on immigration law. He is also an associate editor for the journal *Immigration and Nationality Law and Practice*.

Derek Obadina is Legal Secretary of the Commonwealth Legal Advisory Service, London and is an Associate Research Fellow in Company Law at the Institute of Advanced Legal Studies. He obtained a Doctorate in 1989 from the University of Wales, and has previously taught law at the Universities of Wales and Lagos. He has several publications in the areas of judicial review of administrative action, civil and criminal procedure in Commonwealth jurisdictions, the accountability of prosecutors and company law. He is editor of the *Bulletin of Legal Developments* and a member of the editorial board of the *European Journal of Business Law* and the editorial board of the *Journal of Financial Crime*.

Martin Partington is Professor of Law and Pro-Vice-Chancellor at the University of Bristol. He is also Director of the Centre for the Study of Administrative Justice. He has taught and written on housing law for over 20 years. He was for a time an external assessor for the Institute of Housing. He is currently a member of the Council on Tribunals.

David Pollard teaches public law at the University of Leicester. He is particularly interested in administrative law (co-author of *Constitutional and Administrative Law: Text with Materials*, 2nd edn), social welfare law (author of *Social Welfare Law*, and a long-standing member of the Leicester Social Security Appeals Tribunal), European law (author of *European Community Law: Text and Materials*), and French public law (author of *Source Book on French Law*). He was created Chevalier des Palmes Académiques by the French Republic.

Peter Robson is a Professor of Law in the Law School at the University of Strathclyde. He currently teaches property law; sex, race and the law; housing law; social security law; and jurisprudence. His publications include *Property* (1991), *Residential Tenancies* (1994) and *Homeless People and the Law* (1996). Funded research on landlords in the 1980s (ESRC), domestic violence in Scotland in 1989 (Scottish Office) and ADR in Scotland in 1998 (Citizen's Advice, Scotland). He is a deputy chair of Shelter and a part-time chair of Social Security Appeal Tribunals and Child Support Appeal Tribunals.

Sir Stephen Sedley is a Justice of the High Court, Queen's Bench Division; honorary Professor of Law, Cardiff University and Warwick University.

Prakash Shah is Visiting Lecturer in Law at the School of Oriental and African Studies, University of London, where he teaches immigration, nationality and asylum law and ethnic minorities and the law. He is completing his doctorate on the development of asylum law in the United Kingdom. He is also author of several articles on immigration law and is an associate editor of the journal *Immigration and Nationality Law and Practice*.

Roger Smith is a solicitor, director of the Legal Action Group and an honorary Professor at Kent Law School. He has written widely on matters relating to legal services and access to justice. His most recent book is *Justice: Redressing the Balance*, published by LAG. From 1980 to 1986, he was solicitor to the Child Poverty Action Group and undertook a number of test cases in the fields of judicial review and administrative law.

Foreword

SIR STEPHEN SEDLEY

There has probably been no more deserving beneficiary of the modern expansion of judicial review than social welfare law. Although most forms of social provision possess their own mechanisms for internal review and appeal, those mechanisms themselves are typically subject to the supervisory jurisdiction of the High Court. That it should be so is not uncontroversial. Administrative law – that is to say the law by which public administration is governed – has historical and practical claims to a strong measure of autonomy. Unless Parliament says so, such autonomy cannot be total; but there is both academic and judicial support for the view that within generous limits administrators should be able not only to find facts but to interpret and apply law according to their own lights and culture.

This debate about errors within and without jurisdiction seems an arid and self-referential debate until one recognizes that it is not about legal theory but about administrative and judicial practice. If you look at the carefully crafted accounts in this volume of the interventions and non-interventions of the courts in area after area of welfare law, you will find degrees of preparedness to intervene on legal grounds which it is not easy to allocate to any single theory of jurisdiction, and perhaps easier to relate to perceived merits.

This, it seems to me, is as much a virtue as a vice. It reflects the common law's way of reacting to new issues presented to it by the adaptation of received principles. In administrative law this will sometimes call for considerable deference, especially towards decision-makers deploying a high degree of non-legal expertise. Sometimes – especially in relation to natural justice issues, but also on pure questions of statutory construction – the courts feel confident in second-guessing the administrator. But between these poles lie contested areas in which decision-makers often feel aggrieved at the courts' intervention, but where individuals welcome and depend upon it for their entitlements.

Among these cases, the great majority of which affect nobody but the claimant, issues of wide importance surface from time to time. Many are 'bought off' by the concession of a single claim in order to avoid an adjudication of general effect. It is to public interest groups that people have to look to canvass issues which affect claimants in large numbers, and it is increasingly to these that the courts, too, look for an informed presentation of a case to which government can present an informed response. Public law is only slowly adjusting itself to the value of such interventions and to the rightness of according standing to such groups. This is a process which the Justice/Public Law Project proposals for wider acceptance of third-party interventions may well enhance.

The United Kingdom is hardly in legal terms a unitary state, and it is about to become even less so. The chapters on Northern Ireland and Scotland do a valuable service in describing the often important differences between those jurisdictions and that of England and Wales. Even in this small country the jurisdictions have something to learn from each other.

Both as a handbook and as a study of a vital area of modern public and administrative law in the United Kingdom, this is a volume filled with good things.

Preface

Trevor Buck

The fundamental idea behind this book has been to produce a series of free-standing chapters, readable in their own right, on the main areas of judicial review activity within the broad field of 'social welfare'. In addition, I wanted to produce a book where each of the contributors addressed some of the recurrent themes of social welfare law and policy by means of a persistent focus on the remedy of judicial review. These themes include, for example, the exercise and control of discretionary powers, the role and function of the law in allocating scarce resources in the community, citizens' access to social welfare rights and the function of adjudication in welfare schemes. Finally, the book also contains chapters relating to the Scottish and Northern Ireland jurisdictions respectively; both are clearly sources of rich comparison with the supervisory jurisdiction in England and Wales.

My task as editor has been to ask colleagues to produce their individual chapters within a remit sufficient to attract their academic interest in relating their individual areas to a wider social welfare dimension while ensuring that any guidelines I issued would not be recognized as too prescriptive! As the reader will discover, each contributor advances their own account of substantive or territorial areas in their own style and with their own individual emphases. However, it is also evident that the contributors have in fact addressed issues and themes which will resonate with each other. I believe that such a pluralism of design enriches the whole.

Each essayist touches upon a number of unifying strands which I have attempted to synthesize in the concluding chapter. *Judicial Review and Social Welfare* is a two-way affair; the remedy of judicial review has had much influence on social welfare systems and its application in this sphere has been important in shaping the development of judicial review itself. It must be appreciated that the original writing for this volume was undertaken just prior to the election of the new Labour administration in May 1997. However, it is hoped that this timing will produce a snapshot of the state of public law, prior to the important developments of devolution and the incorporation of the European Convention on Human Rights; which will no doubt both have important consequences for judicial review in the United Kingdom. I hope this volume makes a welcome contribution to the continuing debates concerning both the remedy of judicial review and its particular influence in social welfare law and policy.

Finally, my thanks are due to Oliver Woolhouse, a graduate of the Faculty of Law at Leicester and now barrister, for his assistance in proofreading this volume. Any errors or infelicities of style are, of course, my responsibility.

Trevor Buck
Faculty of Law
University of Leicester
February 1998

1

Judicial Review and Education

NEVILLE HARRIS

EDUCATION AND JUDICIAL REVIEW: THE BROAD CONTEXT OF CHANGE, CONFLICT AND THE SEARCH FOR ACCOUNTABILITY

Over the past two decades judicial review has played a key role in the field of education dispute resolution in England and Wales. As shall be shown, it has reached into many areas of decision-making despite the limits to the courts' powers of intervention. This has been a period of wide-ranging reform and considerable upheaval in the education system. A new statutory framework has widened the scope for legal conflict between those, such as parents and local education authorities (LEAs), who hold at times competing interests. Almost twenty Education Acts have been enacted since 1979 – not including the two major consolidation Acts enacted in 1996. With much of this legislation, the now standard practice of conferring considerable legislative powers on ministers has been adopted. Education orders and regulations have been issued in profusion – generally more than 50 per annum in the past five or six years. In the run-up to the 1997 general election, education was one of the policy areas pushed to the fore in the last Government's final legislative programme, with ministers seeking to resurrect the grammar school ideal and strengthen legal powers in respect of miscreant pupils (but not succeeding in respect of the former, because the relevant provisions were jettisoned in order to ensure the necessarily swift passage of the remainder of the Bill, which became the Education Act 1997).

The changes to the education system during the 1980s and 1990s have been considerable: a new, unitary higher education system, with greater central control over finance and, through it, aspects of quality;

1

autonomous further education institutions no longer in the local education authority sector but, in common with higher education, regulated in part by executive agency; school governing bodies, rather than LEAs, legally responsible for most of the key aspects of managing schools, including control of a school's budget (albeit that head teachers often have a high degree of *de facto* control); a centrally dictated and legally prescribed National Curriculum, although greater flexibility has recently been introduced; the development of a grant-maintained (GM) schools sector, comprising what the Conservative Government liked to call 'self-governing' schools – in the sense that they lie completely outside LEA control and are centrally funded (but are now set for reform under Labour); new quasi-independent and quasi-public city technology colleges; and new and reformed appeal bodies (see below). Change has also resulted from rationalization of local schools provision: the Conservatives put pressure on LEAs to reduce surplus capacity through school closures and amalgamations (reinforced by new central powers) and the Labour Government has now followed the Conservatives in supporting the closure of weak schools which are unable to improve. Nothing is more likely to precipitate recourse to law in this field than the threat of school closure. As Simon Brown LJ said in one case concerning the closure of a 'failing' school: 'Emotions inevitably run high when decisions have to be taken about once treasured institutions.'[1]

One of the most dominant features in the changes to the education power structure has been a reduction in LEA control (see below) and increased institutional autonomy in the schools sector. LEAs have traditionally been regarded as the major providers of education in England and Wales.[2] Their status as 'partners' with central government, which was established under the Butler reforms in the Education Act 1944 (Harris, 1993: ch. 2), has been incrementally undermined by such changes as 'local management of schools' (giving schools delegated budgets and associated powers over the employment of personnel), the introduction of the National Curriculum and the removal of LEAs' control over the secular curriculum in schools, the establishment of GM status (by the general election, in May 1997, 10 per cent of public sector schools had left the LEA sector), and the introduction of a Funding Agency for Schools (FAS) and a Schools Funding Council for Wales (which, *inter alia*, can take over an LEA's duty to ensure the provision of sufficient schools in an area, or share this role with the LEA, once a certain proportion of the children attending state schools in the LEA's area are registered at GM schools[3]). A significant feature of these changes, which have shifted the balance in local–central relations in this field, has been centralization of authority through increased ministerial direction of the education system.[4] Education was at the forefront of central–local government disputes in the courts in the 1960s and 1970s – notably over the issue of comprehensive schooling;[5] in recent years, however, much of the litigation has the appearance of rearguard actions by LEAs standing, as it were, almost powerless to resist a further undermining of their powers but seeking, with very limited success, to protect what remains of their local influence.[6] The reforms proposed by New Labour suggest a revival, albeit a modest one, of LEAs' influence through, for example, monitoring of school performance and the preparation of 'education development plans' as part of the drive towards school improvement (Secretary of State for Education and Employment, 1997: paras 17–24).

The Conservatives' reforms aimed to introduce a market-type system (a 'managed market': Taylor-Gooby, 1993: 114) for the provision and 'consumption' of education, a policy whose stated rationale was that greater competitiveness and consumer choice would produce a more efficient allocation of resources and higher standards, as institutions not only strove to meet performance targets but also competed for the 'custom' on which their funding (because of the link with pupil or student numbers) increasingly depended. To underpin these developments, the Conservatives in effect relied on a new set of 'three Rs' – rights, remedies and regulation. If we take the example of parental choice of school, the Education Act 1980 introduced *rights* for parents to express a preference for a particular school for their child and a *remedy* in the form of appeal to an education appeal committee if dissatisfied, while that Act and the Education (Schools) Act 1992 *regulated* (via numerous statutory instruments) the provision and publication of information about schools, imposing extensive and onerous requirements concerning, for example, information on school performance (presented by the press in school 'league' tables). These basic features are set to continue under the Labour Government, although there will be some changes.

Although the evidence is that the true extent of 'parent power' is more limited than the public have been led to believe (see, for example, Harris, 1993; O'Connor, 1994), there can be no denying that the establishment of numerous rights and remedies has given parents unprecedented opportunities to participate in decisions and promote their individual interests. Whatever the true substance of parental empowerment, parents now enjoy, in relation to a whole range of decision areas – for example, the education of children with learning difficulties, school government, sex education, admission to school and discipline – important rights of access, participation, representation and choice, despite the limitations imposed on them (see Harris, 1993: chs 6 and 7; Meredith, 1992; Harris, 1996b). There are also equally important remedial rights, notably the statutory appeal rights in respect of school admissions, exclusions and special educational needs (see below) and the statutory complaints arrangements introduced under the Education Reform Act 1988 (Harris, 1992a).

The subject of education rights cannot, however, be discussed without remarking on the emphasis which has been placed by the legislation on *parental* rights and remedies. In contrast to other fields and the general policy thrust reflected in the Children Act 1989, children's independent rights have been eclipsed by those of their parents, with children having, for example, very few independent remedial rights, with the notable exception of access to judicial review itself.[7] Students in further education colleges and universities, on the other hand, generally have independent rights and, no doubt encouraged by the climate of consumerism contributed to by the introduction of student 'charters', have become increasingly prepared to assert them.[8]

The individualized focus to relationships between public education providers and parents or pupils/students has given judicial review a particular relevance as a means to securing individual redress of grievance (as Meredith, 1995b: 68–9, notes), albeit that there have also been many occasions when it has been utilized for collective action (most notably over local school closures and other changes). Yet, paradoxically (given that we are talking about an area of public law), these relationships have increasingly assumed private characteristics – as illustrated by the development of home–school agreements (provision for which is made in the Education Act 1997, although at the time of writing the relevant provisions have yet to be brought into force), student contracts (Farrington, 1996) and (until their abolition) education vouchers for nursery education.[9] In any event, the courts in judicial review cases have been reluctant to accept that particular education duties are 'absolute' (see below) and thus might give rise to private causes of action. Both this and the courts' unwillingness to interfere with the exercise of powers conferred by statute, have arguably helped to shift the emphasis in challenges to education decisions further towards claims for private law remedies in the field of contract or tort particularly following recent success in negligence litigation in this field.[10] Yet despite the development and increasing utilization of other avenues of redress (including new appeal and complaints procedures), education has been one of the major areas of growth among judicial review cases. Indeed, education's share of the total judicial review caseload in fact trebled in just four years, according to recent research (Bridges, Meszaros and Sunkin, 1995: 15).

The process of running an education system and catering for the individual and collective needs of children, as well as managing the complex interface between parents' rights and schools' and LEAs' responsibilities, inevitably involves a considerable amount of decision-making which affects various parties' interests. Very often there are decisions which are painful in the way that they impinge upon individual interests. Moreover, the potential incidence of *ultra vires* action is considerable, not least because in an increasingly fragmented education system, decision-making powers and responsibilities are often devolved and exercised by a diverse range of bodies which have many new areas of responsibility but may lack the traditional forms of political accountability associated with LEAs and government ministers (see Feintuck, 1994). Prime examples are the FAS (Johnson and Riley, 1995) and government-appointed education associations, which on appointment have all the wide-ranging powers of school governing bodies and can be sent in to run 'failing schools' and then recommend their removal from the LEA sector or closure. Judicial review may be the only means of ensuring that such bodies are held accountable for the exercise of considerable authority, as in the action brought against the North East London Education Association when it recommended the closure of Hackney Downs School (see below). Furthermore, education is so central to ideals of fundamental human/children's rights that the safeguard which, despite its limitations, judicial review provides through enforcement of the principle that decision-making about a child's education and about local educational provision should involve procedural fairness and be based on rationality, propriety, and so on, must be considered very important. (The human rights dimension to public law disputes would, of course, assume even greater significance if incorporation of the European Convention on Human Rights into English law occurs, via the Government's Human Rights Bill: see below.)

Such is the principle: what of the practice? This chapter assesses the contribution of judicial review to ensuring that the wide range of decision-making bodies in the field of education stay within the law and are accountable to those who depend on the education system. In particular, it analyses the role played by judicial review in determining the extent to which the expectations of individual parents, students and others concerning what they perceive to be their rights of choice (Halstead, 1994), and to acceptable standards of provision, can be upheld.

EDUCATION AND PUBLIC LAW: JURISDICTION

To place this discussion into its proper context, it is first necessary to consider the relationship between the education system and public law. The education system of England and Wales has both private and public sectors. The divide is generally a clear one. Independent (private) schools, defined as any schools which are not LEA-maintained, special or GM,[11] have been left free of much of the statutory regulation governing matters of curriculum, discipline and management applicable to schools in the state sector (Harris, 1995a), obstensibly in the interests of parental choice. Attempts to challenge the exclusion of a child from a private school via judicial review have failed because the courts regard the relationship between parents and such schools as founded on private contractual principles and outwith the scope of their public law supervisory authority.[12] On the other hand, private schools have to be licensed by the state and can be removed from the Register of Independent Schools by the Secretary of State, on specific grounds. Thus a private school was able to utilize judicial review to challenge a decision that its provision was unsuitable.[13]

It was noted above that education has been one of the many areas of state activity subjected to a degree of privatization. The assisted places scheme, first introduced under the Education Act 1980 (see Edwards, Fitz and Whitty, 1989; Smith and Noble, 1996: 64–6), aims to enable children from poorer backgrounds who might not otherwise be able to attend an independent school to have all or part of their fees and expenses paid by the state, subject to a test of means. The scheme, which benefits over 30,000 pupils a year, but which will be phased out over the next seven years following the enactment of the Education (Schools) Act 1997, represents a state subsidy of private education and a partial contracting out of the education of a significant number of pupils. It is indicative of a blurring of the public–private divide in education, to which the nursery voucher scheme (providing parents with up to £1100 per child per year to spend on either public or private nursery education), the contracting out of school inspections (to Ofsted-registered inspectors: see Harris, 1995b) and provision for certain categories of schools to have 'sponsor' governors, have also contributed.

Perhaps the best example of the public–private hybrid is the city technology college (CTC) introduced under the Education Reform Act 1988. CTCs (including city colleges for the technology of the arts) are established under a funding agreement between the promoter/proprietor of the college and the Secretary of State. They must be based in an urban area and cater for pupils in that area with 'different abilities' – although there is quite considerable selection because, under the terms of its agreement, the college will be expected to give priority to those children who it believes will benefit most from the education on offer and who will have the motivation to continue their education to the age of 18 (Walford, 1991). CTCs aim to provide a specialist form of education – one in which there is an emphasis on science and technology or on technology in its application to the performing and creative arts – but they must also offer a 'broad curriculum'. In practice, much of the funding for the fifteen CTCs to have been established to date has come from public funds, because there has been less support from industry than previous governments had suggested would be available. The status of CTCs has been questioned in judicial review proceedings. In *R v Governors of Haberdashers' Aske's Hatcham College Trust ex parte Tyrell*[14] the chief substantive issue concerned a CTC's admissions arrangements. However, Dyson J had to determine as a preliminary issue whether this CTC's decisions were, in principle, amenable to judicial review. Applying relevant authorities,[15] Dyson J reiterated the courts' view that both the source of a body's power and its nature should be looked at in seeking to determine the matter. If the body's authority was derived solely from contract or the consent of the parties its decisions would not be amenable to judicial review. If, on the other hand, the source of the power was statute or secondary legislation made under statute, they would be.[16] In the case of schools, it was easy to distinguish between, on the one hand, county, voluntary or GM schools, the source of whose decision-making authority was statutory, and, on the other, private schools, the source of whose power was consensual and whose decisions 'were not made in the exercise of public law duties or functions'.[17] Although CTCs are, in effect, classed as independent schools,[18] and although the powers and duties of their governing bodies are prescribed by their articles of government and scheme of government rather than by statute, Dyson J considered that the overriding factor was that the existence of CTCs was derived from a statute – then the Education Reform Act 1988 – under which the Secretary of State had exercised his powers to enter into agreements for the provision of education by a CTC, subject to various conditions specified in the agreement. There were no contractual rights: 'even if there is consideration, there is no intention to enter into a contractual relationship on either side'.[19]

The justiciability of decisions of centrally-funded universities, on the other hand, is more problematic, at least in relation to disputes with students. On the one hand, they would appear, on the basis of the decision in *Nolan*[20] (where a student on the Common

Professional Examination course for intending lawyers was successful in having two decisions by the examinations board of the Law department quashed), to be amenable to judicial review. However, despite past doubt over the matter,[21] a student will probably now be regarded as standing in a contractual relationship to the institution concerned (Farrington, 1994: 327–9; Wade and Forsyth, 1994: 642–3) and may thus have private law rights which can be enforced by writ, as in the case of a man who was unexpectedly denied a place on a university course having earlier relied on the university's offer to his detriment.[22] Indeed, in *R v Fernhill Manor School ex parte A*,[23] which concerned justiciability in a judicial review challenge to an independent school's exclusion of a pupil, Brooke J drew analogy with the post-*Roffey*[24] university cases which suggest that the contractual basis to the university–student relationship generally renders inapplicable the court's public law jurisdiction. This view has been criticized for over-simplifying the position (Whincup, 1993). One of the problems is that many of the older universities are subject to visitorial jurisdiction; the university's visitor may have jurisdiction to resolve certain disputes between members of a university, which might include students. Such a jurisdiction was regarded by the House of Lords in *Thomas v University of Bradford*[25] as exclusive (at least in personnel matters, although the Education Reform Act 1988 subsequently cut down this jurisdiction[26]).

The courts' judicial review jurisdiction was subsequently confirmed to be excluded where the visitor had jurisdiction over the dispute in question (a student's failure of a course).[27] (A similar view has been taken of the visitorial jurisdiction in relation to the Inns of Court.[28]) The fact that Manchester Metropolitan University does not have a visitor was referred to specifically by Sedley J in *Nolan* (above) as reinforcing the case for regarding decisions of the university about student discipline or progress as within the judicial review jurisdiction. Other cases have been brought, but as with *Nolan* they all relate to decisions by 'new' universities, which do not have visitors. In *R v Board of Governors of Sheffield Hallam University ex parte R*,[29] Sedley J quashed the decision of the governors to expel R from a physical education training course on the grounds that the governors had failed to provide her with adequate notice of the matters to be relied on against her.[30]

Farrington (1996) argues that a better approach might be to regard disputes in this field as essentially contractual and, in principle, not amenable to judicial review. Such a view is in part predicated on the developing notion of 'contract' in the manner in which students are admitted to universities and served by them. However, it ignores public interest and concern in relation to the operation of our universities; such public interest which would fall squarely within Lord Woolf's justification for the public law–private law divide in the courts' jurisdiction (Woolf, 1986). Indeed, some rights, such as the right to freedom of speech at a university (derived from the duty on a university to take steps to preserve such a freedom), are, on that basis, rightly considered to fall within the general principle of public law justiciability.[31] Another matter is that when universities are at the point of making decisions regarding the admission of a student they have yet to enter into any form of contractual arrangement with him or her; there is a legitimate public interest in ensuring that publicly-funded universities act fairly in making such decisions, and they are undoubtedly exercising public law functions in any event. Thus in *Reilly* v *University of Glasgow*,[32] the Outer House of the Court of Session heard an application for judicial review from a student who had been denied a place on the University's medicine course and gave consideration to, but rejected, the student's claim that there had been a breach of natural justice in the failure of the University's prospectus to explain fully one of the criteria governing admission to the particular course. Private law claims by students may in any event founder in some cases if the university provides a domestic procedure of redress.[33]

A plethora of public or quasi-public bodies now have important powers within the education system, reflecting the widespread introduction of non-departmental public bodies and other develop-ments such as partial privatization across a range of public services since the mid-1980s (Birkenshaw, Harden and Lewis, 1990; Lewis, 1989). The FAS and Ofsted were noted above. Other bodies whose decisions may be amenable to judicial review include the funding councils. They all derive their powers from statute. In one case[34] the Universities Funding Council (UFC) (since replaced by the Higher Education Funding Council) was the respondent to an application for judicial review brought by the University of London's Institute of Dentistry. The Institute was aggrieved at its research rating of 2 and alleged that the failure of the UFC's panel to provide reasons for its decision was unfair and that, in the absence of such reasons, the decision could (in the circumstances) be regarded as irrational. The court held that matters of academic judgment were not within the class of case, exemplified by the decision in *Doody*,[35] where the nature of the decision itself meant that reasons should be given as a matter of routine. Nor was there anything intrinsic in the particular decision taken which would trigger a requirement to give reasons.[36]

Education associations, referred to earlier, are another example of the new breed of education agencies. Their members are selected on an *ad hoc* basis by the Secretary of State to form a small management group to supervise the running of a school which has been found to be failing to provide an 'acceptable' standard of education.[37] Under present legislation the position in relation to such a school would be that following the association's stewardship (which would typically last less than twelve months), the school's fate will be either to become GM (without the usual ballot of parents) or to be closed. The final decision would rest with the Secretary of State. In *R v Secretary of State for Education and Employment and the North East London Education Association ex parte M and Others*[38] the parents of two pupils at a school whose closure had been recommended by an education association and ordered by the Secretary of State made an unsuccessful application for judicial review on the grounds of, *inter alia*, inadequacy of consultation (see below) and that the association had exceeded its powers in making a report to the Secretary of State recommending closure of the school. A further argument, that the closure of the school mid-way through the academic year was *Wednesbury* unreasonable because of the disruption which would be caused to some pupils' education (principally those taking GCSEs at the end of the year), was also rejected, on the ground that the Secretary of State and the association had perceived an overriding need to limit the damage caused by operating a deficient school (see further Harris, 1996a).

Ofsted, on the other hand, is not strictly a statutory body, but carries out administrative functions on behalf of the Chief Inspector of Schools, whose role is statutory.[39] Ofsted contracts out to registered inspectors the work of inspecting individual schools and reporting on standards of education in them. This makes any legal challenge to the way that an inspection has been carried out problematic, albeit that the methods of inspection and the criteria to be applied are strictly regulated and that, on the basis of relevant case law on bodies in a broadly analogous position,[40] the action of Ofsted itself can probably be amenable to judicial review, in particular because of the statutory framework on school standards on which Ofsted's role is centred and because it arguably exercises 'public law functions'[41] and is 'woven into the fabric of public regulation'.[42] A less certain position, however, has existed in relation to the Training and Enterprise Councils (TECs) engaged via contracts with the Training Agency to sponsor local training initiatives involving vocational awards (NVQs etc.). It has been argued that this has meant that 'vocational qualifications have, in essence been privatised' (Unwin, 1989: 252). The limited public accountability of such bodies raises legitimate concerns (see Harden, 1992; Lewis, 1989); it is certainly unclear how amenable their decisions might be to legal challenge (see Cane, 1996: 19–22). Nevertheless, privatization has failed to weaken the overall potential role for judicial review in the field of education.

ACCESS TO EDUCATION: THE NATURE OF THE AUTHORITIES' DUTIES AND DISCRETION

The concept of 'access' to education is a broad one. In simple terms, it refers to the opportunity to receive an education that meets one's needs. Since the Education Act 1993,[43] the Secretary of State has had a duty to exercise his/her powers with a view to, *inter alia*, extending opportunities for choice; thus it might be assumed that, certainly in principle, a citizen might also have a legitimate claim to the education of his or her choice. However, access and choice obviously depend on the availability of educational provision and this, in turn, is affected by the rationing of limited resources. Despite attempts to create a market system for education based on competition and consumer choice, provision is rationed in the interests of economic efficiency, and the legislation facilitates this. It does so either by conditioning choice, so that it can be denied in order to safeguard the 'efficient use of resources' (see 'Choice of school: admission and transport' below[44]), or simply by leaving much discretion as to how education is organized and managed in the hands of education providers, such as LEAs, with the result that some areas of provision may be limited, or even withdrawn, on economic grounds.

Where access is entirely dependent on the exercise of discretion, LEAs and others must act fairly and reasonably in the way that discretion is exercised. The courts have, for example, upheld the right of LEAs to limit discretionary awards (non–mandatory grants) very severely indeed – to wholly exceptional cases, as long as blanket exclusion is not applied and proper account is actually taken of special circumstances.[45] The cases have, for example, confirmed the extreme difficulties facing those who need a grant in order to undertake the legal practice course for intending solicitors.[46] Discretion is also exercised in relation to the nature of the provision to be made available: thus the Secretary of State may, provided public law principles are not infringed in the process, make decisions influenced by policy choices about whether to favour grant–maintained status (see below) or some other change to a school's status.[47]

Judicial review has not, therefore, proved to be a particularly fruitful means of challenging purely discretion-based decisions within the education system. The courts have been understandably reluctant to interfere, because the power is statutory and thus backed by Parliamentary authority. For example, in *R v Secretary of State for*

Education and Science ex parte Avon County Council[48] the Secretary of State approved an application by Beechen Cliff School in Bath for GM status even though the school thereby ceased to feature in the LEA's school reorganization plans and even though those carefully developed plans (which were consistent with the national policy of rationalization of provision) were thrown into chaos as a result. Hutchinson J quashed the Secretary of State's decision in part on the ground that the minister had failed to take proper account of the disruption and uncertainty for children and parents which the conferment of GM status on the school would cause in the circumstances. Following the court's decision, the Secretary of State reconsidered the matter but reached the same conclusion as before. When this decision was also challenged the Court of Appeal not only felt that this time the Secretary of State had taken into account the implications his decision would have, but also held that, in the absence of evidence of irrationality, there was no basis on which the court could interfere: the Secretary of State alone was the judge of the feasibility of the various reorganization schemes put forward by the LEA, which had been rejected following the approval of the GM status application. The court also upheld the right of the Secretary of State to 'have a policy and to apply his policy preference in considering the proposals'.[49] Similarly, in *R v Secretary of State for Education and Science ex parte Newham LBC*,[50] Schiemann J accepted that the Secretary of State was entitled to take the view that the enhancement of parental choice which resulted from the presence of a GM school in an area should take priority over the case for closing a school to achieve greater efficiencies. In *R v Secretary of State for Education and Employment ex parte the Governing Body of West Horndon County Primary School and the NAHT* Harrison J held that the minister's power to determine the information to be shown in primary school performance tables was based on a wide discretionary power (under s. 16 of the Education (Schools) Act 1992) with whose exercise the court would only interfere if the decision was unreasonable or perverse, which amounted to 'a high threshold for the applicants to satisfy'.[51] The challenge to the way that the information had been gathered and set out failed. In yet another case, *R v Secretary of State for Education and Science ex parte Yusuf Islam*,[52] there was a challenge to the Secretary of State's refusal to confer voluntary-aided status on the independent Islamia Primary School in the London Borough of Brent. The challenge succeeded, on the grounds that the promoters of the school had not been provided with all the relevant information by the LEA when making their application to the Secretary of State, with the result that a 'manifest unfairness' had been caused. But

Macpherson J warned in his judgment: 'in the result ... the applicants must realise that the answer may be exactly the same, and the new Secretary of State ... may reach a decision entirely like that of his brother and that will be a matter entirely for him'.[53] Thus, when the Secretary of State reconsidered the application (this time in the correct manner), the renewed application was turned down on pretty much the same grounds as before. The case was one of many where the courts have confirmed that policy choices are matters for the authorities rather than the courts: '[I]t is not for me to say whether the school should become voluntary-aided. Whatever I feel one way or another is wholly irrelevant in that regard; that is a matter entirely for the Secretary of State to decide.'[54]

Often the exercise of discretion will operate via self-imposed policy constraints aimed at rationing resources. Thus, one way or another, the question of resources has been integral to many disputes over access to education which have found their way into the courts, as, for example, in the area of special educational needs. LEAs have, in the case of children with the greatest learning difficulties, a duty to carry out a formal assessment of those needs and a duty to make them the subject of a formal statement if they consider one to be 'necessary'.[55] This is an important duty, because once the provision required to meet the child's needs is specified in the statement the LEA has a duty to ensure that the provision is made (unless the parents themselves have made 'suitable arrangements').[56] LEAs have quite a considerable discretion as regards the provision they specify in the statement – although provision specified must be sufficiently well defined as to meet the identified needs of the child.[57] Policy rules devised by LEAs to provide a consistent approach to these matters and to provide a basis for rationing have been upheld by the courts, on the proviso that they provide scope for individual circumstances to warrant a departure from them. Thus Cumbria LEA's system of banding pupils in accordance with intelligence test scores and allocating specified levels of funding to support provision in particular bands was upheld by the Divisional Court, because, within the arrangements, individual pupils' needs were to be considered by the LEA and could be addressed. The court confirmed that the boundaries between the bands were 'a matter for the local education authority and not easily subject to challenge in the courts'.[58] Similarly, the court refused to strike down one LEA's policy of not paying for children with dyslexia to attend an independent school, on the ground that the LEA's schools would be expected to be able to cater adequately for those needs.[59]

The fact that an authority's reason for failing to comply with its duty is that it has rationed limited resources may deter the court from intervening, particularly because of the nature of many education duties. For example, in one recent case the Brent and Harrow District Health Authority was held to have been, in effect, relieved of its statutory duty to assist an LEA in connection with the exercise of its special educational needs functions because the Act entitles a district health authority to refuse to assist where 'having regard to the resources available to them ... it is not reasonable for them to comply' with the LEA's request for help.[60] Turner J said that the relevant statutory provisions 'do not render it without the power of the district health authority to seek to ration its scarce resources'.[61] Other resource-driven decisions may arise under LEAs' general duty to ensure that local schools provision is 'sufficient'.[62] Under this duty, LEAs must ensure that there are primary and secondary schools in their area which are sufficient in 'number, character and equipment' to meet the local need for primary and secondary education.[63] This means that, *inter alia*, there must be sufficient teachers; when Liverpool City Council issued redundancy notices to all of its teachers the illegality of its action stemmed in part from its failure to take account of this responsibility.[64] There was also an improper motive (to make political capital in its battle with central government).[65] The 'sufficient' schools duty was also tested when, as a result of a shortage of teachers, the Inner London Education Authority (ILEA) was unable to provide sufficient primary school places in Tower Hamlets for all the pupils who needed them.[66] The statute provided a remedy for the failure to perform a duty via complaint to the minister, who had default powers.[67] The minister had declined to intervene in this case. Woolf LJ (as he then was) held that the 'sufficient' schools duty was merely a 'target duty'; provided the LEA was doing all that it could to rectify the situation, within the financial constraints under which it had to operate, and was not acting *ultra vires*, the court had no basis to intervene. This was consistent with *Meade* v *Haringey*, where (following the closure of schools to avoid exacerbating a caretakers' strike) Eveleigh LJ said that 'the local education authority are entrusted with the duty of running the schools, and if what they do is genuinely directed to that end and is a legitimate choice of the various options they would not be in breach of that duty'.[68] The extent of the discretion surrounding the exercise of the 'sufficient' schools duty has been emphasized by decisions confirming that when the LEA makes policy decisions on allocating school places or on whether to provide selective or non-selective schools, such decisions are not amenable to judicial review provided the authority acts *intra vires* and consistent with its other duties, such as the non-discrimination duties under the Sex Discrimination Act 1975.[69] In fact, in one case the court upheld

14

the legality of a school closure which created an imbalance in the availability of single-sex education as between boys and girls, because, *inter alia*, the 'sufficient' school duty could not be fulfilled by keeping the school open (the school's dwindling roll had led to a reduction in the school's resources and its curriculum could no longer be maintained).[70]

Cane (1996: 33) argues that because the choices made by public authorities in the exercise of their functions are often politically or morally contentious, the courts would prefer not to pronounce on the issue when disputes arise, and that in cases where the duty is a broad one (he cites the 'sufficient' schools duty as an example) the courts distinguish between an authority's minimum core duty (failure to perform this will be regarded as justiciable) and the surrounding discretion (which leaves certain decisions to authorities alone). Cane (1981: 18) has explained that the 'sufficient' schools duty has been construed as 'a duty to provide a minimum level of schooling coupled with a discretion to determine, consistent with the fulfilment of that duty and in accordance with the statutory guidelines, what the requirement of sufficient schools entails'. In the Tower Hamlets case (above), Woolf LJ said that LEAs could set their own standards as regards the performance of their 'target' duty, 'as long as those standards were not outside the tolerance provided by the section'. The court was prepared to accept that 'the tolerance provided by the section' allowed the LEA to hold back on provision when constraints made it unavoidable for a 'limited period of time'.[71] It is surprising that the fact that the situation in Tower Hamlets had pertained for over twelve months was not considered to make the LEA's failure to rectify it *ultra vires*. In any event, Woolf LJ's approach was followed recently by Sedley J, who, in considering the LEA's statutory duty to ensure adequate facilities for further education which meets special educational needs in the area,[72] described the notion of a 'target' duty as a 'metaphor [which] recognises that the statute requires the relevant public authority to aim to make the prescribed provision but does not regard failure to achieve it without more as a breach'.[73] In this case, the applicant should, according to Sedley J, have pursued a remedy via complaint to the minister under section 99 of the Education Act 1944 (now section 497 of the 1996 Act), under which the minister may issue directions to an authority or governing body which is in default of its duty; the courts commonly regard the statutory remedy as exclusive in relation to mere non-feasance in respect of target duties[74] and, indeed, in certain other cases (for example, the allegedly defective election arrangements for parent governorship[75]).

Where a duty is more strict, however, the possibility of judicial review will probably not be precluded. In *R* v *London Borough of Harrow ex parte M*[76] the district health authority had refused assistance with regard to the LEA's special educational needs functions on financial grounds (the separate action brought against the health authority was discussed above). The LEA relied on the health authority's failure as an excuse for its own failure to make the provision specified in a statement of special educational needs. The LEA's failure was regarded as justiciable even though complaint could have been made to the minister. Turner J held that the LEA's specific statutory duty to 'arrange that the special educational provision specified in the statement is made for the child'[77] was one which was 'owed personally to the child' and, moreover, was a duty which was 'simply expressed (in the statute) and subject to no qualification' and that it was not delegable.[78] Turner J granted an order of *mandamus* accordingly. Similarly, in *R* v *East Sussex County Council ex parte T*,[79] the LEA was found to have failed in its duty to ensure 'suitable' provision for a child unable to receive normal schooling due to chronic sickness (ME), when it cut its provision of home tuition from five hours per week to three following a £3 million shortfall in its education budget. Suitability did not 'vary according to the financial means of the provider'.[80] However, this decision has recently been overturned by the Court of Appeal,[81] although leave has also been granted for an appeal to the House of Lords. Further judicial consideration of this matter will be particularly valuable in view of the continuing uncertainty over the wider applicability of the House of Lords' decision in *R* v *Gloucestershire County Council ex parte Barry*,[82] distinguished by Keene J at first instance in the *East Sussex* case but applied by the majority in the Court of Appeal. In *Barry* the House held that, in respect of the duty on a local authority under s. 2(1) of the Chronically Sick and Disabled Persons Act 1970 to provide welfare services to meet the needs of a disabled person, a local authority could legitimately consider its financial position as regards the resources it could provide to meet particular needs.

THE IMPACT OF JUDICIAL REVIEW IN PARTICULAR AREAS OF ACTIVITY

There continues to be a steady stream of cases concerned with matters of collective concern, such as school closures and reorganization, as noted above. Although on the face of it, the growth in litigation on such matters seems to have peaked, no one can predict with any certainty what future political and economic changes might precipitate a further impetus towards rationalization.

Cases on changes to local schools over the past decade and a half (at the time of writing) have mostly been concerned with procedural deficiencies, especially lack of consultation.[83] Unfortunately, the courts' fairly strict approach, exemplified by the much-cited decision in *R v Brent London Borough Council ex parte Gunning*,[84] has perhaps given way to a more liberal one. In *R v Secretary of State for Education ex parte London Borough of Southwark*,[85] for example, the Secretary of State wrote to the LEA on 23 December 1993 informing it that he was minded to approve the acquisition of GM status by a particular school with effect from 1 January 1994. The LEA said that, given the proximity of Christmas, it was left with only three working days in which to respond. The court rejected the LEA's claim that a legitimate expectation as to consultation had arisen[86] and that the short time scale helped to make the decision perverse. Similarly, in *R v Secretary of State for Education and Employment and the North East London Education Authority ex parte M and Others*[87] there was a failed attempt to argue a lack of consultation arising from the fact that only periods of ten and fourteen days had been given by the Secretary of State and an education association, respectively, for parents and others to consider and respond to proposals to close the school, which had failed to improve following an Ofsted inspection. Here the Court of Appeal found there to be a duty to consult, but in any event accepted that, in determining whether a failure to consult amounted to a failure to discharge the duty to act fairly, it was necessary to take account of the need to avoid a stultification of the underlying statutory objectives of the new group of powers 'by an over-zealous superimposition of common law procedural requirements'.[88] The powers were intended to enable a seriously deficient school to be dealt with speedily.

What emerges from these recent cases on consultation is that the increased impetus towards change within the education system, exemplified by the last government's ever more streamlined 'opting out' procedures and (in the case of a 'failing' school which has been put under the control of an education association) the streamlined procedure for school closures, has been met with an acceptance by the courts that decisions may have to be implemented quickly and that the appropriateness of the degree of expedition applied in any particular set of circumstances is a matter for the judgment of ministers and not the courts. Ironically, though, the very pace of change makes it all the more important that interested parties are properly consulted – so that over-hasty and ill-judged decisions are avoided.

Despite the importance of the cases on changes to local schools provision, the case law developments affecting individual welfare and entitlement in the fields of school admissions, special educational needs and exclusion from school have in many ways acquired greater significance and they warrant particularly close analysis. In one way or another they touch on the question of access to, and thus the right to, education, and the question of parental choice. There has been less scope for legal challenge in respect of the content of the school curriculum, which is subject to wide-ranging central regulation. It may be noted, however, that religious education and collective worship in the state sector, where the law provides for greater local flexibility (Harris, 1995a: 205–14), have proved contentious and one case was brought to determine the lawfulness of a broadly multicultural approach to collective worship in school.[89]

Choice of School: Admission and Transport

Admission to school is the principal matter over which parents want, and have been encouraged by successive governments to expect, a high degree of individual choice. The fact that parents have a right of appeal to an education appeal committee if denied the school of their choice means that recourse to the courts in England and Wales will arise only in very specific circumstances (on the position in Scotland and Northern Ireland, see Adler, Petch and Tweedie, 1989 and Lundy, 1996, respectively). These would usually be concerned with the legality of the LEA's or school's admissions policy itself, the operation of the exceptions to the general statutory duty to comply with parental preference, or the way in which the local education appeal committee reaches its decision and gives its reasons (Harris, 1995a: ch. 7). There is only space here for a relatively brief review of the cases, which have confirmed the limitations to parental choice under the legislation.

The first matter concerns the nature of admissions policies themselves. These policies provide the basis on which an admissions authority (the LEA, in the case of county schools, and the governing body in respect of voluntary and GM schools) rations school places. The 'open enrolment' requirements introduced under the Education Reform Act 1988[90] require that, in the LEA sector, artificially low admissions limits cannot be set for individual schools. Nevertheless, where schools are oversubscribed there has to be a policy to determine priority between competing claims. In *R v Governors of the Bishop Challoner Roman Catholic Girls School ex parte Choudhury*[91] the admissions policy gave priority to Roman Catholic children in the event of oversubscription. The parents of a Muslim girl and a Hindu girl wanted places at the school (because it offered single-sex education) but were denied on the grounds of religious preference.

The House of Lords confirmed that setting priorities to distinguish between competing claims where there is oversubscription is a legitimate exercise of power by a school and that basing priority for admission on religion in the case of a denominational school was no less lawful than basing it on sibling connection or on proximity of home to school.

Religion was also a factor in two cases where the court upheld as lawful Lancashire County Council's secondary schools admissions policy. Under that policy, where non-denominational secondary schools were oversubscribed, pupils at Roman Catholic primary schools would be considered a lower priority for a place than others. In the first case,[92] Popplewell J held that the education appeal committee had been entitled to apply the LEA's policy (even though the DfE had indicated that the admissions arrangements were not consistent with national policy on admissions), which was entirely rational and within the scope of the LEA's discretionary power. In the second case,[93] Kennedy LJ explained that, because it would be difficult for a non-Roman Catholic child to secure a place in a Roman Catholic secondary school, giving Roman Catholic children equal priority for non-denominational schools could result in some non-Roman Catholic children being left without a school place.

An important group of cases concerns admissions policies which provide that priority of admission is, in the event of oversubscription, to be given to pupils residing within the LEA's area. In R v Shadow Education Committee of the Greenwich London Borough Council ex parte The Governors of John Ball Primary School[94] the Court of Appeal confirmed that, taking account of the wording of the statute,[95] it was not lawful for an LEA to discriminate merely on the basis of the LEA area in which the pupil resided. Subsequently, it was held that, in the light of this judgment, it was not even possible for an LEA's admissions policy to state that its own residents and those living extra-district would have equal priority, if it was subject to the proviso that if its own residents' educational needs could not be met, those residents' preferences would take priority.[96] When the Greenwich decision was implemented in Kingston upon Thames, there were complaints that competition for places at single-sex schools in Kingston would be so tight that some Kingston residents would not secure this form of education for their child, whereas they would have done previously. Watkins LJ confirmed that the LEA was not in breach of its duty by implementing the Greenwich decision, despite its consequences.[97] Greenwich has, in fact, caused many LEAs to change their admissions arrangements and has, to some extent, enhanced parents' rights over choice of school. Nevertheless, it is clear from a very recent decision[98] that where the LEA operates a catchment area policy, *Greenwich* does not preclude it from denying an extra-district applicant a place at one of its schools on the grounds that that person does not live in the catchment area (especially when that person will generally have been offered a place at a school in his or her own area by his/her LEA). The court said that the applicant, who lived in Somerset and sought a school place in Wiltshire, was in the same position as a Wiltshire resident who lived outside the catchment area.

Catchment areas within LEAs have also caused indirect discrimination against ethnic minorities. This will not always be unlawful, thus exposing a weakness in the law's ability to protect minority rights. In *R v Bradford Metropolitan Borough Council ex parte Sikander Ali*[99] the applicant lived in the Manningham area of Bradford. Under the LEA's admissions scheme, Manningham was not associated with any particular secondary school (through community links) and so was not in an identified catchment area. In Manningham, a higher than average proportion of residents were of Asian origin, as compared with Bradford as a whole. The applicant claimed that the admissions policy resulted in indirect racial discrimination because he, and a higher proportion of Asians than whites in Bradford, would not have a high priority for particular schools. Jowitt J said that in determining whether the policy was unlawfully discriminatory one had to compare the position of Asians living in Manningham with that of whites living there, rather than with those living in Bradford as a whole. The case provides another illustration (*Choudhury* (above) also highlighted the problem) of the limitations of the Race Relations Act 1976 to offer adequate protection for ethnic minorities as regards access to education, and especially equality of access. It is also the case that the Race Relations Act is unable to inhibit a racially motivated choice of school. In *R v Cleveland County Council ex parte Commission for Racial Equality*[100] a white mother moved her child from a school with a high proportion of pupils of Asian origin to one in which Asian culture was less prominent, on the grounds of her Christian belief. It had been accepted, on the facts, that her choice of school was not racially motivated but the court in any event held that the LEA's duty to comply with parental preference (the school to which the child was to be moved had spare places) was mandatory, which meant that its performance was excepted from the Race Relations Act.[101]

An admissions authority is entitled to deny parental preference if, *inter alia*, the admission of a child to the school would 'prejudice efficient education or the efficient use of resources'.[102] This represents one of the most severe barriers to freedom of choice.

The other two statutory grounds for denial of preference – religion (where the school is voluntary and admission would not be compatible with admission arrangements agreed between the LEA and the school) and academic ability – have been less problematic.[103] The main problem with the 'prejudice' ground has been finding the right approach to decision-making in cases where, as will generally be the situation in relation to a popular school, there are a number of appeals relating to the same school. In *R v South Glamorgan Appeals Committee ex parte Evans*[104] a two-stage test was developed by Forbes J: first it was necessary for the appeal committee to decide, when the admissions limit for the school had been reached, whether the admission of a further child would cause the 'prejudice' referred to (the onus of proof resting with the LEA); secondly, if there was prejudice, it was necessary to ask whether the reasons put forward by the parent for the child to be admitted to the school outweighed it (see Tweedie, 1986). This approach, and the practice adopted by many appeal committees of hearing all appeals relating to a particular school before deciding which appeals to allow, subsequently received the approval of Woolf LJ.[105] In 1996 approximately 52,000 admissions appeals in respect of LEA-maintained schools were lodged and 36,000 were heard (10,000 others were lodged, and 8000 heard, in respect of GM schools) (Council on Tribunals, 1997: Appendix F). It is likely that a very high proportion of the appeals involve the application of the 'prejudice' test. In the past, some committees have in fact experienced difficulty in applying it correctly (Harris, 1993: 147–8). Recent cases, viewed in conjunction with complaints about appeal procedures investigated by the Local Government Ombudsman, reveal an uneven picture,[106] even though the judicial guidance has been incorporated into the Codes of Guidance on appeals issued by the ACC/AMA (LEA schools) and the DfEE (GM schools). In *R v Appeal Committee of Brighouse School ex parte G; ex parte B*,[107] for example, Sedley J quashed the decision of the appeal committee on the ground that rather than making an independent assessment of 'prejudice', it had relied on the school's admissions limit as being definitive on the matter.

The cases have confirmed the limits to parental choice in relation to school admissions. It is clear that once a school is full it will generally be difficult for more than a very small number of parents to overcome the prejudice test (Beckett, 1994). Recent Government figures are said to show that record numbers of children are being denied a place at their first-choice school[108] and a recent Audit Commission (1996: para. 30) survey concluded that one in five families are unable to secure a place at the school of their choice; not surprisingly, therefore, the number of parents lodging an appeal has more than doubled over the past five years. The fact that, as their Lordships confirmed in *Choudhury* (above), the admissions policy can limit choice in other ways – through catchment areas, proximity of home to school, and so on – means that parental choice will not operate to break down social and economic barriers and racial divides, but will rather widen them.

The cost of transporting a child to a school which is not within walking distance operates as another barrier to choice for some. There have been a number of judicial review challenges to LEA decisions concerning the provision of transport to and from a school chosen by the parent, where the LEA's view is that the child can reasonably attend another school closer to his or her home. The LEA can refuse to provide, or meet the cost of, transport for a child who does not live within 'walking distance' of the school if suitable arrangements have been made for the child to attend a school nearer home.[109] Although there is some conflict between them, the decisions seem to confirm that the LEA does not have to show that the nearer school is 'suitable', contrary to what some parents (who have chosen a more distant school) have argued, and that parental choice may not sway the matter.[110] Nevertheless, the question of suitability is frequently raised in judging the rationality of the LEA's decision. Recently, in *R v Kent County Council ex parte R*[111] a child had been attending a grammar school but the LEA would only meet transport costs for her to attend a school nearer home. The parents objected because the nearer school was not a grammar school and they felt that because of this the arrangements were not suitable. However, McCullough J found no irrationality in the LEA's decision and said that the question of suitability was not one for the courts.

Exclusion from School

The problem of indiscipline in schools and how best to tackle it has been a subject of considerable media and public interest recently. The Education Act 1997 contains a number of measures on discipline. Among them are extensions to schools' and LEAs' disciplinary powers in respect of fixed-term exclusions and detention and provision for home–school 'partnership agreements' which, *inter alia*, may specify the standard of behaviour expected of a pupil. Concern over school discipline has been focused not only on the *degree* of indiscipline in schools (highlighted by the problems at the Ridings School[112]) but also the dramatically increased *use of exclusion* by head teachers in response to it. Official statistics show that the number of permanent exclusions from schools in England and Wales rose from 2910 in 1990–91 to 11,181 in 1993–94;[113] and 12,476 permanent exclusions took place in 1995–96.[114] The new Labour Government believes that 'the present number of exclusions is too high' (Secretary of State for Education and Employment, 1997: para. 19) and it plans to issue new guidance in the near future. Section 156 of the Education Act 1996 gives the head teacher alone the power to exclude a child, either permanently or for a fixed term (not exceeding fifteen days in aggregate in any term – the 1997 Act would, if the relevant parts are brought into force, extend this to forty-five days per year without a specific termly maximum). There is actually some doubt about whether higher levels of pupil misbehaviour and violence are the main cause of this increase in permanent exclusions. Researchers point to the legal limits on fixed-term exclusions and the prohibition (introduced under the Education Act 1993) on indefinite exclusion as making it more likely that exclusion will be permanent. Another, very important, influence seems to be the development of a new 'exclusion culture' in schools, precipitated by competitive pressures and the demands placed on teachers by the National Curriculum (Searle, 1994).

There is now a complex legal framework governing procedures in exclusion cases in state schools. Nevertheless, this offers no guidance to head teachers on when to exclude (with the result that the basic common law rule that punishment at school must be moderate, not excessive, and a reasonable response to the pupil's misbehaviour,[115] including behaviour off school premises,[116] sets the only limits on exclusion). The DfEE's official guidance is structured around the principle that exclusion should be a sanction of 'last resort'.[117] Obviously, the reasonableness of an exclusion must depend on the facts of each case.[118] The case law is still developing; for example, in two recent judicial review challenges the court concluded that alternatives to exclusion should be considered before any decision to exclude is taken, depending on the circumstances.[119]

Different rules on exclusion procedure apply to different schools, but in essence[120] the school must inform the parents (or the pupil if aged 18 or over) of the nature and reasons for the exclusion and of their right to make representations to the governing body and/or LEA.[121] The governing body and/or LEA must consider whether the pupil should be reinstated. The parents (or pupil if aged 18 or over) have a right to appeal against a decision not to reinstate a permanently excluded pupil.[122] The appeal lies to a local appeal committee. There are time limits, to ensure that matters are resolved reasonably quickly. For example, the appeal must be heard within fifteen school days of the date on which the appeal was lodged.[123]

Public law remedies are available in respect of unlawful exclusion from a state sector school.[124] Many of the recent cases have been concerned with the way that appeal committees have performed their role. (The courts have in fact also been willing to entertain judicial review applications where an appeal has *not* first been pursued – if the allegation is of serious procedural unfairness.[125]) In *R v Board of Governors of Stoke Newington School ex parte M*[126] the court struck down, on the grounds of potential bias, a decision not to reinstate an excluded girl, where a member of the committee was the pupil's head of year and thus might have been influenced by knowledge of her. Potts J also confirmed that the merits of exclusion or reinstatement in any particular case were a matter for the education authorities and 'outside the province of this court'.[127] In *R v Governors of St Gregory's Roman Catholic Aided High School ex parte M*[128] the court adopted a lenient approach with regard to an appeal committee's departure from the letter of the Code of Guidance on appeals and its rather terse reasons for decision. Another case, *R v London Borough of Camden and the Governors of Hampstead School ex parte H*,[129] almost certainly led to the inclusion in the 1996/97 Education Bill (now the 1997 Act) of a requirement that the appeal committee should take account of, *inter alia*, the impact that reinstatement would have on the other pupils at the school. Here the Court of Appeal quashed the decision of the committee to reinstate two excluded pupils who were alleged to have fired an airgun at another pupil. The court felt that the committee had placed too much weight on the interests of the perpetrators and not enough on those of the victim, who wanted to remain at the school. The court also felt that the incident itself had not been investigated sufficiently thoroughly by the head teacher. The Education Act 1997 would also require the appeal committee to take account of the school's disciplinary policy. This seems to reflect the court's view in *ex parte M* (above), where Turner J said that in deciding whether an exclusion was a reasonable response, the particular circumstances of the school were of considerable, if not decisive, importance. He referred specifically to the fact that the school operated a strict disciplinary regime. The exclusion of a boy for allegedly using the '"f" word' in the presence of a teacher and then refusing to show any contrition when called to discuss his behaviour was not, in Turner J's view, a response which no reasonable head teacher would adopt in the circumstances of such a school. He said his view would be the same 'even if the principle of proportionality formed part of the domestic law of our courts'.[130]

The extent of the investigation which the head teacher and appeal committee should conduct will depend on the particular circumstances, and because of this, decisions like *ex parte M* (above) inevitably offer little real guidance on this point. Recently, however, Latham J offered some assistance by confirming that their obligation is to ask the right questions and take reasonable steps to become acquainted with relevant information while keeping in mind the central issues in the case.[131]

Schools are often criticized these days for excluding too readily and without any regard to the likely impact of exclusion on the future of the child concerned. Although the duties on LEAs to make provision for excluded children were tightened up under the Education Act 1993, there still tends to be disruption and delay as regards the pupil's education and its proper resumption following exclusion from school.[132] The courts have yet to rule on the question whether, and to what extent, the likely consequences of exclusion for the pupil concerned should be taken into consideration by an appeal committee. The disruption to a 15-year-old's GCSE preparation which would be caused by his exclusion was considered in *ex parte X* (below, note 116), but only in relation to the question of interlocutory relief.

Special Educational Needs

In some ways the field of special educational needs is one which has derived the most benefit from the use of judicial review. The courts have played a vitally important role in clarifying the statutory responsibilities of LEAs in particular, for example on the definition of special educational needs[133] and on the contents of statements of special educational needs.[134] Parents of children with learning difficulties often have very strong views on whether, for example, their child should be educated in a special school (often giving rise to the question of who will pay where the school is independent) or, alternatively, in a mainstream school, which the legislation encourages. Because special education tends to be expensive, disputes over the allocation of resources to meet a child's needs are fairly inevitable[135] and are one reason why as many as 120 judicial review applications in special educational needs cases were sought in 1992–93.[136] Although issues such as the educative duties owed to persons with special educational needs who are above compulsory school age continue to present themselves via judicial review cases,[137] the role of judicial review in the field of special educational needs has declined sharply since the establishment of a statutory right of appeal to the court (via Orders 55 or 56 – originating application or case stated[138]) against the decision of the appeal body. (There is, in any event, a review power vested in the tribunal and its President.[139]) The first-tier appeal body itself has been reformed, with the special educational needs tribunal (SENT) replacing the appellate jurisdiction of local education appeal committees and the Secretary of State in this field (see Harris, 1997). In *R v Special Educational Needs Tribunal ex parte F*[140] Popplewell J held that 'if there is a statutory right of appeal it is to be exercised and, save in exceptional circumstances, judicial review will not be granted where the statutory right of appeal exists and has not been exercised'.[141] The application for judicial review in this case was struck out because the matter should have been pursued via a statutory appeal. In fact, the courts, relying on established judicial authorities such as *Swati*[142] and *Preston*,[143] have followed a consistent line on this point in special educational needs cases,[144] and the matter is now well settled.

This limitation to the amenability of many special educational needs decisions to judicial review has had consequences for legally aided litigation in this field. Because the right of appeal vests in the parents exclusively, and the child has been held not to be a party to the appeal proceedings before the High Court,[145] parents must either be eligible for legal aid (not only legal advice and assistance at the tribunal stage) in their own right or bear the full cost of an appeal (although costs might be awarded). In special educational needs judicial review cases, the applicant has almost always been the child, who will normally qualify for full legal aid. However, it is clear that judicial review will no longer be available in the majority of cases, especially in view of the quite wide grounds of appeal in special educational needs cases since the new appeal arrangements were introduced under the Education Act 1993 (Oliver and Austen, 1996). Judicial review will, however, be possible in respect of certain special educational needs disputes, particularly those concerning the effects of an LEA's policy (for example, involving a change to funding arrangements[146]) or a failure by an LEA to implement a decision of the SENT.

CONCLUSION

The willingness of parents and students to seek redress of grievance and assert their rights as 'consumers' or as 'stakeholders' in the education system, on the scale which has occurred over the past few years, is unprecedented. On the basis of this quite dramatic trend (albeit that the utilization of judicial review has been relatively modest relative to the potential caseload), assertion of these rights is likely to continue to grow, even though there may be a few dispute areas where the number of judicial reviews will fall (notably special educational needs cases, as stated above). Individuals' increased resort to, and success in, contract and tort litigation in this field which has also been witnessed can only serve to heighten public awareness of the potential benefits of mounting legal challenges in general against education providers. Neither the incidence nor the importance of judicial review in the field of education is likely to diminish over the coming years; nor is the diversity in the range of matters which might form the subject of disputes and thus potential litigation.

The difficulties in overturning education decisions, especially those based mostly around discretion/policy, is something which potential litigants will have to bear in mind. The cases discussed in this chapter reveal a limited pattern of success for applicants, with most victories achieving a remedy to procedural deficiencies rather than guaranteeing a different outcome in respect of the substantive issue under dispute. The concept of a parental right of choice, for example, has not stood the test of judicial scrutiny when LEAs and other bodies have taken tough decisions which affect resource allocation and impinge upon individual demands. Furthermore, judicial review does not have any real potential to reallocate power within the education system. The extent of ministerial power over areas like the school curriculum and decisions on a school's status has merely been confirmed by the cases, as has LEAs' and governors' discretionary power over allocation of school places.

Perhaps, though, one ought not overlook what might be termed the judicial review effect on education bodies, in the way that the possibility of such legal action may inhibit some of the more serious potential excesses of power and authority (as Meredith, 1995b: 95 also argues). In areas such as school admissions, exclusions and special educational needs, the judicial review cases must, as well as clarifying the various important duties imposed on them, have caused the generality of LEAs, governors and schools to think twice about the lawfulness of any planned action, although this aspect of the practical impact of judicial review is difficult to measure. Above all, the history of education dispute resolution in recent years has, in common with other areas, highlighted the constitutional importance of judicial review in a field where individual and collective rights compete particularly fiercely against the power of the decision-maker.

The importance of the constitutional role of judicial review will, indeed, increase should incorporation of the European Convention on Human Rights into English law occur via Labour's Human Rights Bill. As education is a field where ministers have wide-ranging discretionary powers and where there is considerable regulation, incorporation could play an important role in enabling basic rights to be safeguarded if they come under threat. Thus, as the Lord Chancellor recently commented, following incorporation 'new issues will be raised on judicial review'.[147] The Convention has only had a limited influence, via the cases, over the education system thus far – notably in relation to sex education[148] and the use of corporal punishment, which has raised questions as to whether such punishment is contrary to the Convention (it is not inhuman or degrading treatment etc., provided it is kept within strict limits[149]) and whether inflicting it contrary to parental wishes amounts to breach of the requirement to uphold parents' religious and philosophical convictions in the course of complying with the duty not to deny the right to education.[150] Should it prove possible following incorporation to argue breach of this latter requirement, and/or the general duty as regards equal treatment on grounds of race, such contentions might well be adopted in a number of the kinds of cases referred to in this chapter. For example, the powers and decisions which were the subject of the dispute over the denial of voluntary-aided status to the Islamia school could be challenged on the basis of a conflict with parents' religious convictions, while it might be argued that the power of exclusion from school might involve a denial of the right to education in some circumstances. The fact that the law failed to prevent the disadvantage to Asians in Manningham resulting from school catchment areas in Bradford (the *Sikander Ali* case above) might, in a similar instance in the future, be considered worth challenging on the basis of a lack of racial equality under the Convention (particularly as a claim of breach of the Race Relations Act 1976 failed in that case). Moreover, in a field where parents have been encouraged (in some cases with the aid of statutory rights) to give free rein to their views on how and where their child should be educated, the duty under the Convention to educate in accordance with parents' 'philosophical convictions' (and possibly also the duty not to interfere with the individual's private and family life[151]) may feature prominently in public law challenges. However, it is clear that in the field of education the UK's reservation in the Convention, to the effect that the principle of adherence to parental convictions is accepted 'only so far as it is compatible with the provision of efficient instruction and training, and the avoidance of unreasonable public expenditure', will be a limiting factor. The Government has argued that the reservation should form part of incorporation, on the basis that 'Its purpose is to recognize that in the provision of State-funded education a balance must be struck in some cases between the convictions of parents and what is educationally sound and affordable'.[152] Nevertheless, there will be huge scope for argument and it is clear that as far as the subject of education and judicial review is concerned, a new dimension will be added to an already vibrant area of public law.

NOTES

1 *R v Secretary of State for Education and Employment and the North East London Education Association ex parte M and Others* [1996] ELR 162 at 205.

2 This chapter focuses on developments in England and Wales. There have been comparable developments in Scotland: see, for example, Alder, Petch and Tweedie, 1989.

3 The proportions are 10 per cent (power sharing – or total transfer of control if the LEA agrees) and 75 per cent (transfer of control, irrespective of the LEA's wishes): Education Act 1996, s. 27. For discussion, see Meredith, 1995a. The FAS is now set for abolition under the School Standards and Framework Bill.

4 The Education Reform Act 1988 alone was said to have conferred over 200 new powers to ministers. This Act introduced greater central government controls not only over schools, but also over further and higher education (see Harris, 1993: 89–98).

5 See, for example, *Lee v Department for Education and Science* (1968) 66 LGR 211 (CA); *Secretary of State for Education and Science v Tameside Metropolitan Borough Council* [1977] AC 1014.

6 See, for example, an LEA's unsuccessful challenge to the legality of the Secretary of State's decision to approve a school's change to GM status at very short notice (*R v Secretary of State for Education ex parte London Borough of Southwark* [1995] ELR 308) and another's failed bid to have the Secretary of State's method of calculating the deduction to its budget resulting from a school's acquisition of GM status overturned (*R v the Secretary of State for Wales ex parte Gwent County Council* [1995] ELR 87).

7 See below. See also, for example, the comments in Bainham and Cretney, 1993: 542: 'No student of children law, looking at education, can fail to be struck by the contrast between the emphasis on parents' *rights* in education alongside the movement from rights to *responsibilities* elsewhere in the law.' Children have no right to express a preference for a school to which they might be admitted, nor to serve on a school governing body (the minimum age is 18), nor (unless aged at least 16) to see their school record, nor to withdraw themselves from sex education or religious education (such rights of withdrawal resting exclusively with parents). A child is not a party to an appeal to a special educational needs tribunal (see below), nor does he or she have an independent right of appeal against his or her permanent exclusion from school. For further discussion, see Harris, 1993: 19–22.

8 See, for example, 'Universities count the cost as students resort to legal action', *The Times*, 7 October 1996.

9 See the Nursery Education and Grant-maintained Schools Act 1996. Labour's white paper announced that nursery vouchers would not be used after summer term 1997: Secretary of State for Education and Employment, 1997, para. 5.

10 On contract, see the *R v Fernhill Manor School ex parte A* [1994] ELR 67 (QBD) and the student cases below. On tort, see for example, *X v Bedfordshire County Council* [etc.] [1995] ELR 404 (HL), *Phelps v The Mayor and Burgesses of the London Borough of Hillingdon* [1988] ELR (QBD) (forthcoming) (£45,650 awarded) and *Christmas v Hampshire County Council* [1998] ELR (QBD) (forthcoming) (negligence claim defeated); and note the widely-reported

settled damages claim (£30,000 settlement) in November 1996 arising out of alleged bullying at school. An earlier claim by a young woman in Derbyshire failed (*Walker* v *Derbyshire County Council*, news report in *The Times*, 7 June 1994). See also S. Hamilton, 'Students sue over course failures', *Sunday Times*, 9 February 1997, also covered by the THES.

11 Education Act 1996, s. 463.

12 *R* v *Fernhill Manor School ex parte A* [1994] ELR 67. Public law remedies may be available in respect of exclusion from a state-maintained school, however: *R* v *Board of Governors of the Oratory School ex parte R*, *The Times*, 17 February 1988.

13 *R* v *Secretary of State for Education and Science ex parte Talmud Torah Machzikei School Trust*, *The Times*, 12 April 1985.

14 [1995] ELR 350.

15 Including *R* v *National Joint Council for the Craft of Dental Technicians (Disputes Committee) ex parte Neale* [1953] 1 QB 704 and *R* v *Panel on Take-overs and Mergers ex parte Datafin (Norton Opax Intervening)* [1987] 1 QB 815.

16 *Datafin*, note 15 above.

17 Note 14 above, at 357F–G.

18 At the time, under s. 105 of the Education Reform Act 1988. See now s. 482 of the Education Act 1996.

19 Note 14 above, at 361F–G.

20 *R* v *Manchester Metropolitan University ex parte Nolan* [1994] ELR 380; and see also *R* v *University College London ex parte Riniker* [1995] ELR 213.

21 Arising, *inter alia*, from the *Roffey* case (*R* v *Aston University Senate ex parte Roffey* [1969] 2 WLR 1418). See Wade, 1969 and Garner, 1974.

22 See *Moran* v *University College Salford (No. 2)* [1994] ELR 187.

23 [1994] ELR 67 (QBD).

24 Note 20 above.

25 [1987] 1 AC 795.

26 See *Pearce* v *University of Aston in Birmingham* [1991] 2 All ER 461 (CA).

27 See the recent case of *R* v *University of Nottingham ex parte Klorides* [1997] 5 March and 28 July (QBD and CA) (unreported). See also *R* v *Lord President of the Privy Council ex parte Page* [1993] 1 All ER 97 (HL); see Wade, 1993. The court granted leave for judicial review of a decision by the University of Cambridge not to award a lecturer a readership; the University does not have a visitor: *R* v *University of Cambridge ex parte Evans* [1997] 22 August (QBD) (unreported). See also *R* v *University College London ex parte Christofi* [1997] 18 June (QBD) (unreported).

28 *Joseph* v *Board of Examiners of the Council of Legal Education* [1994] ELR 407 (CA). See also *R* v *Her Majesty's Judges sitting as Visitors to the Honourable Society of the Middle Temple ex parte Andrew Bullock* [1996] ELR 349 (QBD).

29 [1995] ELR 267 (QBD).

30 See also *R* v *Liverpool John Moores University ex parte Hayes* [1997] 20 June (QBD) (unreported). Other decisions, cited by Farrington, 1996, but unreported, are *R* v *University of Humberside ex parte Cousens*, 29 November 1994 and *R* v *South Bank University ex parte Ifediora* (no date).

31 *Riniker*, note 20 above, *per* Sedley J, at 216; Education (No. 2) Act 1986, s. 43; *R* v *University of Liverpool ex parte Caesar-Gordon* [1990] 3 All ER 831 (QBD).

See also *Educational Institute of Scotland* v *Robert Gordon University* [1997] ELR 1, where a university lecturers' association was permitted by the court to apply for judicial review of a decision of the university to offer new contracts to staff appointed or promoted after a particular date.

32 [1996] ELR 394 (OHSCS).

33 See *Madekwe* v *London Guildhall University* [1997] 5 June (QBD) (unreported).

34 *R* v *Universities Funding Council ex parte The Institute of Dental Surgery* [1994] ELR 506 (QBD).

35 *R* v *Secretary of State for the Home Department ex parte Doody* [1993] QB 157.

36 See also *R* v *Civil Service Appeal Board ex parte Cunningham* [1994] 4 All ER 310.

37 School Inspections Act 1996, ss. 31–33.

38 [1996] ELR 162.

39 School Inspections Act 1996, Chapter I Part I.

40 *Datafin*, note 15 above; *R* v *Advertising Standards Authority Ltd ex parte The Insurance Service plc* (1990) 2 Admin. LR 77; *R* v *BBC ex parte McAliskey* [1994] COD 498. See also the long list of other cases cited in Jones and Thompson, 1996: 192 n. 11.

41 *Datafin*, note 15 above, *per* Lloyd LJ.

42 *R* v *Insurance Ombudsman ex parte Aegon Life Insurance* [1994] COD 426.

43 Section 2; see now Education Act 1996, s. 11.

44 See also Education Act 1944, s. 76 (now Education Act 1996, s. 9), which provides that 'children are to be educated in accordance with the wishes of their parents', provided this is compatible with 'efficient education ... and the avoidance of unreasonable public expenditure'. In general, s. 76 has proved almost impossible to enforce in favour of parental choice: see, for example, *Watt* v *Kesteven CC* [1955] 1 QB 408; *Wood* v *Ealing LBC* [1967] Ch. 364. For a rare instance of s. 76 being applied in favour of an applicant, see *R* v *London Borough of Lambeth ex parte G* [1994] ELR 207 (QBD).

45 See, for example, *R* v *Warwickshire County Council ex parte Collymore* [1995] ELR 217 at 225, *per* Judge J, and *R* v *Shropshire County Council ex parte Jones* [1997] ELR 381.

46 *Ibid.*, and *R* v *Warwickshire County Council ex parte Williams* [1995] ELR 326 and *R* v *Southwark London Borough Council ex parte Udu* [1996] ELR 390 (CA). See also Diamond, 1996.

47 See, for example, *R* v *Secretary of State for Education and the Governing Body of the Queen Elizabeth Grammar School ex parte Cumbria County Council* [1994] ELR 220.

48 (1990) 88 LGR 716 (QBD).

49 *R* v *Secretary of State for Education and Science ex parte Avon (No. 2)* (1999) 88 LGR 737, at 740.

50 *The Times*, 11 January 1991 (QBD).

51 [1997] ELR 374, *per* Harrison J at 378D–E.

52 [1994] ELR 111 (QBD).

53 At 113G.

54 *Ibid.*, at para. D–E.

55 Education Act 1996, ss. 323 and 324.

56 *Ibid.*, s. 324(5)(a); *R* v *Governors of Hasmonean High School ex parte N and E* [1994] ELR 343 (CA). *White and Another* v *Ealing London Borough Council and*

Another; Richardson v *Solihull Metropolitan Borough Council and Another; Solihull Metropolitan Borough Council and Another* v *Finn, The Times,* 1 August 1997 (QBD).

57 *R* v *Secretary of State for Education and Science ex parte E* [1992] 1 FLR 377; *Re L* [1994] ELR 16 (CA); *L* v *SENT and Somerset CC* [1997] 29 August (QBD).

58 *R* v *Cumbria County Council ex parte NB* [1996] ELR 65 at 70; see also *R* v *Cumbria County Council ex parte P* [1995] ELR 337.

59 *R* v *London Borough of Newham ex parte R* [1995] ELR 156 (QBD): the court was satisfied that the policy provided scope for flexibility. Dyslexia was first recognized as giving rise to a special educational need and consequent duty under the legislation, following judicial review proceedings in 1985; *R* v *Hampshire LEA ex parte J* (1985) 84 LGR 547 (QBD). The need for speech therapy was recognized only following the decision in *R* v *Lancashire County Council ex parte CM* [1989] 2 FLR 279 (QBD and CA).

60 Section 160(2) – see now Education Act 1996, s. 322.

61 *R* v *Brent and Harrow Health Authority ex parte London Borough of Harrow* [1997] ELR 187 at 189G (QBD).

62 Education Act 1996, s. 14, formerly Education Act 1944, s. 8.

63 As noted above, that duty may be shared with, or transferred to, the FAS if a sufficient proportion of children in the area attend GM schools.

64 *R* v *Liverpool City Council ex parte Ferguson, The Times,* 20 November 1985 (QBD).

65 See *Meade* v *Haringey LBC* [1979] 2 All ER 1016 (CA).

66 *R* v *Inner London Education Authority ex parte Ali* [1990] 2 ALR 822 (QBD).

67 Education Act 1944, ss. 68 and 99. See now Education Act 1996, ss. 496 and 497.

68 Note 65, at 1028.

69 See *R* v *Birmingham City Council ex parte Equal Opportunities Commission* [1989] AC 1155 and *[Same] (No. 2)* [1994] ELR 282 (CA); *R* v *Secretary of State for Education ex parte Keating* (1985) 84 LGR 469.

70 *R* v *Northamptonshire County Council ex parte K* [1994] ELR 401 (CA).

71 Note 66, at 828–829.

72 Education Act 1996, s. 15 (formerly Education Act 1944, s. 41).

73 *R* v *London Borough of Islington ex parte Rixon* [1997] ELR 66 at 69D (QBD).

74 See *Watt* v *Kesteven County Council* [1955] 1 All ER 473; *Meade* v *Haringey LBC,* note 65 above; *Passmore* v *Oswaldtwistle Urban District Council* [1898] AC 387 (a public health case); *Bradbury* v *London Borough of Enfield* [1967] 3 All ER 434 (CA). In *R* v *Bradford Metropolitan Borough Council ex parte Sikander Ali* [1994] ELR 399, Jowitt J said *(obiter)* (at 315–316) that the possibility of bringing civil proceedings under section 53 of the Race Relations Act 1976 did not preclude an application for judicial review.

75 *R* v *Northampton County Council ex parte Gray, The Times,* 10 June 1986 (QBD).

76 [1997] ELR 62 (QBD).

77 Section 168(5)(a) of the Education Act 1993, now Education Act 1996, s. 324(5)(a).

78 At 64D and 65B–C.

79 [1997] ELR 335 (QBD).

80 *Ibid.*, at 347F, *per* Keene J.

81 31 July 1997: QBCoF 97/0174/D.

82 [1997] 2 All ER 1.

83 As in *R v Secretary of State for Education ex parte Skitt* [1995] ELR 388 and *R v Governing Body of Irlam and Cadishead Community High School ex parte Salford City Council* [1994] ELR 81, where Rose J, as he then was, refused to find irrational the timing of a ballot on opting out which, in fact, resulted in parents of pupils who had started at the school in September 1992 not having a vote in the ballot which took place in October 1992! This curious result was, as Rose J confirmed, a mere quirk of the legislation, which had been applied correctly by the governors.

84 [1985] 84 LGR 211.

85 [1995] ELR 308.

86 Laws J (at 320 *et seq.*) held that neither a clear promise or practice of consultation as would give rise to a legitimate expectation (as *per* the decision in *Civil Service Unions v Minister for the Civil Service* [1985] AC 374) nor any of the other circumstances which might evoke the doctrine applied.

87 [1996] ELR 162 (QBD and CA), discussed above.

88 At 208D, *per* Simon Brown LJ. See also *R v Secretary of State for Wales ex parte Williams* [1997] ELR 100. Consultation over a decision to establish a grammar school in Milton Keynes was a key issue in *R v Buckinghamshire County Council ex parte Milton Keynes Borough Council*, 28 October 1996 (unreported).

89 *R v Secretary of State for Education ex parte R and D* [1994] ELR 495 (QBD).

90 Section 26.

91 [1992] 3 All ER 227, HL.

92 *R v Lancashire County Council ex parte M* [1994] ELR 478 (QBD).

93 *R v Lancashire County Council ex parte F* [1994] ELR 33 (QBD).

94 [1990] 88 LGR 589 (CA).

95 Education Act 1980, s. 6(5).

96 *R v Bromley London Borough Council ex parte C and Others* [1992] 1 FLR 174.

97 *R v Royal Borough of Kingston upon Thames ex parte Kingwell* [1992] 1 FLR 182.

98 *R v Wiltshire County Council ex parte Razazan* [1997] ELR 394 (CA).

99 [1994] ELR 299 (QBD).

100 [1994] ELR 44 (CA).

101 See Race Relations Act 1976, s. 41. The author has discussed this case at length: Harris, 1992b.

102 Education Act 1980, s. 6(3)(a): see now Education Act 1996, s. 411(3)(a).

103 But see *R v Kingston upon Thames Royal London Borough Council ex parte Emsden* [1993] 1 FLR 179 and *R v Metropolitan Borough of Wirral ex parte Pickard* [1991] Lexis CO/1735/91. See also *R v The Governors of La Sainte Union Convent School ex parte T* [1996] ELR 98 (QBD).

104 10 May 1984 (unreported).

105 *R v Local Commissioner for Administration ex parte Croydon London Borough Council* [1989] 1 All ER 1033. Guidance on the constitution of the committee if it cannot get through all the appeals on one day and has to reconvene was offered in *R v Camden Borough Council ex parte S*, *The Times*, 7 November 1990 (QBD).

106 See *W (A Minor) v Education Appeal Committee of Lancashire County Council*

[1994] ELR 530 (CA) at 538 (*per* Hirst LJ); *R* v *Education Appeal Committee of Leicester County Council ex parte Tarmohamed* [1997] ELR 48 (QBD); and *R* v *Essex County Council ex parte Jacobs* [1997] ELR 190 (QBD). Local Government Ombudsman reports of investigations into complaints 96/C/0927 (St Mary's, West Derby); 96/C/1511 and 96/C/1546 (Liverpool City Council); and 95/C/ 1721 (Salford City Council). See also *Commission for Local Administration in England*, 1997: 3 and 13.

107 [1997] ELR 39 (QBD).

108 'Thousands fail to gain places in the schools they choose', *The Times*, 29 December 1995.

109 Education Act 1996, ss. 444 and 509.

110 See *R* v *Rochdale Metropolitan Borough ex parte Schemet* [1994] ELR 79 (QBD); *R* v *Essex County Council ex parte C* [1994] ELR 273; *R* v *Dyfed County Council ex parte S* [1994] ELR 320 (QBD). In *R* v *East Sussex County Council ex parte D*, 15 March 1991 (unreported), Rose J concluded that the arrangements, rather than the alternative school, had to be suitable, but in the Court of Appeal in *R* v *Essex County Council ex parte C* [1994] ELR 54 (QBD) Staughton LJ favoured Roch J's interpretation in *ex parte Schemet* above. Subsequently, in *Re S* [1995] ELR 98 the Court of Appeal distinguished *ex parte C* and Butler-Sloss LJ concluded (at 104D–E) that '"suitable" relates to the arrangements not to the school', an interpretation followed by Collins J in *R* v *Bedfordshire County Council ex parte DE* [1996] 1 July (QBD).

111 14 February 1997 (unreported).

112 This became a front page issue in the broadsheets. For example, on 29 October 1996 the front page headline in *The Guardian* was 'Head closes pupil-row school'. At the height of the matter (in late October and early November 1996), an entire *Panorama* television programme was devoted to it.

113 These figures were published in *The Guardian*, 14 May 1996.

114 DfEE statistics. See also *Times Educational Supplement*, 8 November 1996.

115 *R* v *Hopley* [1860] 2 F&F 202.

116 *R* v *London Borough of Newham ex parte X* [1994] ELR 303, *per* Brooke J at 106H–107A; and *R* v *Solihull Borough Council ex parte W*, 19 May 1997 (unreported) (QBD).

117 DfE, Circular 10/94, *Exclusions from School*.

118 See, for example, *R* v *Governors of St Gregory's Roman Catholic Aided High School ex parte M* [1995] ELR 131 and *R* v *Solihull Borough Council ex parte W*, note 116 above.

119 *R* v *Solihull Borough Council ex parte W*, see note 116 above; and *R* v *Staffordshire County Council Education Appeals Committee ex parte Ashworth* [1997] 9 Admin LR 373 (QBD).

120 The rules are described in some detail in Harris, 1995a: 320–2.

121 The right to make representations includes a right to appear before a meeting where reinstatement is to be considered and make oral representations: *R* v *Governing Body of the Rectory School and the London Borough of Richmond ex parte WK (A Minor)*, 5 February 1997 (unreported), *per* Forbes J.

122 Education Act 1996, s. 159. In some circumstances the governing body may appeal against a decision by the LEA to reinstate the pupil. However, if

enacted, the School Standards and Framework Bill will abolish the LEA's power of reinstatement.

123 Education Act 1996, Sch. 16, para. 7.

124 *R v Board of Governors of the London Oratory School ex parte R, The Times*, 17 February 1988. Decisions of independent schools on exclusions are not amenable to judicial review: *R v Fernhill Manor School ex parte A* [1994] ELR 67 (QBD).

125 See *R v Solihull Borough Council ex parte W*, 19 May 1997 (QBD) (unreported).

126 [1995] ELR 131 (QBD).

127 At 138E–F.

128 [1995] ELR 290 (QBD).

129 [1996] ELR 360 (QBD and CA).

130 At 301G–H.

131 *R v Solihull Borough Council ex parte W*, note 116 above.

132 See 'Exclusions rise relentlessly', *Times Educational Supplement*, 8 November 1996.

133 *R v Hampshire County Council ex parte J* [1985] 84 LGR 547 (QBD); *R v Lancashire County Council ex parte CM* [1989] 2 FLR 279 (QBD and CA).

134 *R v Secretary of State for Education and Science ex parte E* [1992] 1 FLR 377; *Re L* [1994] ELR 16; *R v Hereford and Worcester County Council ex parte P* [1992] 2 FLR 207 (QBD).

135 See, for example, *R v Governors of the Hasmonean High School ex parte N and E* [1994] ELR 343 (CA); *R v Cumbria County Council ex parte NB* [1996] ELR 65 (QBD).

136 Official Report, House of Commons, Standing Committee E, col. 168, 28 January 1993, *per* Mr T. Boswell MP (Under-Secretary of State).

137 See, for example, *R v Oxfordshire County Council ex parte Roast* [1996] ELR 381 (QBD); and *R v Dorset County Council and Further Education Funding Council ex parte Goddard* [1995] ELR 109 (QBD).

138 On the choice of procedure, see *S v Special Educational Needs Tribunal and the City of Westminster* [1996] ELR 102 and *Brophy v Metropolitan Borough of Wirral, sub. nom. R v Special Educational Needs Tribunal ex parte Brophy*, 8 May 1996 (QBD).

139 The review procedure, in Regulations 31 and 32 of the Special Educational Needs Tribunal Regulations 1995, SI 1995, No. 31113 might be preferable to an appeal in some cases: see *South Glamorgan County Council v L & M* [1996] ELR 400 (QBD). Of recent reports of investigations by the Local Government Ombudsman on education complaints, around half have concerned special educational needs, with delay on the part of LEAs in completing assessments and issuing statements of special educational needs being prominent as subjects of complaints.

140 [1996] ELR 213 (QBD).

141 At 217A.

142 *R v Secretary of State for the Home Department ex parte Swati* [1986] 1 WLR 1 (CA).

143 *R v Inland Revenue Commissioners ex parte Preston* [1985] 1 AC 835 (HL).

144 See, for example, *R v Special Educational Needs Tribunal ex parte South Glamorgan*

County Council [1996] ELR 326; *Re M* [1996] ELR 135; *R* v *Barnet LBC ex parte Barnett,* 27 November 1996 (unreported) (QBD).
145 *S* v *Special Educational Needs Tribunal and the City of Westminster* [1996] ELR 228 (CA). See also *R* v *Special Educational Needs Tribunal ex parte South Glamorgan County Council,* note 144 above, and *Council of the City of Sunderland* v *P and C* [1996] ELR 283 (QBD).
146 See *R* v *London Borough of Hillingdon ex parte Governing Body of Queensmead School* [1997] ELR 355 (QBD).
147 '"We should be leading the development of human rights in Europe", says Lord Chancellor', Lord Chancellor's Department Press Release 141/97, 4 July 1997.
148 See *Kjeldsen, Busk Madsen and Pedersen* [1996] 1 EHRR 711.
149 Article 3. *Costello-Roberts* v *United Kingdom* [1994] ELR 1; see also *Warwick* v *United Kingdom* [1986] A9471/81. The law on corporal punishment in independent schools was amended in the light of these developments: see Harris, 1995a: 323.
150 Article 2 to the First Protocol. *Campbell and Cosans* v *United Kingdom* [1982] 4 EHRR 293. In *Kjeldsen, Busk Madsen and Pedersen,* note 148 above, the European Court of Human Rights gave primacy to the state's overriding duty to provide information and promote knowledge on sexual and other matters over the principle of adherence to parental convictions under Article 2 to the First Protocol. In England and Wales, parents were granted an unconditional right to withdraw their children from sex education other than the biological aspects covered under the national curriculum, by s. 241 of the Education Act 1993 (see now s. 405, Education Act 1996).
151 Article 8, breach of which was argued unsuccessfully in *Costello-Roberts,* note 149 above, where the Court commented (at p. 12) that 'the sending of a child to school necessarily involves some degree of interference with his or her private life'.
152 Lord Chancellor's Department (1997), *Rights Brought Home: The Human Rights Bill,* paras 4.6–4.7, Cm 3782.

REFERENCES

Adler, M., Petch, J. and Tweedie, J. (1989) *Parental Choice and Educational Policy.* Edinburgh: University of Edinburgh Press.
Audit Commission (1996) *Trading Places: The Supply and Allocation of School Places.* London: The Stationery Office.
Bainham, A. and Cretney, S. (1993) *Children: The Modern Law.* Bristol: Jordans.
Beckett, F. (1994) 'Hobson's choice', *The Guardian* (Education), 20 September.
Birkenshaw, P., Harden, I. and Lewis, N. (1990) *Government by Moonlight: The Hybrid Parts of the State.* London: Allen & Unwin.
Bridges, L., Meszaros, G. and Sunkin, M. (1995) *Judicial Review in Perspective* (2nd edn). London: Cavendish.
Cane, P. (1981) 'Ultra vires breach of statutory duty', *Public Law*: 11–19.
Cane, P. (1996) *An Introduction to Administrative Law* (3rd edn). Oxford: Oxford University Press.
Commission for Local Administration in England (1997) *Local Government*

Ombudsman Annual Report 1996/97. London: Commission for Local Administration in England.

Council on Tribunals (1997) *Annual Report 1996–97*. London: HMSO.

Diamond, P. (1996) 'The end of discretionary awards', 8(1) *Education and the Law*: 61–8.

Edwards, T., Fitz, J. and Whitty, G. (1989) *The State and Private Education: An Evaluation of the Assisted Places Scheme*. London: Falmer.

Farrington, D. J. (1994) *Law of Higher Education*. London: Butterworths.

Farrington, D. J. (1996) 'Resolving complaints by students in higher education', 1(1) EPLI: 7–10.

Feintuck, M. (1994) *Accountability and Choice in Schooling*. Milton Keynes: Open University Press.

Garner, J. F. (1974) 'Students – contract or status', 90 *Law Quarterly Review*: 6–7.

Halstead, J. (1994) *Parental Choice and Education*. London: Kogan Page.

Harden, I. (1992) *The Contracting State*. Buckingham: Open University Press.

Harris, N. (1992a) *Complaints About Schooling*. London: National Consumer Council.

Harris, N. (1992b) 'Educational choice in a multi-cultural society', *Public Law*: 522–33.

Harris, N. (1993) *Law and Education: Regulation, Consumerism and the Education System*. London: Sweet & Maxwell.

Harris, N. (1995a) *The Law Relating to Schools* (2nd edn). Croydon: Tolley.

Harris, N. (1995b) 'Quality control and accountability to the consumer' in Brighouse, T. and Moon, B. (eds) *School Inspection*, pp. 46–65. London: Pitman.

Harris, N. (1996a) 'Too bad? The closure of Hackney Downs School under section 225 of the Education Act 1993', 8(3) *Education and the Law*: 109–25.

Harris, N. (ed.) (1996b) *Children, Sex Education and the Law*. London: National Children's Bureau.

Harris, N. (1997) *Special Educational Needs and Access to Justice*. Bristol: Jordans.

Johnson, H. and Riley, K. (1995) 'The impact of quangos and new government agencies on education', 48 *Parliamentary Affairs*: 284–96.

Jones, B. L. and Thompson, K. (1996) *Garner's Administrative Law* (5th edn). London: Butterworths.

Lewis, N. (1989) 'Regulating non-governmental bodies: privatisation, accountability and the public–private divide' in Jowell, J. and Oliver, D. (eds) *The Changing Constitution* (2nd edn), pp. 219–45. London: Macmillan.

Lord Chancellor's Department (1997) *Rights Brought Home: The Human Rights Bill*. Cm 3782. London: The Stationery Office.

Lundy, L. (1996) 'Selection on ability: lessons from Northern Ireland', 8(1) *Education and the Law*: 25–38.

Meredith, P. (1992) *Government, Schools and the Law*. London: Routledge.

Meredith, P. (1995a) 'The future of local education authorities as strategic planners', *Public Law* 234.

Meredith, P. (1995b) 'Judicial review and education' in Hadfield, B. (ed.) *Judicial Review: A Thematic Approach*, pp. 67–98. Dublin: Gill and Macmillan.

O'Connor, M. (1994) *Giving Parents a Voice: Parental Involvement in Education Policy-Making*. London: Research and Information on State Education Trust.

Oliver, S. and Austen, L. (1996) *Special Educational Needs and the Law*. Bristol: Jordans.

Searle, C. (1994) 'The culture of exclusion' in Bourne, J. *et al.* (eds) *Outcast England*, pp. 17–28. London: Institute of Race Relations.

Secretary of State for Education and Employment (1997) *Excellence in Schools*. Cm 3681. London: The Stationery Office

Smith, T. and Noble, M. (1996) *Education Divides: Poverty and Schooling in the 1990s*. London: Child Poverty Action Group.

Taylor-Gooby, P. (1993) 'The new educational settlement: National Curriculum and local management' in Taylor-Gooby, P. and Lawson, R. (eds) *Markets and Managers: New Issues in the Delivery of Welfare*. Buckingham: Open University Press.

Tweedie, J. (1986) 'Rights in social programmes: the case of parental choice of school', *Public Law*: 407–36.

Unwin, L. (1989) 'Learning to live under water: the 1988 Education Reform Act and its implications for further and higher education' in Flude, M. and Hammer, M. (eds) *The Education Reform Act 1988: Its Origins and Implications*, pp. 241–550. London: Falmer.

Wade, H. W. R. (1969) 'Judicial control of universities', 85 *Law Quarterly Review*: 468.

Wade, H. W. R. (1993) 'Visitors and errors of law', 109 *Law Quarterly Review*: 155–9.

Wade, H. W. R. and Forsyth, C. F. (1994) *Administrative Law* (7th edn). Oxford: Oxford University Press.

Walford, G. (1991) 'Choice of school at the first city technology college', 17(1) *Educational Studies*: 65.

Whincup, M. B. (1993) 'The exercise of university disciplinary powers', 5(1) *Education and the Law*: 19–31.

Woolf, H. (1986) 'Public law–private law: why the divide? a personal view', *Public Law*: 220–38.

2

Judicial Review and Access to Health Care

BOB LEE

Notoriously, in England and Wales, the courts have been reluctant to intervene in decisions concerning resource allocation within the National Health Service. There is no case in which a person said to be in pressing need of access to medical services has secured such treatment by a successful application for judicial review of a decision to deny access. This chapter examines the role of the courts in relation to such painful problems of allocation, arguing that while the basis for the court's involvement in such decisions is fragile, this fragility extends to much of the court's role in reviewing medical decision-making more generally. It suggests that as the courts expand their involvement in clinical choices, there is little internal logic in maintaining a self-imposed exile in relation to allocation of medicine, and it suggests that there is an ample legal foundation for scrutiny of allocative decisions should the court be minded to intervene. Finally, the chapter suggests the reasons underlying the refusal to review these decisions, and argues that in refuting the possibility of judicial review, rather than standing aside from clinical decision-making, the courts stand alongside and provide a moral basis for the denial of treatment.

THE ROLE OF THE COURTS

Before examining the role of the courts, it is useful to recall the context in which problems of health care allocation arise in the United Kingdom. Disputes surrounding access to health care are not inevitably a matter of public law. In many jurisdictions litigants

39

would seek private law remedies arising out of contract law, or more precisely insurance contract law.[1] For it is in the nature of health care services that they can be provided by the state or by a health care market made up of private enterprises. This is because health is a hybrid economic good, manifesting some of the qualities of a public, and some of a private good.[2] In the United Kingdom a political determination in 1946 chose largely public provision.[3] One consequence of the commitment of the National Health Service to provide health care services freely at the point of delivery was that any determination of rights of access entered the realm of public law.[4]

At the time of the creation of the NHS, this may not have seemed a particularly significant matter. This is not only because those framing the new structure were concerned with greater issues in their grand plan, but also because they seem genuinely to have believed that there could be open and unrestricted access to NHS facilities.[5] The error was to mistake need and demand. Notions of price elasticity dictate that if services are available freely, individuals will consume them to the point that there is no further utility in so doing.[6] Thus from the very beginning in the NHS, although it was enormously successful in eliminating certain patterns of disease by its public provision, it faced problems of insatiable demand. With no framework to isolate true need within the many demands for treatment, doctors were cast, unwittingly and then unwillingly, in the role of gatekeepers – guardians of the services – controlling access to care.[7]

What has developed is a situation which would seem to provide an obvious role for public law. There are people in desperate need of health service facilities which may include life-saving interventions. There are insufficient resources to satisfy all of those who claim (rightly or wrongly) to have such needs. There are doctors and, increasingly, health administrators who control the access to scarce resources. The question, and the central theme of this chapter, is whether or not public law ought then to make such individuals accountable for decisions which have at their heart major issues of distributive justice. Indeed, to go beyond mere accountability, ought we not to strive to open any such decision-making to the glare of public scrutiny, not least so that there can be a wider sharing or participation in the decisions made?

Put like that the case seems to demand an immediate and affirmative answer, but there is another side to the argument and it is not unconvincing. Society may be happy to allocate such a role to doctors for a number of reasons. It might be thought that in many cases there is relative need, and that the ranking of such need, or the elimination of speculative demand, is primarily a medical question, and one which the doctors, rather than the courts, are best equipped to answer. This argument is dependent on the notion that need can be ranked solely in terms which can be defined as 'medical'. In certain cases, this must be so. A patient might become convinced that they have developed a brain tumour, but if all scans show no evidence of it, then doctors are hardly likely to advance treatment. However, in reality, many instances will arise where patients in convincing need of treatment effectively compete for the same resource. If, at this stage, doctors wish to introduce factors such as the patient's age, lifestyle or family circumstances into the decision-making,[8] then what is it in their role of doctors which makes this permissible? And would society share the wider values forming the basis of the decision? It might be preferable to try to ensure fairness in such decision-making by subjecting the choices made to judicial review.

Again, however, there is an argument against judicial review, and although more elaborate than that concerning 'medical' determinations, it is perhaps more compelling. Ultimately in the circumstances outlined above, it may be that treatment cannot be advanced (or at least not in time) to those in dire need. It would follow that, whatever the intervention of the courts, one or more people may be denied treatment capable of furthering their lives and will die in consequence.[9] It is certainly possible to argue that in Calabresian terms we are destined to face certain tragic choices,[10] and it may be that exposing the tragedy does little to help. Doctors always have borne grave responsibilities on behalf of patients and the community. It could be argued that legal interventions which cause us to focus on the nature of tragic choices hardly help resolve the wider problems, and may even hinder attempts to administer limited budgets. Such a case could be made out in relation to Jaymee Bowen, the child seeking treatment in the case of *R* v *Cambridgeshire HA ex parte B*.[11] In the end, although medical intervention was secured as a result of the publicity generated by the litigation (though not through the litigation itself) the child's life ended in the midst of a media circus.[12] Many people bore the news of her death with a heavy heart, since she was clearly a brave little girl who relished life despite her suffering. However, it is less than clear what good knowing about her sad circumstances did for anyone. Only if the courts intervened consistently in favour of the dying patient would this problem be overcome, or so the argument goes, and then what meaning would attach to any such review?[13]

Even setting aside problems of media attention, however, one can question the wisdom of passing responsibility for medical choices over to the courts. There is a discernible move towards what one might call judicialization of the doctor and patient relationship, as the courts rule on sterilization of incompetent patients,[14] PVS cases,[15] enforced caesareans,[16] and other refusals by the patient of the treatment offered.[17] It is not clear what it is that leaves the judge better placed to decide the moral dilemmas inherent in many such applications. Nor indeed do such decisions always resolve such moral questions. Certain difficult cases come before the courts as emergency applications, which the judges insist should not be taken as indicative of a binding determination of the issue[18] (although one might observe that having permitted a course of action it is inevitably more difficult to refuse future similar applications). On other occasions the law demonstrates a remarkable capacity to frame the question in a way which evades the central moral issues. In many ways the recent case of *Blood*[19] is a typical example of this, as an apparently straightforward ethical issue of whether to permit a widow to be inseminated with the sperm of her dead husband is transformed into an issue of her right, in European Union law, to travel elsewhere in the Union for treatment.

Having said that, there is a compelling argument that these cases should come to court precisely because such cases involve moral questions. On this analysis the importance of the courts is the provision of a public and institutional forum within which to hold the debate. That is to say that there may be other possible arenas in which the question could be put, but few which would air the issue quite so formally or would be so well placed to inform a wider public of the resolution of the moral dimensions of medicine.[20] To support this mediating function of the legal process is to refute the 'tragic choices' argument put earlier, and to assume that the language of the law clarifies rather than shrouds the moral issues at stake. However, if the courts are to provide this institutional forum, and if they provide a medium through which society engages with ethical issues in modern medicine, can they afford to be silent in relation to certain selected moral issues? As this chapter will attempt to demonstrate, this is the true dilemma facing the courts in the access to health care cases.

The denial of health care facilities in our system of public provision is unquestionably an ethical as well as a legal issue. This is not merely because of the consequences which may follow (though utilitarians would wish to focus on the outcomes in the circumstances of any case) nor because of reasons of beneficence, nor because it is wrong to deny the treatment, and not simply because allocation decisions may exhibit a lack of respect for particular interests. Rather, it is an ethical issue for all of these reasons,[21] and more besides. Jennings argues that moral decision-making in medicine is increasingly 'embedded as never before in a network of explicit rules and formal procedures and processes'.[22] For Jennings such organizational form itself produces the ethical conclusions, and ethical notions are constructed within these contexts rather than as a result of some neutral process of philosophical reflection. Thus, on one view, legal discourse itself begins to frame ethical choice – no less in consideration of access to treatment than in its denial. More than that, a refusal to involve themselves in decisions concerning access to health care no less contributes to ethical standards than does a refusal, for example, to support euthanasia.

Thus although there is room to question the utility of the courts occupying so central a role in the framing, determining and disseminating news of ethical choices, it is well understood that they do so and that in so doing they form part of the transformation of the ethical concerns of society. This places a heavy responsibility on the legal process, and at the very least it demands of the court an awareness of its own role, especially where it eschews entry to areas of moral debate. This is particularly so as the focus for many moral choices switches away from a power basis located in the doctor/patient relationship and traditionally understood in terms of entrenched notions of medical paternalism and patient autonomy. Just as the big ethical questions arise increasingly not in the surgery but in the research laboratory, genetics clinic or infertility treatment centre, so too where decisions previously involved a doctor, they now concern the multi-disciplinary team, the health economist, the system administrator and the politician. The patient too is now a patient group, or interest group, or part of a genetic linkage involving a number of others or potential others, with disparate needs and concerns. This patient grouping is informed, at a keystroke, from sources which it can access no less easily than those whom we once knew as the professional. However, the approach taken by the courts to questions concerning allocation of medical resources has remained rooted in non-interference in the midst of such dramatic shifts as the following analysis seeks to demonstrate.

RELUCTANCE TO REVIEW

These cultural and contextual changes have a profound impact on decisions about allocation of resources, and they seem to be little understood by the judges. An examination of the case law demonstrates that the courts focus continually on the formal exercise of powers which they class as political, discretionary and beyond their purview and which they locate in centralized choices of expenditure of resources.[23] This denies a reality of the exercise of real power in determining the fate of individuals, vested in those who are accountable only in closed systems of internal review and not in any wider political or legal framework. This is against the background of no accepted formula of establishing treatment priorities, or indeed of assessing health care outcomes.[24] Indeed the health economists, who have worked hard to construct working tools to assist (if not dictate) priorities for treatment, have done so precisely on the basis that the types of cost benefit analysis suggested has its strength in 'its ability to force consideration of the issue of placing values on health outcomes and thereby promote the cause of efficiency in health care'.[25] It seems somewhat ironic that economists should seek to capture this ground by appealing to ethical principles at the same time as lawyers refuse to enter the territory. For Ian Kennedy has written of the most important 'basic moral principle' of 'seeking to do justice or equity among people'.[26] Justice would seem to imply, at least in the view of Rawls,[27] that we should wish to, or may even have a duty, to see that those worst off be given highest priority.

In the few cases brought in which patients seek access to treatment judges have ruled that there is little scope for intervention given the wording of the statutory framework. There is a statutory duty upon the Secretary of State to provide hospital accommodation and other health services detailed in section 3 of the National Health Services Act 1977 in order to meet all reasonable requirements. The difficulty with the section is the qualification of the duty by the words 'to such extent as he considers necessary'. Thus in cases such as *R v Secretary of State for Social Services ex parte Hincks*[28] where orthopaedic patients in Birmingham could show a deterioration in their condition as a result of delays caused by the reversal of plans to build a new orthopaedic unit, previously approved, both at first instance and on appeal the patients' action failed. In spite of this, this case from the first instance decision onwards allowed a route of challenge which technically remains open, namely that in the exercise of discretion the minister might act so unreasonably in the *Wednesbury*[29] sense or might act so as to frustrate the policy of the Act so as to allow redress.

The plaintiff's argument, in *Hincks*, that the Act demands the continuing promotion of 'a comprehensive health service' and that there was no express constraint upon the duty on financial grounds (even though Parliament could have allowed limitations required by financial planning) was said to be 'attractive'.[30] Notwithstanding this, and in spite of judicial activism in vastly extending the ambit of judicial review since the *Hincks* decision in 1980, the grounds for non-intervention given by the Court of Appeal in that case have essentially been reiterated in all subsequent cases.[31] Broadly any action by the Secretary of State was subject to the economic constraints facing the government of the day, since the imposition of an unlimited duty to extend the resources might demand unlimited resources. Moreover, it has been said that the general duties imposed in the statutory framework make it impossible to 'put the spotlight ... upon one particular department of one hospital and to say that conditions there are unsatisfactory'.[32] If this formulation is correct then it may prove impossible to use the section 3 duty to challenge the Secretary of States' action even in the limited terms allowed by notions of *Wednesbury* unreasonableness.

Commenting on the *Hincks* case, Parkin wrote that 'the absence of reporting and comment on this case is perhaps indicative of its orthodoxy, and perhaps the suspicions voiced in the Court of Appeal that the real purpose behind the action was publicity'.[33] Parkin points to the traditional failure of the choice of school cases under the Education Act 1944[34] as an indication of the difficulty in challenging what Lord Woolf was later to describe as 'target duties'.[35] One might add further examples of historic failures to challenge decisions allowing access to social housing[36] or to community care.[37] Note, however, that in these areas statutory reforms have created mechanisms for challenge by concentrating attention on the choices and processes of those administering the resources available.[38]

Yet in relation to health care this has not been so, and even where individual patients seek review of particular decisions made about them in the health care system, the courts have continued to shelter behind the isolation of target duties from review rather than engage with the individual circumstances of the patient-litigant. Thus in two cases both arising also out of Birmingham,[39] and both driven as much by the wish for publicity as the expectation of a remedy, the same response emanates from the courts. Both cases involved heart surgery for infants indisputably in need but repeatedly denied because other cases were given priority access to an admittedly restricted paediatric intensive care facility. 'The balance of available money and its distribution and use' were not matters which the court could investigate, though nor were 'decisions as to staffing'.[40] It was not for the court to substitute its judgment for that of 'those who are responsible for the allocation of resources'.[41] This was something which the court was in 'no position to judge',[42] and what was being suggested was no more than 'somehow more resources should be made available'.[43]

This manner of formulating the problem is rather curious. Elsewhere in the judgments, the individual tragedy is recognized as 'disturbing and distressing'[44] and yet that individual claim for access or relative priority is lost as the courts redefine the problem as some universal and standardized difficulty facing not the child but the system. Newdick puts the matter rather well when he asks 'on what system of priorities was such a refusal to provide care based?' when in *Collier* a district health authority 'with long experience of annual demand for paediatric intensive care' chose not to make available common life-saving cardiac surgery which might be classed as acute fatal treatment to a 4-year-old boy described as being 'desperately needed' by the health authority's own consultant.[45] In such circumstances can the courts go behind the 'target duty' and review the exercise of the duty in practice. In *R v Islington LBC ex parte Rixon*[46] Sedley J stated that it is the nature of a target duty that 'the statute requires the public authority to aim to make the prescribed provisions but does not regard failure to achieve it without more as a breach'.

This dictum is significant; De Smith suggests that 'apart from non-justiciable decisions, the courts will no longer in principle refrain from reviewing any decision'.[47] Although De Smith would include within this non-justiciable element decisions on allocation of scarce resources, pointing particularly to health care, Sedley J's formulation suggests that a target duty is reviewable while leaving open the question of what it is that will constitute the 'more' which provides the basis of review. That this is correct is apparent both from *Hincks*, *Collier*, *Walker*, and the most recent case of *ex parte B*. In the latter case, although the application is described by Bingham MR as a 'wholly understandable but nonetheless misguided (attempt) to involve the court in a field of activity where it is not fitted to make any decision favourable to the patient',[48] Stephen Brown P states that he is 'unable to say that the health authority . . . acted in a way which exceeded its powers or which was unreasonable in the legal sense'.[49] Although we will see later that there is much in the Court of Appeal's language which seems to accept a restricted role, as this dictum indicates, it is not that the decisions themselves are non-justiciable, rather that there are certain limited grounds for review.

At first instance in the case,[50] Laws J had granted the application and quashed the decision of the health authority to refuse a course of treatment which may have held some slight prospects of success for a 10-year-old leukaemia victim. The treatment would have consisted of a course of chemotherapy at a cost of £15,000, which, if effective, would be followed by a bone marrow transplant costing a further £60,000. Laws J stated that the health authority could have treated this as a two-stage process, so that the initial question involved the expenditure of £15,000, and that in refusing to allocate such a sum, the authority had erred in failing to place sufficient weight on the wishes of the parent, in classifying the treatment as a one-stage experimental process and in pointing in far too generalized a way to the limited resources. In the words of the judge: 'where the question is whether the life of a ten year old might be saved ... they must explain the priorities which have led them to decline to fund the treatment'.[51]

Thus, Laws J would wish to see some weighty and objective determination for the decision to deny life described as 'a substantial public interest determination'. This may seem some way from *Wednesbury* principles, but in the view of the judge, 'the decisive touchstone of legality' was never likely to be 'the crude *Wednesbury* bludgeon'.[52] This was because the decision about B involved her right to life, and relying on two judgments of Lord Bridge,[53] which Laws J himself had drawn to the counsel's attention, he argued that the right to life existed not merely as a right to be enjoyed under the European Convention of Human Rights nor as a moral or political aspiration, but as a shared principle within the substance of the common law. He relied in particular on the judgment of Lord Bridge in *R* v *Secretary of State for the Home Department ex parte Bugdaycay*: 'The most fundamental of all human rights is the individual's right to life and when an administrative decision under challenge is said to be one which may put the applicant's life at risk, the decision must surely call for the most anxious scrutiny.'[54]

The Court of Appeal showed no great enthusiasm for extending this line of thinking developed in asylum cases to the area of health care allocation, making no reference to this line of authority but pointing instead to the limitation of the court to question the lawfulness, and the inability to review the merits of any decision.[55] Moreover, it would be 'unrealistic' to require that a health authority demonstrate the relative priorities of patients within their care. There is a stark contrast between these two positions, yet it is undeniable that a life is at stake every bit as much in the *ex parte B* case. Why is it then that the Court of Appeal refused to advance from its position in *Walker* and *Collier*? And would it be open to the courts in the future to scrutinize the substance of allocation decisions made by health authorities?

'TOLLING THE BELL' OF TIGHT RESOURCES[56]

The interventionist line propounded by Sir John Laws in *ex parte B* should be seen alongside his wider advocacy of a judicial role both in testing decisions of administrative bodies against the yardstick of fundamental rights, and also for a more formal transfer of power to the judiciary in order that fundamental rights may be protected from the exercise of public power to sustain democratic principles.[57] It seems probable that this rhetoric proves of concern to at least some of his judicial colleagues who then demonstrate little enthusiasm for the role. However, it is unnecessary to travel all the way along the constitutional road with Laws J in order to arrive at some logic in his position. If as now seems to be the case the courts are willing on occasions to subject to particular scrutiny certain decisions concerning fundamental rights independently protected by the common law, and if as De Smith suggests the right to life is so recognized,[58] it is difficult to explain the decision in *ex parte B*.

One explanation is that the courts would like to intervene in these cases too, but realize the practical impossibility of review. But Bingham MR in the Court of Appeal in *ex parte B* describes the entire application as a 'misguided' attempt 'to involve the court in a field of activity where it is not fitted'[59] – suggesting some wider encumbrance upon the courts' ability to review such decisions. As James and Longley write,

> it may be that the Court of Appeal felt that the health authority had provided sufficient evidence for reaching the decision to which it had come. If that were the case, it would have been preferable to have acknowledged that explicitly, rather than taking a restricted view in the court's role.[60]

Indeed, as this comment suggests, the more one reads the judgment of the Court of Appeal, the harder it is to grasp its rationality. Thus while the Master of the Rolls states that to consider the merits of the decision taken would have the court 'straying far from the sphere which under our constitution is accorded to us' and that medical decisions are not those 'which the court can make',[61] nevertheless he finds it 'impossible to fault [the] process of thinking on their [the health authority's] part'.[62] Consequently while the courts reject their role as a forum to rule upon 'the way in which natural resources are allocated or distributed', every case from *Hincks* onwards has claimed to review decisions taken at least to establish whether there might be a *prima facie* case of *Wednesbury* unreasonableness. All that Law J then argues is that the courts should go further into this process of investigation where a life is at stake. This is hardly greatly different from the greater latitude now allowed in leave hearings in asylum cases because of 'the gravity of the issue which the decision determines'.[63]

The mere fact that a decision has been delegated in the discretionary fashion laid down in the 1977 Act hardly disbars the court from demanding an explanation of how that discretion has been exercised to ensure fairness and distributive justice in the wielding of this power entrusted to deal with competing interests which are as much public as private in nature. In refusing to act in this way, Bingham MR states that where the court then demands reconsideration 'the authority could, on a proper review of all the relevant material reach the same decision'.[64] Putting aside the view of Laws J that the denial of the initial stage of treatment for B could hardly be on a proper basis, this misses the point.

In undertaking a review of the decision, and demanding reconsideration, the courts open up the decision-making. Choices must become transparent, and the values which underpin them are inevitably exposed and subject to question. Sending a decision back for reconsideration may not always lead to a favourable treatment decision but nor is it a 'cruel deception'[65] since it forces *under court scrutiny*[66] internal review of underpinning values which may have become institutionalized in the process of decision-making and which may be a denial of fair and even-handed dealings with people in critical need.

So the practical difficulties facing the courts are not those of rewriting the waiting lists, but can be overcome by subjecting those in charge of allocation to demonstrate some justifiable process which serves the public interest, and, where in doubt as to the substantive quality of the decisions made, to subject them to reconsideration under the public gaze. If this is not possible, and if this form of review is not a matter of great practical difficulty, what underpins the reluctance of the courts in this particular context? It is difficult to locate the judicial reluctance in terms of a constitutional role and in the context of a limited purview of duties delegated by a sovereign Parliament. It seems odd that the courts should pursue strong and inventive attacks on attempts to limit their ability to review administrative decisions,[67] only to buckle before the implied limitation of a target duty. Moreover, of late, the courts have been less fearful of challenging decisions made by those invested with a power. The boundaries of what was once seen as the 'legal' and the 'political' are increasingly blurred in the face of such judicial activism. However, it seems that in areas of resource allocation, the courts show a recognition that in the modern state political power vests increasingly in those who hold the purse strings, and the courts are not yet ready to encroach upon this particular territory. Yet many other judgments of the courts have profound economic conse-quences, and demand not only that funds be reallocated but that new funds be found.[68] In any case, if this were so, it would provide considerable irony. At a time when the courts are so willing to subject to review the activities of government ministers, in their exercise of apparent and generally technical powers, that the issue becomes one of constitutional debate, are they to be seen as slow to make accountable the scores of faceless professionals who exercise real power over the real lives of real people?

A CONCLUSION

There is something much deeper at the heart of these decisions. The argument expressed above is that making decision-makers accountable depends on openness, explanation and justification in order to expose the underpinning values which bolster the choices made. Might it not be that the courts shun such processes because the values involved are essentially moral in nature? Perhaps, even, the courts are aware that often there will be no clear ethical principle informing decisions of who shall live and who shall die, and that consequently no clear criteria supporting choice could be produced if demanded by the court. Indeed the very opening up of the decision-making process would expose a void filled by little more than best guessing, political trade-offs, historic bias and intra-professional or inter-disciplinary rivalries in medicine. On such an analysis, it is not just a case of the courts not wishing to become involved in the merits of the decision, but of not wishing the demerits of present processes of allocation to become apparent as the tragic choices continue.

This is a bleak conclusion; especially so since, if Jennings[69] is correct, the stance not to question decisions about denying life-saving treatment itself forms a strong ethical influence in terms of what it is we permit to happen and how. Not to examine why it is that the intensive care bed or the course of chemotherapy is not made available to a dying infant is as much a moral statement as a decision to allow life support to be withdrawn or to intervene to demand surgery on the mother to preserve the life of the foetus. Whether they wish it or not the courts make these moral choices, and, in so doing, shape those of a society – no less in denying the power to judge as in making the judgment.

NOTES

1 For a comparison with the United States, see D. Fox, *Health Policies, Health Politics: The British and American Experience 1911–1965*, Princeton, NJ: Princeton University Press (1986), and F. H. Miller, 'Competition law and anti-competitive professional behaviour affecting health care', 55 *Modern Law Review* (1992): 453.

2 This is a distinction explored in greater detail in R. Lee, 'What good is health care' (unpublished draft available from author).

3 As laid down in the National Health Service Act 1946. Arguably, with the arrival of internal markets, competition operates within the health care system to produce something other than straightforward public provision – see R. Saltman and C. Van Otter, 'Public competition versus mixed markets: an analysis comparison', 11 *Health Policy* (1989): 43.

4 For an excellent account of the role of administrative law in relation to NHS provision see D. Longley, 'Diagnostic dilemmas: accountability in the National Health Service', (1990) *Public Law*: 527.

5 For further examination of this issue see R. Lee, 'Legal control of health care allocation' in M. Ockleton (ed.) *Medicine Ethics and Law*, Stuttgart: Steiner (1986), at p. 93, and L. Doyal, *The Political Economy of Health* (2nd impression), London: Pluto (1981).

6 A. Pigou, *A Study in Public Finance*, London: Macmillan (1928).

7 R. Lee and F. H. Miller, 'The doctor's changing role in allocating US and British medical services', 18(1)(2) *Law Medicine and Health Care* (1990): 69.

8 See, for example, J. Avron, 'Benefit and cost analysis in geriatric care: turning age discrimination into health policy', 310 *New England Journal of Medicine* (1984): 1294. C. Hall and R. Ernsberger, 'Playing God in the hospital', *Newsweek*, 30 August 1993, p. 4 (comment on refusal to test a 47-year-old smoker for suitability for cardiac bypass operation – Manchester 1993); D. Brahams, 'When is discontinuation of dialysis justified?', *Lancet*, 19 January 1985, p. 176 (following refusal of dialysis to an Oxford vagrant). And see more generally J. Harris, *The Value of Life* (1985), London: RKP.

9 J. F. Childress, 'Who shall live when not all can live?', (1970) *Soundings*: 339.

10 G. Calabresi and P. Bobbit, *Tragic Choices*, New York: Norton (1978). It is important to note, however, that the authors would primarily refer to tragic choices which are inevitable in that we are destined to face them, and that many of the choices to which this chapter refers are of a second order, namely choices implied by scarcity of resource. At least one ethicist would argue that we must 'try to ensure that we have sufficient resources to devote to postponing death, whatever and whenever we can, whether for long or short periods, so that we do not choose between people invidiously': Harris, note 8 above, p. 110.

11 [1995] 2 All ER 129.

12 Although, to be fair, the publicity followed an application by the father to lift any reporting restrictions in the hope that publicity would secure private funding – which eventually transpired.

13 The problem is that this formulation assumes that decision-making in this area is primarily clinical rather than financial, and although there may be certain cases which fall essentially into the clinical category, the courts can hardly discern this without making further enquiry.

14 *Re B (a minor) (wardship: sterilisation)* [1988] AC 199; *F v West Berkshire HA (Mental Health Commission Intervening)* [1990] 2 AC 1; and see Practice Note [1993] 3 All ER 222 requiring prior sanction of the High Court for the sterilization of minors or mentally incompetent adults.

15 *Airedale NHS Trust v Bland* [1993] AC 789; *Frenchay NHS Trust v S* [1994] 2 All ER 403; and see Practice Note at [1994] 2 All ER 413 introducing similar procedures for patients in a persistent vegetative state to those operating for sterilization cases under the 1993 Practice Note, note 14 above.

16 *Norfolk/Norwich (NHS) Trust v W* [1997] 1 FCR 269; *Rochdale Healthcare (NHS) Trust v C* [1997] 1 FCR 274; *Tameside and Glossop Acute Services Trust v C.H.* [1996] 1 FLR 762; *Re S, Independent*, 10 July 1997; *Re L* [1997] 1 FCR 609; *Re MB* [1997] 2 FCR 541.

17 *B* v *Croydon HA* [1995] 1 All ER 683; *Re C* (adult: refusal of medical treatment) [1994] 1 All ER 819; *Re T* [1992] 4 All ER 649 – and see the propositions laid down at 664 on the legal principles applicable to such cases.

18 See the judgment of Lord Bingham MR in *Re S (Hospital Patient: Court's Jurisdiction* [1995] 3 All ER 290 in which he reviews such cases and considers the 'development of a new advisory declaratory jurisdiction'.

19 *R* v *Human Fertilisation and Embryology Authority ex parte DB* [1997] 2 All ER 687; and see D. Morgan and R. Lee, 'In the name of the father? Ex parte Blood: dealing with novelty and anomaly', 60 *Modern Law Review* (1997): 840.

20 The problem with this argument is that, as is mooted above, 'judicialization' necessarily changes the issue under debate – a process of rectification. The author is grateful to Derek Morgan for pointing to the possible exception of the extraordinary judgment of Hoffmann LJ (as he then was) in *Airedale NHS Trust* v *Bland* [1993] 1 All ER 821 at 849.

21 See further R. Gillian and A. Lloyd (eds), *Principles of Health Care Ethics*, London: Wiley (1993).

22 B. Jennings, 'Possibilities of consensus: towards democratic moral discourse', 16 *Journal of Medicine and Philosophy* (1991): 447, at 463. For a consideration of this important work see Morgan, note 20 above, at 203.

23 For an excellent account of this which critically examines the role of the courts in the context of changing patterns of health care delivery see A. Parkin, 'Public law and the provision of health care', [1985] *Urban Law and Policy*: 101.

24 A. Stevens and J. Gabbay, 'Needs assessment needs assessment', [1991] *Health Trends*: 20.

25 G. H. Mooney, 'Cost benefit analysis and medical ethics', [1980] *Journal of Medical Ethics*: 177.

26 I. Kennedy, *The Unmasking of Medicine* (2nd rev. edn), St Albans: Granada (1983).

27 J. Rawls, *A Theory of Justice*, Oxford: Oxford University Press (1972).

28 (1992) 1 BMLR 93 (but case was decided in 1980).

29 *Associated Provincial Picture Houses Ltd* v *Wednesbury Corporation* [1948] 1 KB 223.

30 *Per* Lord Denning MR.

31 See *R* v *Secretary of State for Social Services ex parte Walker* (1992) 3 BMLR 32 (decided in 1987); *R* v *Birmingham Health Authority ex parte Collier* (unreported – 1988 – but see I. Kennedy and A. Grubb, *Medical Law – Text with Materials* (2nd edn), London: Butterworths (1994)), and *ex parte B* (above).

32 *Per* Lord Denning MR in *ex parte Walker*, note 31 above.

33 Parkin, note 23 above, at p. 104.

34 See ss. 8, 36 and 76 of the Education Act 1944 as interpreted in *Watt* v *Kesteven CC* [1955] 1 QB 408; *Wood* v *London Borough of Ealing* [1957] Ch. 364; *Cummings* v *Birkenhead Corporation* [1972] Ch. 12.

35 In *R* v *Inner London Education Authority ex parte Ali* (1990) 2 Admin. LR: 822, at 828, referring to s. 8 of the 1944 Act. Parkin did not adopt this phrase writing in 1985 (note 23 above).

36 See Part V Housing Act 1957 and s. 70 Housing Act 1969, also *Casey* v *Dunganon RDC* (1971) (unreported but cited in D. Hoath (ed.) *Council Housing* (2nd edn), London: Sweet & Maxwell (1982), p. 42).

37 See s. 29 National Assistance Act 1948 and *R v Islington LBC ex parte Rixon*, *The Times*, 17 April 1996.

38 See Education Act 1980, the Housing (Homeless Persons) Act 1977 and the Chronically Sick and Disabled Persons Act 1970.

39 *Ex parte Walker* and *Ex parte Collier*, note 31 above.

40 *Ex parte Walker*, note 31 above, at 34, *per* Macpherson J.

41 *Ibid.*, at 35, *per* Lord Donaldson MR.

42 *Ex parte Collier* (unreported).

43 *Ibid.* Quotation taken from C. Newdick, *Who Should We Treat*, Oxford: Clarendon Press (1995), p. 125.

44 *Ex parte Walker*, note 31 above, at 34 *per* Macpherson J.

45 Note 43 above, p. 127.

46 Above, at note 37.

47 S. A. De Smith, H. Woolf and J. Jowell, *Judicial Review of Administrative Action* (5th edn), London: Sweet and Maxwell (1995), at p. 314 (hereafter referred to as 'De Smith').

48 [1995] 2 All ER 129.

49 *Ex parte B*, note 11 above, at 138.

50 Reported at [1995] FLR 1055.

51 *Ibid.*, at 1065.

52 *Ibid.*, at 1058–9.

53 *R v Secretary of State for the Home Department ex parte Brind* [1991] AC 696 and *R v Secretary of State for the Home Department ex parte Bugdaycay* [1987] AC 514.

54 *Ibid.*, at 531.

55 *Re J (a minor) (medical treatment)* [1992] 4 All ER 614; see also the judgment of Leggatt LJ concerning the 'Absolute undesirability of the court making an order which may have the effect of compelling a doctor or a health authority to make available scarce resources'.

56 This is a reference to the judgment of Laws J in *ex parte B* where he states that however slim the chance for Jaymee Bowen, the health authority must do more than merely toll the bell in this way.

57 See J. Laws, 'Is the Constitution the guardian of fundamental rights', [1993] *Public Law*: 59; J. Laws, 'Judicial remedies and the constitution', 57 *Modern Law Review* (1994): 213; and J. Laws, 'Law and democracy', [1995] *Public Law*: 72.

58 De Smith, note 47 above, pp. 327–8.

59 *Ex parte B*, note 11 above, at 138.

60 R. James and D. Longley, 'Judicial review and tragic choices: *ex parte B*', [1995] *Public Law*: 367, at 371.

61 *Ex parte B*, note 11 above, at 137.

62 *Ibid.*, at 138.

63 *Per* Lord Bridge in *ex parte Bugdaycay*, note 53 above, at 531.

64 *Ex parte B*, note 11 above, at 138.

65 *Ibid.*

66 See the recent case of *R v Human Fertilisation and Embryology Authority ex parte DB* (note 19 above) where Lord Woolf does direct a reconsideration of the HFEA's decision in the Blood affair very much under the scrutiny of the Court of Appeal and with a very strong steer on the public policy issues. This is also

very close to the line which Laws J would have taken in *ex parte B*.

67 Even in the express wording of an ouster clause in a statute – see famously *Anisminic* v *Foreign Compensation Commission* [1969] 2 AC 147 and see De Smith, pp. 237 *et seq*.

68 See *R* v *Gloucestershire CC ex parte Mahfood* and the judgment of McCowan LJ discussed in L. Clements, *Community Care and the Law*, London: Legal Action Group (1996), p. 53. Readers should be aware that this chapter was written prior to the decision of the House of Lords in *R* v *Gloucestershire CC ex parte Barry*, [1997] 2 All ER 1, and also prior to the decision of Dyson J In *R* v *North Derbyshire H.A. ex parte Fisher*, (1997) 38 BMLR 76. This latter case affects parts of the text of this chapter in that it declares a policy decision on the administration of treatment through the drug beta-interferon unlawful. The policy was said not to meet guidance offered by the NHS executive and was not a reasonable way of giving effect to the circular containing the guidance.

69 Note 22 above.

3

Judicial Review and Mental Health

PHIL FENNELL

BACKGROUND: THE LEGISLATIVE FRAMEWORK

The Mental Health Act 1983 is the health and welfare statute which impinges most strongly upon civil liberties, because it allows people to be detained and treated compulsorily if they are suffering from mental disorder of the requisite nature or degree. Like its predecessor, the Mental Health Act 1959, in many ways it reflects a 'medicalist' orientation, conferring wide discretionary powers on mental health professionals to detain and to treat without consent.[1] It provides under one legislative umbrella for the detention of both non-offender and offender patients.

For non-offender patients there is a medically and socially based compulsory admission procedure whereby a social worker or the patient's 'nearest relative', supported by medical 'recommendations', applies for the patient's detention to an administrative authority, the 'managers' of the receiving hospital (the health authority; nowadays the NHS trust). The application is accepted by hospital administrators or other designated staff receiving the statutory documents when the patient is admitted. Except in emergencies, two medical recommendations are necessary, one from a doctor approved as having special experience in the diagnosis or treatment of mental disorder, and the other from any doctor, preferably one with acquaintance with the patient. After admission, patients are entitled to apply to a Mental Health Review Tribunal (MHRT), which must order discharge if satisfied that the criteria for detention are no longer met.

Mentally disordered offenders committing an imprisonable offence can be admitted under a hospital order. Where necessary to protect the public from serious harm, a Crown Court can attach a restriction order to a hospital order, the effect being that the patient may not be discharged (except by an MHRT), transferred or granted leave without the permission of the Home Secretary. Mentally disordered prisoners can also be transferred from prison to hospital with or without restrictions on their discharge. Offender patients have the right to seek discharge by an MHRT.

MHRTs were first constituted in 1959 to introduce a judicial element into review of the need for detention, which would be available during each period for which detention was extended, review being triggered by an application made by or on behalf of the patient. The intention was for the lawfulness of the *initial* detention to be reviewed according to the usual criteria by the High Court through judicial review or habeas corpus, whilst the need for *continued* detention would be reviewed by the MHRTs. Each MHRT hearing takes place before a lawyer president, a medical member of consultant psychiatrist status who examines the patient before the hearing and reports to the panel, and a lay member.

While the 1959 Act was characterized by wide professional discretion to detain (medicalism), the amendments in the 1983 Act are often described as representing a 'new legalism'. This reflected not only concern to protect traditional 'negative' rights in the sense of freedom from arbitrary and unjustified detention, and adequate and effective review of psychiatric decision-making, but also ideas of positive entitlement to care in the least restrictive alternative setting, and the ideology of entitlement – that sufferers had the right to an adequate service.[2]

A major emphasis of the Act is protection safeguards of 'negative' rights *not* to be detained and treated against one's will. The 1983 Act reflects patient entitlement to treatment in the least restrictive setting in the admission and renewal criteria by making it a condition of admission for treatment and renewal that detention may not take place unless it is certified that treatment cannot be provided without resort to compulsory admission. The effect of this provision was considered by McCullough J in *R v Hallstrom ex parte W (No. 2)*.[3] As we shall see, this case has not only had a strong influence on the law on compulsory community care, it also reflects the judicial high water mark of legalism since the 1983 Act. The frequency of patients' entitlement to review of their case by an MHRT was doubled. MHRTs' powers were also increased. Previously their role with regard to restriction order patients had been confined to *advising* the Home Secretary on their suitability for discharge. In 1981 the European Court of Human Rights ruled against the UK in *X v United Kingdom*[4] that all persons detained on grounds of unsoundness of mind, including offenders detained in hospital on a court order, are entitled under Article 5(4) of the European Convention on Human Rights at intervals to seek review of the lawfulness of their detention by a court which must have the power to *order* discharge. The 1983 Act empowers MHRTs to direct absolute or conditional discharge of patients subject to a hospital order with Home Office restrictions on discharge. But it was also provided that such MHRTs should be presided over by judges with experience of sentencing, instead of the existing chairs, who were not judges but experienced solicitors or barristers.

The 1983 Act introduced automatic hearings for patients who do not apply to the tribunal within a specified period of detention, and extended the right to apply for an MHRT review to patients admitted for up to twenty-eight days' assessment. Patients were granted readier access to the report of the responsible authority and its reasons for opposing discharge, and were enabled to be present throughout the hearing unless a specific case based on clear criteria was made for non-disclosure of any of the report or for excluding the patient from any part of the hearing.[5] In any event the patient's representative is entitled to be present throughout and to access to any parts of the report withheld.[6] Changes were made in the legal aid system to enable patients to be represented and in 1994 the Lord Chancellor abolished the means test in MHRT cases.[7] These developments signal an increasing judicialization of the decision to discharge detained psychiatric patients, a process further emphasized by the House of Lords ruling in *Pickering* v *Liverpool Daily Post and Echo Newspapers plc*[8] that MHRTs are courts for the purposes of the law of contempt.

Further emphasis to patients' rights was given by the establishment of a multi-disciplinary Special Health Authority, the Mental Health Act Commission (MHAC), to oversee the exercise of powers and the discharge of duties under the Act in relation to detained patients, visit them in hospital, ensure that their complaints are investigated, and administer the system of statutory second opinions in relation to psychiatric treatment under Part IV. Part IV of the Act made clear that treatment could be given to detained patients without their consent, subject to a statutory second opinion from a consultant psychiatrist appointed by the MHAC. Certain controversial treatments (psychosurgery or surgical implantation of hormones to suppress male sex drive) may only be given with consent and a favourable second opinion.[9]

Despite this emphasis on patients' rights, the new legalism was grafted on to a framework which remains essentially based on medical discretion. Even Part IV grants extensive discretion to treat without consent and the new safeguards for patients' rights were based on medical second opinions. The one provision of the 1983 Act which can be said to reflect positive rights in terms of entitlement to services is s. 117. Section 117 applies to patients who cease to be detained and leave hospital (whether or not immediately after so ceasing) following detention under the 1983 Act for treatment (s. 3), under a hospital order with or without restrictions made by a criminal court (s. 37), or following transfer from prison with or without restrictions (s. 47 or s. 48).[10] The local Health Authority and social services authority are under a joint duty to provide, in co-operation with relevant voluntary agencies, after-care services for patients in the above categories until the authorities are satisfied that they no longer need them. The all-important link between these positive rights to care services and the negative rights of freedom from unjustified detention is provided by the principle of entitlement to care in the least restrictive setting. One key to evaluating judicial review in mental health is the extent to which the jurisprudence reflects the new legalism, and to which it has established links between its two prime concerns, namely protection of traditional negative rights in the sense of freedom from unjustified detention and compulsory treatment, and promotion of positive rights to community care, and care in the least restrictive alternative setting.

DEVELOPMENT OF JUDICIAL REVIEW

Section 139 of the 1983 Act reduced the substantive and procedural hurdles which face anyone seeking to litigate in relation to a purported exercise of powers and duties under the Act. However, the leave of the High Court is still required before proceedings can be instituted against anyone other than the Secretary of State, a health authority or an NHS Trust. In *R v Hallstrom ex parte W* the Court of Appeal held that the language of s. 139 was not sufficiently broad to apply to judicial review. Ackner LJ said that Parliament had not intended to bar the Court's supervisory jurisdiction because, had it done so, 'there would indeed have been no remedy to quash a compulsory admission to hospital made as a result of a reasonable misconception of a public official's powers' and this 'would have disclosed a serious inadequacy in the powers of the courts to protect the citizen from an actual or potential loss of liberty arising out of a serious error of law'.[11]

More judicial attention has been paid to the 1983 Act than to any previous mental health legislation, and the number of applications for judicial review was undoubtedly stimulated by the extension in 1983 of legal aid to Mental Health Review Tribunals. The arrival of lawyers astute to the opportunities for judicial review of MHRT decisions, and the extension of their activities into areas of treatment without consent and lawfulness of detention, have had an important influence on the development of judicial review. It is impossible in a brief compass to survey the entire body of case law involving judicial review of decisions under the Mental Health Act. This chapter therefore focuses primarily on decisions to detain and to release from detention, which I have identified as negative rights. It begins with an examination of the traditional role of the courts in reviewing the lawfulness of decisions of the authorities to detain, to renew detention, or to recall patients to hospital. It then proceeds to look at judicial review of MHRTs. It concludes by considering the extent to which recent case law reflects the new legalism and points the way to the linking of negative rights to freedom from arbitrary or unjustified detention with positive rights to services.

JUDICIAL REVIEW OF DECISIONS TO ADMIT COMPULSORILY OR TO RENEW DETENTION

Habeas Corpus or Judicial Review?

MHRTs review the patient's continued need for detention. Lawfulness of the initial detention or the decision of the responsible authorities to renew is reviewed by habeas corpus or judicial review. Where a challenge is based on jurisdictional fact, habeas corpus is available, and so too is judicial review. In *R v Board of Control ex parte Rutty*[12] the challenge was from a patient detained as a 'borderline high grade mental defective'. Kathleen Rutty had been in institutions since the age of three months, but she could only be detained beyond her seventeenth birthday under the Mental Deficiency Act 1913 if she was both 'mentally defective' and 'found neglected'. A certificate was issued by a magistrate detaining her under the 1913 Act stating that she was a mental defective and had been 'found neglected'. There was no evidence whatsoever to support the latter conclusion, since she had always been in institutional care.

Lord Goddard CJ indicated in the following terms that judicial review should also be available in jurisdictional fact cases:

> If on inquiry the court finds that there was no evidence by which the order or conviction could be sustained, they can release on habeas corpus or quash on certiorari ... But if there is evidence, whatever this court may think of it and no matter what conclusion members of the court might have come to if

they were deciding that case which led to the conviction or order, they cannot disturb the finding, for to do so would be to act as a court of appeal in a matter in which no appeal is given.[13]

In the modern era judicial review of psychiatric decisions to detain must take place in the light of Article 5 of the European Convention on Human Rights. Article 5(1) permits arrest or detention on grounds of unsoundness of mind, provided it is in accordance with a procedure prescribed by law. Unless it is an emergency detention, objective evidence must be presented to a competent authority of unsoundness of mind of a kind or degree warranting detention.[14] Article 5(4) requires periodic review of the lawfulness of detention (both formal legality and substantive merits) before an independent court or tribunal which must have the power to order discharge. Decisions of the Strasbourg institutions in actions based on Article 5 had an important influence on the 1983 Act, and since 1983 have been increasingly referred to by English courts in judicial review cases, even though rarely directly applied in a patient's favour.

Re S-C Mental Patient[15] clarifies the circumstances in which habeas corpus is an appropriate remedy. The procedures for compulsory admission afford a key role to the patient's 'nearest relative'. Only the nearest relative or a specially trained Approved Social Worker (ASW) may make an application for compulsory admission. Unless it is an emergency, that application must be supported by two medical recommendations, stating that the person is suffering from mental disorder of a nature or degree warranting detention in hospital for assessment or treatment.

Where an ASW applies for compulsory admission, he must consult the person appearing to be the nearest relative unless it appears that such consultation is not reasonably practicable or would involve unreasonable delay. An application for detention under s. 3 for treatment for up to six months (renewable) may not proceed if the nearest relative has notified the ASW that he objects to the application being made. The appellant in *Re S-C* was compulsorily admitted under s. 3. The ASW, knowing that the true nearest relative was the patient's father, who objected to admission, had consulted as the nearest relative the patient's mother, who did not object. The ASW's statement on the admission form that the mother was, to the best of her knowledge and belief, the nearest relative, was described by Turner J at first instance as 'disingenuous'.

The Court of Appeal reiterated the distinction between challenge based on the non-existence of a 'jurisdictional' or 'objective precedent fact', and challenge to an 'administrative decision'.[16] Sir Thomas Bingham MR held that habeas corpus was an appropriate remedy since '[t]here is no attempt being made to overturn any administrative decision. The object is simply to show that there was never jurisdiction to detain the appellant in the first place, a fact which upon the agreed evidence appears to be plainly made out.' An objection by the nearest relative deprives the managers of jurisdiction to entertain the application.

Sir Thomas Bingham MR was satisfied, on the facts in *Re S-C*, that an application for habeas corpus was *an* appropriate, and possibly even *the* appropriate course to pursue, implying that judicial review would also be available in a jurisdictional fact case. Where the challenge is to an administrative decision taken within jurisdiction, judicial review is available, but not habeas corpus. The patient's appeal was allowed and his detention held to be unlawful, because the nearest relative had objected and the ASW knew this. However, the case was adjourned to enable the responsible hospital managers to show cause why he should not be released from detention.

A key issue in *Re S-C* was the scope of the protection for hospital managers in s. 6(3) of the 1983 Act which entitles them to act upon any application which appears to be duly made without further proof of the signature or qualification of the professionals signing the admission application or recommendations, or of any matter of fact or opinion stated in them. The Court of Appeal overruled Laws J's decision in *R v South Western Hospital Managers ex parte M*,[17] that s. 6(3) protects the hospital managers against a habeas corpus application. In that case the patient's mother had been interviewed and recorded on the statutory forms as the nearest relative. Because of the mother's place of residence, in law the nearest relative was the patient's uncle. In fact both had been spoken to and neither objected to detention. M sought judicial review, and when leave was refused, applied to habeas corpus addressed to the hospital managers. Laws J held that, because the application to the managers appeared to be duly made, even though the wrong relative had been consulted, the effect of s. 6(3) was that the detention was not unlawful, and habeas corpus could not issue.

In *Re S-C* Sir Thomas Bingham MR rejected Laws J's reasoning in *ex parte M* as being based on a non sequitur. In the Master of the Rolls' view, it was perfectly possible that the hospital managers were entitled to act on an apparently valid application, but that the detention was nevertheless in fact unlawful. The consequences of finding otherwise he described as horrifying, as they might result in a detention being lawful 'even though every safeguard built into the procedure was shown to have been ignored or violated'.[18] This must be right, as Laws J's approach would have meant that there was no effective method of ensuring before a court that detention had in fact been carried out 'in accordance with a procedure prescribed by law' and therefore complied with Article 5 of the Convention. Section 6(3) provides the hospital managers with a defence in civil proceedings if, as Neill LJ put it, 'on careful checking', the application appears to them to be duly made. But it cannot protect them from judicial review or habeas corpus.[19]

The Least Restrictive Alternative: Detention and Compulsory Community Care

Perhaps the most far-reaching cases in terms of their impact on mental health policy have been *R v Hallstrom ex parte Waldron (No. 2)* and *R v Gardner and another, ex parte L*.[20] Both involved patients with long-standing chronic schizophrenic illness, where the psychiatrists were using extended leave to subject patients to a continuing obligation to accept medication, in an arrangement known colloquially as the 'long leash'. The aim was to take advantage of the possibilities for maintaining patients in the community on 'depot medication', so called because one injection can have effect for ten days or more. Patients would be admitted for treatment when the intention was to send them on leave to the community, not to keep them in hospital for treatment.

This was what happened in *Hallstrom*, where the patient was admitted for one night under s. 3, and leave of absence granted the next day, subject to the condition that she accepted medication. The psychiatrist in charge of treatment (the Responsible Medical Officer – RMO) could then recall her from leave if she refused to continue medication, on grounds that it was necessary in the interests of her health or safety or for the protection of others. In *Gardner* the patient had been granted leave of absence in February 1985. In May 1985 the RMO, purportedly acting under s. 20 of the 1983 Act, brought the patient back into hospital for one night to renew the detention for a further six months, and sent her out on leave the next day.

Both patients sought declarations that the doctors had acted *ultra vires*. They argued that, because of the enshrinement of the principle of the least restrictive alternative in the s. 3 and s. 20 criteria for detention and renewal, it was unlawful to detain or renew unless the treatment which they required could not be provided without detaining them in hospital. Since in W's case the detention had only been notional for one night, and in L's case the renewal had taken place while he was resident outside hospital, they argued that the use of compulsory powers was unlawful. McCullough J granted the declarations sought, ruling that the medical recommendation of detention in *Hallstrom* and the renewal of detention in *Gardner* were *ultra vires* and void. The judge ruled that detention and renewal were only lawful for those whose mental condition is believed to require a period of in-patient treatment. Patients cannot be detained in the first place unless they need compulsory in-patient treatment. Although it was perfectly lawful to send a patient who had been lawfully detained on leave with a condition that they accept medication, they could not be returned to hospital unless they needed in-patient treatment under detention.

The immediate political consequence of this ruling was that the Royal College of Psychiatrists lobbied strongly for the introduction of a community treatment order. In 1990, following widespread concern about the failure of community care, the Department of Health issued a circular to health and social services authorities promoting a 'care programme approach' for mentally ill people who have been referred to specialist mental health services, requiring health authorities to draw up written care plans, and to assign a key worker whose task it would be to keep in touch with patients in the community, and review their needs at regular intervals.[21] Social services authorities were to collaborate in this endeavour and, 'as resources allow, to ... expand social care services to patients being treated in the community'.

In August 1993, following a number of incidents of self-harm and homicide by formerly detained patients, the Secretary of State for Health announced a 'ten-point plan to reinforce the care of mentally ill people in the community'. This included a series of shorter-term measures to make greater use of existing powers. Already amendments to the Mental Health Act Code of Practice had been laid before Parliament which encouraged early readmission of patients relapsing following cessation of medication if their mental health was at risk. To prepare the way for supervised discharge, the Department of Health introduced supervision registers, a form of 'at risk' register for mentally disordered adults,[22] and, in May 1994, issued guidance on the discharge of mentally disordered people and their continuing care in the community.[23] The legislative changes proposed in the ten-point plan included the lengthening to twelve months of the period during which detained patients can remain on conditional leave before they are automatically discharged. The centre-piece was the introduction of a statutory power of 'supervised discharge' for patients eligible for s. 117 community care services in the Mental Health (Patients in the Community) Act 1995.[24] The 1995 amendments were designed to require patients to accept s. 117 services by placing them under supervised discharge with a supervisor responsible for ensuring that they receive the services.[25] Patients subject to supervised discharge may be required to attend a specified place for treatment, and if they do not attend may be forcibly taken and conveyed there, but not forcibly treated, unless there is an emergency justifying common law intervention. The 1995 Act came into force almost exactly ten years after the *Hallstrom* ruling.

The Principle in Favour of Personal Freedom

The *Hallstrom* judgment is not only important for its effects on mental health policy. It also contains a passage famous for encapsulating the legalist principle of interpretation in favour of personal freedom. McCullough J said this:

> [C]ounsel for the doctors submits [that] the construction for which he contends should be adopted because it enables doctors in such a situation to do what is, in accordance with good modern psychiatric practice, in the best interests of patients, namely to treat them in the community, but compel them to accept the medication which their condition requires ... There is, however, no canon of construction which presumes that Parliament intended that people should, against their will, be subjected to treatment which others, however professionally competent, perceive, however sincerely and however correctly, to be in their best interests. What there is is a canon of construction that Parliament is presumed not to enact legislation which interferes with the liberty of the subject without making it clear that this was its intention. It goes without saying that, unless clear statutory authority to the contrary exists, no-one is to be detained in hospital or to undergo medical treatment or even to submit himself to medical examination without his consent. This is as true of a mentally disordered person as of anyone else.[26]

This principle has often been referred to in subsequent cases, and many applicants for judicial review have relied on it as expressing a statement of the policy of the 1983 Act which may be relied upon as a *Padfield*-based yardstick against which decision-making under the Act should be measured. As we shall see, however, most of these efforts have been resisted by the courts, and the importance of the passage may be seen as more rhetorical then real. This is not only true where the cases have concerned restricted patients, where the interest in public protection might be expected to outweigh the interest in personal freedom. It has also been evident in cases involving non-offender patients where paternalist considerations for the patient's own welfare have been given greater weight.

No cases illustrate this point more clearly than the series of actions brought by a restricted patient, James Kay, who was subject to a restriction order without limit of time imposed for the manslaughter and rape of a 12-year-old girl in 1970. He was conditionally discharged from hospital in 1985 by a tribunal which found that there was no evidence that he was suffering from mental disorder, but felt that it was appropriate that he remain liable to recall to hospital. Following his conditional discharge he committed two assaults on young women, for which he was sentenced to six years' imprisonment. Whilst serving his sentence he remained subject to the restriction order. In 1986 he applied to an MHRT for absolute discharge, fearing that the Home Secretary would wait until the expiry of his sentence and then recall him to hospital. The tribunal heard his case and expressed itself 'satisfied that the patient was not suffering from any mental disorder', but that it was appropriate for him to remain liable to recall for further treatment, and the conditions imposed in 1985 should be suspended until he was released from prison. K sought judicial review of the tribunal decision on the grounds that as soon as the tribunal found as a matter of fact that he was no longer suffering from mental disorder, he was entitled to absolute discharge. He should not be subject to the Mental Health Act, which can only have effect 'with regard to the reception, care and treatment of mentally disordered patients' defined as persons 'suffering or appearing to suffer from mental disorder'.[27] A conditional discharge must presuppose possible recall to hospital for further treatment, but in the light of the findings of the two tribunals there was nothing to treat.

The Court of Appeal held that 'Section 73 gives to the tribunal power to impose a conditional discharge and retain residual control over patients not then suffering from mental disorder or not to a degree requiring continued detention in hospital'.[28] In Butler-Sloss LJ's view the power to order conditional discharge was designed to support the patient and protect the public, and the tribunal's exercise of this discretionary power should not lightly be set aside. One may question whether this decision complies with Article 5(1)(e) and 5(4) of the European Convention on Human Rights, which provide that where detention takes place on psychiatric grounds there must be objective evidence of unsoundness of mind of a nature or degree warranting detention, and that such detention depends for its continuing validity on the persistence of such a degree of mental disorder. However, national authorities enjoy a 'margin of appreciation' in this regard, and since what K was complaining about was not being subject to continued psychiatric detention but being liable to recall, his complaint on this count probably falls outside the scope of Article 5.

K's concern in bringing these proceedings was to avoid recall to hospital on the expiry of his prison sentence, which is exactly what happened. During the month before his release date the Home Secretary issued a warrant recalling him to Broadmoor on expiry of his sentence. Section 42(3) confers a power on the Secretary of State at any time during the continuance in force of a restriction order by warrant to recall the patient to a specified hospital. It is widely drawn. It does not in express terms require the Home Secretary to act on the basis of medical reports stating that the patient is suffering from mental disorder, and indeed in this case the Home Secretary obtained none. In *R* v *Secretary of State for the Home Department ex parte K*[29] K sought review of the recall.

K relied on the 1981 decision in *X* v *United Kingdom*.[30] Here the UK Government conceded that it was implicit in the equivalent provision of the 1959 Act that no recall power could arise unless the Home Secretary on the medical evidence available to him decides that the patient is mentally disordered within the meaning of the Act. The decision in *Winterwerp* v *The Netherlands*[31] stipulates as one of the minimum conditions of a lawful detention that, except in emergencies, a true mental disorder must be established before a competent authority on the basis of objective medical expertise. X had claimed breach of Article 5(1) in that he had been detained without there being objective evidence of unsoundness of mind. The European Court of Human Rights found that Article 5(1) had not been breached. The Court noted that emergency cases were expressly identified in *Winterwerp* as an exception. Where a provision of domestic law was designed to authorize emergency confinement of persons capable of presenting a danger to others, it would be impracticable to require a thorough examination prior to arrest or detention, and a wide discretion must be enjoyed by the authority empowered to authorize such confinements. X's case was similar to K's in that the patient, who was subject to restrictions, was recalled by Home Secretary's warrant, without prior medical evidence being sought. The difference was that X had been recalled from the community, not prison.

The Court of Appeal rejected K's arguments, holding that the words of s. 42(3) were unambiguous and there was therefore no need to resort to the Convention for assistance in their interpretation.[32] The power could only be subjected to review on grounds of *Wednesbury* irrationality or the principle in *Padfield* v *Ministry of Agriculture Fisheries and Food*[33] that the discretion should only be allowed to be used so as to promote the policy and objects of the Act. The applicant argued that the policy and objects of the Act were to ensure that people were not deprived of their liberty unless they were shown on the basis of objective evidence to be suffering from mental disorder warranting compulsory confinement. The judge at first instance had been McCullough J, who had adopted a much wider view of the policy of the Act than that suggested by his personal freedom statement in *Hallstrom*. In relation to restricted patients he said that the policy of the Act was 'to regulate the circumstances in which the liberty of persons who are mentally disordered may be restricted and, where there is conflict, to balance their interests against those of public safety'.[34] In the Court of Appeal McCowan LJ adopted this wider view of the policy and objects of the Act and K's appeal was dismissed.

In March 1994 in *James Kay* v *United Kingdom* the European Commission of Human Rights upheld Kay's complaint of breach of Article 5 in that the recall had taken place without the Home Secretary first obtaining objective evidence that he was suffering from detainable mental disorder.[35] Unless it is an emergency, before recalling a conditionally discharged restricted patient to hospital, the Home Secretary must first obtain up-to-date medical evidence that he is suffering from mental disorder. Once a patient is recalled, review of his detention must take place speedily for the purpose of Article 5(4), and the Commission re-emphasized the Court's case law to the effect that periods of eight weeks to five months were insufficiently speedy (in this case the applicant had to wait just over two years, and the MHRT review system was found to be inherently too slow).[36]

JUDICIAL REVIEW OF THE DECISIONS OF MHRTS

The statutory route for reviewing MHRT decisions by the High Court is by asking the MHRT to state a case under s. 78(8) of the 1983 Act. Under the 1959 Act only one case stated involving a MHRT reached the High Court.[37] Soon after the 1983 Act came into force, it was established that the preferred route was by judicial review, not the case stated procedure, and there have been four appeals by case stated as against over thirty applications for judicial review which have reached judgment. *Bone* v *Mental Health Review Tribunal*,[38] on the duty to give reasons, established judicial review as the preferred route. Nolan J found himself in a difficult position. His powers under s. 78 were confined to giving any direction which the tribunal ought to have given. It had been decided in favour of the applicant that the duty to give reasons meant reasons which would enable him to find out why his case had been rejected, and not merely rehearsals of the statutory criteria for discharge. No direction could properly be made in this case, because the only direction that the tribunal could make in the applicant's favour was to discharge him, which might have posed a risk to the public. The judge therefore suggested that the case be reheard before a differently constituted tribunal, a course which he could have directed had it been a judicial review. Since then judicial review has been the main route of challenge of an MHRT decision. In terms of impact on applicants, this approach is extremely important, because it means that a finding that an MHRT has acted unlawfully will not necessarily result in the patient's discharge. It is important to note also that leave to review an MHRT decision will be refused if the patient has the possibility of making another tribunal application, unless there is some public interest in exploring the decision.[39]

In order to succeed in an application for judicial review, one of the established grounds must be made out, namely that the MHRT has misdirected itself in law, has behaved *Wednesbury* irrationally,[40] or has failed to act with procedural fairness towards one of the parties.[41] The courts are slow to interfere with a tribunal decision on grounds of *Wednesbury* unreasonableness.[42] Where the decision concerns a restricted patient and the need to protect the public from serious harm comes into play, the courts have declined to interfere with MHRT decisions not to discharge, and have upheld applications by the Home Secretary where he has sought to challenge a creative use by an MHRT of its powers to move a patient into less restrictive conditions. The cases may be divided into four groups on: (a) the duty to give reasons; (b) the effect of a tribunal decision to discharge; (c) the power to recommend, to direct deferred discharge and to adjourn; and (d) the burden of proof.

(a) Duty to Give Reasons

The main successes by patients have been in relation to the MHRT's duty to give reasons, and these triumphs were secured in the three years immediately following the 1983 Act. In *Bone v Mental Health Review Tribunal*[43] Nolan J held that the MHRT's reasons must be genuine reasons and not merely rehearsals of the statutory criteria. They must be adequate and intelligible, and must reasonably be said to deal with the substantial points that have been raised. The overriding question was that enunciated by Donaldson P in *Alexander Machinery (Dudley) Ltd v Crabtree*: 'Is the tribunal providing both parties with the materials which will enable them to know that the tribunal has made no error of law in reaching its finding of fact?'[44] *R v Mental Health Review Tribunal ex parte Clatworthy*[45] involved a restriction order patient. The MHRT decision was quashed on the grounds that the reasons given were inadequate to enable the applicant to know why they had not accepted his contention that he was not suffering from psychopathic disorder.

Clatworthy also establishes an important point which makes it more difficult for patients to succeed in future judicial review cases. It is that the tribunal is entitled to rely on the opinion of its own medical member even if the evidence of the RMO (for the detaining authority) and the independent psychiatrist (for the patient) is all one way that the patient is not suffering from a detainable mental disorder.[46] The impact is softened somewhat in that the court also held that the patient or his representative is entitled to know of the medical member's opinion so that they can present countervailing arguments. Mann J ruled that the reasons given by the tribunal were 'a bare traverse of a circumstance in which discharge could be contemplated' which did not reveal to the applicant why the contentions of the RMO and the psychiatrist who reported on the patient's behalf had not been accepted.[47]

(b) The Effects of an MHRT Decision to Discharge

One of the most significant decisions reflecting support for medical discretion rather than legalist values is *R v South Western Hospital Managers ex parte M*,[48] where Laws J held that, despite MHRTs' status as courts for the purposes of contempt, an MHRT decision to discharge did not preclude an ASW and two doctors from making a decision to re-detain the patient within a day of the MHRT's decision. Such a decision was neither contempt of the tribunal nor an abuse of process. M was detained under s. 2 for up to twenty-eight days' assessment, with treatment if necessary. The MHRT concluded that she was suffering from mental disorder, but not of a nature or degree warranting her detention in hospital for assessment in the interests of her health or safety or for the protection of others. However, they deferred her discharge for three days to enable social services to arrange a suitable support programme for her and for her family.

Within a day of the tribunal's direction to discharge, M's consultant psychiatrist recommended her detention under s. 3 of the 1983 Act. He was concerned that M, believing she was not mentally ill, would not carry out her undertaking to the tribunal to take her medicine. He had heard from a member of the ward staff that she had not been taking her medication, but hiding it under her tongue and spitting it out later. Next day a second medical recommendation was given by a GP in the patient's practice, and an application for compulsory admission was made by an ASW. The

ASW and doctors considered that it was necessary for the patient's own health or safety and for the protection of others that she should receive treatment which could not be provided unless she was detained under the Act. Laws J treated the matter as one of 'pure statutory construction' and held:

> [T]hat there is no sense in which those concerned with a s. 3 application are at any stage bound by an earlier tribunal decision. The doctors, social workers and managers must under the statute exercise their independent judgment whether or not there is an extant tribunal decision relating to the patient. They will no doubt wish to have regard to any such decision, where they know of it, in order to ensure that they have the maximum information about the facts of the case, but . . . it cannot confine or restrict their own exercise of the functions which the Act confers on them.[49]

Laws J went on to hold that even if a s. 3 application would only be good in the event of a change of circumstances, that was sufficiently established here. There was material showing substantial grounds for supposing that the applicant would not abide by her undertaking to the tribunal to continue with her medicine as advised. Although the tribunal was told at the hearing that the applicant had refused much of her medication while in hospital, the fact was that after the tribunal had received her undertaking that she would accept medication, she continued to refuse it.

This creates the possibility of an impasse whereby the MHRT discharges and the patient is readmitted, applies for another tribunal hearing, is again discharged by the MHRT, and is then readmitted. Laws J considered this to be 'unlikely':

> . . . given good faith on all hands and the safeguards which colour the s. 3 process . . . [The] social worker must always conduct a personal interview before making a s. 3 application; there must always be two separate medical recommendations; and there has to be a decision of the managers pursuant to s. 6 . . . [T]he public law safeguards enshrined in *Wednesbury* and *Padfield* apply to all exercises of administrative power by the bodies I have mentioned.[50]

A decision to discharge by a tribunal following inquiry into the justification for detention was a factor to be taken into account by the professionals in exercising their discretion, but it did not preclude them from detaining. However theoretical an impasse might be, the ruling gives mental health professionals the power to 'overrule' an

MHRT decision, a clear reflection of medicalism rather than legalism.

(c) The Power to Make Recommendations, to Direct Deferred Discharge, and to Adjourn

One of the problems with the powers of MHRTs under the 1959 Act was their 'all or nothing' nature, to discharge or not to discharge. The 1983 Act gave new powers to MHRTs to direct discharge on a future date in addition to their power simply to direct immediate discharge or not. *R v Mental Health Review Tribunal for North Thames Region, ex parte Pierce*[51] raised the question whether MHRTs can direct delayed discharge when there is a mandatory duty to discharge. The MHRT considered two applications for discharge, one from the patient and one from her mother. On a patient application the MHRT must discharge if satisfied that detention is not necessary in the interests of the patient's own health or safety or for the protection of others. If the relative applies, the tribunal must discharge if satisfied that the patient would not act dangerously to herself or others. The MHRT rejected the patient's application, but because they were satisfied that she was not dangerous to self or others, decided on the mother's application that the patient should be discharged from liability to be detained in twenty-one days' time. The patient sought judicial review, arguing that, since there was a duty to discharge, it was improper for the tribunal to direct discharge on a future date. Once the patient had been found to be entitled to discharge because one of the preconditions of detention no longer applied, it was a breach of Article 5 of the Convention for her to remain in detention. She should have been released forthwith. The court held that a tribunal has the power to direct the discharge of a patient at a future date in such a case. The power to defer discharge is not confined to cases of discretionary discharge, and there was no breach of Article 5.

In cases involving restricted patients, the Home Secretary is a party to the MHRT proceedings, and there have been several cases where he has used judicial review to protect his own prerogatives and to limit the powers of MHRTs *vis-à-vis* restricted cases. In *R v Yorkshire Mental Health Review Tribunal and another ex parte Secretary of State for the Home Department* and *R v Oxford Mental Health Review Tribunal and Campbell ex parte Secretary of State for the Home Department*, the House of Lords held that the decision to defer conditional discharge is a final decision which cannot be reopened.[52] The Home Secretary succeeded in establishing that, as a party to the proceedings, he is entitled to a copy of all relevant documents received by the tribunal, and to be given the opportunity to be heard as a representative of the public interest before such a decision is reached.

Section 72(3) of the 1983 Act gave tribunals a power to recommend transfer of non-restricted patients to another hospital, and reconvene if their recommendation was not complied with. In practice this power is most likely to be of use where the patient is subject to restrictions and is detained in a secure special hospital. The MHRT may feel that, whilst not ready for discharge, the patient is ready for trial in a less secure setting, such as a Regional Secure Unit or a local psychiatric hospital. In R v *Mersey Mental Health Review Tribunal ex parte O'Hara*[53] the Court held unlawful a tribunal's attempt to use the power in s. 72(3) in the case of a restriction order patient.[54] The Mental Health Unit of the Home Office, which deals with restricted patients, indicated that it would be willing to receive recommendations in such cases, but the MHRT would have no power to reconvene if the recommendation were not complied with.

For restricted patients, the MHRT's only power other than to discharge absolutely or conditionally is to defer conditional discharge until arrangements have been made to the MHRT's satisfaction for the supervision of the offender in the community. The power to defer a conditional discharge differs from the tribunal's power to delay a discharge in the case of a non-restricted patient. Where the tribunal delays the discharge of an unrestricted patient it makes an order which is to take effect at a specified date in the future; discharge must be effected on or by that date, irrespective of whether arrangements for the patient's care have been completed. On the other hand where a tribunal considering the case of a restricted patient defers a direction for conditional discharge, it postpones the coming into effect of the discharge direction until arrangements are made to its satisfaction. If the deferred conditional discharge is not carried into effect by the time the patient's case next comes before an MHRT, the direction lapses.

In *Secretary of State for the Home Department* v *Mental Health Review Tribunal for the Mersey Regional Health Authority*[55] it was held that the tribunal cannot defer a conditional discharge until arrangements are made for admission to another hospital. The patient was detained in a special hospital. The tribunal found that his behaviour had improved substantially over recent months, that he was no longer on any medication, that detention was no longer necessary in the interests of his own health or safety or for the protection of other persons, and that it was appropriate for him to remain liable to recall. However, it also found that the patient would be unable to cope upon discharge from a special hospital direct into the community and a period in a 'half-way house' was essential in the patient's interests and in the interests of the community. In order to facilitate this step, the tribunal directed the patient's conditional discharge, but deferred the direction until arrangements had been made for his admission to a less secure hospital. This was with a view to his subsequent discharge to a local hostel or to his home. The Home Office sought judicial review.

The tribunal had tried to use its power to direct conditional discharge as a way of directing a transfer to a less secure hospital, a power which does not exist for restricted patients, even though it is established good practice for a special hospital patient to be transferred to a local hospital before being discharged so that security can be relaxed gradually and the patient's reaction can be monitored. Although Mann J expressed sympathy with what the tribunal was trying to achieve, he nevertheless declared its approach unlawful.[56]

In *Secretary of State for the Home Department* v *Mental Health Review Tribunal for Wales*[57] the tribunal had directed that the patient, who was severely mentally impaired, be conditionally discharged, on condition that he continue to reside in the hospital where he had been for more than twenty-one years. The grounds of the direction were that he needed supervision, guidance on personal hygiene and social rehabilitation, and the tribunal had decided that this was not treatment within s. 145(1). Mann J held a direction of conditional discharge was inconsistent with a condition of continued residence in hospital, and was therefore unlawful. The finding that the patient needed supervision and training was, in fact, a finding that he needed medical treatment within s. 145(1), and therefore the tribunal had been wrong in deciding that the criteria placing it under a duty to direct conditional discharge had been met. The tribunal must be satisfied that the patient should be released from the hospital before directing conditional discharge.

Under Rule 16 of the MHRT Rules the tribunal may grant an adjournment to obtain further information about the present mental health of the patient. The second limb of Rule 16 allows an adjournment for such other purposes as the tribunal may think necessary. In *R* v *Nottingham Mental Health Review Tribunal ex parte Secretary of State for the Home Department* and *R* v *Northern Mental Health Review Tribunal ex parte Secretary of State for the Home Department*[58] the Court of Appeal declared unlawful an attempt by the MHRT to use the adjournment power to monitor the progress of a restricted patient. The Court of Appeal held that the MHRT has no power to adjourn to give the patient an opportunity to improve or to see whether an improvement already made is sustained, and that the purpose of the power to adjourn was to obtain information about

PHIL FENNELL

the patient's current condition. Where the tribunal is satisfied that
the criteria for discharge are not satisfied at the time of the hearing, it
has no power to adjourn to give the patient an opportunity to
improve. It was the function of the Home Secretary and not the
tribunal to monitor the condition of a restricted patient.[59] The cases
involving the powers of MHRTs in relation to restricted patients
show a steady pattern of success for the Home Office in upholding its
prerogatives in the face of attempts by MHRTs to move patients into
less restrictive environments or legal statuses.

(d) Challenging Decisions not to Discharge: Burden of Proof and 'Treatability'

With non-restricted patients, the tribunal has a discretionary power
to discharge in any case. If the patient wishes to establish entitlement
to discharge, the formal burden of proof is on him to satisfy the
tribunal that the criteria for detention are not met.[60] Under s.
72(1)(b), the MHRT comes under a duty to discharge if at the time
of the hearing the patient is: (1) *not* suffering from mental disorder
(mental illness, psychopathic disorder, mental impairment or severe
mental impairment) of a nature or degree which makes it appropriate
for him to be liable to be detained in hospital for medical treatment
(the 'appropriateness' test); or (2) if it is *not* necessary in the interests
of his health or safety or for the protection of others that he should
receive such treatment (s. 72(1)(i),(ii)) (the 'necessity' test).

The requirement that the patient satisfy the tribunal of a negative,
coupled with the breadth of the concepts of mental disorder and
medical treatment, makes a challenge based on error of law or
Wednesbury unreasonableness all the more difficult to sustain. When
we add the extra ingredients of the need to protect the public from
patients and patients from themselves, it is scarcely surprising that
patients have rarely succeeded in judicially reviewing the substance of
MHRT decisions. Since the justification for psychiatric detention is
the appropriateness of medical treatment for mental disorder, a
significant number of applications for judicial review have been based
on the contention that the patient was not receiving 'medical
treatment for mental disorder' within the meaning of the Act, and
therefore the nature or degree of the disorder did not warrant
medical treatment in hospital.

In *R v Mersey Mental Health Review Tribunal ex parte Dillon*[61]
Russell LJ and Otton J noted the wide definition of medical
treatment in s. 145 of the 1983 Act as being broader than drugs and
ECT, including care, habilation and rehabilitation under medical
supervision, and held that there was no requirement that the medical

treatment envisaged in ss. 72 and 73 of the 1983 Act should be such as might have the effect of alleviating or preventing deterioration in the patient's condition. In *R v South East Thames Mental Health Review Tribunal ex parte Ryan*[62] the patient sought judicial review because he was not receiving medication, an attack held by Watkins LJ to be 'ill-directed' since he needed to be kept in hospital for his own benefit and that of the public even though he was not receiving drugs. Hence the fact of detention in a structured environment with nursing care can be treatment.[63]

The most controversial legal category of mental disorder is psychopathic disorder, a form of personality disorder defined in the 1983 Act as 'a persistent disorder or disability of mind (whether or not including significant impairment of intelligence) which results in abnormally aggressive or seriously irresponsible conduct'.[64] The 1983 Act provides that if a patient is to be detained as suffering from psychopathic disorder under the six-month admission for treatment power in s. 3, a 'treatability' criterion must be met. Medical treatment in hospital must be likely to alleviate or prevent deterioration in his condition.[65] Since, as we have seen, medical treatment is widely defined, the psychiatrist in charge of treatment has considerable discretion as to whether a patient is treatable, as it can be argued in virtually any case that nursing care in hospital is preventing deterioration in the patient's condition. In *R v Cannons Park Mental Health Review Tribunal ex parte A*,[66] A sought judicial review of the MHRT decision not to discharge her, which had stated that it was not likely that the medical treatment she was receiving was alleviating or preventing deterioration in her condition, although she might at some future time accept the only form of treatment which was likely to help her, namely group therapy. She contended that because her condition was not likely to respond to the treatment she was receiving in hospital, it was no longer lawful to detain her. Although it is a precondition of detention and renewal of detention that the patient be treatable, there is no mention of the treatability test in the discharge criteria required by s. 72 to be employed by MHRTs. The question was whether it was impliedly incorporated by the requirement that the disorder be of a nature or degree making treatment in hospital 'appropriate'.

In the Divisional Court Sedley J considered that it was. As he saw it:

The phrase 'appropriate for him to be liable [to be detained]', whilst clumsy, picks up the language of s. 3 and s. 20 which include in their criteria for liability to detention the appropriateness of medical treatment as well as the likelihood of its being effective.[67]

Sedley J referred to the policy behind the relevant provisions of s. 3 and s. 20 that psychopaths should only be detained under compulsory powers when there is a good prospect of benefit from treatment. He was alert to the requirements of Article 5(4) of the European Convention. In *X* v *United Kingdom*[68] the European Court of Human Rights held:

> The right guaranteed by Article 5(4) to test the lawfulness of detention does not incorporate a right for the court to substitute its discretion on all matters for that of the decision-making authority; but the scope of the judicial review must be sufficient to enable enquiry to be made whether, in the case of the detention of a mental patient, the reasons which initially justified the detention continue to subsist.[69]

According to Sedley J, an interpretation in accordance with Article 5(4) required the MHRT to review the legality of detention according to the same criteria which form the basis of the initial admission, renewal or reclassification of the patient. The alternative would mean that:

> far from being a court in which the lawfulness of a patient's detention can be decided, a ... tribunal would be a primary decision-making body, judging a patient's liability to be detained on criteria different from and wider than those by which the authorities whose decision is being reviewed were empowered to cause the patient to be detained.

The tribunal had not found that medical treatment would alleviate A's condition, but had instead expressed the hope that she would agree to appropriate treatment by being kept in hospital. This was not a lawful ground of detention according to the principle of construction in favour of personal freedom enunciated by McCullough J in *Hallstrom*. The Divisional Court held that the tribunal's findings obliged them to release the applicant and quashed the decision not to discharge, remitting the case to the tribunal with a direction that A be discharged.

The Court of Appeal granted the tribunal's appeal. The majority did not find the wording of s. 72(1)(b) to be unclear. Hence there was no doubt to be resolved by reference to the history of the legislation, or the *Hallstrom* principle of construction in favour of personal liberty. Kennedy LJ questioned whether the principle has 'any part to play in the construction of a section which in terms seeks to have regard to the potentially conflicting interests of the health or safety of the patient on the one hand and the protection of other persons on the other'.[70] Equally, because there was no doubt, there was no need to have to resort to materials relating to the history of the present legislation, and the court could not invoke the assistance of Article 5 of the Convention.[71]

Kennedy and Nourse LJJ held that the decision of an MHRT whether it is under a duty to discharge a patient might involve some consideration of treatability in that, if medical treatment could do nothing to alleviate or prevent deterioration, the MHRT might more readily conclude that the patient's liability to detention was inappropriate. Roch LJ was less dismissive of the European dimension to the question and accepted that Parliament would have failed to meet the criticisms in *X* v *United Kingdom* if a tribunal was not required to employ the treatability test in deciding whether it was under a duty to discharge.

All three judges in the Court of Appeal considered that, because it was for the patient to satisfy the tribunal of entitlement to discharge, the tribunal was only under a duty to discharge if satisfied that treatment was *not* likely to alleviate or prevent deterioration in the patient's condition. The duty did not arise if they were merely *not satisfied* that the patient *was* treatable. Although the precise meaning of treatability had not been extensively canvassed at first instance, the Court of Appeal considered that too narrow an approach had been adopted by the Divisional Court, Roch LJ said this:

> 'Treatment in hospital' will satisfy the 'treatability test' although it is unlikely to alleviate the patient's condition, provided that it is likely to prevent a deterioration. The treatability test will still be met, even though the treatment will not immediately alleviate or prevent deterioration, provided that alleviation or stabilisation is likely in due course, and even if initially there is some deterioration due to the patient's initial anger at being detained.

Roch LJ noted the broad definition in s. 145(1) and held that a patient is treatable, even if the only treatment is nursing care which is unlikely to alleviate the patient's condition, as long as it is likely to prevent deterioration. It will be hard to argue that any patient is not treatable where the fact alone that they are detained in hospital under supervision of doctors and nurses can always be said to be likely to prevent deterioration.

In *ex parte A* the Court of Appeal fixed on the fact that in order to establish entitlement to discharge it was for the patient to establish the absence of mental disorder of a nature or degree making liability to detention appropriate or that detention was not necessary on the health or safety criteria. This and the fact that the MHRT must give reasons for a decision to discharge was, as Roche LJ put it, 'consistent with proper weight being given to the views of the RMO'.[72] Kennedy LJ spoke more openly of the 'onus of proof', whereby:

> The tribunal is only required to discharge if it is satisfied of a negative – first, that the patient is not then suffering from psychopathic disorder. If he may be, the obligation to discharge does not arise. The approach is not surprising because the tribunal is not intending to duplicate the role of the responsible medical officer. His diagnosis stands until the tribunal is satisfied that it is wrong. If the diagnosis may be right, may the disorder be of a nature or degree which makes it appropriate for him to be liable to be detained in a hospital?

In other words, the tribunal does not have to be satisfied that the patient *is* suffering from mental disorder of the required nature or degree, merely that he *may be* so suffering.[73] Equally they need not be satisfied that detention *is* necessary on health or safety grounds merely that it *may be*. As long as they are *not satisfied that it is unnecessary* they are under no duty to discharge.

At the admissibility stage in *James Kay* v *United Kingdom*, one of the applicant's contentions before the Commission was that the tribunal cannot provide an effective remedy 'because it does not have to find positive evidence that the patient is suffering from mental disorder'.[74] This point has yet to be argued in full before the Strasbourg institutions, but the absence of sufficient evidence to satisfy the MHRT that the patient is not suffering from mental disorder of a nature or degree warranting detention is not the same as the presence of positive evidence satisfying them that he is.

CONCLUSION – THE NEW LEGALISM: NEGATIVE AND POSITIVE RIGHTS AND THE FUTURE OF JUDICIAL REVIEW

There are two aspects of the new legalism: the protection of negative rights of freedom from arbitrary or unjustified interference with individual liberty, and upholding of positive rights to care in the least restrictive setting. Judicial review of decision-making under the 1983 Act reveals that the first part of that project, the subjection of therapeutic power to more rigorous control, has not been a particular success. Despite the judicial rhetoric reflected in McCullough J's famous principle in favour of personal liberty, the legislation remains imbued with wide discretionary power to detain and treat without consent. Many of the cases have been successful applications by the Home Secretary to maintain the control exercised by the Home Office Mental Health Unit over restricted patients. Even in cases where applicants have established points in favour of patients' rights, this has rarely resulted in discharge from detention. This results from the understandable desire of the courts to avoid decisions which might result in harm to the patient or others in a social context of increasing concerns about suicide, self-harm, and homicides by former psychiatric in-patients.

The jurisprudence under Article 5 of the Convention provides a yardstick against which the 1983 Act can be measured, but by applying *Brind* principles, with rare exceptions the English courts have avoided direct application of its provisions, necessitating recourse to the Strasbourg institutions for effective redress. With incorporation a number of new possibilities will be opened up, including forcing speedy hearings before MHRTs as required by Article 5(4). If treatability is an essential element of detainable psychopathic disorder, does it contravene the Convention that a MHRT is not required to discharge if satisfied that the patient is not having treatment which is likely to alleviate or prevent deterioration?

There must also be serious doubt as to whether the current positioning of the burden of proof in MHRTs satisfies the requirement in *Winterwerp* v *The Netherlands*,[75] namely that review must be sufficient to enable enquiry to be made whether the reasons which justified the detention continue to subsist. Can it meet the requirements of Article 5(4) review if a tribunal can continue detention even though not satisfied that a patient *is* mentally disordered and *does* require detention, as long as they are *not* satisfied that he is *not* mentally disordered and *not* satisfied that he does *not* need detention (the famous double negatives of MHRT decision-making)? We may question whether Article 5(4) is contravened by arrangements whereby, instead of the burden being on the detainers to justify detention by establishing that the conditions originally authorizing it continue to be met, the burden is on the detainee to justify discharge by showing that they are not met. This surely contravenes the requirement specified by the European Court of Human Rights in *Winterwerp* v *The Netherlands*,[76] that the validity of continued detention depends on the persistence of mental disorder of a nature or degree warranting detention (para. 37 of the judgment). The Government has indicated its intention to review the 1983 Act, and although their intention in doing so is probably to increase rather than limit therapeutic discretion, *Ex parte A* and *Kay* indicate the need to re-examine the fit between the admission and renewal criteria and those governing discharge, especially in relation to treatability. Any review should consider the current position of the burden of proof and its compatibility with the European Convention as a central issue. Placing the burden on the responsible authority to justify detention would also increase the incentive for the authority more actively to present the case for detention and increase the quality of information available to the tribunal.

The European and English jurisprudence has largely been concerned with negative rights, freedom from arbitrary arrest or detention; rights not to be done to. The ideology of entitlement to care in the least restrictive setting is most clearly reflected in the 1983 Act by the correlative duty under s. 117 of the 1983 Act to provide after care. The key case on s. 117 is *R v Ealing District Health Authority ex parte Fox*,[77] involving an offender patient detained in Broadmoor under a restriction order. It illustrates the connection between the 'negative right' not to be deprived of liberty without sufficient cause and due process, and the 'positive right' to community care services. A MHRT reviewed *Fox*'s detention and directed conditional discharge, deferred until a number of conditions were met, including social work support and supervision by a consultant psychiatrist who would act as the patient's RMO. All the consultants at the patient's local Regional Secure Unit considered that he would not be amenable to supervision and declined to supervise him, as did the consultant general psychiatrist for his local area. The health authority therefore refused to supply psychiatric supervision, and the MHRT's order for discharge could not take effect. The applicant sought judicial review.

In the health authority's view, the duty under s. 117 did not apply because the patient had not yet left hospital. *Fox* establishes that the duty under s. 117 is to consider the individual needs of each patient to whom the section applies. Otton J rejected the contention that it only came into effect once the patient was discharged from hospital. He considered it to be a continuing duty in respect of any patient who may be discharged and falls within s. 117, although the duty to any particular patient was only triggered at the moment of discharge.[78]

The judge also concluded that the mere acceptance by the authority of their consultants' opinions was not of itself sufficient to discharge their obligations to proceed with reasonable expedition and diligence and to give effect to the arrangements specified and required by the tribunal. If the health authority's doctors did not agree with the conditions imposed by the tribunal and were disinclined to provide supervision, the authority could not let the matter rest there. They were under a continuing obligation to make further endeavours to provide arrangements within their own resources or to obtain them from other authorities, or, at the very least, to make inquiries of other service providers. If they still could not make the necessary arrangements they were not entitled to let the matter rest there, but were to refer the matter to the Secretary of State to enable him to exercise his power under s. 71 of the 1983 Act to send the case back to the tribunal. This represented a significant limitation on the victory for patients, because it would result in the benefit of the deferred discharge being lost. Once the tribunal commences considering the reference from the Secretary of State, the original deferred discharge automatically lapses, and the MHRT considers the matter afresh.

Although the applicant was entitled to have the health authority's decision quashed, Otton J refused mandamus compelling them to provide psychiatric supervision in the community. That would in effect compel a doctor to supervise a patient against the doctor's will which was based on an honestly held clinical judgment that the treatment was not in the patient's best interests or was not in the best interests of the community in which the supervision would take place. However, he granted a declaration that: (1) the authority had erred in law by not attempting with all reasonable expedition and diligence to make arrangements so as to enable the applicant to comply with the conditions imposed by the tribunal; and (2) a district health authority is under a duty under s. 117 to provide after-care services when a patient leaves hospital, and acts unlawfully if it fails to seek to make practical arrangements for after-care prior to that patient's discharge from hospital where such arrangements are required in order to enable the patient to be conditionally discharged from hospital. *Fox* establishes that once the authority has assessed individual needs and the patient is discharged, the authority is under an absolute duty to provide them until it is satisfied, on reassessment, that he no longer needs them.

Section 117 services are community care services under the National Health Service and Community Care Act 1990. Local authorities, in assessing and meeting need for services, are required to act in accordance with policy guidance issued by the Secretary of State.[79] That guidance reflects the ideals of care in the least restrictive alternative setting, by setting out an order of preference for the care of people with problems of mental ill health, whereby treatment in hospital should be seen as a last resort. Lawyers acting for community care clients have pursued a strategy of 'hardening' up this form of 'soft law' to develop client entitlement. In *R v London Borough of Islington ex parte Rixon*[80] Sedley J held that in exercising their powers and duties under community care legislation local authorities were bound to follow policy guidance issued by the Secretary of State unless there was a good reason for not doing so, articulated in the course of some identifiable decision-making process. In *R v London Borough of Sutton ex parte Tucker*[81] a local authority was found to have acted unlawfully in breach of the guidance by failing to make a care provision decision, having assessed the needs of a non-detained but mentally incapacitated patient as involving transfer from long-stay hospital care into a community-based facility.

Stanley Johnson v *United Kingdom*[82] has again raised the issue of entitlement to discharge if the tribunal finds that there is no mental disorder. The case shows the link between negative rights and positive rights. Johnson was found by three MHRTs (1989, 1990, 1991) not to be suffering from mental disorder, but each considered him to require community care. They therefore conditionally discharged him but deferred the discharge until a suitable hostel could be found. None ever was. He was finally released following a tribunal hearing in 1993. He complained to the European Commission on Human Rights that his detention contravened Articles 5(1) and (4) because the unsoundness of mind which formed the necessary basis of his continued detention was no longer present. The Court delivered judgment in October 1997, holding that there had been a breach of Article 5(1). The court rejected the argument that a finding by an expert authority that a person is no longer suffering from the form of mental illness which led to his confinement must inevitably lead to his immediate and unconditional release into the community. This would be an unfortunate curtailment of the expert authority's discretion to assess, part of the 'margin of appreciation' left to the national authorities. Nevertheless, discharge must not be unreasonably delayed, and there must be safeguards, including judicial review, to prevent this. The tribunal had to have the powers to ensure that a placement could be secured within a reasonable period of time.

Very often MHRTs find patients to be suffering from mental disorder which would not be of a nature or degree warranting detention if only community care provision could be made. Often the reason for non-provision of community care is lack of resources. In *R* v *Gloucestershire County Council ex parte Barry*[83] the House of Lords held that a local authority could take its resources into account in meeting need for community care under s. 2 of the Chronically Sick and Disabled Persons Act 1970, which like s. 117 is a community care duty owed to individuals. The fact that a person would not require detention given adequate community care support could be used to base an argument based on Article 5. Failure to provide, and failure to fund that care, are breaches of Article 5 because they are consigning a person to detention which they would not otherwise need. By failure to provide positive rights the patient's negative rights would be infringed. The Mental Health Act has recently been amended to introduce new compulsory community powers, and the intersection between mental health and community care legislation has become an increasingly fertile field for judicial review. Subject always to the Government's legal aid 'reforms', it may be that we are about to see judicial review reflect the new legalism by pursuing the inter-relationship between the negative right of freedom from unjustified detention and the positive right of entitlement to community care services.

NOTES

1   For a fuller discussion of medicalism and the competing philosophy of legalism see P. Fennell, 'Law and psychiatry' in P. A. Thomas (ed.) *Legal Frontiers*, Aldershot: Dartmouth (1996), pp. 208–64.

2   L. O. Gostin, 'Perspectives on mental health reforms', 10 *Journal of Law and Society* (1983): 47–70.

3   [1986] 2 All ER 306.

4   (1981) 4 EHRR 188, 1 BMLR 98.

5   Interdepartmental Committee Report on Mental Health Review Tribunal Procedures (DHSS) 1978; The Mental Health Review Tribunal Rules 1983, SI 1983, No. 942.

6   *Ibid.*, rr. 23 and 12.

7   Legal Advice and Assistance (Amendment) Regulations 1994, SI 1994, No. 805.

8   [1991] 1 All ER 622; [1991] 2 WLR 513; (1991) 6 BMLR 108, 1991, All ER Annual Review 237–9.

9   Two applications have been made employing traditional *Wednesbury* principles to review MHAC decisions: unsuccessfully in respect of its task of investigating complaints about the exercise of powers and duties in relation to detained patients (*R v Mental Health Act Commission ex parte Turner* CO/1945/92, QBD 10 January 1993); and successfully in relation to its second opinion functions for controversial treatment for mental disorder (*R v Mental Health Act Commission ex parte W, The Guardian*, 27 May 1988; *The Independent*, 27 May 1988; *The Times*, 27 May 1988. Reported sub nomine *R v Mental Health Act Commission ex parte X* (1988) 9 BMLR 77. For further discussion of the issues in this case see P. Fennell, 'Sexual suppressants and the Mental Health Act', [1988] *Crim. Law Rev.*: 660–76).

10   That is, those detained under Mental Health Act 1983, ss. 3, 37, 47 or 48.

11   [1986] QB 824, at 846.

12   [1956] 1 All ER 769, [1956] 2 QB 109.

13   [1956] 1 All ER 775.

14   *Winterwerp* v *The Netherlands* (1979) EHRR 387.

15   [1996] 1 All ER 532.

16   See *R v Secretary of State for the Home Department ex parte Muboyayi* [1991] 4 All ER 72 [1992] QB 244, *Khawaja v Secretary of State for the Home Department* [1983] 1 All ER 765; [1984] AC 74.

17   [1994] 1 All ER 161, [1993] QB 683, All ER Annual Review 1994, Medical Law, 280–8.

18   [1996] 1 All ER 532, at 543.

19   *Ibid., per* Neill LJ at 544 and *per* Sir Thomas Bingham MR at 539.

20   [1986] 2 All ER 306.

21   HC(90)23/LASSL(90)11, 'Care Programme Approach for People with a Mental Illness Referred to the Specialist Psychiatric Services'.

22   NHS Management Executive, Health Service Guidelines HSG(94)5, 'Supervision Registers'.

23   NHS Management Executive, Health Service Guidelines HSG(94)27.

24   For a full discussion of the background to the 1995 Act, see P. Fennell, 'Community care, community compulsion and the law' in Ritter, Hervey *et al.*, *Collaborative Community Health Care*, London: Edward Arnold (1996), ch. 6.

25   Mental Health (Patients in the Community) Act, s. 25A(4).

26   *R v Hallstrom ex parte W (No. 2)* [1986] 2 All ER 306, at 314.

27   Mental Health Act 1983, ss. 1(1) and 145(1).

28   *R v Mersey Mental Health Review Tribunal ex parte K* [1990] 1 All ER 694, *per* Butler-Sloss LJ at 699f.

29   [1990] 1 All ER 703 (QBD), [1991] 1 QB 270, [1990] 3 All ER 562, 6 BMLR 1 (CA).

30   (1981) 4 EHRR 188, (1981) BMLR 98.

31   (1979) EHRR 387.

32   *R v Secretary of State for the Home Department ex parte Brind* [1990] 2 WLR 787, [1990] 1 All ER 469.

33   [1968] AC 997, [1968] 1 All ER 694.

34   [1990] 1 All ER 703 at 709, [1990] 1 WLR 168, at 174.

35   *James Kay v United Kingdom*, Application No. 17821/91, Admissibility Decision 7 July 1993, Decision on the merits 1 March 1994.

36   Commission Report, paras 50 and 63–65. There have been two other cases concerning recall of conditionally discharged restricted patients. In *R v The Managers of the North West London Mental Health NHS Trust ex parte Stewart, The Times*, 19 July 1996, CO/1825/95 (transcript: Smith Bernal), Harrison J held that it was open to the authorities to detain a conditionally discharged restricted patient under the civil power in s. 3 rather than go through the recall procedure, and this did not involve any breach of Article 5(4) of the Convention in that the patient was not deprived of the right to challenge that detention before an MHRT. In *Dlodlo v Mental Health Review Tribunal for the South Thames Region and Others, The Times*, 12 August 1996 (transcript: Smith Bernal), the Court of Appeal held that it was open to the Home Secretary to recall a patient to hospital under s. 42, notwithstanding that the patient was already detained there under s. 3.

37   *Re VE* [1973] 1 QB 452.

38   [1985] 3 All ER 330.

39   *Re Jones* QBD, 8 March 1991, CO/102/91.

40   *Associated Provincial Picture Houses v Wednesbury Corporation* [1948] 1 KB 223.

41   See per Lord Diplock in *Council of Civil Service Unions v Minister for the Civil Service* [1985] AC 374, 410–11.

42   *R v Mental Health Review Tribunal ex parte London Borough of Haringey*, 4 April 1995, CO/892/95, where the Court dismissed an application by a London Borough for review of a decision of the tribunal to direct discharge of a patient detained under a hospital order without restrictions, but to delay it in order to

provide time for appropriate community support services and hostel arrangement to be set in place to support the patient. Subsequent to the tribunal decision, the health and social services authorities had decided to apply for the patient to be admitted for treatment under s. 3 of the 1983 Act, and to displace the nearest relative, who was objecting to the application. A nearest relative may block an admission for treatment, but the application may proceed if the nearest relative has been displaced on grounds of unreasonable objection (s. 29).

43 [1985] 3 All ER 330.
44 [1974] ICR 120, at 122.
45 [1985] 3 All ER 699.
46 *Ibid.*, at 703. In *R v South East Thames Mental Health Review Tribunal ex parte Ryan*, Queen's Bench Divisional Court, 19 March 1987 (CO/98/87), it was held that the MHRT was entitled to reject the RMO's opinion on the basis of its own medical member's views. The patient sought judicial review because he was not receiving medication. The attack was held by Watkins LJ to be ill-directed since the patient needed to be kept in hospital for his own benefit and that of the public even though not receiving drugs. See also *R v Trent Mental Health Review Tribunal ex parte Ryan*, QBD CO/445/91 (transcript: Marten Walsh Cherer).
47 See also *R v Mental Health Review Tribunal (Mersey Region) ex parte Davies*, QBD 21 April 1986 (unreported), CO/1723/85; *R v Mental Health Review Tribunal ex parte Pickering* [1986] 1 All ER 99 where (at 104) Forbes J said that when a tribunal gives reasons 'one must somehow be able to read from the reasons the issue to which the reasons are directed'.
48 [1993] QB 683, [1993] 3 WLR 376, [1994] 1 All ER 161.
49 [1994] 1 All ER 161 at 173.
50 *Ibid.*
51 20 May 1996, CO/1467/96 (transcript: Smith Bernal).
52 [1986] 3 All ER 238, 1 WLR 1170, Appeal to House of Lords reported *sub nomine Campbell v Secretary of State for the Home Department* [1988] 1 AC 120, [1987] 3 WLR 522.
53 *The Times*, 28 April 1986.
54 See also *Grant v Mental Health Review Tribunal of Trent*, 23 April 1985, CO/489/85, *R v Mental Health Review Tribunal ex parte O'Hara*, *The Times*, 28 April 1986, and *R v Oxford Mental Health Review Tribunal ex parte Smith* (transcript: John Larking), 25 January 1995.
55 [1986] 1 WLR 1160, [1986] 3 All ER 233.
56 [1986] 3 All ER 233, at 238c.
57 [1986] 1 WLR 1160, [1986] 3 All ER 233.
58 Reported together (CA) *The Times*, 12 October 1988.
59 On the power to adjourn, see also *R v Mental Health Review Tribunal ex parte Cleeland*, Court of Appeal (Civil Division), 28 June 1989.
60 *Perkins v Bath District Health Authority, R v Wessex Mental Health Review Tribunal ex parte Wiltshire County Council* (1989) 4 BMLR 145, *R v Cannons Park Mental Health Review Tribunal ex parte A* [1994] 1 All ER 481 (QBD DC) and [1994] 2 All ER 659 (CA).
61 Unreported, 16 March 1986, CO/1381/86 (QBD).

62 Unreported, 19 March 1987, CO/98/87.
63 See also *R v Trent Mental Health Review Tribunal ex parte Ryan*, QBD, CO/445/ 91 (transcript: Marten Walsh Cherer) and Gostin and Fennell, *Mental Health: Tribunal Procedure* (2nd edn), London: Longman (1992), pp. 86–8.
64 Mental Health Act 1983, s. 1(2).
65 Mental Health Act 1983, s. 3(2)(b).
66 [1994] 1 All ER 481 (QBD DC) and [1994] 2 All ER 659 (CA).
67 *Ibid.*, at 490c.
68 (1981) 1 BMLR 98, 4 EHRR 188.
69 4 EHRR 188, at 189.
70 [1994] 2 All ER 659, at 684c.
71 *Brind v Secretary of State for the Home Department* [1991] 1 All ER 720, [1991] AC 696.
72 [1994] 2 All ER 659, at 677b.
73 See also *R v Trent Mental Health Review Tribunal ex parte Ryan*, QBD, CO/445/ 91 (transcript: Marten Walsh Cherer).
74 *James Kay v United Kingdom*, Application No. 1782/91, Admissibility Decision 7 July 1993.
75 (1979) 2 EHRR 387.
76 *Ibid.*
77 *R v Ealing District Health Authority ex parte Fox* [1993] 1 WLR 373. The *Mental Health Act Code of Practice* (2nd edn) (1993), paras 27.1–27.11.
78 NHS Management Executive/HSG(94)27, 'Guidelines on the Discharge of Mentally Disordered People from Hospital and their Continuing Care in the Community', para. 19.
79 Local Authority Social Services Act 1970, s. 7(1). See also s. 7A.
80 (1996) 32 BMLR 136.
81 Unreported, Queen's Bench Division, 29 October 1996.
82 European Commission on Human Rights Decision on Admissibility, 18 May 1995, 32520/93. Judgment of the European Court of Human Rights, 24 October 1997.
83 [1997] 2 WLR 459.

BIBLIOGRAPHY

Department of Health and Social Security and the Home Office, *Interdepartmental Committee Report on Mental Health Review Tribunal Procedures* (1978).
Fennell, P., 'Sexual suppressants and the Mental Health Act', [1988] *Criminal Law Review*: 660–6.
Fennell, P., 'Community care, community compulsion and the law' in Ritter, S., Hervey *et al.* (eds) *Collaborative Health Care*, ch. 6. London: Edward Arnold (1996).
Fennell, P., 'Law and psychiatry' in Thomas, P. A. (ed.) *Legal Frontiers*, pp. 208–64. Aldershot: Dartmouth (1996).
Gostin, L. O., 'Perspectives on mental health reforms', 10 *Journal of Law and Society* (1983): 47–70.
Gostin, L. O. and Fennell, P., *Mental Health: Tribunal Procedure* (2nd edn). London: Longman (1992).

LEGISLATION

Legal Advice and Assistance (Amendment) Regulations 1994, SI 1994, No. 805.
The Mental Health Act 1959.
The Mental Health Act 1983.
The Mental Health (Patients in the Community) Act 1995.
The Mental Health Review Tribunal Rules 1983, SI 1983, No. 942.

GUIDANCE

HC(90)23/LASSL(90) 11, 'Care Programme Approach for People with a Mental Illness Referred to the Specialist Psychiatric Services'.
NHS Management Executive, Health Service Guidelines HSG(94)5, 'Supervision Registers'.
NHS Management Executive HSG(94)27, 'Guidelines on the Discharge of Mentally Disordered People from Hospital and their Continuing Care in the Community'.
Department of Health, *The Mental Health Act Code of Practice* (2nd edn) (1993).

CASES

Alexander Machinery (Dudley) Ltd. v *Crabtree* [1974] ICR 120.
Associated Provincial Picture Houses v *Wednesbury Corporation* [1948] 1 KB 223.
Bone v *Mental Health Review Tribunal* [1985] 3 All ER 330.
Campbell v *Secretary of State for the Home Department* [1988] 1 AC 120, [1988] 3 WLR 522.
Council of Civil Service Unions v *Minister for the Civil Service* [1985] AC 374, 410–11.
Dlodlo v *Mental Health Review Tribunal for the South Thames Region and Others, The Times,* 12 August 1996 (transcript: Smith Bernal).
Grant v *Mental Health Review Tribunal of Trent* CO/489/85.
James Kay v *United Kingdom,* Application No. 17821/91, Decision of Commission on admissibility 7 July 1993; Report of the Commission adopted 1 March 1994.
Khawaja v *Secretary of State for the Home Department* [1983] 1 All ER 765, [1984] AC 74.
Padfield v *Ministry of Agriculture Fisheries and Food* [1968] AC 997, [1968] 1 All ER 694.
Perkins v *Bath District Health Authority, R* v *Wessex Mental Health Review Tribunal ex parte Wiltshire County Council* (1989) 4 BMLR 145.
Pickering v *Liverpool Daily Post and Echo Newspapers plc* [1991] 1 All ER 622, [1991] 2 WLR 513, (1991) 6 BMLR 108, 1991 All ER Annual Reviews 237–9.
R v *Board of Control ex parte Rutty* [1956] 1 All ER 769, [1956] 2 QB 109.
R v *Cannons Park Mental Health Review Tribunal ex parte A* [1994] 1 All ER 481 (QBD DC) and [1994] 2 All ER 659 (CA).
R v *Ealing District Health Authority ex parte Fox* [1993] 1 WLR 373.
R v *Gardner ex parte L* [1986] 2 All ER 306.
R v *Hallstrom ex parte W* [1986] QB 824.
R v *Hallstrom ex parte W (No. 2)* [1986] 2 All ER 306.

R v Mental Health Act Commission ex parte Turner QBD, 10 January 1993, CO/1945/92.

R v Mental Health Act Commission ex parte W, The Guardian, 27 May 1988; *The Independent,* 27 May 1988; *The Times,* 27 May 1988. Reported sub nomine *R v Mental Health Act Commission ex parte X* (1988) 9 BMLR 77.

R v Mental Health Review Tribunal ex parte Clatworthy [1985] 3 All ER 699.

R v Mental Health Review Tribunal ex parte Cleeland, Court of Appeal (Civil Division), 28 June 1989.

R v Mental Health Review Tribunal ex parte London Borough of Haringey, 4 April 1995, CO/892/95.

R v Mental Health Review Tribunal ex parte O'Hara, The Times, 28 April 1986.

R v Mental Health Review Tribunal ex parte Pickering [1986] 1 All ER 99.

R v Mental Health Review Tribunal for the North Thames Region ex parte Pierce, 20 May 1996, CO/1467/96 (transcript: Smith Bernal).

R v Mental Health Review Tribunal (Mersey Region) ex parte Davies QBD, 21 April 1986 (unreported), CO/1723/85.

R v Mersey Mental Health Review Tribunal ex parte Dillon QBD, 16 March 1986 (unreported), CO/1381/86.

R v Mersey Mental Health Review Tribunal ex parte K [1990] 1 All ER 694.

R v Mersey Mental Health Review Tribunal ex parte O'Hara, The Times, 28 April 1986.

R v Oxford Mental Health Review Tribunal ex parte Secretary of State for the Home Department [1986] 3 All ER 238, 1 WLR 1170.

R v Oxford Mental Health Review Tribunal ex parte Smith, 25 January 1995 (transcript: John Larking).

R v Secretary of State for the Home Department ex parte Brind [1990] 2 WLR 787, [1990] 1 All ER 469.

R v Secretary of State for the Home Department ex parte K [1990] All ER 703 (QBD) [1991] 1 QB 270, [1990] 3 All ER 562, 6 BMLR 1 (CA).

R v Secretary of State for the Home Department ex parte Muboyayi [1991] 4 All ER 72 {[1992] QB 244.

R v South East Thames Mental Health Review Tribunal ex parte Ryan, Queen's Bench Divisional Court, 19 March 1987 (unreported), CO/98/87.

R v South Western Hospital Managers ex parte M [1994] 1 All ER 161 [1993] QB 683 [1993] 3 WLR 376 All ER Annual Review 1994, Medical Law, 280–8.

R v The Managers of the North West London Mental Health NHS Trust ex parte Stewart, The Times, 19 July 1996, CO/1825/95 (transcript: Smith Bernal).

R v Trent Mental Health Review Tribunal ex parte Ryan QBD, CO/445/91 (transcript: Marten Walsh Cherer).

R v Yorkshire Mental Health Review Tribunal and another ex parte Secretary of State for the Home Department, reported with *R v Oxford Mental Health Review Tribunal ex parte Secretary of State for the Home Department* [1986] 3 All ER 238, 1 WLR 1170, Appeal to House of Lords reported sub nomine *Campbell v Secretary of State for the Home Department* [1988] 1 AC 120, [1987] 3 WLR 522.

Re Jones QBD, 8 March 1991, CO/102/91.

Re S-C (Mental Patient; Habeas Corpus) [1996] 1 All ER 532.

Re VE [1973] 1 QB 452.

Secretary of State for the Home Department v Mental Health Review Tribunal for the Mersey Regional Health Authority [1986] 1 WLR 1160, [1986] 3 All ER 233.

Secretary of State for the Home Department v *Mental Health Review Tribunal for Wales* (CA) [1986] 1 WLR 1160, [1986] 3 All ER 233.

Stanley Johnson v *United Kingdom*, European Commission on Human Rights, Decision on Admissibility 18 May 1995 32520/93, Judgment of the Court 24 October 1997.

Winterwerp v *The Netherlands* (1979) EHRR 387.

X v *United Kingdom* (1981) 4 EHRR 188, 1 BMLR 98.

4

Judicial Review and Social Security

PETER ROBSON

PROLOGUE

The role of the courts in defence of the poor has in the past been direct. In February 1873 Mary Clark, a deserted wife, applied to the Relieving Officer at about 4 p.m. for a workhouse order, telling him that she was without food or means. He gave her no relief, but told her to come back the next morning and he would see what he could do for her. On the next day she went to him again and applied for relief, and he asked her where she had slept during the past night; she said she had slept nowhere but had walked up and down the streets. He replied that if a police constable had seen her the constable would have sent her to the casual ward. She said that a police constable had seen her, but had taken no notice of her. The woman again told the Relieving Officer that she had no food or home or means, that she had previously been in the Whitechapel Workhouse, and that she wished to be admitted into the Workhouse until she could get an order made on her husband for her maintenance. The Relieving Officer was, on conviction, fined forty shillings and costs for the offence of having refused, as a case of urgent necessity, the woman relief.[1] Worse than a fine was the possibility of an indictment for manslaughter if death had followed upon a Relieving Officer's refusal of relief.[2] An adverse finding at a judicial review hearing or in an anonymized Report from the Ombudsman is the nearest modern equivalent. It rather pales by comparison.

INTRODUCTION

In the past twenty years after a brief flurry in the use of judicial review in social security a marked decline has followed. Use of judicial review in social security law has been limited during an era when judicial review has become the focus of considerable interest. This form of court supervision has been described as having transformed the face of administrative law and led to a 'torrent' of cases against public bodies (Bridges, Meszaros and Sunkin, 1995: 1) and as 'a great weapon in the hands of judges'.[3] The Public Law Project has documented these developments in a variety of fields (Sunkin, Bridges and Meszaros, 1993a; Bridges, Meszaros and Sunkin, 1995; Hadfield and Weaver, 1994; Mullen, Pick and Prosser, 1996). The conclusion for England and Wales, which is also reflected in the other studies, is that the paucity of litigation is one of the main puzzles associated with judicial review. Why, ask Bridges, Meszaros and Sunkin, are there so few challenges in this key area of governmental activity affecting vital rights and interests of individuals and groups (Bridges, Meszaros and Sunkin, 1995: 71)? This apparent absence of challenge through judicial review occurs during a period when the number of appeals against decisions of the social security authorities has risen and when the number of volunteer and professional advisers has expanded rapidly. There is now a vigorous literature on welfare rights in books, journals and magazines (Appendix 4.2). This chapter explores the paradox. We have, however, a mere handful of social security cases being brought in an area where we have witnessed 'an increasing need to resort to the courts for protection against alleged abuse by public bodies of their public duties' (Woolf, 1986: 222). There is a marked contrast, for instance, with the volume of litigation on homelessness (Robson and Poustie, 1996). It does seem, however, likely that the current level of use may well be increased.

In order to appreciate why the role of judicial review in social security has been markedly different from other areas it is necessary to look at the mechanisms for adjudication which exist in those areas where citizens have rights in relation to the areas traditionally covered by social security. It is worth also pointing out that in this collection of essays there is separate coverage of two recent developments in the social rights field which are in line with the expansion of judicial review experienced generally. These two areas themselves, housing benefit and the Social Fund, represent a particular trend to move potential areas of conflict into areas where there is 'soft adjudication'. In these fora there are rules in operation but the process of challenge is a review without any form of further appeal. There has been much professional and academic scepticism about these mechanisms (Drabble and Lynes, 1989).

THE DEVELOPMENT OF SOCIAL SECURITY PROVISION IN BRITAIN

It is important to bear in mind that the various parts of the income support system which exists in Britain were introduced in a haphazard and unsystematic manner. It may be currently advisable, in political terms, to talk in terms of a welfare system but this is misleading. This is a theme discussed at greater length below. Welfare practice in twentieth-century Britain, however, has been characterized by consistency in avoidance of the courts as far as adjudication is concerned. Neither practitioners nor Government have been keen to involve the judiciary.

Modern methods of providing financial support during those times when individuals are not able to participate in the world of waged work are complex. There is, at the end of the 1990s, only a vestige of a coherent system and no vision evident of how to deal with ageing, disability and child support. The day-to-day struggle for poor and marginalized people to secure what limited rights they have continues to dominate the work of poverty law practitioners.[4] The various channels of challenge to decisions on benefits are complex and varied. The role of judicial review needs to be located within the existing structure and its possible future role assessed in this context.

The Poor Law, with its confinement of paupers in segregated institutions, is no longer with us. It was replaced from 1908 over the ensuing forty years on a pragmatic *ad hoc* basis by a patchwork mix of rights and discretion (Gilbert, 1970). Social security was then systematized in the 1940s. The core principles in the Report of Sir William Beveridge (Beveridge, 1942) were implemented in the legislative programme of the post-war Labour Administration of Clement Attlee.[5] A range of universal social security benefits was to be made available to cover the major incidences of involuntary absence from waged work – sickness, unemployment, old age and childbirth.[6] These events were funded by non-means-tested benefits made available on the basis of workers having paid a National Insurance contribution.[7] There was also recognition of other life expenses which were to be borne by the community for the broad public interest such as Family Allowances to help meet the cost of child-rearing.[8] The Beveridge Report did note that there would be gaps in this provision which would be met by a new discretionary system to be called National Assistance.[9] Introducing the new system, the Minister of Health, Aneurin Bevan, indicated that the work to be left to the Assistance Board after the whole of the needs had been met by all the other measures – insurance allowances, old age pensions, sickness benefits – would be limited to certain 'residual categories'.[10] The income support role was not expected to be a major issue as there would only be a limited number of cases not covered by social insurance.[11] At this juncture it was possible to describe this as a social security system.

The continuing financial significance of contributory insurance-based benefits must not be forgotten despite their decline. By 1978–79 the budget of the whole social security system budget was £15 billion. This amounted to £11.5 billion covering retirement pensions, sickness, unemployment and child benefit. Only 15 per cent of the budget was taken by means-tested income payments to the poor (Donnison, 1982: 13). In 1994/95 overall expenditure had risen to £84 billion. Between 1980 and 1994 the percentage of expenditure on contributory insurance-based benefits declined from 64 per cent to 47 per cent (statistics from the DSS, 1995).

Despite, however, the intention that the social insurance system be comprehensive, a whole range of gaps has been identified, including groups with no contribution record or whose entitlement is used up[12] – first-time job seekers, congenitally disabled people and those who are long-term unemployed (Parker, 1993: 183). The inadequate coverage of the social insurance concept in these areas of social life has led to some legislative innovations. The income problems of chronically sick and disabled people have been recognized as being inadequately covered by the social security system. In a survey conducted in 1968–69 by the Office of Population, Censuses and Surveys (OPCS) it was revealed that, of the 1 million-plus people who were disabled in such a way that they were not able to enter the workforce, some 35–40 per cent of these were forced to subsist on means-tested state benefit (Harris, Smith and Head, 1972). One of the central themes of Beveridge had been to remove the need for people to rely on the means test. Its degrading nature had been recorded in both popular culture (Brierley, 1935) and academic studies (Bradshaw and Deacon, 1983).

The Governmental response was to introduce the invalidity pension[13] which reversed the previous position whereby the long-term sick had received a lower rate of benefit after six months. Another major problem identified in the OPCS work was the problem of the people who never qualified for national insurance benefits as they were unable to satisfy the contribution conditions. To meet this deficiency a non-contributory benefit was introduced in 1975.[14] It was available on a non-means-tested basis. It was, however, also paid at a lower level than invalidity pension to preserve the principle of non-means-tested benefits being insurance-based.[15] The benefit was extended in 1977 to cover disabled housewives. This was not without its controversial aspects involving as it did a sexist additional test for women only centring on their inability to 'perform normal household duties'. This discrimination was removed and these benefits were merged to form the Severe Disablement Allowance in 1984.[16]

Specific benefits were also introduced aimed to meet the financial needs of severely disabled people with the introduction of Attendance Allowance and Mobility Allowance.[17] These broke significantly with the insurance concept, offering benefits that were neither contributory nor means-tested. In addition they were neither taxable nor taken into account for the purposes of making an income support claim. Hence the policy changes which have been introduced since 1970 have drastically altered the nature of social security and have led to the situation where it is not a coherent system. The major change in the 1990s has been to extend the range of disabled people who are entitled to such benefits with both mobility and care components in the Disability Living Allowance.[18] Laudable though these moves may be, there is an absence of any clear underlying principles behind the legislation. This can be seen, for instance, in the existence of two benefits to subsidize the wages of the working poor. Family Credit and Disability Working Allowance are non-contributory and act as means-tested wage supplements for fixed periods of six months. They add to the mixture of insurance benefits, strict means testing and universal non-contributory benefits, seen in the rest of British social security.

The centrality, then, of the insurance principle has been significantly undermined (Clasen, 1994). The commitment to providing social rights without means testing has disappeared. It seems entirely possible that retirement pensions, child benefit and unemployment benefit will become means-tested in the none-too-distant future. The muted protests at the reduction in unemployment benefit from a twelve-month to a six-month benefit and the abolition of one-parent benefit do not bode well for the future. In Britain in 1997 there is now a mix of taxable and non-taxable benefits. Some benefits are means-tested while others are payable irrespective of income. A number of benefits are taken into account in determining entitlement to income support while others are disregarded. Benefits are both contributory and non-contributory. There is no obvious underlying rationale for ascribing benefits to these various categories (Appendix 4.1).

These policy developments have been abetted by the emergence of the phenomena which have called into question the effectiveness of the insurance-based nature of welfare provision in Britain. Long-term unemployment has become a feature of economic life in a way which was not anticipated by Beveridge and the structure of unemployment benefits which was adopted. This has produced a situation where those relying on the modern version of national assistance, income support, amounted to 9 million in 1994.[19] At the same time there have been reductions in the effectiveness of insurance benefits. The purchasing power of social insurance benefits has been affected by changing the link between waged work and benefits. Benefits are now linked to the Retail Price Index rather than average wages (Atkinson and Micklewright, 1989: 125). In addition, as mentioned, the erosion has occurred in the substance of benefits such as the six-month Jobseeker's Allowance replacing the year-long Unemployment Benefit.

DEVELOPMENTS IN ADJUDICATION

Although, as noted (Appendix 4.1), benefits can be distinguished along using various different lines, including means testing and taxability, for the purposes of adjudication the distinction between insurance-based and non-insurance-based benefits has been most significant. The adjudication systems used by these two branches of social security administration have traditionally been quite distinct. National Insurance benefits have provided a range of benefits which has expanded from the first legislation in 1911 covering sickness and unemployment. In the event of disputes about entitlement, provision was made for initial decisions by Board of Trade insurance officers. Appeal lay to a court of referees. This was a three-member tribunal with a chair, one member from an employers' panel and one from a workmen's panel.[20] When the original means-tested pensions were made contributory in 1925, decisions as to entitlement were made directly by the Minister. Appeals against rejection were heard by an independent referee, a senior lawyer. This system was adopted for disputed claims under the Family Allowances Act 1945 with the additional proviso that the referee could state a case on a point of law for the High Court.[21] When the social insurance system was expanded to its full range under the Attlee Government the National Insurance Act 1946 made provision for claims to be determined initially by an insurance officer. Appeal lay to an independent national insurance tribunal. There was a further level of appeal to a National Insurance Commissioner.

Running parallel with the insurance benefits the safety net system of social assistance varied considerably during the first four decades of the century. The traditional source of financial support, the Poor

Law authorities, were subject to challenge in the courts. Disputes about the responsibility for the maintenance of paupers were a major source of litigation during the nineteenth century (Mackay, 1904: ch. XVI). This source of assistance was, however, in danger of complete bankruptcy with the financial pressures of the depression and its role was superseded by a national benefit called 'uncovenanted benefit' (Gilbert, 1970). The treatment of those who had run out of the initial insurance-based unemployment and sickness benefits was also made uniform with the introduction of the Unemployment Assistance Board in 1934. It employed its own staff and fixed benefit rates in consultation with the Government. As far as challenging decisions was concerned, the system was remarkably deficient. Unlike the Poor Law with its range of direct intervention by magistrates, the non-insurance clients had a less direct form of redress. This continued under the Unemployment Assistance Board with Boards of Referees. These operated as an arm of the administration operating in an administrative capacity rather than judicially. This stemmed both from the dominance of appointment by the Unemployment Assistance Board of tribunal members (Lynes, 1975) and from the considerable political problems involved in imposing a household means test (Gilbert, 1970: 182ff.). After the abolition of the final vestiges of the Poor Law under the National Assistance Act 1948, a similar kind of arrangement continued. Lawyers were not central as with insurance benefits. Precedent and further appeal were absent from the system. There was a strong element of administrative continuity underlying the development of adjudication in the area of means-tested benefits until 1966 (Bradley, 1975) and extending beyond until legislative amendment in 1980. From the mid-1960s this part of the tribunal system became a focus for political action to secure changes in the allocation of goods to poor people through challenges on exceptional needs payments and exceptional circumstances additions.[22]

AVOIDING THE USE OF THE COURTS

One feature of the struggle of the working classes for social rights has been doubts about the courts' ability to provide fair and impartial decision-making. Suspicion regarding the courts as a forum for the working man has existed from writers looking at the background as well as pronouncements of the judges interpreting both common law and statute (Ensor, 1933; Pritt, 1971a; Robson, 1979). These pronouncements often seemed to confirm the notion of courts as the accomplices of the employing classes (Sachs and Wilson, 1978; Griffith, 1985).

This was reflected in the problems encountered in the use of the courts under the first mass benefit available to workers under the Workmen's Compensation legislation. The effect of the court process on the rights of injured workers under the Workmen's Compensation Acts of 1897 and 1906 meant that what was conceived as a simple, immediate and effective measure turned out to be 'complex, slow and often ineffective' (Abel-Smith and Stevens, 1967). This absence of the courts was a feature of the early insurance-based benefits and continued with the Beveridge restructuring. There was no provision in the national insurance legislation at that time nor in the social assistance provisions for appeal to the courts from decisions of the adjudicating authorities. The Franks Committee commented favourably on this concentration on the speedy resolution of conflicts (Franks Committee, 1957: para. 108).

THE EMERGENCE OF JUDICIAL REVIEW CHALLENGES

The role of judicial review in this area was dormant until the 1950s. It emerged in the context of disablement benefit. The appeal mechanism for this benefit was the medical appeal tribunal used in connection with disablement questions which had the additional feature that two of the members have medical expertise. These tribunals, however, provided no appeal to Commissioners. A challenge by way of judicial review was successfully mounted in 1956 concerning the decision of a medical appeal tribunal in connection with the level of injury assessed where there was an injury to one of two 'paired' organs.[23] In those areas where there was appeal to Commissioners, the relationship between the courts and Commissioners was curiously deferential. There was a marked reluctance to interfere with Commissioners' decisions.[24]

The intention and expectation of the post-war Beveridge-based welfare system was that the various common financial calamities that befall people throughout their lives would be met by universal benefits. These would be available as of right without a means test. Significantly, however, the emergence of long-term unemployment altered the operation of this model. The benefit targeted at unemployment was, from its original inception in 1911, time-limited. After a year's unemployment benefit, entitlement ceased.[25] This contrasts with the position of those who were long-term sick. Here, in fact, the benefit not only continued but also increased in its value from 1971. Unemployment levels increased. This had a major impact on the use of the basic mechanism of means-tested income benefits. The numbers of those who depended on means-tested benefits rose from 1 million in 1945 to 3 million by the end of the 1970s.[26] A resultant problem for those on these benefits for an extended period of time was the inadequacy of the rate of benefit. To meet this, the system of additional lump sums and weekly payments which had been available from the introduction of unemployment assistance became the focus for claims in the 1970s.

One of the central features of the means-tested income replacement benefit, supplementary benefit, was the existence of discretion within its framework on a number of issues. In terms of the Ministry of Social Security Act 1966 every person in Great Britain whose 'resources are insufficient to meet his requirements shall be entitled to benefit'.[27] This was subject to the discretion of the Supplementary Benefits Commission to depart from the criteria laid down. The range of discretion is neatly summed up by Cranston (1985):

> ... the Supplementary Benefits Commission had discretion under other sections to depart from them. Thus where it appeared reasonable in all the circumstances, supplementary benefits could be paid to a person by way of a single payment to meet an exceptional need; supplementary benefits could be paid in urgent cases, notwithstanding the limitations normally obtaining: and in exceptional circumstances, supplementary benefits could be awarded at an amount exceeding that calculated in accordance with the Schedule, or a supplementary allowance could be reduced below the amount so calculated, or withheld altogether, as was appropriate to those circumstances.
> (At p. 169)

The question of how such discretion was operated was a major concern for activists in the 1970s (Adler and Bradley (eds), 1975). The appeal to Supplementary Benefits Appeals Tribunals were often unsuccessful and the absence of satisfactory decision-making processes was identified as a problem (Adler, Burns and Johnson, 1975).

Although there was no right of appeal from the decision of Supplementary Benefit Appeal Tribunals the supervisory jurisdiction of the High Court was always available. Until 1973 no application was reported (Calvert, 1978: 457). The first decision in this area was *R v Birmingham Appeal Tribunal ex parte Simper*.[28] Here the Divisional Court quashed a tribunal decision which had automatically offset the appellant's Exceptional Circumstances Addition for heating against a long-term addition. This success was ratified into legislation. From April 1975 the long-term addition was incorporated into the long-term scale rates.

This initial success in the Divisional Court was not followed in the Court of Appeal in subsequent litigation. In the first cases to reach the Court of Appeal, the view was expressed, however, that this was an area in which the courts should not interfere. In *R v Preston Supplementary Benefits Appeal Tribunal ex parte Moore and Shine*,[29] the question of how students in different circumstances should be treated by the benefits system was looked at. The Court of Appeal decided against both the students and took the opportunity to discourage use of the courts for questions under the supplementary benefit scheme. Lord Denning was at the height of his crusade against trade unionists, homeless people and other enemies of the *status quo*. His preference was for the courts to be used by people like George Ward and John Gouriet to defend certain kinds of rights of the 'little man' (Robson and Watchman (eds), 1981). He opined that

> It is plain that Parliament intended that the Supplementary Benefit Act 1966 should be administered with as little technicality as possible. It should not become the happy hunting ground for lawyers. The courts should hesitate long before interfering ... with the decisions of the appeal tribunals ... The courts should not enter into a meticulous discussion of the meaning of this or that word in the Act. They should leave the tribunals to interpret the Act in a broad reasonable way, according to the spirit and not to the letter ...[30]

It was conceded that it was helpful if there was uniformity in the decisions of those applying the legislation each day and that the courts should be ready to consider points of general application. The courts, however, while being ready to lay down broad guidelines for tribunals, 'should not be used as if there was an appeal to them. Individual cases of particular application must be left to the tribunals.'[31]

Despite this discouragement, a variety of issues were brought before the courts in the 1970s. In *R v West London Supplementary Benefits Appeal Tribunal ex parte Clarke*[32] the court was faced with an applicant whose son had promised to support her when she came to Britain from India. After living with her son-in-law and daughter for over two years she fell out with them and was ordered to leave the family home. The social security authorities took the view that she had resources notionally available from her son-in-law who had previously supported her. Their decision to offset her benefit entitlement by a sum was upheld by the Supplementary Benefit Appeal Tribunal which accepted the official view that it was up to the family to meet the financial support undertaking to the immigration authorities as there had been no changes in the family's circumstances. This was, however, rejected by the Divisional Court as disclosing a clear error by the authorities. In the circumstances the court, despite *Moore*, felt compelled to interfere in this case.

The question of a student's rights to support where the parental contribution was not forthcoming was raised in *R v Barnsley Supplementary Benefit Appeal Tribunal ex parte Atkinson* at both Divisional Court[33] and Court of Appeal[34] levels. The Divisional Court was unwilling to interfere with the decision of the social security authorities and adopted the Denning approach. In the particular circumstances of this case, however, the Court of Appeal noted that the social security authorities had not actually exercised discretion in their treatment of parental contributions. They had applied a blanket rule that such resources were to be assumed without the possibility of considering whether they were indeed resources available to the claimant. They did not, however, suggest that the attitude in *Moore* was in any way displaced. Further approaches to the courts met with limited success.

Despite the limited approach of the Court of Appeal one might have expected a steady build-up of business just as occurred with challenges to the Housing (Homeless Persons) Act in spite of the dire warnings of Lord Bridge in *Puhlhofer*.[35] That this did not occur is attributable to a significant degree to the pragmatic decision to alter drastically the method of social security adjudication. One of the by-products of the decision to put a ceiling on the costs of additional payments in the means-tested supplementary benefits area was a shift to replace discretion with formal rights. The Government was keen to put a brake on these additional payments which were made available after 1980 only by satisfying detailed regulations contained in statutory instruments.[36] Accordingly, in 1980 a right of appeal was introduced from the tribunals dealing with means-tested benefits in the Social Security Act 1980.[37] This right of appeal is to Social Security Commissioners with a further right of appeal to the Court of Appeal or, in Scotland, to the Court of Session.[38] Opening up the process to appeal rather than judicial review has not, to date, greatly altered the approach of the courts. The cautious approach which was found in relation to insurance-based benefits[39] has been continued,[40] although where questions of sex discrimination have been identified the European Court of Justice has been used.[41] Finally, the reservation of certain matters for decision by the Secretary of State is one which avoids the use of the tribunal appeal system. There may be appeal on a point of law to the High Court. Such matters, it is argued, have no very clear rationale (Ogus, Barendt and Wikeley, 1995: 585) and are only a source of complication.[42]

Specific issues have been taken beyond the level of Commissioners on the interpretation of crucial questions in social security law. These include unemployment benefit questions such as whether a claimant should be disqualified from benefit for being in prison,[43] when an involuntary striker was deemed to be barred from benefit,[44] what amounted to being employed to the full extent normal[45] and the nature of care required by a blind person to qualify for financial assistance.[46] In relation to attendance allowance claims there was an appeal to the House of Lords on what amounted to 'attention in connection with his bodily function'.[47] There is, however, a much greater reliance on the cheap access to the expertise of the Social Security Appeal Tribunals and the Social Security Commissioners. The number of appeals lodged annually has risen in the 1990s from 67,000 to 77,000 (statistics from the DSS, 1995).

In addition there are other cheap methods of 'maumauing the flakcatchers'[48] which have been used to a significant degree. Internal review can be of great significance, with 25 per cent of decisions being revised on review in the claimant's favour (Wikeley and Young, 1994: 242). The introduction in 1967 of the Parliamentary Commissioner or Ombudsman offered an alternative method of relief when claimants were dissatisfied with the operation of the social security system. The range of issues where there have been successful outcomes for claimants includes delays and abuse as well as matters of substance such as misinformation.[49] The Department of Social Security has been the subject of a significant proportion of the complaints to the Parliamentary Commissioner for Administration (Parliamentary Commission for Administration, 1994: 45).

THE USE OF JUDICIAL REVIEW IN SOCIAL SECURITY IN THE 1990S

The rise in the use of judicial review has been extensively documented (Hadfield (ed.), 1995; Buck, 1996). It is worth, however, noting the major patterns which have occurred in the use of this remedy as they relate to social security matters. In England and Wales there has been a rise in the use of judicial review generally during the 1980s and 1990s from some 533 in 1981 to 3208 in 1994 (Bridges, Meszaros and Sunkin, 1995: 7). This disguises the fact that there have been a number of areas where use has not been extensive. This includes social security, which is described as being largely untouched by judicial review (Sunkin, Bridges and Meszaros, 1993: 444). The Home Office, the Department of the Environment and the Inland Revenue were the subject of 90 per cent of judicial review challenges. Only three departments – Social Security, Transport and the Welsh Office – received no more than ten challenges in any single year (*ibid.*: 42). The percentage of applications for leave to seek judicial review has generally been below 1 per cent as far as social security benefits are concerned. During 1993 social security tribunals dealt with 161,208 cases and hence the Public Law Project's conclusion that the figures also highlight the exceptional nature of recourse to judicial review (Bridges, Meszaros and Sunkin, 1995: 11). There did not appear any particular problem in relation to the obtaining of legal aid (*ibid.*: 71). In Scotland, with a slightly later database, the same kind of picture emerges despite the fact that there is here no need to seek leave (Mullen, Pick and Prosser, 1995 and 1996). While the published figures do not provide a breakdown between social security and social fund reviews, the number of petitions under the category 'Welfare' has been very small, ranging from two to four per year between 1988 and 1993 (Mullen, Pick and Prosser, 1996: 19). These include, as indicated, social fund petitions in several instances. In Northern Ireland, between 1987 and 1991 the position was generally different as far as the major areas of use were concerned. The lack of challenges over social security, however, does not appear to be markedly different (Hadfield and Weaver, 1994).

The issues which have come up before the courts cover a wide range of matters. These include matters of principle where poverty lobbyists have sought to alter the standards applicable across the board through use of judicial review. The courts have continued their arms-length relationship with the administration of benefits. They rejected the case brought by the Child Poverty Action Group to require decisions to be given within fourteen days of the claim. The legislation provided for this. It was, however, not to be strictly applied in the view of the Court of Appeal.[50] Nor have the courts been prepared to require a Social Security Commissioner to give reasons for a decision to refuse leave to appeal.[51] The courts have, not unexpectedly, rejected attempts to use judicial review where the claimant still has outstanding the avenues of appeal to a Social Security Appeal Tribunal. Where there are separate proceedings taking place or available as an option the Social Security Appeal Tribunal has been preferred.[52] There have also been questions of less general impact concerning the backdating of pension claims[53] and the extension of time to bring an appeal.[54] While the House of Lords has not been prepared to find that regulations about overpayment were unlawful,[55] they have rejected the notion that the lawfulness of delegated legislation could only be discussed in judicial review proceedings.[56] While the restricted view taken by the Court of Appeal was dismissed as 'mistaken',[57] the impetus to proceed via judicial review has been further weakened by this broad approach.

Not all actions, of course, are brought strictly on their merits.

Where there is a threat of court action the Department of Social Security may well at this stage concede the specific case. They may do so because they do not wish a clear principle to be laid down or they may simply wish to avoid the lottery of court process.[58] Practitioners in social security as well as homelessness litigation recognize this civil action version of plea bargaining as a normal part of the negotiating process. Hence, particularly where the number of actions is small, it is necessary to investigate the extent to which these are raised on their substantive merits and where they are part of the negotiation process. Practitioners acknowledge this practice. They are, not surprisingly, coy about which category particular actions fall into.

STRATEGIES FOR CHALLENGING SOCIAL SECURITY DECISION-MAKING

The individual welfare benefits' appeal mechanisms provide the principal opportunity for shifting the interpretation of the specified rules. Where these challenges have been successful there is a tendency to alter the benefit and the method of adjudication, making it more difficult to challenge on a daily basis. Until 1980, as has been noted, there was a range of additional payments to those existing on the poverty line.[59] These payments were either one-off grants known as exceptional needs payments or exceptional circumstances additions paid weekly. They were administered by the DHSS. They followed detailed undisclosed rules which were produced by the Supplementary Benefits Commission who were given discretionary powers under the Supplementary Benefits Act 1976. Claims for help with exceptional needs were considered in the light of individual and local circumstances and no comprehensive list of the needs which the Commission would meet was provided, although they included, in practice, such things as the replacement of clothing and footwear and essential items of bedding and furniture and household equipment (DHSS, 1970: paras 85–89). Weekly payments could be sought for such things as extra dietary or laundry needs (DHSS, 1970: paras 62–72). Appeals as to when and what individuals were to be provided with were fertile ground for the nascent welfare rights movement in the 1970s. The number of claims rose from 470,000 in 1968 to 1,130,000 in 1979. The level of payments increased from an average of £5.80 to £33.59 during this same time. The tribunals were subject to intensive criticism (Lister, 1975; Bradley, 1975). There was, as has been noted above,[60] a limited recourse to the courts using judicial review.

The response of the Government was to replace the discretionary system with a set of detailed statutory rules. In place of Supplementary Benefits Appeal Tribunals operating with few guidelines, the appeal system was radically altered. They were provided with lawyer chairs. They were to operate by way of detailed procedural rules interpreting formalized tests within a precedent-based system. In terms of claimants many of the criticisms voiced during the 1970s were met. The reformed system proved to be even more extensively used, with claims rising from 1 million to over 4.7 million.[61] The average payment increased to over £75. Replacing discretion with rules did not limit the payouts as Government would have hoped. The costs of these additional payments for recurrent needs rose from £37m to £370m between 1979 and 1986. The response of the Government was to declare that 'everyone was agreed that the single payments system was a mess'[62] and to replace the formal rule-centred single payments system with a discretionary scheme. This scheme had a fixed annual ceiling. Once the fund is exhausted the payments halt (Buck, 1996). This time challenges were not to be heard by an independent tribunal but were limited to internal review hearings to which representations could be made. Where systems are in danger of benefiting claimants financially, it seems, the rules are changed (Piven and Cloward, 1972).

The same kind of dilemma faces those working with Incapacity Benefit. In the pursuit of a drastic reduction of those relying on long-term sickness benefit, the Government introduced a new way of assessing eligibility. In place of the test as to whether an individual was 'capable of work' as determined by their likely capacity to perform in a job, the new entitlement depends on whether or not claimants meet a required number of points on a functional scale.[63] The scale covers both physical and mental issues. Points are awarded outwith the context of work. Appeals against the decisions of adjudication officers operating these rules with the benefit of a medical report from the Benefits Agency Medical Service are heard by Social Security Appeal Tribunals. The early results seem to suggest that the Government's fear that many of those claiming invalidity pension were capable of work do not appear to have been realized. The Government were of the view that over 240,000 claimants were truly fit for work. Early results from the new medical tests and the appeals in the first years suggest that this is wildly overestimated. Fifty per cent of the claimants satisfy the 'all work test' and it is accepted by the Benefits Agency that they are not able to work. Of the remainder 73 per cent of appeals have been successful where the claimant and representative are present and there has been an overall success rate of 58 per cent. Changes have already been introduced. The right to an automatic oral appeal has been removed.

Paper hearings take place unless an oral hearing is specifically requested. One would be surprised if there is not a fall in appeal hearings. At the time of writing, the Government threatens to dispense with the right to independent adjudication. As we have noted, this kind of internal control has a history in social security adjudication. The unglamorous daily battles in the trenches of poverty litigation will continue. There is, however, a role for the showpiece cavalry charge.

ASSESSING JUDICIAL REVIEW IN SOCIAL SECURITY IN THE 1990S

The value to those working in the poverty movement of judicial review is not its everyday value or its ability to effect long-term changes. Its value lies in the ability of the high-profile public nature of judicial review to provide a focus for campaigns on specific issues. The administration of social security is highly politicized. It is a direct reflection of the Government's political agenda. In the past twenty years there has been an increasing identification of the Government with the daily administration of welfare. The trend has been for the rules to reflect political ideology rather than simply efficient service delivery to consumers of welfare services. The advantage from the point of view of politicians is that the political policy moves of welfare are far from accessible. Welfare rules are transmitted in arcane and often impenetrable language. The decisions are diffused in statutory instruments. These contain no ringing phrases of political intent. They are not journalist-friendly for the most part.

In noting the limited impact of judicial review on most Government departments, Bridges, Meszaros and Sunkin conclude that it is misleading to see judicial review as being primarily a tool for challenging and constraining central government. Rather, they suggest that it is more accurate to view judicial review as an additional constraint on local government which now carries much of the administrative burden of recent pressures on the social welfare system (Bridges, Meszaros and Sunkin, 1995). This is indeed the case so far as allocating housing to homeless people is concerned, where the problems can be localized. There appear to be, however, rather different explanations when looking at the largely centralized administration of social security, the vast majority of which goes unchallenged (Sainsbury, 1994: 340). The reasons which have been identified centre much more on the expansion of the accessible alternative channels of challenge which are available to volunteer and paralegal expertise as well as to unassisted claimants. This relates to an interesting point made in the judicial review study of England and

Wales which suggested that the existence of accessible appeal rights may well have an impact on the level of demand for judicial review (Bridges, Meszaros and Sunkin, 1995: 193).

Judicial review, however, does have a quite distinct function in social security. Its users seek to stop Government in its tracks. It provides a focus which translates into headlines of unlawful Government action. It is, however, a weapon which can only be used sparingly. Other developments may complicate matters and require noting. The Government have reactivated the notion that challenges in the courts may not automatically lead to changes (Harlow, 1981) with their reluctance to implement court rulings on unlawful deductions.[64] The application beyond the parties and existing appellants has already been limited. How one assesses the various challenges and findings of unlawfulness in the actions of the State in social security depends on what view one takes of the significance of the political process to the lives of poor people.[65] The attempts to humanize the public face of the poverty agencies dealing with benefits seem fraught, given the nature and level of public welfare in Britain in the 1990s (Swift, Grant and McGrath, 1994). The long-term impact beyond the 1990s may well expand as Government seeks to provide cost ceilings and the predictability of budgets in social security matters. At the time of writing the extension of the use of judicial review in social security is recognized by practitioners as limited. It is, nonetheless, seen as a serious and often necessary option.[66]

NOTES

1   *Clark* v *Joslin* (1873) 27 LT (NS) 762 from Editors of the Poor Law Officers' Journal (1927) *The Law Relating to the Relief of the Poor* (3rd edn), p. 28. London: Law and Local Government Publications.
2   *R* v *Curtis* – 15 Cox's CC 746, September 1885 – *ibid*.
3   *Nottinghamshire County Council* v *Secretary of State for Environment* [1986] AC 240, *per* Lord Scarman at 251.
4   See the columns of the journals in Appendix 4.2 over the years and the dominance of technical over policy issues.
5   For a brief discussion of the differences between what was adopted by the Labour Administration and the Beveridge plan see MacGregor, 1981: ch. 1.
6   National Insurance Act 1946, c. 67.
7   Employers and the Government also made a significant contribution to the Insurance Fund: Kincaid (1975): ch. 5.
8   Family Allowances Act 1945, c. 41.
9   National Assistance Act 1948, c. 29.

10 *Hansard* 444 (24 November 1947), col. 1603.
11 Beveridge, *Social Insurance and Allied Services*, at para. 19.
12 *Category*   *Reason for exclusion*
    Carers   Not available for work
    Children (including school students)   Not available for work
    Students   Not available for work
    Trainees   Not available for work
    First-time job seekers   No contribution record
    Lower paid   Already in work
    Uninsured lone mothers (except widows) Absent parent still alive
    Congenitally disabled   No contribution record
    Long-term unemployed   Entitlement used up
13 National Insurance Act 1971, s. 3.
14 Social Security Benefits Act 1975, c. 11.
15 Social Security 1975, c. 14, s. 3.
16 Housing and Social Security Act 1984, c. 48, s. 11.
17 National Insurance Act 1970, c. 51.
18 Social Security Contributions and Benefits Act 1992, c. 4.
19 DSS Social Security Statistics, 1995.
20 Committee on Procedure and Evidence for the Determination of Claims for Unemployment Insurance Benefit (1929, Cmd 3415), paras 61–69.
21 This only occurred four times over the next fourteen years: Ogus and Barendt, 2nd edn, 1982: 582.
22 Notes 28 and following below.
23 *R v Medical Appeal Tribunal ex parte Gilmore* [1957] 1 QB 574.
24 *R v Industrial Injuries Commissioner ex parte Amalgamated Engineering Union (No. 2)* [1966] 2 QB 31; *R v National Insurance Commissioner ex parte Michael* [1977] 2 All ER 420.
25 The reduction of this period to six months with the depoliticizing/sanitizing of unemployment benefit into the Jobseeker's Allowance occurred under the Jobseekers Act 1995, c. 18.
26 SBC Annual Report 1979 (Cmnd 8033), paras 8.1–8.33.
27 Section 4(1).
28 [1974] QB 543.
29 [1975] 1 WLR 624.
30 *Ibid.*, at 631.
31 *Ibid.*
32 [1975] 1 WLR 1396.
33 [1976] 1 WLR 1047.
34 [1977] 1 WLR 917.
35 *Puhlhofer* v *Hillingdon LBC* [1986] AC 484, at 518.
36 See Ogus and Barendt, 3rd edn, 1988 for a detailed account of the operation of the interpretation of single payments.
37 Section 14 (now Social Security Administration Act 1992, s. 24).
38 Either court can be used depending on which is most convenient to the business in hand. The same sort of split function exists in the context of the common Child Support Act 1991 – G. Jamieson, 'The Child Support Act 1991 and the Act of Union', 37 JLS (1992): 484, at 485.

39 R v *National Insurance Commissioner ex parte Stratton* [1979] QB 361.

40 *Crewe* v *Social Security Commissioner* [1982] 2 All ER 745; *Presho* v *Department of Health and Social Security* [1984] AC 310; *Cartlidge* v *Chief Adjudication Officer* [1986] QB 360 but contrast with the Court of Session's approach in *Watt* v *Lord Advocate* 1979 SLT 137.

41 *Drake* v *Chief Adjudication Officer 150/85* [1987] QB 166; *R* v *Secretary of State for Social Security ex parte Equal Opportunities Commission* [1992] 3 All ER 577.

42 They have, however, led to an upsurge in judicial review challenges in the 1990s discussed below.

43 *R* v *National Insurance Commissioner ex parte Warry* [1981] 1 All ER 229.

44 *Cartlidge* v *Chief Adjudication Officer* [1986] 1 QB 360.

45 *Chief Adjudication Officer* v *Brunt* [1988] 1 All ER 466 (CA); Buck, 1987.

46 *Mallinson* v *Secretary of State for Social Security* [1994] 2 All ER 295.

47 *Woodling* v *Secretary of State for Social Services* [1984] 1 All ER 593.

48 See Tom Wolfe's classic account of the methods of disrupting the operation of the welfare system's operation in the United States in the 1960s: Wolfe, 1971. For further discussion see Piven and Cloward, 1972.

49 See the Annual Reports of the Parliamentary Commissioner for Administration.

50 *R* v *Secretary of State for Social Services ex parte Child Poverty Action Group* [1990] 2 QB 540 (CA).

51 *R* v *Secretary of State for Social Services ex parte Connolly* [1986] 1 All ER 998 (CA).

52 *R* v *Secretary of State for Social Security ex parte Khan*, 27 April 1990 (QBD); *Badibanga* v *The Ipswich Department of Social Security*, 6 June 1995 (CA).

53 *R* v *Secretary of State for Social Security ex parte Foe*, 7 November 1995 (QBD); *R* v *Department of Social Security ex parte Edwards*, 10 July 1992 (QBD).

54 *R* v *Social Security Appeal Tribunal ex parte O'Hara*, 13 July 1994 (QBD).

55 *Britnell* v *Secretary of State for Social Security* [1991] 2 All ER 726.

56 *Chief Adjudication Officer* v *Foster* [1993] 1 All ER 705 (HL).

57 A. Bradley, 'Social security tribunals and administrative legality', [1993] *Public Law*: 218–20.

58 *De Roe* v *Department of Social Security*, 9 October 1989 (CA) (treatment of lump sum and weekly payment of disablement benefit as resources); *R* v *Social Security Appeals Tribunal ex parte Gordon*, 17 April 1989 (QBD) (entitlement to benefit for children when claimant abroad and children staying with grandparents).

59 Supplementary Benefits Act 1976, c. 71, s. 3(1).

60 Notes 19 and following.

61 Statistics from the DSS, 1987.

62 'Panorama', August 1987, Tim Yeo, Minister of State for Social Security, speaking on the 1980 reforms.

63 Social Security (Incapacity for Work) Act 1994, c. 18.

64 *Guardian*, Saturday 9 November 1996, *per* Peter Lilley.

65 Judicial review may not be the answer very often for the social security client but to the critical legal scholar it demonstrates how the impasse of flippable concepts can be negotiated without excessive self-contradiction by the

adjudicating authorities. It also offers an opportunity for the post-modern theorist to observe the operation of different discourses in practice on issues of conflict.

66 S. Martin, 'Suspension of benefit and judicial review', 237 *Scottish Legal Action Group* (1996): 140–2.

BIBLIOGRAPHY

Abel-Smith, B. and Stevens, R. (1967) *Lawyers and the Courts*. London: Heinemann.

Adler, M. and Asquith, A. (eds) (1981) *Discretion and Welfare*. London: Heinemann.

Adler, M. and Bradley, A. (eds) (1975) *Justice, Discretion and Poverty*. London: Professional Books.

Adler, M. Burns, E. and Johnson, R. (1975) 'The conduct of tribunal hearings' in Adler, M. and Bradley, A. (eds) *Justice, Discretion and Poverty*. London: Professional Books.

Alcock, P. and Harris, P. (1982) *Welfare Law and Order*. London: Macmillan.

Atkinson, A. B. and Micklewright, J. (1989) 'Turning the screw: benefits for the unemployed 1979–1988' in Atkinson, A. (ed.) *Poverty and Social Security*. Hemel Hempstead: Harvester Wheatsheaf.

Baldwin, N., Wikeley, N. and Young, R. (1992) *Judging Social Security: The Adjudication of Claims for Benefit in Britain*. Oxford: Clarendon Press.

Beveridge, W. (1942) *Social Insurance and Allied Services*. London: HMSO.

Bradley, A. (1975) 'National Assistance Appeal Tribunals and the Franks Report' in Adler, M. and Bradley, A. (eds) *Justice, Discretion and Poverty*. London: Professional Books.

Bradley, A. (1993) 'Social security tribunals and administrative legality', *Public Law*: 218–20.

Bradshaw, J. and Deacon, A. (1983) *Reserved for the Poor*. London: Routledge.

Bridges, L., Meszaros, G. and Sunkin, M. (1995) *Judicial Review in Perspective*. London: Cavendish.

Brierley, W. (1935) *Means-Test Man*. Nottingham: Spokesman.

Buck, T. (1987) 'Unemployment benefit: the "Full-Extent" Normal Rule', *Journal of Social Welfare Law*: 23–36.

Buck, T. (1996) *The Social Fund: Law and Practice*. London: Sweet and Maxwell.

Calvert, H. (1978) *Social Security Law*. London: Sweet & Maxwell.

Clasen, J. (1994) *Paying the Jobless*. Aldershot: Avebury.

Cranston, R. (1985) *Legal Foundations of the Welfare State*. London: Weidenfeld & Nicolson.

Deacon, A. and Bradshaw, J. (1983) *Reserved for the Poor: the Means Test in British Social Policy*. Oxford: Blackwell.

DHSS (1970) *Supplementary Benefits Handbook*. London: HMSO.

Donnison, D. (1982) *The Politics of Poverty*. Oxford: Martin Robertson.

Drabble, R. and Lynes, T, (1989) 'The social fund – discretion or control?', *Public Law*: 297–322.

Editors of the Poor Law Officers' Journal (1927) *The Law Relating to the Relief of the Poor*. London: Law and Local Government Publications.

Ensor, R. C. K. (1933) *Courts and Judges in France, Germany and England*. London: OUP.

Field, F. (1982) *Poverty and Politics*. London: Heinemann.

Franks Committee (1957) *Administrative Tribunals and Enquiries* (Chairman: Lord Franks). Cmnd 218. London: HMSO.

Gilbert, B. B. (1970) *British Social Policy 1914–1939*. London: Batsford.

Griffith, J. A. G. (1985) *The Politics of the Judiciary*. London: Fontana.

Hadfield, B. (ed.) (1995) *Judicial Review: A Thematic Approach*. Dublin: Gill and Macmillan.

Hadfield, B. and Weaver, E. (1994) 'Trends in judicial review in Northern Ireland', *Public Law*: 12–16.

Harlow, C. (1981) 'Administrative reaction to judicial review', *Public Law*: 116–32.

Harris, A., Smith, C. and Head, E. (1972) *Income and Entitlement to Supplementary Benefit of Impaired People in Great Britain*. London: HMSO.

Hill, M. (1969) 'The exercise of discretion in the National Assistance Board', 47 *Public Administration*: 75–90.

Jamieson, G. 1992 'The Child Support Act 1991 and the Act of Union', 37 JLS 484 (1992).

Kincaid, J. (1975) *Poverty and Equality in Britain*. Harmondsworth: Penguin.

Lister, R. (1975) 'SBATs – an urgent case for reform' in Adler, M. and Bradley, A. (eds) *Justice, Discretion and Poverty*, pp. 171–82. London: Professional Books.

Lynes, T. (1972) *The Penguin Guide to Supplementary Benefits*. Harmondsworth: Penguin.

Lynes, T. (1975) 'Unemployment Assistance Tribunals in the 1930s' in Adler, M. and Bradley, A. (eds) *Justice, Discretion and Poverty*. London: Professional Books.

MacGregor, S. (1981) *The Politics of Poverty*. London: Longman.

Mackay, T. (1904) *A History of the English Poor Law*. London: King.

Martin, S. (1996) 'Suspension of benefit and judicial review', 237 *Scottish Legal Action Group*: 140–2.

Mullen, T., Pick. K. and Prosser, T. (1995) 'Trends in judicial review in Scotland', *Public Law*: 52–6.

Mullen, T., Pick, K. and Prosser, T. (1996) *Judicial Review in Scotland*. London: Wiley.

Ogus, A., Barendt, E. and Wikeley, N. (1995) *The Law Relating to Social Security*. London: Butterworths. (Earlier editions: 1978, 1982 and 1988.)

Parker, H. (1993) 'Citizen's income' in Berghman, J. and Cantillon, B. (eds) *The European Face of Social Security*, pp. 181–98. Aldershot: Avebury.

Parliamentary Commissioner for Administration (PCA), *Annual Report for 1994* (HC 07). London: HMSO.

Partington, M. (1975) 'Supplementary benefits and the Parliamentary Commissioner' in Adler, M. and Bradley, A. (eds), *Justice, Discretion and Poverty*, pp. 155–82. London: Professional Books.

Piven, F. and Cloward, R. (1972) *Regulating the Poor*. New York: Vintage.

Pritt, D. N. (1971a) *Law, Class and Society: The Apparatus of the Law*. London: Lawrence and Wishart.

Pritt, D. N. (1971b) *Law, Class and Society: Law and Politics and the Law in the Colonies*. London: Lawrence and Wishart.

Pritt, D. N. (1972) *Law, Class and Society: The Substance of the Law*. London: Lawrence and Wishart.

Prosser, T. (1981) 'The politics of discretion: aspects of discretionary power in the supplementary benefits scheme' in Adler, M. and Asquith, S. (eds) *Discretion and Welfare*, pp. 148–70. London: Heinemann, London.

Prosser, T. (1983) *Test Cases for the Poor*. London: CPAG.

Robson, P. (1979) *Housing and the Judiciary*. Glasgow: University of Strathclyde.

Robson, P. and Poustie, M. (1996) *Homeless People and the Law*. London: Butterworths.

Robson, P. and Watchman, P. (eds) (1981) *Justice, Lord Denning and the Constitution*. Aldershot: Gower.

Sachs, A. and Wilson, J. (1978) *Sexism and the Law*. London: Martin Robertson.

Sainsbury, R. (1994) 'Internal reviews and the weakening of the social security claimants' rights of appeals' in Richardson, R. and Genn, M. (eds) *Administrative Law and Government Action*. Oxford: Clarendon Press.

Social Trends (1996). London: HMSO.

Sunkin, M., Bridges, L. and Meszaros, G. (1993a) 'Trends in judicial review', *Public Law*: 443–6.

Swift, P., Grant, G. and McGrath, M. (1994) *Participation in the Social Security System*. Aldershot: Avebury.

Whiteley, P. and Winyard, S. (1987) *Pressure for the Poor*. London and New York: Methuen.

Wikeley, N. and Young, R. (1992) 'The administration of benefits in Britain: adjudication officers and the influence of Social Security Appeal Tribunals', *Public Law*: 228–62.

Wolfe, T. (1971) *Radical Chic and Mau-Mauing the Flakcatchers*. New York: Bantam.

Woolf, H. (1986) 'Public law–private law: why the divide? A personal view', *Public Law*: 220.

APPENDIX 4.1

	CONTRIBUTORY	MEANS-TESTED	TAXABLE	COUNTED FOR INCOME SUPPORT
Retirement Pension	YES	NO	YES	YES
Jobseeker's Allowance – contributory	YES	NO	YES	YES
Jobseeker's Allowance	NO	YES	N.A.	YES
Incapacity Benefit	YES	NO	YES (long term) / NO (short term)	YES
Statutory Sick Pay	NO	NO	YES	YES
Maternity Allowance	YES	NO	NO	YES
Statutory Maternity Pay	EMPLOYMENT CONDITION	NO	YES	YES
Non-contributory Retirement Pension	NO	NO	YES	YES
War Pension	SERVICE CONDITION	NO	NO (WIDOWS)	NO
Attendance Allowance	NO	NO	NO	NO
Invalid Care Allowance	NO	NO	YES	YES (IS PREMIUM)
Severe Disability Allowance	NO	NO	YES	YES (IS PREMIUM)
Disability Living Allowance	NO	NO	NO	NO
Disability Working Allowance	NO	YES	NO	N.A.
Income Support	NO	YES	N.A.	N.A.
Child Benefit	NO	NO	NO	YES (IS PREMIUM)
Family Credit	NO	YES	NO	N.A.
Housing Benefit	NO	YES	N.A.	N.A.
Community Charge Benefit	NO	YES	N.A.	N.A.
Widow's Payment	YES	NO	NO	YES
Widow's Pension	YES	NO	YES	YES

APPENDIX 4.2

Books

Benefits – CHAR's guide to means-tested benefits for single people without a home. London: CHAR.

Bonner, D., Hooker, I. and White, R., *Non-Means Tested Benefits: The Legislation*. London: Sweet & Maxwell.

Mesher, J. and Wood, P., *Income Related Benefits: The Legislation*. London: Sweet and Maxwell.

National Welfare Benefits Handbook (CPAG).

Ogus, A., Barendt, E. and Wikeley, N. *The Law Relating to Social Security* (4th edn). London: Butterworths (1995) [earlier editions: 1978, 1982 and 1988].

Rights Guide to Non-Means-Tested Benefits (CPAG).

Journals/magazines

Adviser
Journal of Social Welfare and Family Law
Journal of Social Security Law
Legal Action
Poverty
SCOLAG
Welfare Rights Bulletin

5

Judical Review and the Discretionary Social Fund: The Impact on a Respondent Organization

TREVOR BUCK

INTRODUCTION

Academic commentators have argued for more work to be done on the under-researched area of the impact of judicial review.

> In the first place some understanding of its impact is essential to inform the current theoretical debate concerning the constitutional role of judicial review. Secondly, judges do make and act upon intuitive assumptions concerning the impact of their intervention and it is of the utmost importance to provide the court with some independent alternative. (Richardson and Sunkin, 1996: 102)

The aim of this chapter is to provide an account and analysis of the impact of judicial review challenge on the Independent Review Service[1] (IRS) from 1988 until the present as a contribution towards the understanding of the impact of judicial review on respondent organizations. IRS is the public agency which has responsibility for the Social Fund Inspectors' (SFIs') reviews of discretionary social fund decisions. The legal framework was established by the Social Security Act 1986. The regulated social fund scheme (maternity and funeral expenses) was introduced in April 1987 and the discretionary scheme in April 1988.[2] The primary legislation was consolidated and can now be found in the relevant parts of the Social Security Contributions and Benefits Act 1992 (SSCBA 1992) and the Social Security Administration Act 1992 (SSAA 1992), as amended by the Social Security Act 1998 (SSA 1998).[3] The extent to which the social fund provides an efficient targeting of resources for persons on low income remains of course a contentious area and one which has proved difficult to identify. The traditional measures of 'take-up' have proved inadequate in relation to the social fund due to its discretionary nature and cash-limited budget (see Huby and Whyley, 1996). However, certain conclusions can also be made on the relevance of this case study to the wider concerns about the role of judicial review in social welfare matters and the issue of achieving consistency in approach to the exercise of discretionary powers.

This chapter focuses in particular on the effects of judicial review on the behaviour, development and culture of IRS. The more formal outcomes of judicial review challenge of the social fund and detailed accounts of case law development have been dealt with elsewhere (Buck, 1996: ch. 4).

The methodology employed in writing this chapter could be said to be both a product of documentary research and my own 'participant observation' (May, 1993: ch. 7) within IRS over the last five years.[4] I shall have to leave the reader to assess whether the known weaknesses or strengths of these methods predominate. I believe it has been a considerable advantage to observe the development of this organization over a long period of time compared with the 'snapshot' views available to most researchers.

THE STRUCTURE OF AN SFI REVIEW

It has been argued that the SFI review approaches the Donough-more Committee[5] definition of 'judicial' and the Franks Report[6] criteria of openness, fairness and impartiality (Hadfield, 1995: 268). Other commentators have been more cautious in their appraisal of this departure from the mainstream social security adjudication system (see Sainsbury, 1994). Whatever the classification, the social fund review process contains four[7] key points of decision-making activity. The first three are conducted within the local offices and the last, the SFI review, is conducted by an Inspector at the IRS located in their Birmingham headquarters. The SFI's review is essentially the final statutory remedy available to discretionary social fund applicants. It is predominantly a paper review. There is no oral hearing although there will usually have been an 'interview' with the applicant, conducted by the reviewing officer in the local office at the internal review stage. An SFI review, it should be noted, has a special poignancy in the context of judicial review. The relevant secondary legislation,[8] in the form of Secretary of State's Directions 1 and 2 to the SFIs,[9] contain a replication of the judicial review and merits tests respectively. The Inspector has three options; to confirm the internal review, to substitute his/her own decision or to refer the case back to the internal reviewer.[10] The complexity of the review structure is paralleled by the fact that there are three distinct types of payments – Community Care Grants (CCGs), Budgeting Loans (BLs) and Crisis Loans (CLs) – all with their own eligibility and qualification rules. However, an application for a social fund payment, typically for clothing and household equipment, may well be treated as an application to the fund as a whole[11] and therefore all three types of payment will fall to be considered by the social fund officer (SFO), social fund review officer (SFRO) and SFI up the review ladder.

The legal structure of decision-making involves applying a distinct order of consideration.[12] First, there are *jurisdictional* matters to consider; the 'time, form and manner' of the application is prescribed by regulations.[13] The root jurisdictional point lies in whether the item(s) or services requested by the applicant can reasonably constitute an 'other need' within the meaning of s. 138(1)(b) of the SSCBA 1992. Finally, Direction 7 prevents repeat applications for the 'same item or service'.[14]

Second, there are matters of *eligibility* to consider, for example, an applicant is eligible for a CCG and BL if he or she is 'in receipt' of a qualifying benefit.[15] For BLs there is an added requirement that the applicant must have been in receipt for a period of twenty-six weeks preceding the date of determination of the application.[16] Third, even if eligible, the applicant must also *qualify* for a payment via Directions 2 (BL), 3 (CL) or 4 (CCG). Direction 3, for example, allows a CL to be considered to assist an applicant to meet expenses 'In an emergency, or as a consequence of a disaster, provided that the provision of such assistance is the only means by which serious damage or serious risk to the health or safety of that person, or to a member of his family, may be prevented'.[17] Even if the applicant is both eligible and qualified, the items or services applied for may be *excluded items/services*, e.g. medical items (Direction 12(j)) and housing costs (Direction 12(h)), and in Northern Ireland only, certain security items (Direction 12(q)).

Once these hurdles have been passed, the SFOs must consider 'all the circumstances' of the particular case; the 'principles of determination'[18] structure this discretion by setting out a legal duty to have regard to several particular matters contained in s. 140(1)(a)–(e) of the SSCBA 1992. I have referred to this stage of the decision-making, for the sake of clarity, as *the 'priority' stage*. It is in essence the heart of the discretionary social fund scheme.[19] When all the relevant factors have been balanced at this stage – for example, the nature, extent and urgency of the need, the existence of resources of the applicant, the possibility of some other body wholly or partly meeting the need, the state of the local budget, the priorities contained in any local guidance – then it only remains to make an award and apply capital rules[20] to the amount of the award.

THE ORGANIZATIONAL FRAMEWORK

The organization, now called IRS, was established in 1988.[21] There were 40 SFIs, six managers and eighteen support staff in 1988–89. There are currently 78 SFIs, ten managers and 41 support staff.[22] The administrative head is the Social Fund Commissioner,[23] appointed by the Secretary of State for Social Security for a term of three years.

The core task of IRS is to process the requests for SFI reviews from applicants against the decisions of an internal review performed in the local social security offices by SFROs. The SFRO internal review is, in turn, an attempt to redress grievances from the initial SFO's decision.

The structure of the review process therefore can be contrasted with the more established procedure adopted in respect of most of the mainstream social security benefits, i.e. determination by an adjudication officer (AO) subject to appeal to the social security appeal tribunals (SSATs) and Social Security Commissioners.

In addition to the different grievance procedure (see Council on Tribunals, Special Report, 1986) there were four other principal elements to the discretionary social fund which marked radical departures from previous practice: the introduction of loans; a cash-limited fund (Mullen, 1989); a system for setting priorities in disbursing the funds; and the novel use of 'directions' and 'guidance'[24] in describing the detailed rules and operation of the scheme.

The publication of a DSS consultation paper (DSS, 1996) and the introduction of the SSA 1998 have focused attention again on the IRS 'model' for adjudication within the social security system. However, it is important to understand the changing environment of public debate on these matters. The IRS model of review is now ten years old and an increasing number of commentators are (perhaps reluctantly) conceding it has some merit (Dalley and Berthoud, 1992).

IRS has developed under the leadership of two influential Social Fund Commissioners, Mrs Rosalind Mackworth CBE (1988–95) and Mr John Scampion (1995–). The vision provided by the first Commissioner was to build an organization which could support SFIs in their quasi-judicial role. Much needed to be done, and was done, to persuade the public, the Benefits Agency (BA) and the DSS social fund policy branch that civil servants could perform this role as well (and more cheaply[25]) as the legally qualified chairmen of the Independent Tribunal Service (ITS). From May 1990 recruitment exercises for SFIs were advertised externally in the welfare rights press and a national newspaper in addition to the usual internal civil service channels. Now about 25 per cent of the total number of SFIs are recruited externally.[26] The general conception of the SFI's role was of a professional adjudicator located within an expert system. The statutory monitoring function of the Commissioner,[27] training and legal services were all directed to servicing the needs of the SFIs. The perception was of a group of highly trained, semi-autonomous, but atomized specialists; an administrative version of a barrister's chambers.

By contrast, the second Commissioner has been anxious to introduce a 'customer care' philosophy into IRS.[28] The *Social Fund Commissioner's Annual Report for 1995–96* reflects the desire to mould an organization around the customer's view which

> could well be summed up by saying they expect a quality decision, a full and fair consideration of their case and circumstances, a good sound answer that is right the first time and as early as possible in the social fund process.[29]

The Report includes a 'mission statement' and notes the necessity to critically examine 'the culture that underpins the delivery of our business'. The 'guiding principles' adopted are that IRS aims to be an expert body that is an open and listening organization and uses objective standards in the review and is an organization recognized as a quality organization 'with expertise that influences the administration of the social fund and so improves the service for customers'.[30]

This self-conscious attempt to change the ethos of IRS centres around the organizational aim to provide the customer with a 'quality' decision. This is given further definition by IRS – 'consistent, clear, expeditious, independent and cost effective'. Quality Assurance is now stated to be supported by four elements: Inspectors' team-working,[31] a Quality Team, Case Reading and Statistical Data.

However, in addition to the new customer focus of the organization other influences are apparent, in particular the desire to stabilize or even reduce the unit cost of an SFI review, reported as £149 for 1995/96.[32] The economics of decision-making are quite simple – productivity is increased by arranging work so that each SFI can clear a greater number of decisions in the same time. One way in which this has been achieved is to significantly reduce the average length of SFIs' decision letters. There was some concern that the organization was becoming 'over-legalized'. Indeed, some SFIs appeared to be producing increasingly lengthy decisions as a defensive reaction to the messages emanating from judicial review challenge.[33] More concise decision-making, however, was perceived to be both consistent with the organization's construction of customer needs and the need to increase SFIs' clearance rates.[34] Further, the argument over whether such a policy shift generated more or less judicial review challenge is quite even. On the one hand, shorter decisions may simply provide the petitioner with less potential ammunition. On the other hand, there is a difference between concision and bowdlerization. If SFI decisions skip vital elements of the decision-making process (e.g. qualification or 'priority') or fail to give sufficient reasons, they will become more vulnerable to judicial review challenge.[35] Essentially IRS have tried to steer a steady course between the two objectives of cost-effectiveness and quality reasoning. The overall aim has been to produce more user-friendly[36] decision letters which effectively address the key points with both clarity and concision.

THE INCIDENCE OF JUDICIAL REVIEW CHALLENGE

It has been said that the matters on which judical review cases have been heard have been of a routine nature. However,

> this albeit limited input into the system is nevertheless of importance – a system largely insulated from external perceptions of 'legality', 'fairness' and 'reasonableness', and 'good administration' needs at least an occasional transfusion of ideas or the application of a goad or a tap on the shoulder – whichever metaphor one prefers – in terms of both an impetus for growth and the joint formulation of standards of good administration on the one hand and of external validation and the enhancement of transparency of decision making on the other. (Hadfield, 1995: 267–8)

Table 5.1 represents the numbers of judicial review challenges in respect of SFI decisions since April 1988. It should be noted that the *total* figure for applications for leave (i.e. including unsuccessful applications) is not known. However, applying the Public Law Project's findings[37] on the yearly aggregate numbers of applications for leave allowed since 1989, it is estimated there ought to be in the region of at least another sixty applications for leave which have failed since 1989. The total balance of nineteen decisions upheld and seven decisions[38] which were found to be flawed is a final reminder of the way in which a successful judicial review is a rather remote possibility.

However, these figures alone cannot explain the shifts in IRS' perception of the role and function of judicial review. Looking at the flat landscape of such statistics it would not be surprising if such an organization felt under no immediate threat from such litigation. The best possible presentational spin would be that only seven out of

Table 5.1 Applications and disposal of judicial review challenges to SFI[39] decisions in England and Wales, Scotland and Northern Ireland 1988–97

	Appln for leave granted	Appln withdrawn/ lapsed	SFI decision upheld	SFI decision quashed	Adjourned
1989/90	4	1	1	2	0
1990/91	11 (1)	4	3 (1)	0	0
1991/92	5 (3)	1 (1)	4 (1)	0	0
1992/93	5	5	3	1	1
1993/94	6 (1)	3 (1) [1]	1 [1]	1 (1)	0
1994/95	13	7	0 [1]	1	0
1995/96	4	7	1	0	0
1996/97	2[40] (1)	0	1 (1)	0	0
1997/98	1	0	0	1	0
Totals	51 (6)	28 (2) [1]	14 (3) [2]	6 (1)	1
UK Total	**57**	**31**	**19**	**7**	**1**

( ) = Northern Ireland cases.
[ ] = Scottish cases.
Source: Derived from the Social Fund Commissioner's *Annual Reports* 1988–96.

about 145,000 SFIs' decisions issued since 1989 have been met with the formal disapproval of the court's supervisory jurisdiction. Of course, a low strike rate of judicial review cases tells us little about the quality of decision-making under challenge. Other factors have more significance in explaining low activity, not least the structural obstacles faced by social security customers in gaining access to the High Court's jurisdiction and the SFI's use of a 'judicial review proofing' power (see below). However, it is the case that professional policy-makers and politicians do regard the avoidance of judicial review as an impressive measure of the organization's ability to manage its caseload without incurring the essentially unpredictable results of such challenges.

In social welfare matters there is perhaps always the prospect of exposing the classic 'hard case' to media scrutiny. Customers of the discretionary social fund are inherently hardship cases to some extent. It is inevitable that the judicial view of which fact situations amount to real hardship will differ from the public agency view which will suffer, in varying degrees, from 'case hardening'.[41]

JUDICIAL REVIEW PROOFING

If the customary restrictions on access to the High Court were not enough, the discretionary social fund also provides an intriguing example of a judicial review-proofing power. There is a permissive power contained in s. 66(5) of the SSAA 1992[42] enabling the SFI to review his own or another SFI's decision. There is nothing in the law, directions or guidance issued by the Secretary of State to indicate in what circumstances this power ought to be employed. The provision was introduced in the latter stages of the passage of the Social Security Bill 1986 ostensibly to correct the 'minor defect' in the Bill that an SFI's decision was incapable of being changed. The amendment was made 'so that problems could be avoided'.[43]

IRS has frequently struggled to produce a sensible formulation of the circumstances in which the power might be appropriately used. In fact the power has been used as a potent instrument to resolve cases without the need to have them aired in the High Court. The published figures illustrate how the numbers of 's. 66(5)' decisions have increased over the years.[44] On occasion the IRS has agreed to undertake a s. 66(5) review several months after the initial SFI decision has been issued.

The existence of the 's. 66(5) review' is generally not well known and has only recently been publicized.[45] An aggrieved applicant is often encouraged to formally request a s. 66(5) review before becoming engaged on the expensive course of High Court litigation. Indeed, it may be the case that a petitioner taking judicial review proceedings without requesting a s. 66(5) review could be in danger of having their application dismissed on the ground that the normal statutory remedy has not been exhausted. An application for leave was set aside in the High Court of Justice in Belfast on this ground.[46] Initially, there was a reluctance to use the s. 66(5) review beyond correcting SFI decisions for clerical errors. However, the power is now used more robustly and has implications for litigation strategy (see below).[47] The use of this power may well be to the advantage of both petitioner and respondent in certain cases.

However, the power may be seen as unsatisfactory in several respects. There is no time limit within which to apply for a second review; it is unclear the extent to which circumstances arising *after* the SFI's initial decision can be taken into account.[48] Finally, the power provides the IRS with a powerful tool in their litigation strategy. There will no doubt be situations where there are temptations to avoid a High Court hearing because of some embarrassment factor in an SFI's decision is present; a 'hard case' element may present stronger attention to alternative methods of resolving the dispute.

On occasion the IRS has been willing to risk having decisions quashed because of a perception that it may be in the wider public interest to have a day in court.[49] But without formal mechanisms of accountability within such organizations it is likely that such a strategy may be too highly dependent on the views of the incumbent Social Fund Commissioner and his/her management team. A different view of priorities within the organization, prompted perhaps by adjustments in the organization's finances, the priorities set by the Commissioner or limitations on the virement of budgets, may well tend to submerge such a public interest stance and allow a narrow focus on costs or simply '*ad hocery*' to drive litigation strategy. A s. 66(5) review can save all the parties much time and expense; it can also be used to 'kill off' otherwise meritorious challenges which arguably ought to be aired in court.

DEVELOPING LITIGATION STRATEGY

The development of litigation strategy within IRS has broadly followed three chronologically overlapping phases. These can be characterized as: 'crisis management' (1989–91); 'consolidation' (1991–95); and 'customer focus' (1995–present).

Crisis Management

There is a sense in which a well-formulated judicial review challenge will *always* be perceived as a potential crisis for a respondent public service organization, especially where those challenges are numerically few. However, it is fair to say the initial challenges to the discretionary social fund were perceived to be linked to a more substantial political agenda which deplored the basic principles of the fund. The Child Poverty Action Group soon identified several themes critical of both the nature and detailed structure of the social fund (see Lister and Lakhani, 1987). It was therefore unsurprising that fundamental issues such as the *vires* of the Secretary of State's directions and guidance (in particular guidance relating to the social fund budget) and the nature of the SFI's review were the main points of legal debate.

In addition, the participants in the earlier litigation were acutely aware of the potential significance of the 'guideline' judgment delivered by Woolf L J.[50] The judgment caused, *inter alia*, the announcement of an increase of £12m in the gross budget for 1990/91.[51] The confluence therefore of a politicized context and the imminence of a guideline judgment prompted a litigation strategy which could be generally described as 'defensive'. Although there were efforts to facilitate the test cases brought by Child Poverty Action Group[52] there were inevitably other applications which were carefully managed in order that they might be resolved without the need for court appearance. The

122

Commissioner and her management team were faced with the unknown. The organization had not really begun to work out its relationship with the other key organizations it would have to liaise with: i.e. the BA, the social fund policy branch, the solicitors' branch of the DSS, and organizations representing the interests of claimants. It was perhaps inevitable with respect to the earlier litigation that the initiative passed to the DSS to guide these cases through the courts,[53] given the potential impact on policy and administration which they posed. During this period of 'crisis management' there was a steady stream of legal advice to the IRS from the DSS solicitors' branch in relation to interpretational and procedural points which arose while the scheme was 'settling in'.[54] The IRS view was that the quality of the advice received had varied and was sometimes perceived to be out of touch with the practical problems which the SFIs were confronted with in their review work.

Some dissatisfaction with the conduct of these cases and the advice emanating from the DSS helped IRS to identify the need for good, independent legal advice.[55] The experience of the Social Fund Commissioner and management team in relation to this litigation strengthened the view that the organization itself should attempt to achieve the maximum independence of operation at other levels too.

The upshot of this phase of crisis management for litigation strategy was the development of a regular procedure to handle judicial review challenges.[56] Essentially, this involved the legal adviser consulting with a few key officials (including, of course, the SFI responsible for the decision under challenge) on the merits of each application and reporting back to the Commissioner. According to the results of this consultation the legal adviser would seek counsel's opinion. On occasion an SFI would be advised to undertake a s. 66(5) review in the light of such consultation.[57]

Consolidation

Once the cases of *Stitt* and *Healey* and associated applications had been heard by the Divisional Court and the Court of Appeal (see Appendix 5.1), there followed a period of organizational consolidation. During this period there was less contact with the DSS solicitors' branch or social fund policy branch with regard to litigation strategy. To some extent this was due to a clearer understanding of the legal territory occupied by the Secretary of State, the SFO and the SFI respectively in the social fund scheme.[58] During this period of 'consolidation' there were judicial review challenges against the SFI alone, the Secretary of State and the SFO.[59] The cases received little national publicity. Nevertheless, the experience of disseminating and deciphering the lessons of *Stitt (No. 1)* and *Healey* had been formative. The pattern of unpacking the judgments and feeding back the appropriate messages to SFIs was formalized through the issue of training notes. These analysed the court's judgments in some detail and highlighted relevant learning points.

Training in the general principles of judicial review for new SFIs was regarded as a key part of their induction.[60] In short, judicial review was being regarded by the SFIs as the ultimate and authoritative source of quality control. A judgment when issued would be eagerly 'squeezed' to offer up any possible learning points (in addition to any obvious points of clear law). This period of organizational development was characterized by the emphasis on the positive aspects of judicial review. The Commissioner was committed to the view that a respondent organization should welcome the test of judicial review. Indeed 'withstanding judicial review' became the accepted test applied in carrying out the formal monitoring of SFI decisions. The 'dual culture' of civil servants and externally recruited SFIs assisted in developing a public service mentality on this issue rather than a more embattled position.

The policy of utilizing judicial review judgments as a deliberate training method relied crucially upon an appropriate mediation of this material to the SFIs. It was soon realized that the manner in which the judicial review cases was communicated to staff had implications beyond merely the knowledge gained of the constructional points. The process therefore of this mediation of the legal messages came to be viewed as not merely a legal service because wider management issues were raised. Many of the learning points identified would have a direct impact on the delivery of SFIs' decisions. This inevitably had resource implications within the organization. For example, *Connell* implied a more comprehensive approach in decision letter-writing to ensure the 'transparency' of decision-making indicated in that case. On the other hand, how far could this decision be dismissed as exceptional? In fact the case did lead to management expectations that SFIs would be more explicit in their decision letters in relation to the consideration of local guidance priority client groups (see Appendix 5.1). *Connell* also prompted a management decision to devise a procedure whereby the legal adviser would be alerted to all cases where judicial review had been mentioned in correspondence at a much earlier stage than had been the previous practice.[61] SFIs had more autonomy over which problems in their review work were taken for legal advice and at what stage. Finally, the nature and potential role of the SFI's s. 66(5) review power were critically examined within the organization and new, internal guidelines were issued.

In May 1993 it was decided that any further legal advice on general points to SFIs would be made available to the public and a series of Advice Notes, prepared by the legal adviser in consultation with IRS staff, were issued.[62] Some of the Advice Notes contain a direct response to judicial review judgments, often attempting to work through some of the loose ends or gaps in the judgments.[63] However, the dividing line between ensuring that the organization had workable definitions available to it which could be acceptably applied in a consistent manner and, in effect, making policy was a narrow one. It ought to be questioned whether it is appropriate for any social welfare agency to be placed in the position of having to generate its own interpretation on important issues in order to 'make discretion work'.

Customer Focus

The focus on a customer-orientated approach in the organization has to some extent detracted from judicial review as a key influence in the development of the organization. The priorities of IRS have inevitably changed owing to the arrival of the second Commissioner with a different but distinct leadership style and the absence of any full judicial review hearing throughout 1996.

The lull in litigation has been caused by a combination of the increasing difficulty petitioners faced in obtaining legal aid and the increasing success of preventative work undertaken within IRS in identifying and settling difficult cases. This long pause in litigation activity had several effects on IRS. First, it released management and other staff time for a more thorough, reflexive investigation into 'quality issues' and the detailed practicalities of achieving consistency[64] of decision-making in SFIs' determinations within a customer- rather than court-orientated framework. Second, it enabled a fuller digestion of the lessons of judicial review to be achieved. In particular, an increasingly sophisticated appreciation of the *limitations* of judicial review developed. Third, it appeared to confirm the new policy to produce more concise decisions written in 'plain English' which would address the points actually at issue rather than indulge in too much legalism.[65] It can be noted that this policy relied on a calculation that a diminution of reasoning given in SFI decision letters will not necessarily prompt any significant increase in litigation. Indeed, the aim was to increase quality by enhancing clarity and concision. Finally, the pause in litigation allowed the organization to be less dominated by what was at times perceived as the rather arbitrary intervention of a judicial review judgment into regular work procedures. IRS, under the leadership of a new

Commissioner, was in a good position to reach maturity by defining its own quality standards and taking the lead on a number of management issues without the disruptive effects of judicial review challenge.

The almost capricious and arbitrary nature of judicial review was reflected in *Connell* where the judge alighted upon a feature of the case which had not been explicitly identified at all by the petitioner or respondent in the grounds for application. It is fair to say that the perception, rightly or wrongly, within IRS was that the judge had seized upon a convenient peg to quash the decision while at the same time indicating that there would be no substantive change caused by a re-run of the case. It may be that in such cases the judicial view is that this demonstrates an even-handedness: a brokerage of the competing interests of the parties. However, it would appear both the petitioner and respondent viewed the result as disappointing.

The 'fallow' period of a little over a year without judicial review challenge has been followed by renewed activity at the time of writing. One case involved the interpretation of 'other needs', the fundamental jurisdictional gateway to the discretionary social fund contained in s. 138(1)(b) of the SSCBA 1992. There were two possible interpretations available. (See *Harper* in Appendix 5.1.) The judge concluded however that there was not even any *ambiguity* in the construction of this phrase in the legislation, despite hearing complex conflicting arguments from three silks and despite the continuing problems (see Buck, 1997b) that had been experienced by those with responsibility for administering the social fund for many years.[66] In fact the judge's conclusion in *Harper* was similar to advice given to IRS in an opinion of counsel several years earlier. What has developed in the intervening period is a narrow interpretation of 'maternity'[67] and 'funeral' expenses[68] within IRS in order that the perceived ambiguity of interpretation is settled in favour of the applicant. Items which fall outside of this narrow definition can therefore be considered for payment under the discretionary scheme. The IRS' general perception of this case was that the constructional issue was one upon which the courts should provide a final authoritative ruling.[69] There was, however, some disappointment that the judicial consideration of the implications of this ruling had not been more thorough.

THE IMPACT OF JUDICIAL REVIEW ON IRS

The judicial review challenges to SFI decisions are briefly summarized in Appendix 5.1; a more detailed account of the case law can be found elsewhere.[70] The overall picture is not particularly coherent. The cases, since *Healey*, have tended to alight on narrow constructional points of varying significance for the administration of the social fund. Two of the cases raised issues which might well have produced a more complete analysis if they had been allowed to proceed to the Court of Appeal.[71] The overall impression which has been communicated to specialist, social welfare organizations such as IRS is that even when the court is presented with a fundamental problem to determine it appears to resile from fully working through the administrative implications. The respondent organization has to be carefully educated to understand from the outset the limitations of judicial review.[72] In any discretionary scheme there will always be a tendency for the decision-maker to want to offload the responsibility on to some other body or person. The courts cannot be blamed for failing to fill a vacuum created by organizational inertia. As can be seen in many other areas of social welfare law, the courts will frequently wish to point out where responsibility for the exercise of discretionary powers ultimately lies – with the body in which Parliament has vested those powers. This is especially the case with social security matters which must always necessarily confront an enormous range of practical difficulties generated by the very large numbers of applicants and a wide range of circumstances presented to the decision-maker.

However, the judicial review judgments have provided useful training material for the IRS. A close analysis of each case carefully presented to the SFIs can yield a rich source material, not only in relation to the strictly legal points, but also in respect of procedural, stylistic and other quality standards. However, the collective experience of the organization soon appreciated the 'hit-and-miss' nature of judicial review after the excitement of the early cases subsided. The growing awareness of the capricious nature of judicial review has tended to weaken its direct influence on the organization's behaviour. At the same time this knowledge has strengthened the view that such activity ought to be carefully managed and controlled largely by employing more freely the s. 66(5) power to undertake a further SFI review. There is a sense in which the SFI's perspective is that of an arbitrary 'judge over your shoulder'[73] who can appear at any time, without warning and with equal probability in respect of any decision, irrespective of whether it would be regarded internally as a good-quality or a poor-quality one.

If that probability is perceived as low the temptation may be to ignore the possibility of it ever occurring. On the other hand, the uncertain incidence of judicial review may also enforce a disciplined approach and extra willingness to listen to advice and improve quality. These two possibilities appear logically as mutually exclusive ones, but in practice they exist side by side within the fabric of a public agency.

The content and style of SFI decision letters has been greatly influenced by the judicial review cases. The judicial norms reflected in the substantive grounds for judicial review, together with a political resolution to achieve an independent organization in this field, have resulted in a deliberate attempt to incorporate standards of quality decision-making within the structure of an SFI decision.

A recurring issue has been the lengths to which the decision-maker ought to give reasons[74] for the decision (Buck, 1995). Arguably, all the main elements to an SFI's decision should be properly addressed.[75] This would mean that the rationales for the decisions on jurisdictional issues, eligibility, qualification, priority and the amount of the award (if any) should be clear in each SFI decision letter. However, as we have seen, each application to the social fund was, prior to SSA 1998, an application to the fund as a whole,[76] therefore this process would have to be triplicated in the same decision letter. Such a policy would also result in very lengthy decision letters.

The central tendency in the development of administrative law is to raise the requirement of decision-makers to produce fuller reasons for their decisions.[77] However, the case law provides very little help in relation to complex decision-making structures as to which particular elements of that legal structure require full explanation, which partial explanation and which no explanation at all. A customer focus, as developed by IRS, implies fuller treatment of those points of contention as defined by the applicant and the BA internal reviewers. However, these are not invariably the points seized upon in the High Court.

The new methods developed by IRS to achieve quality assurance are, in concept, an outgrowth of the standards of administrative justice advanced by the remedy of judicial review. They reflect the organization's desire to achieve a consistency of approach to decision-making, a value which is highly prized in the administration of social security benefits.[78] As part of the new customer care culture adopted by IRS, the approach to 'monitoring' SFI decisions was radically changed in 1995–96. As we have seen, the basic test applied by the Commissioner and managers was to assess whether an SFI decision would stand up to judicial review.[79] The new approach, however, proceeds from IRS' own definition of quality. It is also designed to be less intimidating to SFIs. The old categorization into 'acceptable' and 'unacceptable' decisions was perceived by SFIs as being somewhat arbitrary. Given that it is difficult to determine any real uniformity in the way in which the courts themselves apply administrative law principles, it is unsurprising that the second-guessing by the Commissioner and managers of how decisions might hypothetically stand up to court scrutiny would produce uneven results. Now 'monitoring' has been replaced by 'case reading'.[80] Sample cases are read by the Commissioner and senior managers. Standard forms with commentary boxes relating to the elements of the definition of quality e.g. clarity, consistency are filled in by the case readers after discussion with the SFIs. Issues arising from case reading are fed back for further discussion to the Quality Forum meeting.[81]

EVALUATION OF JUDICIAL REVIEW REMEDY

There seems to be little doubt about the enduring political utility of judicial review as a remedy, in particular as it applies to social welfare agencies such as IRS.[82] The earlier judicial review cases provided a forum by which opposing political views concerning the nature and form of last resort support could be channelled. The legal challenges enabled certain features of the scheme to be adjusted but it also spelled in political terms the realization that the new scheme was in place and would be continued. However, the social fund remains a source of political concern because of the inherently difficult tasks it seeks to undertake. The responsible Minister is naturally in fairly regular contact with the senior staff of the social fund policy branch and the Social Fund Commissioner. It would be surprising if the overriding concern of the politicians when there is a threatened judicial review was anything other than the potential political embarrassment.

Although a political weather eye is kept on judicial review challenges in this field, IRS experience demonstrates that where political controversy has diminished there is greater capacity for social welfare agencies to adopt a public interest stance and embrace 'facilitative' strategies to judicial review within their organizations.

It has been stated that,

Although the ability of juridical norms to infiltrate administrative cultures is likely to be limited, it may be that certain values, those associated with process for example, are more readily internalised than others. (Richardson and Sunkin, 1996: 103)

The development of IRS certainly resonates with that proposition. Indeed, I believe the level of internalization of judicial norms in IRS has been comparatively high. The experience of IRS also demonstrates, in my view, the great limitations of judicial review in providing all that will be needed to achieve the consistency in approach required to ensure full public acceptance of the exercise of a complex structured discretionary power. That conclusion surely indicates the need for lawyers and judges to work towards a greater coherence and consistency of application of the general principles of judicial review themselves if the beneficial effect of the supervisory jurisdiction applied to social welfare agencies is to be maximized.

NOTES

1   Originally known as the Office of the Social Fund Inspectors, the name was changed in October 1992 shortly after the Office of the President of Social Security Appeal Tribunals changed its designation to the Independent Tribunal Service.

2   Cold weather payments were added on to the regulated scheme in November 1988; see the Social Fund Cold Weather Payments (General) Regulations 1988 (SI 1988, No. 1724).

3   SSCBA 1992, ss. 138–40 and SSAA 1992, ss. 64–66, 78, 167–69; as amended by the Social Security Bill 1998, clauses 36–38, 68, 69 and 73. The reader should note that at the time of writing, the Social Security Act was completing its parliamentary passage.

4   Consultant Legal Adviser to IRS, 1992–97.

5   *The Report of the Committee on Ministers' Powers*, Cmd 4060 (1932), s. III, para. 10.

6   Franks Committee, Administrative Tribunals and Inquiries, Cmnd 218 (1957).

7   Until September 1995 there was an *additional* tier of social fund review conducted within the local offices. See Buck, 1996: 536–8 for flow chart relating to the system in force September 1994 to September 1995.

8   The Secretary of State's Directions are currently published in the *Social Fund Guide* along with national guidance. There are forty Directions and two separate Directions addressed specifically to the SFIs.

9   *SFI Direction 1*:
'In reviewing a determination a social fund inspector must have full regard initially to:
(a) whether the SFO applied the law correctly in arriving at his decision on review. In particular:
    that the decision is sustainable on the evidence;
    that the SFO took all relevant considerations into account and did not take irrelevant considerations into account;
    that the SFO interpreted the law including Secretary of State directions correctly;
(b) whether the SFO acted fairly and exercised his discretion to arrive at a conclusion that was reasonable in the circumstances – *i.e.* a decision that a reasonable SFO could have reached;
(c) whether the required procedural steps have been followed; that the applicant had sufficient opportunity to put his case; and there has been no bias.'

SFI Direction 2:
'If in reviewing a determination initially, a social fund inspector is satisfied that

the decision was reached correctly, having regard to the factors in direction 1, the social fund inspector in reviewing the determination thereafter must have full regard to

(a) all the circumstances, including the state of the budget and local priorities that existed at the time the original decision was made;

(b) any new evidence which has since been produced; and

(c) any relevant change of circumstances.'

10 S. 66(4) SSAA 1992. See now clause 38(4), Social Security Bill 1998.

11 See *Social Fund Guide*, paras 3000, 4000 and 5000. However, the principle that an application is treated as one for all three types of payment has been changed by the recent legislation.

12 See *Social Fund Guide*, para. 3002 and Buck, 1996: Appendix 5.

13 The Social Fund (Applications) Regulations 1988 (SI 1988, No. 524) and Social Fund (Application for Review) Regulations 1988 (SI 1988, No. 34).

14 This Direction has caused enormous practical difficulties of interpretation yet has received no attention whatsoever in the judicial review cases. See *Advice Note No. 17* and the annotation to Direction 7 published in Buck, 1996: 525–32 and 332–6 respectively. It is believed the purpose of this provision was originally to prevent welfare rights campaigners flooding the social fund with repeat applications.

15 I.e. Income Support or income-based Job Seeker's Allowance.

16 See Direction 8 (eligibility for BLs) and 25 (eligibility for CCGs).

17 Most of the wording has been carried over from a discretionary default power contained in the 'single payments' scheme which preceded the discretionary social fund; see Regulation 30 of the Supplementary Benefit (Single Payments) Regulations 1981 (SI 1981, No. 1528). The wording of the 'medical ... items and services' exclusion was the subject of judicial challenge. The court considered the application of Social Security Commissioners' Decisions in respect of the single payments version of this exclusion. See *Connick* in Appendix 5.1.

18 This is the wording of the marginal note to s. 140, SSCBA 1992.

19 In practice eligibility and qualification conditions will filter out many applicants and in 1996/97 as much as 82.6 per cent of CCG applications were refused on the ground they did not meet Direction 4 (i.e. the qualification condition) (*Annual Report by the Secretary of State for Social Security on the Social Fund, 1996/97*: Annex 5).

20 Directions 9 and 27 in relation to BLs and CCGs respectively. There is no equivalent Direction in respect of CLs.

21 The first Social Fund Commissioner was appointed from 1 December 1987 four months in advance of the legislation coming into effect.

22 IRS, *Organisation Chart* (1 March 1997). The peak year for numbers of staff at IRS was 1992–93, a total of 168 in all: 7 managers, 103 full-time and 14 part-time SFIs and 44 support staff. See Buck, 1996: Table 5, p. 109.

23 The Social Fund Commissioner's powers are found in s. 65 of the SSAA 1992 (see now clause 37, Social Security Bill 1998). Essentially the legal duties of the Social Fund Commissioner are constrained to appointing staff, monitoring the quality of decisions, providing advice and assistance and training to the SFIs.

The Social Fund Commissioner, unlike the Social Security Commissioners, has no judicial authority under the legislation. For the provenance of this office, see Buck, 1996: 111–14.

24 Directions are binding in law but unlike Statutory Instruments are not laid before Parliament, they are simply issued by the Secretary of State. The legislation provides a legal duty for SFOs to take account of general guidance (contained in the *Social Fund Guide*) and any local guidance issued by the Area SFO; see SSCBA 1992, s. 140(2) and (5). For the relationship between local and national guidance, see *Advice Note No. 16* in Buck, 1996: 516–25.

25 See Note 32 below for calculation of the cost of an SFI review.

26 However, these SFIs will mostly be on fixed-term contracts of one or two years' duration.

27 See note 23 above.

28 It must be said that the first Commissioner's regime also involved attention to, for example, Citizen's Charter principles and a 'user survey' was conducted in 1994–95; see *The Social Fund Commissioner's Annual Report for 1991–92*, para. 1.11 and *1994–95*, para. 7.11 respectively.

29 *Annual Report of the Social Fund Commissioner for 1995–96 on the Standards of Reviews by Social Fund Inspectors*, p. 2.

30 However, it is observed that the Social Fund Commissioners Annual Reports for 1995–96 and 1996–97 lack the statistical detail of previous Reports; no doubt a product of the new ethos but a disappointment to the researcher!

31 See generally, 'Delivering quality through teams', *The Social Fund Commissioner's Business Plan 1997/98*.

32 Calculated by dividing total expenditure of IRS (£4.194m) by the numbers of cases cleared (28,064). It is intended to produce an SFI's case review 'at a unit cost of £130 for 1997/98'; see 'Delivering quality through teams', *The Social Fund Commissioner's Business Plan 1997/98*, p. 3.

33 In particular, *Connell*: see Appendix 5.1.

34 In 1996–97 29,436 cases were cleared in the office by SFIs and of these 94 per cent were cleared within fifteen working days: *IRS State of Work* (31 March 1997). The speed of the SFI review must always remain one of its principal advantages, especially when compared with appeal tribunal adjudication (see Sainsbury, 1994: 293).

35 See, for example, *Taylor*.

36 For many years the IRS has employed the services of the Plain English campaign in their training. It should be noted however, that SFIs are also encouraged to use the wording of the legislation, Directions and Guidance where this is appropriate. The identification of the elements in any one decision where it is best to quote the legislative wording is sometimes not an easy one.

37 See Sunkin, Bridges and Meszaros, 1993; Bridges, Meszaros and Sunkin, 1995.

38 *Roberts, Sherwin, Ali, Ward* (NI), *Connick, Connell* and *Taylor* (see Appendix 5.1 below).

39 The power to recover social fund loans is exercised by the Secretary of State, not the SFI. There was a judicial review challenge of this power in Scotland; see *In Petition of Mulvey*, Outer House, Court of Session, 1995 SLT 1064; overturned on appeal to the Inner House, Court of Session, 1996 SLT 229; Inner House

decision confirmed by the House of Lords. *Mulvey* v *Secretary of State for Social Security* 1997 SLT 753. Similarly the SFO's power to initiate a review under s. 66(1)(b) of the SSAA 1992 was the subject of judicial review challenge in *R* v *Social Fund Officer, ex parte Hewson* (22 June 1995).

40 At the time of writing, an application for leave has been granted in *Carruthers* (see Appendix 5.1) but the case has not yet reached full hearing.

41 The McKim case (*In Petition of Gray*) was regarded internally as a hard case. An opposite organizational response was present in *Ali* where the judge clearly was of the view that the applicant's circumstances made him a 'wholly exceptional case', a view not shared within IRS.

42 '(5) A social fund inspector may review a determination ... made by himself or some other social fund inspector.' The same wording is promised in clause 38(5) of the Social Security Bill 1998.

43 Baroness Trumpington, *Hansard*, HL Vol. 479, col. 431 (24 July 1986).

44 Only 0.6 per cent of all SFI reviews were subject to a second s. 66(5) review in 1989/90, whereas in 1995/96 this percentage had risen to 3.9 per cent (1085 out of 28,064 cases cleared in that year) (Buck, 1996: 71 and *The Social Fund Commissioner's Annual Report 1995–96*, p. 24).

45 Since November 1996. See leaflet IRS 3.

46 *Re Foley*: see Appendix 5.1.

47 The greater numbers of s. 66(5) decisions also adds further complications to the way in which the statistics are collected and recorded.

48 Generally, internal advice has stressed the approach of looking at the circumstances existing at the time of the initial SFI decision. However, there are technical difficulties. For example, the District may be paying high- and medium-priority applications by the time the s. 66(5) is issued, although the budget guidance issued at the time of the initial SFI decision states only high-priority applications will be paid. Which guidance document should have more weight?

49 E.g. *In Petition of Gray, Harper* and *Carruthers* (Appendix 5.1).

50 *Stitt (No. 1), Sherwin* and *Roberts* (Appendix 5.1).

51 A detailed account on the impact of Woolf LJ's judgment is provided in Buck, 1996: 157–62.

52 *Stitt (No. 1)*'s application proceeded to the High Court even though there had been no SFI decision made in his case.

53 Although it must be said that IRS secured separate representation for the SFI in *Roberts*.

54 It has been surprising how, ten years on, many of these points still remain unresolved; for example, the contentious interpretation of the 'date of determination' and the precise meaning of 'in receipt' contained in Direction 8.

55 Stuart Pinder was the IRS consultant legal adviser from February 1990 to August 1992 and he undertook much of the earlier consolidation of advice and training work. His contribution had an important impact on the development of IRS and confirmed the organization's desire to have their own independent adviser.

56 A flow chart was circulated within IRS to consolidate the procedures.

57 Generally, SFIs would be willing to listen carefully to advice from the in-house lawyer and counsel. In theory, if an SFI refused to take advice which might

have avoided a court hearing IRS might be left with no choice but to refuse financial assistance on costs.

58 In *Stitt (No. 1)*, Secretary of State for Social Services was cited as the respondent whereas in *Healey* the Secretary of State *and* the SFI were respondents. Lawyers advising petitioners also developed a clearer understanding of whether it was more appropriate to serve papers on the SFI, the SFO and/or the Secretary of State.

59 *Connick, Mulvey* and *Hewson* respectively: see Appendix 5.1.

60 Training in the principles of dealing with evidence was also given. This has been extended in recent years and a Practice Note on Evidence has been issued to SFIs and circulated more widely within the DSS and elsewhere.

61 My estimation is that this yielded about seventy case referrals in 1995 and 1996 respectively.

62 See *Advice Notes Nos 1–17* in Buck, 1996: Appendix 3. *Advice Note No. 18* (Excluded Housing Costs) was also issued in November 1995. This series of Advice Notes was discontinued as a result of the establishment of the 'Quality Team' and other organizational changes within IRS. The *IRS Journal and Digest* now covers many of the ongoing developments within the organization and has a wide circulation within the DSS and welfare rights groups.

63 *Advice Note No. 7* deals with the interpretation of the medical items and services exclusion. The Note and the judgment both affected the national guidance issued; see *Social Fund Guide*, paras 4230–4235. Advice Note No. 9 deals with some of the unresolved points observed in *Mohammed*.

64 E.g. the SFIs' approach to the interpretation of 'family' and the implementation of Direction 4(a)(iii) has achieved an impressive level of consistency; see Buck, 1997a.

65 This was reflected in a series of Delivery of Decisions training sessions which emphasized the importance of delivering clear, concise and user-friendly decision letters.

66 The Secretary of State issued new Directions with effect from 5 June 1995 which expressly excluded funeral expenses from payment other than funeral directors' fees in excess of the prescribed limit under the regulated scheme or any other reasonable funeral expenses not prescribed under the regulated scheme. The exceptions to this exclusion, by implication, indicated that funeral (and therefore possibly also maternity) expenses which were not prescribed ones under s. 138(1)(a) SSCBA 1992 could be considered for payment under the discretionary scheme. The DSS received counsel's opinion on the point and in the light of that advice decided to withdraw the new Directions on 1 August 1995.

67 Items are only regarded as maternity expenses if they will meet the immediate needs of a new-born child. Maternity clothing for the mother would not be regarded as within the definition of maternity expenses and therefore *would* fall to be considered for a discretionary social fund payment. See also *Social Fund Guide*, paras 4205–4210.

68 See *Social Fund Guide*, paras 4211–4213.

69 Indeed there was some surprise within IRS when the Child Poverty Action Group were initially refused legal aid to run this case. There was much

commonality of interest between IRS and the Child Poverty Action Group in seeing this case in court.

70　See generally Buck, 1996: ch. 4, and references therein.

71　*Harper* and *Ledicott*. In each case it is fair to say that both petitioner and respondent would have been content to see it proceed to the Court of Appeal.

72　The organization benefited greatly from training sessions in the early years provided by Maurice Sunkin, now Professor of Law, Essex University, and Stuart Pinder, now full-time Tribunal Chairman with the ITS.

73　See Treasury Solicitors' Department and Cabinet Office, 1994.

74　In *Re Jenett* (NI) the SFI's decision narrowly escaped being quashed on the ground that insufficient reasons for the decision had been offered.

75　This was certainly the view which emerged in argument before Brooke J in *Connell*.

76　See note 10 above.

77　See N. R. Campbell, [1994] *Public Law*: 184; R. Gordon and C. Barlow, (1993) NLJ: 1005; P. Craig, [1994] LQR: 12; A. Bradley, 138 Sol. Jo.: 88 (1994).

78　The problem of consistency frequently appears as a problem of 'territorial justice' in social security. The Social Policy Research Unit at the University of York, for example, has undertaken valuable work on the geographical inequities caused in the administration of the single payments scheme (Huby and Walker, 1991).

79　See Buck, 1996: 118–20 for a detailed account of the practice of monitoring from 1988 to 1995.

80　The statutory provisions of course still retain the word 'monitor'; see s. 65(5)(a) SSAA 1992 (clause 37(5) Social Security Bill 1998).

81　A monthly meeting consisting of the Social Fund Commissioner, and the senior managers, the Quality Team and legal advisers.

82　Indeed, the expertise of IRS in handling judicial review challenge is thought to be one of the reasons why the government reversed its original plans to withdraw the social fund inspector's review powers from the 'modernized' budgeting loan scheme introduced by the SSA 1998.

REFERENCES

Annual Report by the Secretary of State for Social Security on the Social Fund 1995/96 (1996). London: HMSO.

Annual Report of the Social Fund Commissioner for 1995–96 on the Standards of Reviews by Social Fund Inspectors (1996). London: HMSO.

Bridges, L., Meszaros, G. and Sunkin, M. (1995) *Judicial Review in Perspective* (2nd edn). London: Cavendish.

Buck, T. G. (1993) 'The Social Fund and judicial review', *Journal of Social Welfare and Family Law*: 159–73.

Buck, T. G. (1995) 'The duty to give reasons', *Independent Review Service Journal*: 10–11, 19.

Buck, T. G. (1996) *The Social Fund: Law and Practice*. London: Sweet & Maxwell.

Buck, T. G. (1997a) 'Defining the "family" and families under exceptional pressures' (unpublished paper).

Buck, T. G. (1997b) 'R v *Social Fund Inspector, ex parte Harper* (Casenote)', *Journal of Social Security Law*: 134–8.

Council on Tribunals, Special Report (1986) *Social Security – Abolition of Independent Appeals Under the Proposed Social Fund*. Cmnd 9722.

Dalley, G. and Berthoud, R. (1992) *Challenging Discretion: The Social Fund Review Procedure*. London: Policy Studies Institute.

DSS (1996) *Improving Decision-Making and Appeals in Social Security*. Cm 3326.

Hadfield, B. (ed.) (1995) *Judicial Review: A Thematic Approach*. Dublin: Gill & Macmillan.

Huby, M. and Walker, R. (1991) 'The social fund and territorial justice', 19 *Policy and Politics*: 87–98.

Huby, M. and Whyley, C. (1996) 'Take-up and the Social Fund: applying the concept of take-up to a discretionary benefit', 25 *Journal of Social Policy*: 1–18.

Lister, R. and Lakhani, B. (1987) *A Great Retreat in Fairness: A Critique of the Draft Social Fund Manual*. London: Child Poverty Action Group.

May, T. (1993) *Social Research: Issues, Methods and Process*. Buckingham: Open University Press.

Mullen, T. (1989) 'The Social Fund – cash-limiting and social security', *Modern Law Review*: 64–92.

Richardson, G. and Sunkin, M. (1996) 'Judicial review: questions of impact', *Public Law*: 79–103.

Sainsbury, R. (1994) 'Internal reviews and the weakening of social security claimants' rights of appeals' in Richardson, R. and Genn, H. (eds) *Administrative Law and Government Action*. Oxford: Clarendon Press.

Sunkin, M., Bridges, L. and Meszaros, G. (1993) *Judicial Review in Perspective*. London: Public Law Project.

Treasury Solicitors' Department and Cabinet Office (1994) *Judge Over Your Shoulder* (2nd edn). London: HMSO.

APPENDIX 5.1: SUMMARY OF MAIN POINTS – JUDICIAL REVIEW CHALLENGES OF SFI DECISIONS IN THE UNITED KINGDOM 1990–97

1990

R v Secretary of State for Social Services and Social Fund Inspector, ex parte Stitt (No. 1), Sherwin* and Roberts*, (1990) *The Times*, 23 February, DC

- Secretary of State did have power to frame directions in wide terms, including power to exclude whole categories of need for the proper control and management of the social fund.
- The mandatory tone of budget allocation guidance was held unlawful.

*Cases where the SFI's decision was quashed.

- A technical interpretation of Direction 4(a)(i) to be avoided; this conflicted with the obvious policy intention of 4(a)(i) and (ii) when read together. Directions should be construed in a common sense manner to give effect to their obvious intent.

R v Secretary of State for Social Services and the Social Fund Inspector, ex parte Stitt (No. 1), (1990) *The Times*, 5 July, CA

- Divisional Court judgment was upheld but different views as to the precise source of the Secretary of State's power to make directions.

1991

R v Social Fund Inspector and Secretary of State for Social Security, ex parte Healey, Smith and Stitt (No. 2), (1991) *The Times*, 22 April, DC

- Direction 4(a)(i) required that '. . . a claimant should be, actually or imminently, in the community following a stay in care'. Residence in a 'half-way house' was not sufficient.
- A single claimant could not qualify for a CCG via Direction 4(a)(iii), the meaning of '. . . *and* his family' in the Direction was conjunctive.
- The exclusion of 'housing costs' did not only extend to permanent structures but also to mobile ones; a caravan therefore was an excluded housing cost.

Re Jenett, QBD (Crown side) Northern Ireland, 10 May 1991 (unreported)

- The judge conceded that the SFI's decision failed to give full reasons, however, it would be upheld as it was neither wrong nor unreasonable.
- The challenge to the national guidance concerning priority groups failed.

R v Social Fund Inspector and Secretary of State for Social Security, ex parte Healey, Stitt (No. 2) and Ellison, (1991) *The Times*, 31 December, CA

- Divisional court upheld. Noted *obiter* that those representing Mr Healey might want to make representations to the Secretary of State but court's hands were tied.
- The words 'in the community' must bear the same meanings in both Directions 4(a)(i) and (ii).

- On a true reading of SFI Directions 1 and 2, the SFI's review function was not solely supervisory.

1992

Re Friel, QBD (Crown side) Northern Ireland, 3 April 1992 (unreported)

- National and local guidance concerning priority in domestic violence cases considered. Local guidance said to be '... given purely to inform the officer of the sort of general situation that he looks at'.

R v Social Fund Inspector, ex parte Ali, ★ *Broadhurst, Rampling, Mohammed and Semplis*, (1992) *The Times*, 25 November, QBD

- An SFI's decision in *Ali*'s application that an award of a payment for a fridge would not ease exceptional pressures on the applicant and his family was quashed as *Wednesbury* unreasonable.
- The judge observed that the SFI's post-decision letter in *Broadhurst*'s application issued after her decision was in retrospect 'more kindly than wise' but he was not prepared to overturn the decision.
- *Rampling*'s application was adjourned as in the course of proceedings a potential breach of natural justice arose which had not been raised in the grounds of application.
- *Mohammed*'s application that an Ethiopian refugee should have qualified under Direction 4 for a CCG was dismissed; it could not be properly said that when a refugee came to the UK for the first time that she would be 're-establishing' herself in the community within the natural meaning of Direction 4(a)(i).
- The relationship between old and new guidance was considered in *Semplis*' application. Judge held that the new emphasis in the guidance was within the intended framework of Direction 4.

1993

Re Ward, ★ QBD (Crown side) Northern Ireland, March 1992, judgment delivered 4 June 1993 (unreported)

- No error in law in finding that clothing was low priority on the facts in this case.
- SFI ought to have inquired further into the evidence available to show why applicant required a generator, cooker and gas tank.

- The cost of an empty cylinder (£4.00) was not an excluded cost under Direction 29(c).

R v Social Fund Inspector, ex parte Connick,★ QBD, 8 June 1993 (unreported)

- SFI had applied the wrong test in concluding that an application for incontinence pads was caught by the 'medical ... item or service' exclusion in Direction 12(j).

R v Social Fund Inspector, ex parte Ibrahim, QBD, 9 November 1993 (unreported)

- The interpretation of 'institutional or residential care' in Direction 4(a) was considered. Relying on the wording of national guidance, a 'rationale test' was adopted.

1994

Petition of James William Gray (curator ad litem to Alexander McKim), Outer House, Court of Session, 23 February 1994.

- It was not an error of law for the SFI to have made a broad assessment of the applicant's outgoings and resources, including Attendance Allowance.

Petition of Donald Murray, Outer House, Court of Session, 27 April 1994 (unreported)

- A challenge to the SFI's decision on priority failed. The judge found no basis for the suggestion the SFI was not entitled to regard the matter *de novo* on review.

R v Independent Review Service, ex parte Connell,★ QBD, 3 November 1994 (unreported)

- SFIs were not at liberty to ignore the guidance given by the Secretary of State in relation to priority groups, '... the way [the SFI] takes account of [national] guidance should be made transparent'.

1995

R v *Social Fund Inspector, ex parte Ledicott*, (1995) *The Times*, 24 May, QBD

- The correct construction of s. 66(4)(b) of the SSAA 1992 (the SFI's power to substitute his/her own determination) did not preclude SFI applying an amended Direction issued by the Secretary of State *after* the SFO's and SFRO's determinations.

R v *Social Fund Inspector, ex parte Tuckwood*, QBD, 27 April 1995 (unreported)

- SFI had correctly interpreted the phrase 'provision of heating, including central heating' as excluding the costs of repairs to the applicant's central heating system.

Re Bullock, QBD (Crown side) Northern Ireland, 21 September 1995 (unreported)

- Application for judicial review was dismissed by consent. Petitioner had maintained that Direction 12(q) which excludes certain specialist security items (in Northern Ireland only) was *ultra vires* the Department's power to issue Directions.

1996 None.

1997

Re Foley, QBD (Crown side) Northern Ireland, 22 January 1997 (unreported)

- Petitioner had failed to disclose the standard document used by the Office of the Social Fund Commissioner to elicit further observations on the papers from the applicant. There had been no request for the SFI to undertake a further discretionary review. Counsel for the respondent SFI successfully applied for leave to be set aside.

R v *Secretary of State for Social Security and the Social Fund Inspector, ex parte Harper*, (1997) *The Times*, 31 March, QBD

- The judge concluded that s. 138(1) of the SSCBA 1992 was not ambiguous. 'Other needs' contained in s. 138(1)(b) did not mean needs other than funeral and maternity expenses as *prescribed* in s. 138(1)(a). The regulated and discretionary schemes therefore provide 'mutually exclusive methods of making payments to meet particular needs, the former meeting the need for maternity and funeral expenses [of whatever nature] and the latter meeting other needs'.

- *Obiter* statement that certain *Hansard* material would have been admissible to show 'that an amendment which was intended to give precisely the same legal effect as that now advanced by the applicant was rejected on the merits by Parliament'.

R v Social Fund Inspector, ex parte Taylor,★ (1998) *The Times*, 20 January, QBD

- It was held that the guidance clearly provided that 'needs' should be assessed and their priority determined *before* budget considerations were taken into account. The case of *R v Gloucestershire County Council ex parte Barry* [1997] 2 All ER 1 was distinguished. In that case the relevant statute imposed a duty on the local authority to meet the needs of chronically sick and disabled persons, but made no reference to the cost of meeting those needs as a relevant criterion to be considered. In the social fund scheme Parliament has expressly directed that resources should be taken into account and the Secretary of State had drawn a clear distinction between the assessment of need and the cost of meeting it.
- In determining the application as a medium-priority case the Inspector had given little weight to medical evidence. In the circumstances the judge held that he ought to have given the applicant the opportunity of dealing with those matters that were troubling him. That was particularly so because the review procedure was essentially inquisitorial. However, ultimately the decision whether to make an award and the amount of that award was for the inspector.

R v Social Fund Inspector, ex parte Carruthers, QBD (forthcoming)

- The court will consider two points; whether a single person can meet the conditions of Direction 4(a)(iii) (see *Healey*, DC above); and the meaning of 'institutional or residential care' in Direction 4(a)(i) and (ii) (see *Ibrahim* above).

6

Judicial Review and Legal Services

ROGER SMITH

Examination of the role of judicial review in legal services requires consideration of three different but linked themes:

- the use of judicial review in the context of legal aid and legal services
- the role of legal aid in the use of judicial review; and
- the use of judicial review in the development of legal services.

Hence, each of these are discussed below.

JUDICIAL REVIEW AND LEGAL SERVICES

Judicial review has been developed in the field of legal services, as elsewhere, to police the operation of public decision-makers. Into its maw have been successfully dragged local authorities wishing to close law centres; legal aid authorities (first the Law Society and then the Legal Aid Board) administering legal aid; and, finally, the Lord Chancellor himself on that issue of supreme public and professional importance – the rate of lawyers' remuneration.

Let us begin with the deployment of legal aid against the Lord Chancellor in his own courts. In 1986, the Bar Council and the Law Society had the hubris to issue proceedings against Lord Hailsham. Politically, this was rather daring though an 'anonymous correspondent' to the Bar's journal *Counsel* drawled, somewhat superciliously, that the 'case involved little more than a "textbook" application of established principles of administrative law'.[1]

The applicant on behalf of the Bar was its then chairman, Robert (now Lord) Alexander QC. His case was that the Lord Chancellor could not reasonably have come to the decision that his members were entitled to a 5 per cent annual increase on their legal aid fees for criminal work. This, he felt, was particularly outrageous given that a respectable firm of accountants, albeit instructed by himself, had indicated that an increase of between 30 and 40 per cent would have been more reasonable. The Law Society, caught a little unawares by the Bar's gung-ho attitude to litigation, tagged along with a similar application.

The Bar advanced two grounds: a legitimate expectation of the professional bodies to proper consultation and negotiation and a failure by the Lord Chancellor to pay heed to any reasonable construction of the words of s. 39(3) of the Legal Aid Act 1974 that required him 'to have regard to the principle of allowing fair remuneration'.

The result was a classic illustration of the ups and downs of judicial review litigation. The short-term result was victory – though judicial etiquette required that neither case was actually decided and the Lord Chancellor thereby spared total judicial humiliation. The Lord Chancellor caved in to the Bar when it became apparent that the court, led by a characteristically trenchant Lord Lane, was not going in his direction. The turning point came with his Lordship's remarks on adjourning for lunch on the second day of the hearing: 'We have now got down to the narrowest of narrow points. I wonder why we have been spending a day and a half over these matters.'[2]

The parties used the recess to come to agreement, though Lord Hailsham jibbed at liability for the Bar's costs. It did him no good: costs were awarded against him as the matter was adjourned generally with liberty to restore. The Law Society's case went the same way and its then president, Alan Leslie, expressed his satisfaction: 'solicitors will be relieved to know that we are to have proper discussions on criminal legal aid rates'.[3]

As many a judicial review litigant has discovered, however, the doctrine of Parliamentary sovereignty allows a determined politician to have the last word. The profession's success with increased remuneration rates was short-lived. The Legal Aid Act 1988, designed mainly to substitute the Legal Aid Board for the Law Society, was used to settle a few scores. Out went the amenable provisions of the 1974 Act and in came the somewhat more indeterminate requirements of s. 34(9) of the 1988 Act. These blocked any repetition of Lord Alexander's venture by adding such considerations as 'the cost to public funds' to the list of criteria of which the Lord Chancellor could take account in setting rates of remuneration. That was the end of that.

At a more humble level, the courts have deployed judicial review to prowl around the legal aid administration, tidying up the sort of inadequacies that they have tackled in other areas of government function. A 1970 case established that the grant or refusal of legal aid certificates was a potential subject of prerogative orders.[4] The court was happy to intervene from time to time in order to tune up the standards of legal aid administration. Hence, a 1990 case decided that a legal aid appeal committee which was minded to refuse a certificate in the face of counsel's strong opinion to the contrary must at least give extended reasons.[5] The financial capital test must take account of the consequences of other outstanding legal proceedings.[6] Civil legal aid, available under statute only for legal proceedings, can be obtained for an interlocutory application.[7]

Legal aid and judicial review stand in a particularly close relationship. In practice, legal aid is the gatekeeper for an individual applicant who wants to mount a judicial review challenge. Without it, the potential liability of costs is considerable. Unsurprisingly, the relative test of merit for the two has been explored by judicial review litigation. This is essentially the same, i.e. a *prima facie* arguable case.[8] As far as legal aid is concerned (see below), in practice, this is rather generous. It means that if an applicant can get leave to issue judicial review then legal aid is likely to be forthcoming. This overlap may not last all that long. The man who would be Lord Chancellor under a Labour Government, Lord Irvine of Lairg QC, told the 1996 Bar Conference that he was attracted to the idea of strengthening the legal aid merits test:

> There may be a case for tightening the merits test so that, for example, legal aid should be granted if counsel can advise that on current information the prospects of success are at least 60/40.[9]

This would put more distance between the two, making leave much easier to obtain than legal aid. Already, the courts have resiled slightly from too great an identification of the two tests. It is now clear that the Legal Aid Board is not bound simply to look at the decision on leave or the *prima facie* case, they can have regard to the likely final result of the judicial review application in deciding to grant or refuse legal aid.[10]

On two issues, the courts have been drawn into decisions that are crucial policy matters for the future development of legal aid. First, the courts have upheld the Legal Aid Board's ruling that fees for the legal advice of commercial paralegals to solicitors should not be allowed as a disbursement under the 'green form' legal advice scheme.[11] This stopped the development of such services in their tracks. Second, the court asserted its right to require the Legal Aid

Board to follow fair procedures in the grant of a legal aid contract for multi-party actions.[12] It, thus, rejected the Board's argument that the grant of such contracts did not raise public law issues, a finding of some importance given the government's intention to require most legal aid practitioners to operate under similar contracts.[13]

As a result, the Legal Aid Board faces a potential welter of litigation if there is ever implementation of the proposal of the government for compulsory competitive tenders for exclusive contracts to provide legal aid. Already, there is regular litigation in multi-party action cases by disappointed firms of solicitors where contracts are awarded for 'generic' work. The consequences of failure to obtain a more general legal aid contract will be such that disappointed firms are bound to take action as a way of seeking to protect the livelihood of their partners and staff.

There have been at least two cases in which judicial review has been deployed by law centres against local authorities in disputes over their funding. In legal terms, these were not exceptional but they emphasize the breadth of the impact of judicial review in the field of legal services. Highfields and Belgrave Law Centre challenged the decision of its funder, Leicester City Council, to close it with almost immediate effect in 1986. The case settled and the Centre is still operational. In 1991, Brent Community Law Centre, whose Kate Markus had earlier acted for the Highfields and Belgrave Centre, successfully fought off a similarly snap decision to de-fund taken when a Conservative administration captured its previously-Labour-controlled council. Again, the Centre still survives.

LEGAL AID AND JUDICIAL REVIEW

For most applicants, legal aid is as much, if not more, of a hurdle to the commencement of a judicial review action as is the requirement for leave. This is because legal aid provides a guarantee of payment for an applicant's costs, win or lose, as well as an indemnity for the litigant in relation to the costs of the respondent if the case is lost.

In practice, the costs indemnity is the most important part of this dual function for social action groups wishing to take cases on public interest and general principle. Many would be willing to run litigation on what effectively would be a contingency basis if only their clients could be indemnified against potential liability for costs or that liability waived. As a result, there has been a consistent stream of argument supporting a relaxation of the indemnity costs rule in appropriate 'public interest' cases. Among the proponents of such a reform have been Lord Woolf, who argues that:

> Those who legitimately seek the assistance of the court for
> [public interest judicial review applications] should receive
> protection as to the costs of bringing proceedings.[14]

The Law Commission has provided some support in a recent report on administrative law which recommended that costs could be awarded from central funds as well as from the parties, thus providing the possibility of protection while maintaining the indemnity principle.[15]

The Public Law Project has continued to press for reform,[16] supporting among other mechanisms a Law Commission recommendation that the legal aid test be amended to include a public interest criterion.[17] An alternative proposal, advanced by CPAG lawyer David Thomas, has been for the idea of a 'pre-emptive costs order', i.e. a statement at the beginning of a case that the judge will not be inclined to exercise the discretion to award costs should the applicant lose.

In the absence of legal aid or pre-emptive costs orders, there are limited possibilities for providing adequate protection for a potential litigant against an order for costs. Government departments, once relatively open to agreeing that costs would lie where they fall in cases for which their lawyers had some sympathy, are now much tougher and agree much more rarely to waive costs in advance. The problem of cost protection necessarily arises in every case taken other than by an individual. Unlike the situation in some other countries (such as Canada, in the province of Quebec), legal aid is not available for incorporated or unincorporated bodies, even if they operate on a not-for-profit basis. Thus, pressure groups like the Child Poverty Action Group (CPAG) have been barred from obtaining legal aid for cases taken in their own right. The two cases taken in its own name to extend *locus standi* were thus taken under conditional grants, i.e. sums to be payable in the event of defeat by local authorities such as the (now deceased) Greater London Council.[18] A further CPAG case, where the individual applicant was a striking miner who was not legally aidable, was brought with an indemnity from his union.[19] The extent to which third parties provide such indemnities for litigation costs is unknown.

Some idea of the practical importance of legal aid in judicial review can be obtained from the statistics. In 1995–96, legal aid certificates were issued to 5481 applicants.[20] In the calendar year 1995, there were, however, only 3604 applications received by the court.[21] Some explanation for the discrepancy in numbers may be indicated by the fact that just over a third of the legal aid certificates were first issued on an emergency basis. Presumably, the 1800 cases for which legal aid is granted but proceedings are not issued settle between grant and issue of an application.

Legal aid is not, however, easy to obtain. The test of means becomes increasingly stringent as eligibility declines. In practice, therefore, a social action group seeking to take a test case generally needs to find a potential applicant who is in receipt of basic income support benefits in a situation where change to their financial circumstances is unlikely. Pensioners, thus, become particularly attractive litigants. Practitioners report that it is increasingly difficult to obtain a favourable decision from the Legal Aid Board on the merits of a judicial review case. CPAG's lawyer David Thomas says, for example, that he almost as a routine now has to proceed to appeal in order to get legal aid granted. This seems a common experience and a result of the growing bureaucratization of the procedures of the Legal Aid Board. No doubt the diverse nature of judicial review presents particularly difficult problems because it defies easy routinization of procedure.

The test of merit requires following a route that begins with statute; passes through regulation; and ends, ambiguously as to legal effect but dominantly in practice, with guidance from the Legal Aid Board. The main statutory provisions are set out in s. 15(2) and 15(3) of the Legal Aid Act 1988. These set a 'positive' and a 'negative' test of reasonableness:

> A person shall not be granted representation for the purposes of any proceedings unless he satisfies the [Legal Aid] Board that he has reasonable grounds for taking, defending or being a party to proceedings ... [and]
> may be refused representation for the purposes of any proceedings if, in the particular circumstances of the case it appears to the board ... unreasonable that he should be granted representation ...

The reasonableness criteria are then further expanded by provisions of the Civil Legal Aid (General) Regulations 1989 which include the following provisions particularly relevant to judicial review applicants. Regulation 29 allows an application to be refused 'where it appears ... that ... only a trivial advantage would be gained by the applicant from the proceedings to which the application relates'. Regulation 32 requires that:

> When determining an application, the Area Director shall consider whether it is reasonable and proper for persons concerned jointly with or having the same interest as the applicant to defray [all or part of] the costs.

The Board's guidance on these provisions has been the subject of some analysis and comment, notably by the Public Law Project.[22] Over the years, it is clear that the Board has tightened up the operation of the merits test in practice, expanding on the well-established 'private client test' (i.e., judging the reasonableness of a case by reference to the likely decision of a 'person with adequate means to meet the probable costs of the proceedings, but not with over-abundant means, so that paying the costs would be possible, although something of a sacrifice').[23]

The specific guidance on judicial review begins by following the law stated above and specifically quoting *ex parte Hughes* as authority for the generally overlapping tests for legal aid and leave:

> The Board is not bound by the decision as to leave but in general, if a court grants leave and the Board has no additional information casting doubt on the merits of the claim, it is likely that the application will satisfy the legal merits test (though not necessarily the reasonableness test).[24]

The guidance stresses the need to warn potential respondents of impending applications for judicial review and requires 'a proper letter before action'.

These provisions, as such, rarely prove too great an obstacle to the determined applicant or litigator. Problems arise most often in relation to 'public interest' litigation, on which the Board issues specific guidance. Here the Board takes a line that is arguably stronger than the provisions in statute and regulation require:

> The purpose of legal aid is to assist individuals who might otherwise be unable to take proceedings on account of their means ... Legal aid is devised to assist those whom it finances in the course of litigation and not directly to assist other parties to the proceedings or other members of the public who are not parties to the proceedings in determining points of general interest ... indeed, it would be an abuse of process to pursue proceedings with legal aid which are only of academic interest to lawyers and which no reasonable paying client would fund privately.
>
> There are cases where the existence of other claims can have a bearing on the merits or cost benefit of the applicant ... but public interest in the more general sense will rarely be a significant consideration in legal aid decisions.[25]

The language of this passage is interesting. The target elides from 'public' interest to 'general' and, even more pejoratively, 'academic' interest. The reluctance to allow litigation based on principle rather than personal interest indicates one of the reasons why most judicial review applications relate to immigration and housing questions. These are types of case with high personal engagement by the applicant in the decision being contested. In 1995, the two categories accounted for about half of all the review applications made. A citizen who wishes to argue that a government decision is *ultra vires* but can show little personal gain from a decision in their favour, whatever their interest from the point of view of the judicial review or the wider public interest in undoing the wrong, will find it very difficult to obtain the legal aid necessary to cover their costs.

The Public Law Project researchers comment that the guidance (actually in a milder form in the version which they considered than in the current 1996 version) indicates the lack of fit between the legal aid provisions and the fundamental purpose of legal aid:

> Judicial review owes its origins to the supervisory role of the High Court to ensure that subordinate courts and tribunals and other bodies exercising administrative decision-making functions perform their functions within the rule of law. Conceptualised in this way, there is an inherent public purpose in judicial review proceedings which can be said to transcend the individual applicants' interests in particular cases or the direct benefit they may gain from them.[26]

JUDICIAL REVIEW AND LEGAL SERVICES

The growth in the use of judicial review over the last twenty years is a well-observed phenomenon. Table 6.1 shows how striking it has been and the numbers continue to grow. The number of civil applications for 1995 was up 14 per cent on 1994, at 3283.

Table 6.1 Use of civil judicial review or equivalent[27]

Year	Number
1964	59
1974	160
1984	703
1994	2887

Behind this expansion in jurisdiction lies the story of which legal institutions and organizations have been taking judicial review cases. In the 1960s and 1970s relatively few cases were taken. Thus, individual lawyers and organizations could play a disproportionately large role in opening up the field. Among the early pioneers were a number of pressure groups, most notably the CPAG, which deliberately used the prerogative orders as part of test case strategies. In doing this, they were much influenced by the United States where lawyers, often working in a civil rights' context, had been doing the same. The CPAG formed a Legal Department in 1968. Henry Hodge, now a prominent private practitioner, was the most celebrated early holder of the office of the CPAG's solicitor. He set out the intention:

> Thus, although losses could be expected, the strategy always assumed that success would come in the long run in the sense that favourable changes would occur for the poor. Legislators would be shamed into amending harsh legislation; administrative practices would alter; and families who had received no help might get such help as the knowledge gained from the cases spread.[28]

The early cases were not necessarily in the form of applications for prerogative orders but the absence of any statutory appeal rights from supplementary benefits appeal tribunals until 1977 meant that certiorari was a common form of challenge to wayward appeal decisions. From the mid-1970s, the cases poured off the production line.

Many of the early attempts fell by the wayside as judges proved reluctant to accept jurisdiction over what they clearly regarded as irritatingly parochial matters of concern only to marginal groups in society, i.e. the poor and powerless. Thus, a couple of early challenges to the 'cohabitation rule' failed with Lord Widgery moved to say in the second that the phrase ' "cohabiting as man and wife" ... is so well known that nothing I could say about it could possibly assist in its interpretation hereafter'.[29] The high water mark of judicial indifference to the fate of those passing through supplementary benefit appeal tribunals was reached in two cases, *ex parte Moore* and *ex parte Shine*.[30] Lord Denning opined:

> This seems to me a good instance of where the High Court should not interfere with a tribunal's decision even though it may be erroneous in law.

Gradually, however, the tide turned. Among the failures there were successes, at least at the judicial level. As early as 1974 the fact that there was a possibility of success was indicated by a resounding victory in *ex parte Simper*.[31] This was a winning challenge to the computation of the rate of benefit for those in receipt of long-term and other additional payments. The bureaucracy was, however, proving reluctant to respond:

> Evidence that the court's decision was not implemented is a report of the Ombudsman and a parliamentary debate on the later legislative change.[32]

The Government was not disposed to be compliant either and brought forth immediate statutory remedy.[33] Foreshadowing the brief success of the legal profession's cases on remuneration, this set the trend for legislative intervention to overrule its effect. Henry Hodge's early enthusiasm for the power of shame soon proved naïve. Legislative overruling by statute was always inconvenient but possible. Where regulations could be changed, this could be done particularly easily. The CPAG's record appears to have been 72 hours between the promulgation of an offending decision and its amendment by regulation.[34]

In consequence, the major long-term effect of the strategic effect of test cases involving judicial review has probably been procedural rather than substantive. The implementation of an appeal process from supplementary benefit appeal tribunals, first in 1977 to the High Court and then in 1980 to Social Security Commissioners, was the direct result of the onslaught of concerted judicial review cases.

Another example of the shift from the substantive to the procedural can be derived from a later CPAG case, R v Chief Adjudication Officer ex parte Bland.[35] This case was actually taken to publicize the fate of striking miners whose benefit was reduced to minimal levels during the miners' strike of 1984 and 1985. It was successful to a degree in relation to this. The Guardian, The Times and the Financial Times all covered the case and provided a degree of publicity for its facts. The case was, however, fairly comprehensively lost on its main point of argument. However, it did lead to the development of an accelerated appeal process that had been missing in supplementary benefit cases.[36] This was implemented soon afterwards as a way of blocking recourse to judicial review and ensuring that cases were kept within the appeal framework. The Department of Health and Social Security, as then it was, had previously proved hostile to such a provision.

The CPAG's role in judicial review was such that it played a creditable role in extending locus standi by taking, relatively successfully, two cases in its own name.[37] Such success represented a considerable advance in administrative law at the time of the decisions but provides an ironic commentary on the hopes of Henry Hodge that litigation would achieve substantive results for the CPAG's constituency. The group's legal legacy has proved perhaps of

151

more interest to lawyers and legal academics than to the poor and needy. Interestingly, very few social action groups have followed the CPAG in taking cases in their own name. An exception was the National Association of Citizens Advice Bureaux who joined the CPAG in its second judicial review application in 1986.

The CPAG's work in social security was followed in other fields by law centres. They developed judicial review in the late 1970s and early 1980s, particularly in the field of homelessness and other areas of local authority housing policy. Particularly active were law centres in local authority areas that implemented harsh housing policies. Thus, the south London Borough of Wandsworth became a judicial review battleground in the early 1980s as a flagship Thatcherite council slugged out its precise legal obligations to its tenants and homeless first with the three law centres that it inherited and then, after their demise, with a combined centre, the Wandsworth Legal Resource Project.

The result was a series of keystone cases on local authority duties, such as two cases involving the same applicant, Mr Winder, an obstreperous Wandsworth tenant.[38] Although ultimately unsuccessful, the good Mr Winder fronted a spirited attack on the manner in which the council had pushed through rent rises in a way designed to encourage a shift to home ownership rather than tenancy.

It was not only right-wing councils which felt the lash of the law centre. Faced with cuts to its resources, the London Borough of Camden, a long-time Labour council, implemented cost-saving policies such as the somewhat cynical closing of its homelessness unit. The council appeared to believe that reducing the opening hours of its homelessness bureaucracy would reduce the problem of homelessness, or at least the numbers for which it had to take responsibility. The council tried various combinations of closing hours, from days in the week to hours in the day. Camden's Law Centre, somewhat exposed as a recipient of grant aid from the Borough, attacked these arrangements as unlawful in the light of the Borough's statutory obligations under the then current homelessness legislation.[39]

Russell Campbell, the housing specialist solicitor at Camden Law Centre during this period, reports that, although he and the Law Centre opened up the field of judicial review in homelessness cases and began the first few cases, private practitioners soon took up the torch. A major advance achieved by the Law Centre was the implementation of an emergency application procedure involving judges being on duty and willing to hear applications prior to the filing of the full documentation. Once the procedure was established, private practitioners took over the bulk of the cases and Russell

Campbell himself soon left the Centre to become the lawyer at the national housing pressure group Shelter. The degree of involvement by the Centre diminished severely as a result.

There is some evidence that this is suggestive of a common pattern. Research undertaken for the Public Law Project produced statistics for representation in judicial review cases for 1987, 1988 and 1989. It found that law centre involvement in judicial reviews varied between 6 and 8 per cent, showing some evidence of dropping further in data for the first quarter of 1991. In homelessness, there was a marked fall in the proportion of cases undertaken, with the proportion of cases taken by law centres falling from a quarter to a tenth over the three-year period as the numbers grew. The researchers were rather damning about the role of law centres outside these two areas:

> Taking the three-and-a-quarter years covered by the research as a whole, law centres were responsible for 17 judicial reviews relating to welfare benefits out of a total of 58 such cases in the period, 10 education judicial reviews out of a total of 124 such cases, and seven judicial reviews in relation to utilities. In no other field did law centres, taken as a group, represent applicants in more than five judicial reviews ...[40]

The researchers found relatively limited specialization among private practice solicitors in judicial review. Use of the procedure seemed to be in the process of becoming dispersed rather than concentrated during their period of research:

> The overall impression gained from our research is that only very limited degrees of specialisation in judicial review have been developed by solicitors in private practice, whether representing individuals or companies, or indeed by law centres.[41]

Indeed, judicial review is now a relatively widespread technique among solicitors in private practice. Notably, areas that have been opened up to its operation in the 1990s have seen much less involvement by law centres. Luke Clements, for example, has explored judicial review from private practice in Hereford, first in relation to gypsies and then 'when I found it so easy to use and so powerful' he extended its reach into challenging community care decisions, on which he has written one of the early, leading texts.[42] Similarly, the leading lawyer developing education law is Jack Rabinowicz, a private practitioner in London. The various groups of specialist lawyers such as the Housing Law Practitioners Associations, the Social Security Law Practitioners Association and the

Immigration Law Practitioners Association are all dominated by private practitioners.

Judicial review has moved into the mainstream of legal practice. Although it accounts for only around 3.25 per cent of all non-matrimonial certificates, it is well established in a number of specialist jurisdictions. More broadly, litigators have lost both their fear and their ignorance of the technique.

CONCLUSION

Both judicial review and legal aid exist along the faultlines of power within the constitution and the state. The form and content of either depends at any particular point in time on the balance of underlying forces, many of which may have a somewhat contradictory nature. For example, the effectiveness of judicial review as a mechanism for challenge of the executive depends upon the view taken of their role by the judiciary (on which there are likely to be different views taken by different judges), the cases taken by lawyers and the extent of actions of governments and governmental bodies.

As a procedurally-orientated remedy, judicial review can be largely marginalized as a campaigning tool of use to social action groups by the simple expedient of, on the one hand, taking care that decisions are not procedurally challengeable and, on the other, *ex post facto* legislation in the event of most losses. A common pattern is discernible in the response by Government to the use of judicial review by lawyers at the cutting edge of legal services' development. Once review becomes established as a routine challenge to executive action or inaction, the statutory response is, where possible, to establish an appeal procedure that will avoid the embarrassment and cost of judicial review cases. Thus, the CPAG's use of review against tribunals led to appeal procedures in the late 1970s. Similarly, homelessness challenges are about to be redirected into the county courts through the latest Housing Act. One might predict that, eventually, other areas that give rise to consistent review applications, such as housing benefit decisions by review boards, will also be brought into appeal processes that currently do not exist.

Such a move is, overall, desirable. People should have more easily accessible ways of challenging decisions than traipsing off to the courts. Adjudicating bodies should follow acceptable procedures in arriving at their decisions. It means, however, that for the campaigner judicial review becomes one of a variety of territories over which skirmishes with the executive take place. Its role changes over time, according to the value placed by Government on reviewable decision-making. This is an unending battle where victories in one area are often balanced by defeats elsewhere. Social security appeal procedures were radically improved in the mid-1980s. A few years later, the whole area of what had been single payments was removed from a rights-based, appeal-friendly scheme to the realm of the Social Fund involving discretionary judgments from a capped fund, a mechanism deliberately introduced to avoid appealable or reviewable decisions. Immigration remains an area of law where the executive prefers to sustain wide attack by means of judicial review rather than giving appeal rights to such groups as asylum-seekers. The perceived balance of advantage shifts back and forth over time.

Legal aid is, as we have seen, crucial to the use by the poor of judicial review as a remedy. Again, the coverage which it provides is a balance of different forces. Most obviously, the Government controls eligibility and scope although individual decision-making by the Legal Aid Board is relatively autonomous. A further factor in controlling availability is the willingness of practitioners to undertake cases in this field. In the 1970s, solicitors were slow to use judicial review: it now appears that they are more willing. Here the main issue is the rising pressure of cost. Other areas of work have expanded in the same way as has judicial review. For example, significant numbers of expensive medical negligence cases are now taken under legal aid in a way that did not occur twenty years ago. The result is a clampdown on spending, the results of which can be seen in the Legal Aid Board's increasingly tough line on merits. As mentioned above, the introduction of tightly drafted contracts for limited amounts of work by defined practitioners could well threaten the flexible use of judicial review in opening up new areas of legal challenge in the way that we have seen over the last two decades.

There is likely never to be a final resting place in the balance of power that sets the context for the use of judicial review and legal aid. It will always be in the process of negotiation and battle. And this is quite right. Both are powerful supports for the individual against the state, the powerful against the powerless. Together they represent a major way in which legal services and their state funding for the poor represents, in the civil field, not only public assistance in the resolution of private disputes but also an integral part of the constitutional fabric of rights that are meaningful and duties that are enforceable.

NOTES

1 A correspondent, 'Ex Parte Alexander', *Counsel*: 24–5 (Easter 1986).
2 *Ibid.*, quotation.
3 Alan Leslie quoted in *Law Society's Gazette*, 9 April 1986.

4 *R v No. 9 (North Eastern) Legal Aid Area ex parte Foxhill Flats (Leeds) Ltd* [1970] 2 QB 152.

5 *R v Legal Aid Area No. 8 (Northern Appeal Committee) ex parte Parkinson, The Times*, 13 March 1990.

6 *R v Legal Aid Assessment Office ex parte Croder, The Independent*, 23 July 1993 (DC).

7 *R v Legal Aid Committee No. 1 (London) Legal Aid Area, ex parte Rondel* [1967] 2 QB 482 (DC).

8 *R v Legal Aid Board ex parte Hughes* (1992) 24 HLR 698 (CA).

9 28 September 1996.

10 *R v Area No. 8 Committee of the Legal Aid Board ex parte Megarry and Others* (1 July 1994) unreported but see, e.g., Public Law Project, *The Applicant's Guide to Judicial Review*, London: Sweet & Maxwell (1995), p. 75.

11 *R v Legal Aid Board ex parte Bruce* [1992] 1 WLR 694 (HL).

12 'Court rejects LAB Gulf War ruling', *Law Society Gazette*, 21 February 1996.

13 As set out in Lord Chancellor's Department, *Striking the Balance: The Future of Legal Aid in England and Wales*, Cm 3305, London: HMSO (1996).

14 Child and Co. lecture, 19 February 1996.

15 Law Commission, *Administrative Law: Judicial Review and Statutory Appeals* (HC 669), London: HMSO (1994), p. 85.

16 See, e.g., Public Law Project, *A Memorandum to Lord Woolf on the Question of Costs and Access to Justice in Judicial Review Cases* (1996).

17 L. Bridges, G. Meszaros and M. Sunkin, *Judicial Review in Perspective*, London: Cavendish (1995), p. 195.

18 *R v Secretary of State for Social Services ex parte CPAG and the GLC, The Times*, 16 August 1985.

19 *R v Chief Adjudication Officer ex parte Bland, The Times*, 6 February 1985.

20 Legal Aid Board, *Annual Report 1995–96*, London: HMSO, p. 63.

21 Lord Chancellor's Department, *Judicial Statistics 1995*, Cm 3290, London: HMSO (1996), p. 16.

22 See, e.g., Public Law Project, *The Applicant's Guide to Judicial Review*, London: Sweet & Maxwell (1995), pp. 71–83.

23 Legal Aid Board, *Legal Aid Handbook 1996/97*, London: Sweet & Maxwell (1996), p. 62.

24 *Ibid.*, p. 73.

25 *Ibid.*, p. 69.

26 Note 22 above, p. 108.

27 Taken from *Judicial Statistics*, note 21 above. Measures civil prerogative orders in 1964 and 1974; judicial review in civil cases in 1984 and 1994.

28 Quoted in T. Prosser, *Test Cases for the Poor: Legal Techniques in the Politics of Social Welfare*, London: CPAG (1983) and originally in R. Lister, *Justice for the Claimant*, London: CPAG (1974), p. 242.

29 Prosser, note 28 above, p. 28.

30 [1975] 1 WLR 624.

31 *R v Greater Birmingham SBAT ex parte Simper* [1974] QB 543.

32 Prosser, note 28 above, p. 62.

33 *R v Greater Birmingham Appeal Tribunal ex parte Simper* [1974] QB 543.

34 It has probably been done quicker. This is just my personal record. Decision
    R(SB) 26/48 was made on 2 November 1983 and overruled by amending
    regulations by the 5 November.
35 *The Times*, 6 February 1985.
36 See further R. Smith, 'How good are test cases' in J. Cooper and R. Dhavan
    (eds) *Public Interest Law*, Oxford: Basil Blackwell (1986), pp. 271–85.
37 *R v Secretary of State for Social Services ex parte CPAG and GLC*, *The Times*, 16
    August 1985 and *R v Secretary of State for Social Services ex parte CPAG* [1990]
    QB 540.
38 *London Borough of Wandsworth v Winder* [1985] AC 461 and *ex parte Winder (No.
    2)* HLR 400, both concerned with the method to be adopted for setting rents.
39 See, e.g., *R v. London Borough of Camden ex parte Wait* (1986) HLR 434 and *ex
    parte Gillan* (1989) HLR 114.
40 L. Bridges, G. Meszaros and M. Sunkin, *Judicial Review in Perspective*, London:
    Cavendish (1995), p. 61.
41 *Ibid.*, p. 62.
42 L. Clements, *Community Care and the Law*, London: Legal Action Group
    (1996).

7

Judicial Review and Homelessness

DAVID POLLARD

INTRODUCTION

In one sense, this chapter is the odd chapter out in this book, in that it will be seen that the role of proceedings for judicial review in relation to homelessness is now so curtailed as to have little or no relevance to the central issues faced by applicants for housing accommodation. In another sense, however, this chapter is central to any discussion of the role of judicial review in welfare-orientated situations because it will describe a welfare scheme of immense importance where, for twenty years, the only form of legal redress against decisions of the welfare provider was judicial review. This chapter will, in the context of homelessness situations, discuss the immense contribution to dispute settlement by judicial review, and will question whether, and to what extent, the exercise of a supervisory jurisdiction by the High Court is less appropriate than an appellate jurisdiction exercised by some lower tribunal.

In many welfare-providing schemes which are discussed here, the enabling legislation took account of the development of principles of fair administration (or administrative justice) and provided a common form of administrative law dispute settlement machinery, namely a mechanism for the citizen to make a first application to the appropriate authority to be considered under the scheme, a mechanism for seeking to question initial decisions which were unwelcome (whether by way of administrative review within the hierarchy of the administrative authority or by way of appeal to a court or tribunal), and an appellate mechanism to correct errors of law.

The homelessness scheme, introduced by the Housing (Homeless Persons) Act 1977,[1] fitted in well with the welfare rights ethic of its time. It provided a method of allocating, to those defined as most in need, resources which were scarce, both because of the finance involved and the time in which housing can be physically provided, by imposing on housing authorities certain duties. By imposing such duties, the potential recipients of such resources saw the scheme in terms of rights, rights which it was claimed must be enforced in some way or another. Although, as will be seen, the homelessness scheme did provide a proper mechanism for the citizen to make a first application to the housing authority to be considered under the scheme, that scheme went no further and challenges to adverse initial decisions had to be mounted, first, by using the informal review machinery established by many housing authorities and, then, by applications for judicial review.

To describe the operation of judicial review in relation to homelessness, it is first necessary to describe the principal elements of the statutory and administrative scheme which made provision for dealing with housing authority duties towards the homeless from 1977 to 1997. This scheme has been replaced, as from 20 January 1997, by Part VII of the Housing Act 1996, which makes considerable amendments to the scheme, in terms of both substantive and procedural rules.[2] This chapter will concentrate on legal concepts which are to be continued in the 1996 Act scheme and, because of this (and for literary purposes), the pre-1996 Act homelessness scheme will be chronicled in the present tense. Whether a homelessness duty is owed to an applicant and the form any duty should take will depend on the applicant's circumstances and the answers to a number of questions. First, is the applicant homeless or threatened with homelessness? If the applicant is neither homeless nor threatened with homelessness, no homelessness duty whatsoever is imposed on the housing authority.[3] If the applicant is in fact homeless or threatened with homelessness, a second question arises, namely, has the applicant a priority need? If the housing authority decide that they are not satisfied that the applicant has a priority need, their homelessness duty is to furnish the applicant with advice and such assistance as they consider appropriate in the circumstances in any attempts he or she may make to secure that accommodation becomes available (or does not cease to be available) for the occupation of the applicant and any household.[4] If the applicant has a priority need, a third question arises, namely, has the applicant become homeless (or become threatened with home-lessness) intentionally? If the housing authority decide that they are satisfied that the applicant has a priority need but are also satisfied that he or she became threatened with homelessness intentionally, their homelessness duty is to furnish the applicant with advice and such assistance as they consider appropriate in the circumstances in any attempts he or she may make to secure that accommodation does not cease to be available for occupation by the applicant and any household.[5] If the housing authority decide that they are satisfied that the applicant has a priority need but they are also satisfied that the applicant became homeless intentionally, they are under a 'limited duty' to do two things. First, they must secure that accommodation is made available for occupation by the applicant and any household for such period as they consider will give the applicant a reasonable opportunity of securing accommodation for the household's occupation. Second, the authority must furnish the applicant with advice and such assistance as they consider appropriate in the circumstances in any attempts the applicant may make to secure that accommodation becomes available for occupation.[6] If the housing authority are satisfied that the applicant has a priority need and are not satisfied that the applicant became homeless intentionally, they are under a 'full duty' to secure that accommodation becomes available for the occupation of the applicant and any household and if the housing authority are satisfied that the applicant has a priority need and are not satisfied that the applicant became threatened with homelessness intentionally, they are under a duty to take reasonable steps to secure that accommodation does not cease to be available for occupation by the applicant and any household.[7] At each stage in the process the housing authority are under a statutory duty to give reasons for their decisions (see below).

The most immediate method of 'enforcing' a housing authority's duty is by the normal administrative process of applying to the authority for accommodation (or for assistance in obtaining accommodation) and by adducing evidence (on any application form, at the initial interview or during the authority's subsequent inquiries) that an applicant's circumstances are such that the authority are under a homelessness duty towards the applicant. If a housing authority's decision is adverse to the applicant (e.g., that the applicant is not homeless, has no priority need, or is intentionally homeless) and the authority notify him or her of their decision that no homelessness duty arises or that a duty arises which is less advantageous than that claimed by the applicant (e.g., a 'limited housing duty' rather than the 'full housing duty'), the applicant may take further administrative action. The applicant may make representations to the authority's homelessness officers, the Director of Housing or the Housing Committee (however named). The authority may have their own informal internal appeals or review structure and there may be administrative machinery for a meeting with housing authority officials or councillors. In addition an approach may be made to a local councillor or to the Commissions for Local Administration (but an examination of administrative redress, though of immense importance in practice, is outwith the scope of this chapter).

As stated earlier, if administrative redress failed, then under the pre-1996 Act scheme, for an applicant wishing to take legal action to challenge the housing authority's decision there was no statutory right of appeal to a court or tribunal. The only method of challenge was an application for judicial review. This system continued for twenty years and during that time, the courts overtly pursued the twin roles of interpreting the legislation and imposing standards of procedural propriety and rationality (but it may be noted that, in following those roles in the many mixed law and fact situations which arose, the courts may covertly have pursued something approaching an appellate jurisdiction).

THE IMPACT OF JUDICIAL REVIEW

The Interpretation Role

It is obvious that whether a homelessness duty arises and, if so, the extent of that duty, depends on the applicant coming within certain categories of applicant (of fitting into certain boxes). Housing authorities have been given considerable guidance by a series of Codes of Practice[8] as to central government views regarding how the appropriate statutory provisions are to be interpreted but many of the key phrases have been left for interpretation by the courts, and in the early years this was the principal role of judicial review applications and decisions.

To be within the homelessness scheme an applicant must be homeless or threatened with homelessness. A person is homeless if that person has no accommodation and a person cannot be treated as having accommodation unless it is accommodation which it would be reasonable for him or her to continue to occupy. Furthermore, regard may be had, in determining whether it would be reasonable for a person to continue to occupy accommodation, to the general circumstances prevailing in relation to housing in the district of the housing authority to which he or she has applied for accommodation or for assistance in obtaining accommodation. A person will be treated as having no accommodation if there is no accommodation which that person (together with any other person who normally resides with him or her either as a member of the family or in circumstances in which it is reasonable for the persons to reside together) is entitled to occupy, *inter alia*, by virtue of an interest in it, by an order of a court, or by an express or implied licence. A person is homeless if he or she has accommodation but cannot effectively use or occupy that accommodation in three sets of circumstances, namely he or she cannot secure entry to it, it is probable (i.e., not certain) that occupation of it will lead to violence from some other person residing in the accommodation or to threats of violence from some other person residing in the accommodation and likely to carry out the threats, or it consists of a moveable structure, vehicle or vessel designed or adapted for human habitation (e.g., a mobile home, caravan or houseboat) and there is no place where he or she is entitled or permitted both to place it (or moor it) and to reside in it.[9] A person is threatened with homelessness if it is likely that that person will become homeless within twenty-eight days.[10] Since there is no statutory definition of the word 'accommodation', the courts were called upon to assist. It was held that 'accommodation' must, by definition, be capable of accommodating and that if a place is properly capable of being regarded as accommodation from an objective standpoint, but is so small a space that it is incapable of accommodating the applicant together with other persons who normally reside with the applicant as members of his or her family, then on the facts of such a case the applicant would be homeless because he or she would have no accommodation in any relevant sense.[11] To be homeless and to have found some temporary accommodation are not mutually inconsistent concepts and homelessness does not cease if a person has a roof over his or her head. An obviously temporary letting or licence will not necessarily cause homelessness to cease[12] and, although a tenancy may still exist on paper, 'accommodation' must refer to habitable accommodation and premises which have been completely vandalized, during a person's temporary absence, are not 'accommodation'.[13] However, 'accommodation' does not mean settled or permanent accommodation.[14] Other cases brought other situations within the 'homeless box', namely women living in temporary emergency refuges for battered women[15] and a man living in an overnight shelter which accepted persons in order of arrival but who would not be given lodging there if the shelter was full when he arrived.[16]

To be within the homelessness scheme an applicant must have a priority need for accommodation by reason of coming within certain categories: a pregnant woman or a person with whom a pregnant woman resides or might reasonably be expected to reside, a person with whom dependent children reside or might reasonably be expected to reside, a person who is vulnerable as a result of old age, mental illness or handicap or physical disability or other special reason, or with whom such a vulnerable person resides or might reasonably be expected to reside (below), or a person who is homeless or threatened with homelessness as a result of an emergency.[17] Housing authorities have been given considerable guidance on vulnerability by the Code, but, since the statute does not provide an exhaustive definition of vulnerability, certain guidelines have been laid down by the courts. For example, where a man aged 59, with a drink problem, suffered a severe head injury and, from then onwards, could not fend for himself, it was held that he was vulnerable,[18] but a person with a history of drug dependence where there was no evidence that she was less able to obtain suitable accommodation than the ordinary person was held not vulnerable.[19] With regard to mental handicap, it has been held that this does not mean mental illness but rather subnormality or severe subnormality and where an applicant with a record of incompetence was subnormal and was incapable of articulating in either English or her native language, it was held, in the circumstances of the case, that no housing authority properly instructing themselves by means of adequate inquiries could have come to any other conclusion but that the applicant was vulnerable.[20]

A person who is homeless (or threatened with homelessness) and has a priority need must then pass the next hurdle, that of unintentional homelessness and because of the effect of a finding of intentional homelessness, there have been many cases on this subject. A person becomes homeless intentionally if that person deliberately does or fails to do anything in consequence of which he or she ceases to occupy accommodation which is available for his or her occupation and which it would have been reasonable to continue to occupy. A person becomes threatened with homelessness intentionally if that person deliberately does or fails to do anything the likely result of which is that he or she will be forced to leave accommodation which is available for his or her occupation and which it would have been reasonable to continue to occupy. For the purposes of the above rules, an act or omission in good faith on the part of a person who was unaware of any relevant fact will not be treated as deliberate. In determining whether it would have been reasonable for a person to continue to occupy accommodation, regard may be had to the general circumstances prevailing in relation to housing in the district of the housing authority to whom the person applied for accommodation or for assistance in obtaining accommodation.[21]

As was seen above, an undoubtedly homeless person with priority need may find that intentional homelessness is a key factor in his or her housing problems and this, coupled with the language of intentional homelessness ('deliberately does or fails to do', 'in consequence of which', 'the likely result of which', 'accommodation which is available for his or her occupation', 'which it would have been reasonable to continue to occupy', 'in good faith', 'unaware of any relevant fact', and 'the general circumstances prevailing in relation to housing in the district of the housing authority') has resulted in many judicial review applications being made, which have involved a very thorough examination of the, often complicated and long-running, sets of facts leading to something akin to the exercise of an appellate jurisdiction in that the finding by way of judicial review is either 'yes' or 'no' and there is no way the housing authority can act other than to accept that finding and its consequences.

Sometimes intentional homelessness cases raise a question as to the intentions of an applicant and involve an investigation into the applicant's mind. Problems arose with regard to acquiescence in a deliberate act or omission made by one person to the detriment of his or her family or household resulting in homelessness (or threatened homelessness). Sometimes, acquiescence was found, for example, the failure to terminate a partner's right to remain in the accommodation and permitting that person to remain in the accommodation despite repeated warnings that his conduct (nuisance to neighbours when drunk) could well lead to possession proceedings,[22] a cohabitee causing nuisance when the applicant (in prison) had not sought to show his disapproval of the cohabitee's conduct and had done nothing to prevent the nuisance from continuing,[23] and co-operation by both spouses in a decision to move home.[24] Sometimes, acquiescence was not found, for example, a wife who was not a party to the decision to leave accommodation[25] and an applicant rendered homeless by the vandalism of premises by her husband, when in no way was she a party to the vandalism.[26] The phrase 'unaware of any relevant fact' also involves an investigation into the mind of an applicant, for example, an applicant arriving from Jamaica unaware that her proposed accommodation was inadequate[27] or an applicant's knowledge of methods of finance (including social security benefits) which might lead to retaining accommodation.[28]

The courts, in their role of interpretation, have had to define (or list) the types of deliberate acts and omissions 'in consequence of which' or 'the likely result of which' is the loss (or threatened loss) of available accommodation. Examples include failure to pay rent,[29] failure to seek a contribution from nondependants whose presence in the household resulted in a reduction in housing benefit entitlement, despite having been informed of the effect of nondependants in the household,[30] persistent failure to make mortgage payments,[31] breaches of covenants resulting in an order for possession of the property,[32] eviction because of misbehaviour of an applicant's children,[33] eviction because of violent and intimidatory behaviour by both an applicant and his wife, plus complaints of vandalism on the part of the applicant's children,[34] abandoning the property,[35] and loss of tied accommodation because of loss of relevant employment (and here the reasonableness of an employer's act of dismissal will have an obvious importance).[36]

In many cases, the causal connection between the act or omission and the loss (or threatened loss) of accommodation is strong and straightforward, with nonpayment of rent or mortgage payments and breach of a covenant leading immediately or inexorably to eviction or foreclosure. However, the further the act or omission becomes an act or omission in the past, the more tenuous becomes the causal connection between a past act or omission and present or current homelessness. It may happen that there is a series of events leading up to a state of homelessness. People may deliberately give up secure accommodation (e.g., for family or employment reasons) and move to other accommodation which they subsequently have to leave. For the ensuing homelessness to be intentional, there must be a continuing causal connection between the deliberate act in consequence of which homelessness resulted and the homelessness existing at the date of the inquiry made when the applicant requests the housing authority for accommodation (or for assistance in obtaining accommodation).[37] Some of the most difficult decisions have had to be made with regard to the 'causal connection' question and here, once again, applications for judicial review have most resembled applications for appeals against findings (or at least inferences to be drawn from findings) of facts. For example, whether homelessness was directly attributable to matrimonial breakdown rather than to the earlier leaving of secure accommodation in order to emigrate with a husband,[38] the effect of voluntarily leaving a flat in which there was entitlement to occupy and signing a temporary holiday letting tenancy agreement for another flat,[39] leaving a caravan site to live at a number of addresses, including a bed and breakfast establishment which had subsequently closed down,[40] making no arrangements to keep current accommodation available pending return from a long holiday abroad,[41] whether homelessness was due to anti-social behaviour or a threat by the IRA to kill because of that behaviour,[42] whether homelessness was directly attributable to non-payment of rent or sexual harassment,[43] taking up precarious accommodation,[44] and whether an applicant's financial activity in dealing with a second mortgage was such as to put retention of accommodation at risk.[45] Occasionally, it has been specifically held, in an action for judicial review, that on the facts the local housing authority's decision ought to have been that an applicant's home-lessness was not intentional (e.g., because the court held that the applicant had acted in good faith).[46]

As stated above, if a person leaves accommodation which was then available for occupation, intentional homelessness will depend on whether it was reasonable for that person to continue to occupy that accommodation. If it was not so reasonable, there can be no finding of intentional homelessness. In determining whether it would have been reasonable for a person to continue to occupy accommodation, regard may be had to the general circumstances prevailing in relation to housing in the area of the housing authority which received the application for accommodation or for assistance in obtaining accommodation. Such questions raised both an objective test comparing the applicant's situation with that of others and a subjective test of the applicant's perceived view of his or her situation. With regard to the objective test, inevitably *Wednesbury* reasonableness raised its head. Overcrowding in the applicant's previous accommodation was held to be a relevant factor,[47] and where a family consisted of a man, his wife and four children (aged, respectively, 12, 7, 4 and four months) it was considered astonishing that a housing authority should regard it as reasonable that a family of that size should live in one room 10 ft by 12 ft in size. Although reasonableness must take account of the general circumstances prevailing in relation to housing in the area, there was no evidence that accommodation in the relevant area was so desperately short that it was reasonable to accept overcrowding of that degree.[48] In addition to the physical nature of the accommodation, in deciding whether it would have been reasonable for an applicant to continue to occupy accommodation, the courts have held that regard may be had also to the applicant's lack of employment prospects and lack of entitlement to social security benefits,[49] whether there was any evidence of violence from a husband making it unreasonable to continue to occupy the matrimonial home,[50] whether it was reasonable to leave accommodation in the face of proceedings for possession,[51] whether a person suffering from an acute back condition should continue to live in a house on a very steep hill,[52] and whether sectarian violence made it reasonable to leave home.[53]

As was seen above, a housing authority may be under a duty (whether 'limited' or 'full') to secure accommodation for an applicant. In determining whether accommodation is suitable the authority must have regard to housing and public health legislation relating to housing standards.[54] Occasionally the initial decision as to the appropriateness or suitability of accommodation of the housing authority has been the subject of judicial review proceedings, once again raising the mixed law and fact elements with regard to *Wednesbury* unreasonableness.[55] Occasionally, it has been held on the facts that no reasonable authority could have determined that the accommodation actually offered was suitable (and this is tantamount to a direction that the housing authority cannot force the applicant to live there).[56] It has been held that, whereas it may, on the facts, be unreasonable to refuse an offer of accommodation, suitable with respect to size, in the applicant's own area where he or she has a local connection, and whereas the offer of accommodation need not be in the area of the housing authority to whom the application was made, it is different when the offer is only of accommodation in a far-off area in which the applicant has no connection and has been given only a few days in which to consider the offer,[57] that the housing authority must take into account strong evidence of racial harassment[58] and of all relevant social and medical factors.[59]

Procedural Safeguards and Propriety

It will have been obvious that, in order for an applicant to come within the inclusionary categories (homeless or threatened with homelessness, priority need and non-intentional homelessness) or for the housing authority to determine that the applicant does not come within those categories, there has to be an investigation into the situation of the applicant. So many factors may be relevant: the size and structure of the household, the age of the applicant, the number of any dependants, the nature and location of the accommodation last occupied, the reason for leaving it, the prospect of return, the question of the availability of accommodation elsewhere, any particular problems such as illness or handicap, any need for accommodation at some distance from a violent partner, the place and type of employment, family connections, or attendance at hospitals and schools, and financial status. Obviously it is important for an applicant to provide as much information as possible to the housing authority but many applicants may not be able to draw up a list of better particulars and a fact-finding duty is imposed on the authority, a truly important procedural requirement, since applicants may often be under considerable strain, may be confused, may not find it easy to explain their position clearly and logically and, in certain areas, the presence of an interpreter may be desirable. Consequently, if an applicant applies to a housing authority for accommodation, or for assistance in obtaining accommodation, and the authority have reason to believe that the applicant may be (i.e., not is) homeless or threatened with homelessness, they are under a duty to make such inquiries as are necessary to satisfy themselves as to whether he or she is in fact homeless or threatened with homelessness. If they are satisfied that the applicant is in fact homeless or threatened with homelessness, the authority must then make any further inquiries necessary to satisfy themselves as to whether the applicant has a priority need and also whether the applicant became homeless or threatened with homelessness intentionally.[60]

Failure to make adequate inquiries may lead to a decision being quashed on the *Wednesbury* ground that no reasonable housing authority, properly instructed, could have made the decision. It is significant to note that, once the inclusionary categories had been more or less defined with certainty during the first few years of the original homelessness scheme, a very large proportion of judicial review applications in the second decade of that scheme centred on allegations that inadequate inquiries have been made by the housing authority, with the result that an adverse determination had been made, whereas, had those inquiries been adequate, a different determination would, or might, have resulted. These applications were presumably designed to obtain an instruction to the housing authority to look again.

The extent and degree of the duty to make inquiries has been detailed by the courts. It has been held that a housing authority are under a duty to make adequate administrative arrangements to receive applications and that in heavily populated areas this may mean 24-hour cover.[61] Generally, an applicant should be interviewed personally but failure to interview is not fatal to the decision if other inquiries are adequate.[62] It has been held that a housing authority should make their inquiries vigorously and elicit all relevant facts. Where a question of intentional homelessness arose in the case of a couple living with one set of parents, it was held that a ten-minute conversation with those parents was inadequate.[63] However, the test is to make such inquiries as a reasonable housing authority would make and the authority are under no positive duty to conduct 'CID-type' inquiries. There is no obligation imposed on the local housing authority to seek the standard of evidence required in a court of law and there is no requirement for evidence to be corroborated or to ignore hearsay evidence.[64] If the applicant provides no evidence or information on a particular matter the housing authority may be excused for not investigating it.[65] Where an applicant has come to Great Britain from abroad, it may not be possible to make as full inquiries as will be possible in the case of an applicant already within Great Britain and authorities must do their best in such circumstances,[66] but 'their best' must be sufficient.[67]

It has been held that, in making their inquiries, a housing authority must comply with the *audi alteram partem* rule and that an applicant should be given the opportunity to see and comment on material information gathered during the inquiries.[68] Inquiries should be made in a caring and sympathetic way.[69] The applicant must be given an opportunity to explain matters which the housing authority are minded to regard as weighing substantially against him or her,[70] but the authority are under no obligation to present for comment by the applicant every fact obtained during their inquiries[71] and there is no rule of general application that if bad faith is attributed to an alleged intentionally homeless applicant that the matter must be specifically put to that applicant.[72] However, if a matter is 'decisive' (e.g., the state of an applicant's health) that must be put to the applicant.[73] The *audi alteram partem* rule would appear most important in cases where a determination of intentional homelessness may be made but it has been held that there is no obligation to give an applicant an oral hearing before such a determination is made.[74] Where an application was resubmitted for further consideration to a meeting of council officials in order to make inquiries to obtain information to present to the appropriate housing authority committee, the applicant was not invited but the meeting was attended by a professional housing aid adviser who was permitted to play an active part in representing his interests and who, because of her professional ability, was assumed to put his case much better and more forcefully than he would ever have done, there was no reason to doubt that full natural justice was afforded to the applicant.[75]

In certain situations, more specific duties have been imposed. If there is evidence that an applicant might have dependent children living with him or her (raising the question of priority need), that must be fully investigated,[76] as must any claim that an applicant is vulnerable (again raising the question of priority need), based on medical facts[77] or drug dependency.[78] Where evidence in a medical report stated that an applicant was subnormal, it was held that if the authority had had some doubts as to the degree of subnormality, then the duty was upon them to make the appropriate inquiries: either they ought to have accepted that the applicant was subnormal or, if they were not sure about the degree of subnormality or whether it was present at all, they ought to have made the inquiries. In not making such inquiries, the housing authority did not properly instruct themselves and were in error in law in that respect.[79] Whether an applicant is intentionally homeless is to be measured objectively and, in the case of an applicant stating that she was frightened of sectarian violence in Belfast, the (English) housing authority were enjoined to make sufficient inquiries so as to appreciate the effect of such violence on the particular applicant (who had a young daughter).[80] Furthermore, allegations of the risk of domestic violence should be fully investigated,[81] as should allegations that sexual harassment resulted in an applicant leaving accommodation.[82] If there is a possible question of an applicant stating that he or she was unaware of an important fact, then the housing authority are obliged to make such inquiries as are necessary to satisfy themselves whether the applicant was unaware of the fact and whether the fact was indeed a material one,[83] for example, whether an applicant was genuinely unaware as to entitlement to housing benefit[84] or as to the realities of the financial world.[85] In the context of an employee occupying tied accommodation and being dismissed from that employment and accommodation, resulting in a determination of intentional homelessness, there must be a thorough examination as to why the person was dismissed, since not every dismissal is as a result of a deliberate act or omission, and if there is doubt or uncertainty after making the necessary inquiries that uncertainty is to be resolved in favour of the applicant.[86] In the case of a reapplication, facts found after a previous application will, if unchanged, be relevant to the housing authority's subsequent action. A reapplication which is not made on fresh grounds or with fresh material may be rejected by the authority if they have done all that was necessary to inquire into the matter on the previous application; if an application is made on new grounds or with new material, the authority are bound to look into the matter again. The authority are entitled to reopen the matter of their own accord if they take the view (e.g., after representations being made to them) that they are no longer satisfied upon the matters which they had to be satisfied and in relation to which appropriate inquiries had to be made.[87]

The homelessness scheme imposes a number of duties on housing authorities to notify the applicant of those decisions and to give reasons for their decisions. The authority are under a duty to notify the applicant of their decision whether the applicant is homeless or threatened with homelessness, whether there is a priority need and whether the applicant became homeless or threatened with homelessness intentionally.[88] The notice must be given in writing. Normally the housing authority will notify the applicant of their decision (and, where required, their reasons) by delivering or sending it to his or her place of residence. However, notification and/or reasons will, if not actually received by the applicant, be treated as having been given to him or her only if they are made available at the authority's office (e.g., the housing department office or a housing aid centre) for a reasonable period for collection by or on behalf of the applicant.[89] The duty to give reasons is an important one as the reasons may show that an authority has misinterpreted or misused the appropriate legal provisions, and thus enable the applicant to seek redress. The reasons must explain the housing authority's decision clearly and intelligibly,[90] they must state the facts on which the decision is based and state why an applicant does or does not come within an inclusionary category,[91] particularly if the decision appears to contradict strong evidence raised by an applicant (in this case the relevance of medical evidence and suitability of accommodation offered).[92] If the reasons are inadequate, the decision will be quashed.[93] To state, in a determination of intentional homelessness, merely that 'regard has been given to the general circumstances prevailing in relation to housing' in a particular area has been held to be manifestly defective.[94]

HOMELESSNESS CASES AND ADMINISTRATIVE LAW

The fact that under the pre-1996 Act homelessness scheme, if administrative redress failed, an applicant wishing to take legal action to challenge the local housing authority's decision had no statutory right of appeal to a court or tribunal and that the only method of challenge was an application for judicial review resulted in many applications for, and decisions on, that homelessness scheme which have made a significant contribution to the development of general principles of administrative law. In particular, such decisions have made a contribution to the grounds for judicial review and by interpreting key words and phrases in the former scheme have laid a firm basis for guidance to the special appellate jurisdiction (to be described below, where it will be seen that a right of appeal lies 'on a point of law'). Early on, homelessness cases raised the dichotomy between a housing authority's public law and private law functions and contributed to what has become known as the principle of procedural exclusivity. It was held that the homelessness duties of a housing authority are public law duties. The power of decision in such matters is committed exclusively to the authority, there being no statutory right of appeal, and as such can only be challenged before the courts on the general principles relating to judicial review of administration. It is inherent in the homelessness scheme that an appropriate public law decision of a housing authority is a condition precedent to the establishment of any private law duty. The homelessness public law functions must, therefore, be challenged by means of an application for judicial review. Once a decision has been reached by a housing authority which gives rise to the temporary, limited or full housing duty, rights and obligations are immediately created in the field of private law. Each of the above duties, once established, is capable of being enforced by injunction and the breach of it gives rise to liability in damages.[95] In addition to the exclusionary principle, a number of cases, where the action or inaction of a housing authority was clearly susceptible to judicial review, have been of particular relevance to general rules of administrative law, according to the now-accepted division of illegality, procedural impropriety and irrationality: misinterpretation of the provisions of the homelessness legislation,[96] fettering discretion,[97] breach of statutory and common law rules of procedural propriety,[98] decisions not taking into account matters which clearly should have been taken into account,[99] decisions based on a conclusion unsupported by the facts,[100] and decisions so unreasonable that no reasonable housing authority could have taken them.[101]

However, despite the fact that judicial review cases mapped out the homelessness scheme, added flesh to the legislative provisions and insisted on standards of procedural propriety and rationality and despite the fact that the plight of the homeless is a desperate one, there has been judicial warning that, in view of the nature of the application for judicial review, which is a discretionary remedy, it is not appropriate to use judicial review to monitor the actions of housing authorities, save in the most exceptional or perverse cases.[102] Consequently, towards the end of the twenty-year period in which the impact of judicial review on the homelessness scheme operated, some started to question whether the same impact could not have been achieved to the same degree and in a more efficient and user-friendly manner by another judicial forum. In particular, questions were raised as to the expense of proceedings for judicial review (the effect of such expense on the budgets of housing authorities allocated for housing purposes in general and the thorny question whether money expended on legal proceedings might be better devoted towards the provision of housing), on the London-based High Court and on the delays involved in coming to a decision for the applicant by way of judicial review. These views were taken up by the Law Commission and by the Government when it was preparing the new homelessness scheme (in what is now the Housing Act 1996, Part VII).

In its Report *Administrative Law: Judicial Review and Statutory Appeals*,[103] the Law Commission pointed out that in 1993 out of 2414 applications, 447 related to homelessness (with 668 immigration and 472 criminal cases), that leave was granted in 40.8 per cent of the homelessness cases, with 23.2 per cent being withdrawn, and concluded that the figures demonstrated the extent to which the resources of the High Court (both judges and deputies) were being devoted to homelessness cases because Parliament had provided no other right of recourse to those who were dissatisfied with a local authority's decision. They referred to the fact that in the earlier Consultation Paper *Administrative Law: Judicial Review and Statutory Appeals*,[104] they had (in view of the large increase in applications for leave to move for judicial review and the long delays in hearing cases) invited views on the question of whether Parliament ought to provide some form of appeal to a court or tribunal. A number of persons responding to the Consultation Paper had discussed the desirability of creating an intermediate right of appeal (to a county court or tribunal) in homelessness cases, from which appeal on a point of law might possibly lie to the Court of Appeal. The absence of an internal mechanism of review by a senior official or other body was also identified as contributing to the problems in cases where there is no right of appeal, since, although an internal review is not a substitute for an appeal to an independent adjudicative body, it is likely to lead to a better standard of decision-making. While an internal review would be welcomed, the Law Commission did not believe that the provision of an internal review could be regarded as a proper substitute for a right of appeal to a court or an independent tribunal and recommended the creation of such a right of appeal in homelessness cases. This might lie either to an independent tribunal or to the county court. Although there were certain advantages in an appeal to a tribunal, there was no obvious candidate and the cost implications in creating a new tribunal, particularly a locally-based one, had to be set against the benefits of a tailor-made body. The Law Commission backed the county court proposition since the advantages of the county court were that it already dealt with other housing matters (including breach by a housing authority of its statutory duty to provide accommodation once the existence of a statutory homelessness duty is established) and it is a local court. As far as the scope of the appeal was concerned, the Law Commission believed that, as a minimum, there should be a right of appeal on a point of law and recommended this. The Law Commission noted that as an error of law is almost invariably likely to be *ultra vires*, the effect of this would primarily be a change of forum from the High Court.

The Government had also been considering the question as to how to lessen the present reliance on judicial review as part of its review of the homelessness legislation and proposed that housing authorities should be required to establish a formal mechanism whereby a person can challenge a decision by the authority's officers on a homelessness application and that this would be followed up by a right of appeal on a point of law.

THE NEW PROVISIONS

It may be noted than many housing authorities had established internal review systems or internal appeal machinery, of a variety of nomenclature, and that these in so many cases provided an applicant with a second chance to press his or her claim (especially an opportunity to question the factual or legal basis of the original adverse decision). The Housing Act 1996 places this on a mandatory statutory footing and an applicant has the right to request a review of specified decisions of a housing authority. These decisions, of course, are decisions under the Housing Act 1996, Part VII, which in some cases has extended and in some cases has limited the homelessness duties of housing authorities under the former scheme discussed above. What follows must be read subject to this qualification. A right to request a review applies to the following decisions.[105] First, decisions of a housing authority as to a person's eligibility for assistance, which incorporates a reference to new provisions relating to persons from abroad and certain asylum seekers.[106] Second, decisions of a housing authority as to what homelessness duty (if any) is owed to an applicant (and this incorporates findings as to homelessness, threatened homelessness, priority need and intentional homelessness).[107] Third, decisions of a housing authority which bring into play provisions allowing for the referral of cases to another local authority and duties owed to an applicant whose case is considered for referral or referred.[108] Fourth, any decision of a housing authority as to the suitability of accommodation offered to the applicant in discharge of the duties mentioned above.[109] Certain homelessness decisions are not subject to the mandatory review procedure[110] and, therefore, judicial review may in the future have a role to play in such circumstances. There is no right to request a review of the decision reached on an earlier review.[111] A request for review must be made before the end of the period of twenty-one days beginning with the day on which the applicant is notified of the authority's decision (or such longer period as the authority may in writing allow).[112] On a request being duly made to them, the authority (or authorities) concerned 'shall' (i.e., there is a duty) review their decision.[113]

A statutory right to request a review is, on principle, to be approved as it gives the applicant a second opportunity to present his or her case in the light of the reasons given by the housing authority. This mandatory requirement, coupled with the prospect of an automatic appeal, may, in the future, lead housing authorities to determine to get it right at this stage (rather than, as has been suggested, await a successful application for leave to apply for judicial review before so proceeding).

The procedure to be followed on a review is of great importance in that it must afford the applicant every opportunity to put his or her case at a hearing which to all intents and purposes will be the last opportunity to obtain a definitive finding of fact. If the review is conducted by an officer of the housing authority (as opposed to the authority or any emanation thereof), the decision on review must be made by a person senior to the person who made the original decision and who was not involved in the original decision. On receipt of any request for a review, the housing authority are under a duty to inform the applicant that the applicant (or any representative) may make written representations to the authority. Any such representations must be considered by the authority which must carry out the review on the basis of the factual situation as at the date of review. It may happen that the authority consider that, although the original decision was made irregularly, nevertheless the authority consider that they will make a decision which is adverse to the applicant and in such a situation the authority must notify the applicant of the applicant's right to make oral representations on the matter.[114] The authority (or, as the case may be, either of the authorities) concerned must notify the applicant of the decision on the review within eight weeks of the day on which the request for a review was made (or such longer period as may be agreed). If the decision is to confirm the original decision on any issue against the interests of the applicant, they must also notify him or her of the reasons for the decision (reasons must also be given if the decision is to confirm a previous decision to refer the case to another authority). In any case they must inform the applicant of his or her right to appeal to a county court on a point of law, and of the period within which such an appeal must be made. Notice of the decision can not be treated as given unless and until the above rules relating to the giving of reasons and appeal rights have been complied with. Notice required to be given to a person under the above must be given in writing and, if not received by him or her, will be treated as having been given if it is made available at the authority's office for a reasonable period for collection by the person or on his or her behalf.[115]

If an applicant who has requested a review is either dissatisfied with the decision on the review or is not notified of the decision on the review within the time limit stated above, he or she may appeal to the county court on any point of law arising from the decision or, as the case may be, the original decision. An appeal must be brought within twenty-one days of the applicant's being notified of the decision or, as the case may be, of the date on which he or she should have been notified of a decision on review. On such an appeal, the court may make such order confirming, quashing or varying the decision as it thinks fit.[116]

As has been seen, both the Law Commission and the Government preferred the county court as the appellate authority to existing tribunals or – an alternative long canvassed by some involved in housing law – the establishment of a specialized Housing Court with a comprehensive jurisdiction along the lines of the Social Security Commissioners. Therefore, the principal research question for the next few years is to what extent the new review and appeal provisions form a more effective and efficient dispute settlement machinery for homelessness than that previously provided by judicial review. The county court has certain obvious advantages over existing tribunals since it is a local judicial forum of easy access and county court judges have wide experience of analogous housing law actions, and this may offset one argument for retaining judicial review, namely that a centralized bench can create and apply a more cohesive system of principles. It has been noticeable that a high proportion of applications for judicial review emanated from certain housing authorities which were faced with a greater number of applications for housing assistance and, as it is probable that this state of affairs will continue, the county courts for those areas will develop a high degree of expertise. Furthermore, it might be that a local court is better able to adjudge local housing conditions, where these are relevant to a homelessness determination. One factor which will be important is the extent to which county court cases on homelessness will be reported. The reporting of homelessness judicial review cases, particularly in the *Housing Law Reports*, has resulted in the comprehensive development of homelessness administrative law being made available to those advising local housing authorities on that law and being incorporated in successive Codes of Practice issued by the Department of the Environment. It has not been so normal to report county court cases on housing matters and it is to be hoped that those responsible will change this situation, rather than to permit a dearth of first instance reporting.

An appeal on a point of law will, it is suggested, cover the same grounds of *ultra vires* applied by the High Court in judicial review proceedings, the grounds of illegality, irrationality and procedural impropriety (and their various sub-headings). For many years, appeals on the ground that a decision of one of the several appeal tribunals dealing with social security appeal matters was 'erroneous in point of law' have resulted in the Social Security Commissioners creating a catalogue of errors identical to those created by the High Court.[117]

With regard to procedure, a number of matters should be raised.

(It should be noted that what follows will, of course, be subject to any consequential amendments to county and other court procedural rules.) First of all, it must be emphasized that, if an appellate jurisdiction has been provided by Parliament, that jurisdiction must be used first by the aggrieved applicant who should first exhaust whatever other rights he or she has by way of appeal. It was a long-standing principle that the prerogative orders of certiorari and mandamus will lie only where there is no other equally effective, beneficial and convenient remedy[118] and it has been referred to as 'a cardinal principle' that, except in the most exceptional circumstances, the supervisory jurisdiction will not be exercised where other remedies were available and have not been used.[119] The factors which the courts will take into account when deciding whether to grant relief by way of judicial review, when an alternative remedy is available, are whether the alternative statutory appeal remedy will resolve the question at issue fully and directly, whether the statutory procedure would be quicker, or slower, than by way of judicial review, and whether the matter depends on some particular or technical knowledge which is more readily available to the alternative appellate body.[120] The above factors would all appear to be present in the new appeal system, and judicial review proceedings should, on principle, become something of a residual nature, relating only to any matter not within the scope of internal review (since the appellate provisions only relate to matters within the review jurisdiction). Second, an appeal must be brought within twenty-one days and this is a shorter period than that allowed for the commencement of judicial review proceedings. One important question for future research is whether this short period (albeit following what could be a lengthy time during which the review takes place) might tempt applicants to 'bung in an appeal' in cases where there may be little foundation, especially as there is no requirement for leave (which in judicial review proceedings acted as a filter to weed out unmeritorious applications). Finally, since the right of appeal is that of the applicant who has requested a review, such an applicant will automatically have *locus standi* (to use judicial review terminology), even if the appeal is instigated or supported by an organization or pressure group wishing to undertake a test-case strategy.

In some ways, it is not so much the grounds on which the county court will act and the procedures that it will follow which are to be the subject of future analysis but the statutory power given to the court. The former have already been mapped out by the application of general principles of administrative law and are well established. What is not so established, especially within the context of the problems of dispute settlement in homelessness situations, is the extent of the court's powers. 'Confirm' and 'quash' are analogous to the findings of validity and invalidity of housing authorities' decisions by way of judicial review. An appellate jurisdiction means that the county court can substitute its decision for that of the housing authority (or review authority) and the use of the word 'vary' may be seen by some as resulting in homelessness decisions on matters of fact being taken by the county court rather than by the authority – that, of course, is for the future.

NOTES

1 And then consolidated in the Housing Act (HA) 1985, Part III.
2 Housing Act 1996 (Commencement No. 5 and Transitional Provisions) Order 1996 (SI 1996, No. 2959).
3 HA 1985, s. 64(4), (5).
4 HA 1985, s. 64(4), (5); s. 65(4); s. 66(3).
5 HA 1985, s. 64(4), (5); s. 66(3).
6 HA 1985, s. 64(4), (5); s. 65(3).
7 HA 1985, s. 65(2); s. 66(2), (4); s. 75.
8 See *Homelessness: Code of Guidance for Local Authorities* (Department of the Environment) (various editions and recently revised in December 1996 to meet the 1996 Act scheme).
9 HA 1985, s. 58(1); s. 58(2); s. 58 (2A), (2B), both as inserted by the Homeless Persons Act (HPA) 1966, s. 14(2); s. 58(3).
10 HA 1985, s. 58(4).
11 *Puhlhofer v Hillingdon LBC* [1986] 1 All ER 467 (HL).
12 *Din v Wandsworth LBC* [1983] 1 AC 657, *per* Lord Lowry, at 677.
13 *R v Gloucester City Council, ex parte Miles* (1985) 83 LGR 607 (CA).
14 *R v Brent LBC, ex parte Awua* [1996] 1 AC 55.
15 *R v Ealing LBC, ex parte Sidhu* (1982) 80 LGR 534.
16 *R v Waveney DC, ex parte Bowers* [1982] QB 238 (CA).
17 HA 1985, s. 59.
18 *R v Waveney DC, ex parte Bowers* [1983] QB 238 (CA).
19 *Ortiz v City of Westminster* (1993) 27 HLR 364 (CA).
20 *R v Bath City Council, ex parte Sangermano* (1984) 17 HLR 94.
21 HA 1985, s. 60.
22 *R v Swansea City Council, ex parte John* (1982) 9 HLR 56.
23 *R v Swansea City Council, ex parte Thomas* (1983) 9 HLR 64; *R v East Northamptonshire DC, ex parte Spruce* (1988) 20 HLR 508.
24 *R v Tower Hamlets LBC, ex parte Khatun* (1993) 27 HLR 344 (CA).
25 *Lewis v North Devon DC* [1981] 1 WLR 238.
26 *R v Gloucester City Council, ex parte Miles* (1985) 83 LGR 607 (CA).
27 *R v Wandsworth LBC, ex parte Rose* (1983) 11 HLR 107.
28 *R v City of Westminster, ex parte Moozary-Oraky* (1993) 26 HLR 213.
29 *R v Wandsworth LBC, ex parte Hawthorne* [1994] 1 WLR 1442 (CA).
30 *R v West Somerset DC, ex parte Blake*, 10 July 1986 (McCowan J).

31 *R v Eastleigh BC, ex parte Beattie* (1984) 14 Fam. Law 115.

32 *R v Swansea City Council, ex parte Thomas* (1983) 9 HLR 64.

33 *R v Salford City Council, ex parte Devenport* (1984) 82 LGR 89 (CA).

34 *R v Southampton City Council, ex parte Ward* (1984) 14 HLR 114.

35 *Lally v Kensington and Chelsea Royal Borough Council, The Times*, 27 March 1980; cf. on the facts, *R v Gloucester City Council, ex parte Miles* (1985) 83 LGR 607 (CA).

36 *R v Thurrock BC* (1981) 1 HLR 128; *R v Thanet DC, ex parte Reeve, The Times*, 25 November 1981.

37 *Din v Wandsworth LBC* [1983] 1 AC 657, *per* Lord Fraser, at 672.

38 *R v Basingstoke and Deane DC, ex parte Bassett* (1984) 14 Fam. Law 90.

39 *Dyson v Kerrier DC* [1980] 1 WLR 1205 (CA).

40 *R v London Borough of Harrow, ex parte Holland* (1982) 4 HLR 108 (CA); cf. *R v City of Gloucester, ex parte Miles* (1985) 83 LGR 607 (CA) (applicant already homeless when she ceased to occupy accommodation because the premises had then been vandalized by her husband: held not intentional homelessness).

41 *R v Wycombe DC, ex parte Mahsood* (1988) 20 HLR 683.

42 *R v LB of Hammersmith and Fulham, ex parte P* (1989) 20 HLR 21.

43 *R v Newham LBC, ex parte Campbell* (1993) 26 HLR 183.

44 *R v Croydon LBC, ex parte Graham* (1994) 26 HLR 286 (CA).

45 *R v Wandsworth LBC, ex parte Onwudiwe* (1994) 26 HLR 302 (CA).

46 *R v Exeter City Council, ex parte Tranckle* (1993) 26 HLR 244 (CA).

47 *R v Eastleigh BC, ex parte Beattie* (1984) 14 Fam. Law 115 (DC).

48 *R v Westminster City Council, ex parte Ali* (1983) 11 HLR 83.

49 *R v Hammersmith and Fulham LBC, ex parte Duro-Rama* (1983) 81 LGR 702.

50 *R v Wandsworth LBC, ex parte Nimako-Boateng* (1984) 14 Fam. Law 117.

51 Din v *Wandsworth LBC* [1983] 1 AC 657; *R v Portsmouth City Council, ex parte Knight* (1984) 82 LGR 184; *R v Surrey Heath BC, ex parte Li* (1984) 16 HLR 83 (DC).

52 *R v Wycombe DC, ex parte Queenie Homes and Dean Homes* (1990) 22 HLR 150.

53 *R v Newham LBC, ex parte McIlroy* (1991) 23 HLR 570.

54 HA 1985, s. 69(1), as substituted by the HPA 1986, s. 14(3).

55 *R v Exeter City Council, ex parte Glidden* [1985] 1 All ER 493; *R v Ryedale DC, ex parte Smith* (1983) 16 HLR 69; *R v London Borough of Ealing, ex parte McBain* (1985) 85 LGR 278 (CA); *R v LB of Lewisham, ex parte Dolan* (1992) 25 HLR 68.

56 *R v Brent LBC, ex parte Omar* (1991) 23 HLR 446.

57 *R v Wyre BC, ex parte Parr, The Times*, 4 February 1982 (CA).

58 *R v Tower Hamlets LBC, ex parte Subhan* (1992) 24 HLR 541.

59 *R v Lewisham LBC, ex parte Dolan* (1992) 25 HLR 68.

60 HA 1985, s. 62(1), (2). In addition, the local housing authority may, if they think fit, also make inquiries as to whether the applicant has a local connection with the district of another local housing authority in England, Wales or Scotland (HA 1985, s. 62(2)). It may be noted that a local connection with the area of another local housing authority may result in the transfer of homelessness responsibility to that other authority.

61 *R v Camden LBC, ex parte Gillan* (1988) 21 HLR 114.

62 *Reynolds v Sevenoaks DC* (1990) 22 HLR 250 (CA).

63 *R v Dacorum BC, ex parte Brown, The Times,* 1 May 1989.

64 *R v Hillingdon Homeless Families Panel, ex parte Islam, The Times,* 9 February 1981; *R v Southampton City Council, ex parte Ward* [1984] FLR 608; *R v Nottingham City Council, ex parte Costello* (1989) 21 HLR 301.

65 *R v London Borough of Harrow, ex parte Holland* (1982) 4 HLR 108 (CA); *R v Wandsworth LBC, ex parte Henderson,* 10 April 1986.

66 *De Falco v Crawley BC* [1980] QB 460 (CA), *per* Sir David Cairnes, at 484.

67 *R v Westminster City Council, ex parte Iqbal* (1990) 22 HLR 215; *R v Tower Hamlets LBC, ex parte Bibi* (1991) 23 HLR 501.

68 *R v Tower Hamlets LBC, ex parte Rouf* (1989) 21 HLR 294.

69 *R v West Dorset DC, ex parte Phillips* (1984) 17 HLR 336; *R v Tower Hamlets LBC, ex parte Hoque, The Times,* 20 July 1993.

70 *R v Wyre DC, ex parte Joyce* (1983) 11 HLR 75 (DC).

71 *R v Southampton City Council, ex parte Ward* [1984] FLR 608; *R v Newham LBC, ex parte Bones* (1993) 25 HLR 357.

72 *Hobbs v Sutton LBC* (1993) 26 HLR 132 (CA).

73 *R v Tower Hamlets LBC, ex parte Sabor* (1992) 24 HLR 611.

74 *R v Harrow LBC, ex parte Hobbs, The Times,* 13 October 1992.

75 *R v West Somerset DC, ex parte Blake,* 10 July 1986.

76 *R v Lewisham LBC, ex parte Creppy* (1991) 24 HLR 121 (CA).

77 *R v Lambeth LBC, ex parte Carroll* (1988) 20 HLR 142.

78 *R v Islington LBC, ex parte Trail* [1994] 2 FCR 1261.

79 *R v Bath City Council, ex parte Sangermano* (1984) 17 HLR 94; *R v Wyre BC, ex parte Joyce* (1983) 11 HLR 73 (DC).

80 *R v Brent LBC, ex parte McManus* (1993) 25 HLR 643.

81 *Patterson v Greenwich LBC* (1993) 26 HLR 159 (CA); *R v Tynedale DC, ex parte McCabe* (1992) 24 HLR 384.

82 *R v Northampton BC, ex parte Clarkson* (1992) 24 HLR 529.

83 *R v Wandsworth LBC, ex parte Rose* (1983) 11 HLR 107.

84 *R v City of Westminster, ex parte Moozary-Oraky* (1993) 26 HLR 213.

85 *R v City of Westminster, ex parte Ali and Bibi* (1992) 24 HLR 109; *R v Tower Hamlets LBC, ex parte Ullah* (1992) 24 HLR 680.

86 *R v Thurrock BC, ex parte Williams* (1981) 1 HLR 128.

87 *R v Hambleton DC, ex parte Geoghan* [1985] JPL 394; *R v Dacorum BC, ex parte Walsh* (1991) 24 HLR 401.

88 HA 1985, s. 64(1), (2), (3), (4).

89 HA 1985, s. 64(5). For other reason-giving duties, see HA 1985, s. 67(1), (2); s. 68(3), (4); s. 70(6), (7).

90 *R v Tower Hamlets LBC, ex parte Ojo* (1991) 23 HLR 488.

91 *R v Islington LBC, ex parte Trail* [1994] 2 FCR 1261.

92 *R v Lambeth LBC, ex parte Walters* (1993) 26 HLR 170.

93 *R v Hillingdon LBC, ex parte H* (1988) 20 HLR 554; *R v Tynedale DC, ex parte Shield* (1990) 22 HLR 144.

94 *R v Northampton BC, ex parte Carpenter* (1993) 25 HLR 350.

95 *Cocks v Thanet DC* [1983] 2 AC 286. See also *Ali v Tower Hamlets LBC* [1992] 3 WLR 208; *LB of Tower Hamlets v Abdi* (1992) 25 HLR 68; *LB of Hackney v Lambourne* (1992) 25 HLR 172 (CA).

96 R v *London Borough of Ealing, ex parte Sidhu* (1982) 80 LGR 543.

97 R v *Newham LBC, ex parte Gentle* (1993) 26 HLR 466; R v *Newham LBC, ex parte Laronde* (1994) 27 HLR 215; R v *Islington LBC, ex parte Aldabbagh* (1994) 27 HLR 271; cf. R v *Bristol City Council, ex parte Johns* (1993) 25 HLR 249.

98 R v *Tower Hamlets LBC, ex parte Rouf* (1989) 21 HLR 294; R v *Wyre DC, ex parte Joyce* (1983) 11 HLR 75 (DC); R v *Tower Hamlets LBC, ex parte Sabor* (1992) 24 HLR 611; R v *Harrow LBC, ex parte Hobbs, The Times*, 13 October 1992.

99 R v *Wandsworth LBC, ex parte Rose* (1983) 11 HLR 107; R v *Bath City Council, ex parte Sangermano* (1984) 17 HLR 94; R v *Tower Hamlets LBC, ex parte Khalique* (1994) 26 HLR 517; cf. *Robinson v Torbay BC* [1982] 1 All ER 726, where the court was 'impressed with the amount of time and care and thought given by' the local housing authority in making a determination which took into account all relevant matters and did not take into account anything which should not have been taken into account.

100 R v *London Borough of Hillingdon, ex parte Islam* [1983] 1 AC 688.

101 R v *Westminster City Council, ex parte Ali* (1983) 11 HLR 83; R v *Tower Hamlets LBC, ex parte Ali* (1993) 25 HLR 218.

102 See, e.g., *Puhlhofer v Hillingdon LBC* [1986] 1 All ER 467 (HL).

103 Law Com. No. 226 (1994, HC No. 669 of 1993–94).

104 No. 126, 1993.

105 HA 1996, s. 202(1).

106 See HA 1996, ss. 185–7.

107 See HA 1996, ss. 190–3 and ss. 195–7.

108 See HA 1996, s. 198(1), s. 198(5), s. 200(3) or (4).

109 See HA 1996, ss. 206, 210.

110 See HA 1996, s. 188(1), (3) (interim duty to accommodate in case of apparent priority need); s. 194 (exercise of power to secure accommodation after the end of the minimum period of two years' duty to secure accommodation for persons with priority need and who are not homeless intentionally); s. 202(3) (exercise of power to extend the period of twenty-one days within which to request a review); s. 211 (exercise of power and duty to protect the property of persons).

111 HA 1996, s. 202(2).

112 HA 1996, s. 202(3).

113 HA 1996, s. 202(4).

114 Allocation of Housing and Homelessness (Review Procedures and Amendment) Regulations 1996 (SI 1996, No. 3122), Regulations 7, 8.

115 HA 1996, s. 203; SI 1996, No 3122, Regulation 9.

116 HA 1996, s. 204(1), (2), (3).

117 For a discussion, see Pollard, *Social Welfare Law*, §§C.3371–C.3410.

118 R v *Paddington Valuation Officer, ex parte Peachey Property Corp. Ltd* [1966] 1 QB 380; R v *Hillingdon London Borough, ex parte Royco Homes Ltd* [1974] QB 720.

119 R v *Epping and Harlow General Commissioners, ex parte Goldstraw* [1983] 3 All ER 257; R v *Chief Constable of the Merseyside Police, ex parte Calveley* [1986] QB 424; *Preston v IRC* [1985] AC 835.

120 R v *Hallstrom, ex parte W* [1986] QB 824; R v *Birmingham City Council, ex parte Ferrero Ltd* [1993] 1 All ER 530 (CA).

8

Judicial Review and Housing Benefit

MARTIN PARTINGTON

INTRODUCTION

This essay considers the impact that proceedings taken by way of judicial review may have had on the administration of housing benefit. It is not proposed to offer a detailed analysis of every decision – reported or unreported[1] – but rather to focus on cases of particular relevance. The chapter is divided into four parts:

(1) an account of the development of the housing benefit scheme, highlighting those aspects of the structure of the scheme that have particular significance for the way in which it is administered;
(2) a brief review of the functions of judicial review;
(3) a consideration of selected judicial review decisions relating to housing benefit; and
(4) conclusions about the impact of the procedure in this area of social policy.

OUTLINE OF THE HOUSING BENEFIT SCHEME

The legal structure of the housing benefit scheme has been the subject of detailed analysis elsewhere;[2] here, a summary of the development of housing benefit is provided to highlight two particular aspects of the scheme of relevance to the argument – the administrative framework and the subsidy structure. At the end of this part, some data are provided about the current use of the scheme.

182

The Development of the Housing Benefit Scheme

Although housing benefits have existed for many years, there has been a number of transformations, both of the benefits themselves and the policy context within which they are set. Four distinct stages can be identified:

- the situation before 1983;
- Housing Benefit Mark 1: 1983–87;
- Housing Benefit Mark 2: 1987–96;
- the 1996 and subsequent amendments.

The Situation Before 1983

Before 1983, two quite different schemes were in place. The payment of rent (as well as mortgage interest) for those out of work and in receipt of Supplementary Benefit (the predecessor of Income Support) was made through the Supplementary Benefit scheme. Both the policy and the administration of Supplementary Benefit were undertaken directly by Central Government through the Department of Health and Social Security (DHSS). Appeals against adverse decisions went to Supplementary Benefit Appeal Tribunals. A further right of appeal to the Social Security Commissioners on a point of law was introduced in 1980.[3]

In addition, a scheme of *rent rebates and rent allowances* for, respectively, council tenants and private sector tenants, provided subsidies for the costs of renting accommodation for those in low-paid employment. These had been introduced under the Housing Finance Act 1972, to compensate for the then Conservative Government's policy of increasing local authority rent levels, to bring them closer in line with private sector rents. This scheme was administered by local authorities themselves. The policy underpinning the scheme was developed within the Department of the Environment. Unlike Supplementary Benefits, there were no formal appeal rights against adverse decisions, save to the limited extent afforded by the procedure of judicial review.

Housing Benefit Mark 1: The 1983 Scheme

Housing Benefit itself was first introduced in 1983.[4] It is a means-tested social security benefit, designed to assist the poor – whether in work or out of work – with their housing costs. The major policy reason for its creation was that the Conservative Government had, by then, introduced its 'right to buy' policy for the privatization of council housing. Thus, in addition to their 1970s goal of seeking to bring public sector and private sector rents closer in line, they were now anxious to ensure that – in general – rent levels were at least as high as, or even higher than, mortgage repayment levels. This would provide added incentives to council tenants who could afford to do so to exercise their right to buy.

Two particular points need to be stressed. First, responsibility for the policy development of the scheme was vested in the DHSS; the Department of the Environment was no longer directly involved, though it retained an active watching brief.

Second, the administration of housing benefit was transferred to local authorities. Although it would have been perfectly possible to have retained it as a Central Government function, there was a plausible argument that, given the predominance of housing benefits going to those residing in council housing, and the experience of local authorities in administering the former rent rebates and rent allowance schemes, local authorities should take over all the administrative functions. It also had the effect that the total number of civil servants employed in the (then) DHSS could be reduced – a major objective of the Thatcher administration.[5]

This decision had three profound consequences:

First, there was an obvious separation between the branch of Government responsible for the development of the law and policy relating to housing benefit (then the DHSS) and the branch of government responsible for its administration (local authorities). Unlike most of the rest of the social security system, Central Government was unable directly to administer the scheme it had created. The normal managerial chains of command, supplemented in more recent years by the work of the Central Adjudication Services – with their responsibilities for the direct monitoring of standards of decision-taking – simply did not exist in the context of Housing Benefit.

Instead, Central Government had to rely on indirect modes of control over administrative standards. The three primary mechanisms adopted were:

(a) the publication of detailed written *Guidance* intended to assist local authority decision-takers in their administrative tasks;
(b) the discipline provided by local authority audit and the work of the National Audit Office; and
(c) the imposition of financial controls on local authorities through the Housing Benefit Subsidy system.

While the first may have some effect, it is frankly hard to gauge the relative weight of such guidance set against in-house instructions on how to carry out defined administrative tasks. The role of audit can provide some discipline, and when a major inquiry is undertaken can be dramatic, but it is not the same as day-to-day managerial control. The use of subsidy became the main mechanism of control; it is examined in more detail below.

Second, despite the very close similarities between the law on Supplementary Benefit (now Income Support) and that on Housing Benefit, decisions on entitlement to housing benefit were made, not by staff operating within what might be described as the 'social security culture', but by local authority staff with an inevitably much more limited understanding of that tradition.[6]

Third, the mainstream system of social security decision-making and adjudication – with initial decisions being taken by Adjudication Officers, with appeals going to Social Security Appeal Tribunals and thence, on a point of law, to Social Security Commissioners – did not apply to housing benefit. Instead new and parallel systems were created for the making and review of decisions. However, there was no mechanism for decisions on points of law to be made by the Social Security Commissioners, even though – as just noted – much of the law relating to housing benefit was essentially the same as that applying to the other income-related social security benefits. The only way of seeking such rulings was by judicial review.

Housing Benefit Scheme: Mark 2: 1987–96

The original Housing Benefit scheme underwent detailed change in 1987 following the Fowler Review of Social Security,[7] though the fundamental administrative structure sketched in the foregoing paragraphs was not altered. The 1987 reforms were driven by a number of other important policy issues.

The first related to social security policy. One of the Government's principal aims was to integrate, even more than had been done before, the detailed rules which applied across the range of the main means-tested social security benefits – Income Support, Family Credit and (now) Council Tax Benefit, as well as Housing Benefit. As a result of the changes brought into effect in 1987, many more of the legal rules which relate to housing benefit were made similar or identical to those found in the other social security benefits.[8]

Despite the desire to integrate the rules, however, the distinctions between the bodies responsible for making policy and those taking and reviewing decisions remained; Housing Benefit was kept outside the mainstream social security decision-making and adjudicative structure.[9]

The second related to public sector housing policy. By the time of the 1987 reforms, Housing Benefit had become an increasingly significant feature of the Government's policy for subsidizing the cost of public sector housing. Put very crudely, the provision of finance to subsidize the capital costs of housing provision, thereby keeping down the costs of local authority housing, had been replaced by a policy of providing subsidies directly to those who lived in those houses. In addition Government had become even more determined to see a closer alignment of public and private sector rent levels. The result of these policies were sharp upward trends in local authority rent levels; Housing Benefit was now the principal means of protecting the poor from the impact of those increases.

The third related to private sector housing policy. At roughly the same time as the 1987 social security reforms were passing through Parliament, significant changes were also being made to the regulation of the private rented sector of the housing market. Most relevant for this chapter was that the Government was preparing for the introduction, under the Housing Act 1988, of the concept of the 'assured tenancy' in relation to which rents were to be 'regulated' – subject to very limited statutory controls – solely by the operation of the housing 'market', rather than by the former fair rent scheme.[10] As a consequence, it was anticipated – quite sensibly – that there would be a significant increase in the levels of private sector rent levels which would also make the existence of a robust Housing Benefit scheme essential for those who would otherwise be unable to afford the new private rent levels.

All these factors relating to housing policy had the effect of increasing the costs of the Housing Benefit scheme, since the underlying policies led both to the exertion of upward pressures on public sector rents and to a marked uplift of private sector rents. However, as a result of the delegation of administrative responsibility to local authorities, Central Government lacked a degree of control over Housing Benefit that it was not lacking in other areas of social security law.

Changes in 1996 and Subsequently

To a considerable extent, rent levels in the public sector – though theoretically set under discretionary powers given to local authorities[11] – are in practice controlled by Central Government by its housing subsidies mechanisms. In addition, rent levels of housing associations are set at 'affordable' levels, as a result of the policies of the Housing Corporation, to which housing associations effectively have to sign up. To a degree, therefore, Central Government has a direct influence over the rent levels in these two sectors.

However, the move to reliance on market rents in the private rented sector created a major policy problem for Government with

Housing Benefit: what should be the basis for limiting the amount of Housing Benefit payable in relation to particular properties? Unregulated rent levels combined with a Housing Benefit scheme which paid 100 per cent of contractual rents to the landlords of low-income tenants could potentially be as distortive of 'true' housing market rent levels as any 'fair rent' scheme might have been prior to the 1988 changes, albeit in the opposite direction. Although the original Mark 1 and Mark 2 Housing Benefit schemes did have rules relating to 'excessive' and 'unreasonable' rents which would not be met by Housing Benefit, there developed increasing worries about the interaction of the Housing Benefit scheme and the existence of 'market rents' in the private sector of the housing market.

These concerns led to further important changes to the scheme, introduced in 1996. First, Rent Officers were given significant new powers to determine both general and specific rent levels which were to be used as the basis for determining in particular areas of the country particular levels of private sector rents which would be paid for by the Housing Benefit scheme. Although 'fair rents' in the old Rent Act sense – which sought to eliminate the distortion of rent levels caused by housing shortages – were not reintroduced, these changes in effect create a form of rent regulation, at least for Housing Benefit purposes, which is likely to impact on the contractual rents which will realistically be sought in the market place. From January 1996, 100 per cent Housing Benefit for those in the private rented sector is only payable to the level of the 'local reference rent' – an average of local rents as determined by the Rent Officer. If a contractual rent exceeds that level, the Housing Benefit scheme will pay only 50 per cent of the difference between the contractual rent and the local reference rent.[12]

Second, a strict limit has been set on the level of Housing Benefit payable to single people under the age of 25. These restrictions were to have been extended to all single people under the age of 60 in October 1997, but this idea was dropped by the new Labour government.

In short, both of these measures are designed to ensure that those on low incomes live in accommodation at the poorer end of the housing market, thereby – it is hoped – putting some limit to this area of Housing Benefit expenditure.

Housing Benefit Subsidies[13]

While control of Housing Benefit expenditure at the macro level operates, as just noted, through mechanisms for controlling the rental levels of public sector, housing association and private sector tenancies, more detailed control is exercised by Central Government through the provisions of the Housing Benefit Subsidy Order. This sets out the basis on which the costs incurred by local authorities in administering the Housing Benefit scheme – including payment of the benefit itself – are reimbursed by the Central Government to local authorities.

The details of the Housing Benefit Subsidy Order are extremely complex. In outline it provides for two principal amounts of subsidy to be paid: an amount to cover expenditure on the benefits provided by way of rebates and allowances;[14] and a further amount in respect of the costs of administering the scheme.[15]

Central Government could have decided that the subsidy level would meet all expenditure incurred by local authorities on both benefit provision and administration; indeed this was, broadly, the situation under the Mark 1 scheme. But officials realized that that amounted to writing local authorities a blank cheque, and it is no longer the basis on which subsidy is calculated.

Instead, the Order now provides that the element attributable to administration costs is an amount determined, not by the authority's actual expenditure, but by a complex formula set out in detail in the Order itself.[16] The element attributable to the cost of the benefit itself is also not the total cost of that provision but, in normal cases, 95 per cent of the actual expenditure on housing benefit.[17]

In specific contexts the 95 per cent provision is amended:

(i) where a claim has been back-dated for good cause[18] the amount of subsidy payable is only 50 per cent of the actual expenditure on any payments so back-dated.[19]

(ii) in the case of defined classes of private sector tenancies, a threshold is set above which local authorities receive significantly reduced levels of reimbursement of their Housing Benefit expenditure.[20] Where eligible rents exceed the threshold, local authorities receive only 25 per cent of the amount by which the eligible rent met by Housing Benefit exceeds the threshold.[21]

(iii) where rent officers have made determinations, the subsidy available for any Housing Benefit payable in relation to properties where the contractual rent exceeds the level of such determination is also very severely restricted.[22]

(iv) there are specific rules which restrict payment of subsidy in cases of over-payment of rent rebates or rent allowances.[23]

(v) there are also rules preventing payment of subsidy in relation to defined items such as certain charges for services, or discretionary additional payments.[24]

There is no relief from these rules in cases where the decision is taken by a Review Board.

The theory underpinning these rules is that the provision of less than 100 per cent compensation for the costs of the benefits should encourage efficient administration by local authorities.[25] But the effect of these subsidy rules is to cause a significant tension, between the legal requirements to administer the Housing Benefit scheme according to the rules of the scheme, and the financial and practical imperative not to 'waste' subsidy by taking decisions that do not result in a maximum subsidy return. Indeed, there is at least some evidence that, because of the very difficult financial situation in which many local housing authorities find themselves as a result of broader policy decisions in relation to local government finance, the 'legal' has had to yield to the 'practical'.

Data on the Housing Benefit Scheme[26]

Before turning to examine the impact of judicial review in Housing Benefit, it is worth just setting the current scheme in context. At the end of February 1996, there was a total of 4,785,000 Housing Benefit recipients in Great Britain. This was an increase from a total of 3,925,000 in November 1990. In tenure terms, the number of local authority tenants in receipt of benefit on these two dates was almost the same: 2,918,000 in February 1996, against 2,919,000 in November 1990. The bulk of the increase was attributable to increased receipt of Housing Benefit by private sector tenants, where there had been a rise from just over 1 million in November 1990 to just under 2 million in February 1996. Within the 'private sector' figure, 694,000 were housing association tenants; 932,000 were 'deregulated' private sector tenants (i.e. in assured or assured shorthold tenancies created after 15 January 1989); and 230,000 were 'regulated' tenancies (under the Rent Act 1977). Perhaps surprisingly, given the perception that poorer people live in accommodation rented from local authorities or housing associations, about 20 per cent of those in receipt of Housing Benefit were renting from private landlords. These figures also reveal why the Government has been so anxious to find mechanisms for limiting the level of private sector rents met by Housing Benefit.

The average amount of weekly Housing Benefits in Great Britain in May 1995 was £39.60 a week. This disguises the fact that the average local authority tenant received £33.09 a week, whereas the average private sector tenant (or more realistically their landlord) received £50.49 a week. Sums paid to those in work (and therefore not in receipt of Income Support) were on average noticeably lower than those paid to the unemployed (who were receiving Income Support). Although the largest group of recipients received levels of

Housing Benefit close to the average amount (about 1.5 million received between £25 and £35 a week), a significant group (over 500,000) received over £60 a week, of which a clear majority were under 60, and a significant proportion of whom were lone parents.

Total spend rose, in cash terms, from £6.4bn in 1991–92, to £10.8bn in 1995–96. While some of this increase reflects inflation of benefit levels, some the increase in the number of claimants, and some the increase in local authority rent levels, much of the increase must be attributable to increases in the levels of private sector rent levels.

THE FUNCTIONS OF JUDICIAL REVIEW

Having noted important features of the Housing Benefit scheme, it is necessary to consider briefly the functions of judicial review, before proceeding to consider the use of judicial review in the specific context of Housing Benefit.

Taking proceedings by way of judicial review has been a significant growth area for legal practice over the last thirty to forty years.[27] The factors responsible for this development are many and complex. Partly they result from changes internal to the legal system, including the response of practitioners, the judiciary and scholars to developing this area of law, but also they are due to procedural change and the availability of legal aid. There have also been profound changes external to the legal system, and the growth of a 'rights' culture. The relentless growth in the regulatory activity of the state and the increasing variety of bodies with jurisdiction over aspects of citizens' lives have given further impetus to the use of judicial review. Now almost any new area of social or public policy will be subject to judicial review proceedings, as those affected by such policies and their legal advisers seek to test the boundaries of the law established by Government.[28] The essays in this volume provide ample testimony to this general proposition.

The primary purpose of judicial review is to support adherence to the basic constitutional doctrine of the *rule of law* which asserts that, in taking the decisions which affect the lives of the ordinary citizen, officials must act within the law whose legitimacy is itself underpinned by the principle of the *sovereignty of Parliament*. The role of the judges in enforcing the rule of law through use of judicial review is in turn justified by that other great constitutional principle – the *separation of powers*.[29]

Put more concretely, it may be suggested that, although clearly interrelated and often confused in practice, the following conceptually distinct functions for judicial review may be identified:[30]

(i)   determining the boundaries for the exercise of legislative powers, particularly in the making of delegated legislation;

(ii) ensuring that officials act in compliance with statutory provisions;

(iii) providing interpretations of the meaning of particular statutory provisions;

(iv) setting limits to the use of discretionary powers and deciding whether such discretionary powers have been reasonably used;

(v)   establishing and enforcing procedural norms, such as the principles of fairness.

Those who take judicial review proceedings usually do so with just a particular case in mind. However, some practitioners seek to use judicial review in a more strategic fashion by bringing *test cases* which seek to identify particular issues which impact on substantial numbers of individual cases. This may be described as the 'political function' of judicial review.

Furthermore, considerable use is made of judicial review as a part of a litigation strategy, in which proceedings are contemplated, and even taken to the leave stage, without any necessary intention of getting to a full hearing. It becomes part of the process of reaching a settlement in a dispute. This may be described as the 'covert function' of judicial review.

There are two further functions which it could be argued that the judicial review procedure has, though which have not as yet been adequately developed in the courts:

(a)   seeking to enhance the quality of administrative decision-taking; and

(b)   protecting certain fundamental human rights values.

These issues will not be pursued in detail here, but should not be overlooked in any overall evaluation of the impact of judicial review on the administrative process.

THE USE OF JUDICIAL REVIEW IN HOUSING BENEFIT CASES

To understand the uses to which judicial review has been put in Housing Benefit cases, it is necessary to provide a little more detail about the legal framework of Housing Benefit.

The Legal Framework of Housing Benefit: A Brief Résumé

As with the bulk of modern welfare legislation, the relevant Act of Parliament, now the Social Security Contributions and Benefits Act

1992, Part VII, sets out only the barest outline of the Housing Benefit scheme, as part of the overall package of income-related benefits. The detailed regulatory framework is determined by the Department of Social Security and set out in detail in Regulations, principally the Housing Benefit (General) Regulations 1987 and the Housing Benefit Subsidy Order.[31]

The basic legal conditions for entitlement to Housing Benefit are:

(a) the claimant must be *liable* to make payments for accommodation in Great Britain;
(b) the claimant must *occupy* the accommodation 'as his home';
(c) the payments must relate to *eligible housing costs* as defined for the purposes of the Housing Benefit scheme, principally the rent;
(d) the appropriate *maximum housing benefit* must be determined in relation to his claim;
(e) either the claimant's income must be the same as or less than the applicable amount which applies in his case, or if his income does exceed the applicable amount, then there must still remain a positive sum after the deduction, from the maximum Housing Benefit, of 65 pence for each £1 of excess, known as the *taper*;
(f) the claimant's capital must not exceed the prescribed amount – currently £16,000;
(g) claimants who are already in receipt of Income Support receive by way of Housing Benefit 100 per cent of their eligible rent less deduction for any *non-dependant* who may be living in the accommodation, if appropriate;
(h) in no case may the amount of Housing Benefit exceed the *maximum rent*;[32] and
(i) the claim must be made in the prescribed manner.

Many of these basic principles and the detailed regulatory provisions which amplify them have generated the disputes which have come before the courts. They may be considered using the functional classification of uses of judicial review noted above.

The Uses of Judicial Review

Reviewing the Regulation-making Process

The one Housing Benefit case which falls in this category is *R v Secretary of State for Social Security, ex parte The Association of Metropolitan Authorities*.[33] There the courts held that the Secretary of State had failed to follow statutory requirements relating to consultation prior to the making of amendments to the Housing Benefits Regulations. Although the Secretary of State had the power to make Regulations without completing the consultation in a case of urgency, he or she could not use this power where the reason for the urgency was that the Secretary of State himself/herself had delayed making a decision until the last moment, and had thus in a sense created the urgency himself/herself.

There have as yet (at the time of writing) been no direct challenges to specific Housing Benefit Regulations on the grounds that they are *ultra vires* the parent legislation, as has occurred in other areas of social welfare law.

Reviewing the Decision-taking Process

An example of a decision in this category is *R v Housing Benefit Review Board of the London Borough of Sutton ex parte Keegan*.[34] In that case, the claimant, an elderly lady, lived in accommodation owned by her son-in-law and daughter. The son-in-law could not allow her to live there rent-free, so charged her rent. It was accepted that the applicant could not have afforded to pay the charge without the provision of Housing Benefit. The council decided the arrangement was caught by the rule that payments 'not on a commercial basis' prevented liability for rent arising. However, Potts J held that the mere fact that she could not pay the rent was not determinative of the issue. After all, by definition, Housing Benefit claimants are not in a position to pay rent. The judge stated that the Review Board should have reviewed the means, circumstances and intention of both the landlord and the tenant, and made findings on fact on those matters; and also made findings as to the consequences of Housing Benefit not being paid in the particular case (e.g. that the landlord might evict and that therefore the authority might have to rehouse). If it transpired that the landlord would sell the property or re-let it to another, this would be evidence that the specific tenancy was not contrived.

In short, this case gave detailed guidance as to how decision-makers should approach the decision-making task in such cases.

Interpreting statutory Provisions

The bulk of the judicial review cases on Housing Benefit have, in essence, involved the interpretation of specific statutory provisions as they apply to particular factual situations. For example what does or does not fall within the definition of 'eligible rent' has been the subject of a number of determinations.[35] The meaning of 'service charges' was considered in *R v North Cornwall DC ex parte Singer*.[36] The meaning of 'occupies' was considered in *R v Penwith District Council ex parte Burt*.[37] What was 'income' was considered in *R v West Dorset CC ex parte Poupard*.[38]

Setting Limits to the Use of Discretionary Powers

There have been few decisions dealing specifically with the reasonableness of the exercise of discretionary power in the context of Housing Benefit. A decision that might be included here is the *Connery* decision, discussed at greater length below.

Developing Procedural Norms

A number of cases have sought to establish procedural norms in the context of Housing Benefit decisions, particularly decisions taken by Housing Benefit Review Boards. The clearest example is, perhaps, *R v Sefton MBC ex parte Cunningham*[39] which dealt with the adequacy of reasons in a decision letter. There have been a number of other cases on the same general issue: for example, *R v Housing Benefit Review Board of East Devon ex parte Gibson*;[40] and *R v Solihull MBC Housing Benefit Review Board, ex parte Simpson*.[41]

There have also been cases dealing with procedural questions relating to the bringing of judicial review cases themselves: for example, *R v London Borough of Haringey ex parte Azad Ayub*[42] had, as one of the issues to be determined, the question of whether Mr Ayub had standing to bring proceedings at all.

More important, perhaps, are decisions relating to the nature and extent of the evidence to be taken into account in certain types of decision: for example, the *Gibson* case, above; and also, under the Mark 1 scheme, *R v South Hertfordshire Housing Benefit Review Board ex parte Smith*.[43] (Such cases might also be classified under the heading 'Reviewing the Decision-taking Process' above.)

The Tension Between the Subsidy Rules and the Scheme Rules

Although there has been a range of issues thrown up by the Housing Benefit scheme which has resulted in reported litigation, there is a dearth of cases which directly focus on what may be regarded as the most difficult question arising in Housing Benefit law: where there is conflict between the rules of the scheme and the subsidy rules, which should have priority?

The case which has to date focused most directly on the issue was *R v Housing Benefit Review Board of the London Borough of Brent ex parte Connery*.[44] The issue there involved a consideration of the circumstances in which a claimant's prima facie entitlement to have 100 per cent of his rent paid by Housing Benefit – as being the 'eligible rent' – could be reduced. (It should be stressed that the detail of the law has now been amended; however, the case is still of significance for the argument advanced in this chapter.)

Under the then wording of the Housing Benefit (General) Regulations 1987, Regulation 11, the eligible rent could be reduced in two different sets of circumstance, which may be paraphrased thus: (1) where the accommodation was larger than needed by the claimant; (2) where the rent paid was unreasonably high. The case dealt with the latter issue.

The question posed in the case was whether, in coming to its decision on the matter, the local authority was entitled to take into account its own financial position, which in turn raised the question of whether the amount of subsidy payable in relation to that particular claim should be allowed to influence the authority in reaching its determination.

On the particular legal point, the regulation then stated:

> ... [W]here the appropriate authority considers ...
> that the rent payable for [the] dwelling is unreasonably high by
> comparison with the rent payable in respect of suitable
> alternative accommodation elsewhere,
> the authority may treat the claimant's ... eligible rent as
> reduced by such amount as it considers appropriate having
> regard in particular to the cost of suitable alternative
> accommodation elsewhere ...

In analysing this provision, the judge, Schiemann J (as he then was), found that these provisions involved the exercise by the authority of two separate discretions: the first was concerned with deciding whether the rent payable for the applicant's dwelling was unreasonably high; the second concerned whether, in the light of the first decision, the authority should reduce the rent. It was conceded on all sides that, in reaching a decision on the first point, the authority was not entitled to take its financial position into account.

Having reached that decision, Schiemann J decided that a second discretionary decision then had to be taken, namely whether or not to exercise its power to reduce the rent. The learned judge, in an extempore judgment which is frankly not entirely easy to follow, stated that counsel for the claimant did draw the court's attention to the fact that the scheme itself and the subsidy rules were to be found in different statutory instruments. However, the judge does not seem to have been asked to consider the implications of this: did one set of rules have primacy over the other?

Instead the judge merely stated that as the hearing had proceeded, counsel for the claimant had come to accept a rather vaguer submission – presumably made by counsel for the authority – that 'the crucial question was whether [in exercising its discretion] the authority could take its own financial situation into account'. Further, and somewhat mysteriously, 'If it can take projected rate income into account it can take projected subsidy income into account'. It is not at all clear how this latter sentence follows from the previously quoted sentence.

The judge then turned to the arguments made for the local authority. He held that in exercising their discretion the local authority could not reduce the level of 'eligible rent' below the cost of suitable accommodation elsewhere; but the judge accepted that in deciding whether or not the eligible rent was to be brought down to that level – whatever that might be – 'a relevant consideration was the state of the authority's own finances'.

The judge then amplified the implications of this conclusion: 'Authorities, generally, in the carrying out of their functions are bound to have regard to the financial implications of any action or inaction on their part save in those cases ... where there is an absolute duty to do something and to raise the appropriate funds to enable that duty to be fulfilled ... [The] present case is not, in my judgement, such a case.'

The question must be asked: why not? The fact is that the central issue, whether the rules of the Housing Benefit scheme, as embodied in the Housing Benefit (General) Regulations, did create a duty to be fulfilled whatever the financial implications (i.e. were to have priority over the subsidy rules in the Housing Benefit (Subsidy) Order), was not clearly addressed. For the issue to have been dealt with properly, there should have been a much more detailed examination of the structure of the Subsidy Order, and a much more explicit examination of the tensions created by the interaction of the scheme and the subsidy rules.

The precise point that arose for consideration in *Connery* cannot now arise because, as has been noted, the detailed terms of the Regulation have been altered. In particular the word 'may' which then appeared in the Regulation – which gave the authority the discretion to act or not – has been replaced by the word 'shall' which makes a decision to reduce the eligible rent level a mandatory one. In addition the details of the subsidy rules have been amended.

However, if one poses the question: 'What *should* the eligible rent be of a dwelling where the rent was unreasonably high?', the answer should surely be: 'The eligible rent should be set at the level of the rent of suitable accommodation elsewhere.' I would argue that this is a question of fact, which should *not* be influenced by the subsidy implications of the decision. Yet it would seem that the basis on which decisions would now have to be taken could still be influenced by the reasoning in the *Connery* case, which – somehow – concludes that taking the subsidy implications into account is possible.

The point of this analysis is a short one: despite the perceived importance of the procedure of judicial review in general, in the context of Housing Benefit the really crucial issue – about the relative priorities of the scheme rules and the subsidy rules – has been ducked.

In the specific context of the levels of 'unreasonable rents' the issue will be less likely to arise in future, as a result of new powers given to Rent Officers to make determinations – which are binding on the authority – as to the level of rent to be regarded as 'eligible' for Housing Benefit purposes.

But there are other areas where the authority has to exercise discretion and/or judgment – for example in deciding whether a claim for Housing Benefit can be back-dated for good cause. The crucial issue – can such judgmental or discretionary decisions be influenced by taking subsidy considerations into account? – has not been addressed directly and unequivocally by the courts. The judicial review procedure is at best a haphazard means of getting these key issues addressed.

CONCLUSIONS

From the foregoing analysis, there are four main points to be drawn which relate to the use of judicial review in the context of housing benefit:

(1) As is indicated at the end of the first part of this chapter (see under sub-heading 'Data on the Housing Benefit Scheme'), Housing Benefit is an enormous operation, in terms of both the numbers who receive the benefit and the amount of cash spent on it. It should be noted that the vast bulk of cases are, it seems, dealt with wholly satisfactorily. However, while the statistical information suggests that the typical case is dealt with entirely properly by those bodies charged with the duty to administer the Housing Benefit scheme, it is equally important that the non-typical case is properly dealt with within the rules as laid down by Parliament.

(2) What the decided cases on judicial review do show is that the sorts of issue that get dealt with by the Divisional Court (and Court of Appeal) in relation to Housing Benefit are usually dealt with perfectly satisfactorily and equally as authoritatively in the context of social security adjudication by the Social Security Appeal Tribunals and the Social Security Commissioners.[45]

Thus the need to use judicial review in the context of Housing Benefit means that the relatively inexpensive and straightforward means for having an issue of law resolved, which is available in the context of other social security benefits, is quite simply denied to claimants in the context of Housing Benefit. Only those with the limited level of resources to get legal aid to take judicial review proceedings can do so; and in cases where legal aid is obtained, local authorities will have to divert resources to respond to such proceedings and the time taken to reach final conclusions is far too long.

In short, although judicial review is a potential means to challenge local authority decisions, it is not a sensible means in the context of a scheme of mass application. Judicial review is a remedy which should be reserved for the unusual and difficult case; there should be cheaper alternatives for the more straightforward issues.

(3) There is undoubtedly tension between the rules of the scheme itself and the subsidy rules. The latter are arguably needed because of the lack of alternative means of controlling administrative behaviour, given the decision to devolve that responsibility to local authorities. But officials are, in a number of situations, caught between taking decisions that will not adversely affect their councils in financial terms and taking decisions which should be taken under the rules of the scheme. Although this issue has been visited once by the courts, the only reported decision, discussed above, is not particularly clear and does not, in my view, clearly establish the principle of the supremacy of the scheme over the subsidy provisions.

Experience in practice suggests that when such cases arise, local authorities will usually seek to settle the individual case without a formal court ruling, rather than risk the possibility of a clear decision adverse to their interests. For example, the Audit Commission found that 82 of the 355 local authorities it has studied had never used the power to back-date a late claim for Housing Benefit; and that a further 236 had paid less than 0.5 per cent of their total payments as back-dated payments.[46] These figures do not reflect the practice in social security administration, and suggest strongly that local authorities are failing to apply the late claim rules properly, certainly not in the way social security officials would apply them.

In that sense, the process of judicial review must be regarded as a less than satisfactory means to tease important issues out, since the courts only take jurisdiction over those matters referred to them.

(4) These tensions are a specific example of an issue that arises frequently in modern public administration whenever Central Government creates legal entitlements, which have to be delivered by local government or other agencies. Where such agencies are dependent on levels of funding determined by Central Government, the tensions between entitlement and resource, noted here in the context of Housing Benefit, can be recognized in other policy areas such as education, health services, social services and the provision of community care.

It is unrealistic to expect the judicial review procedure to resolve the tensions that arise between the promise and the delivery of legal rights. But the judges should not pretend that such tensions do not exist. If Governments promise entitlements but do not provide realistic levels of resource for their delivery, that is a cruel deception on the public. Practical reality and political honesty may both require that legal entitlements have to be replaced by more rather than less discretion – as arguably has occurred with the creation of the Social Fund. The judicial review procedure could be an important mechanism to persuade Government to confront these challenges head on. Experience to date suggests that, at least in the context of Housing Benefit, judicial review has not in this respect achieved its full potential.

NOTES

1 A Lexis search revealed over 100 reported and unreported cases.
2 See, for example, ch. 4 in A. Arden and M. Partington, *Housing Law* (2nd edn 1994, annual updates); *CPAG's Housing Benefit and Council Tax Legislation* (annual); *SHAC Guide to Housing Benefit and Council Tax Benefit* (annual); A. Ogus, E. Barendt and N. Wikeley, *The Law Relating to Social Security* (4th edn), London: Butterworths (1995), ch. 13.
3 Social Security Act 1980, ss. 14 and 15.
4 The enabling legislation was passed in 1982.
5 The fact that local authority staff numbers increased, according to some estimates, by as many as 3500 in order to carry out the new work did not feature in the headline figures, which had showed a reduction of 2500 in the numbers of civil servants employed within the DHSS.
6 I. Loveland, 'Discretionary decision taking in the housing benefit scheme: a case study', 16 *Policy and Politics* 99 (1988) takes a slightly different view.
7 *The Reform of Social Security*, Cmnd 9691, London: HMSO (1985).
8 Similar links can be found with the Disability Working Allowance, introduced in 1991, and the income-related component of the Jobseeker's Allowance, introduced in 1996.
9 Social Security Appeal Tribunals, and the Social Security Commissioners. On social security adjudication, see J. Baldwin, N. Wikeley and R. Young, *Judging*

Social Security: The Adjudication of Claims for Benefit in Britain, Oxford: Clarendon Press (1992).

10   Rent Act 1977. Fair rents were determined by Rent Officers, and on appeal by Rent Assessment Committees: Arden and Partington, note 2 above, ch. 3.

11   Housing Act 1985, s. 24 (as amended).

12   Housing Benefit (General) Regulations 1987, Regulation 11 (as substituted by SI 1995, No. 1644, Regulation 5). The 50 per cent 'uplift' was abolished in October 1997.

13   The pioneering article examining the links between subsidy and decision-taking is by S. Rahilly, 'Housing Benefit: the impact of subsidies on decision-making', 2 *Journal of Social Security Law* (1995): 196.

14   Housing Benefit and Council Tax Benefit (Subsidy) Order, 1996, Article 3(a).

15   *Ibid.*, Article 3(2).

16   *Ibid.*, Schedules 1 and 2.

17   *Ibid.*, Article 4(1).

18   Possible under Housing Benefit (General) Regulations 1987, Regulation 72(15).

19   Housing Benefit and Council Tax Benefit (Subsidy) Order 1996, Article 5.

20   *Ibid.*, Article 7 and Schedule 5. These provisions effectively only apply to assured tenancies created under the Housing Act 1988, or to tenancies created before 15 January 1989 which have not been submitted to the Rent Officer for the assessment of a fair rent. For a recent review of these issues, see Lord Irvine of Lairg, 'Judges and decision-makers: the theory and practice of *Wednesbury* review' [1996] *Public Law*: 59–78.

21   Housing Benefit and Council Tax Benefit (Subsidy) Order 1996, Article 5.

22   See *ibid.*, Article 8 and Schedule 6.

23   *Ibid.*, Article 10.

24   Article 11.

25   Housing Benefit Review Team, *Review of Housing Benefit*, Cmnd 9520, London: HMSO (1985).

26   The data are taken from *Social Security Statistics, 1996*, London: HMSO.

27   It is important to keep this statement in perspective. By comparison with the thousands of cases dealt with annually by tribunals and inquiries, or the variety of ombudsmen at both central and local government levels, or other review, inquiry or complaints procedures, the quantitative use of judicial review is still trivial; the qualitative importance of the procedure cannot, however, be denied.

28   What the appropriate limits for judicial review should be is, inevitably, the subject of often sharp debate, not least amongst Ministers and others whose decisions may be called in question. For a recent review of these issues, see Irvine, note 20.

29   For a critique of conventional thinking about the doctrine of the separation of powers see the thought-provoking discussion in J. M. Jacob, *The Republican Crown*, Aldershot: Dartmouth (1996), at pp. 17–18. He argues that a more constructive way of conceptualizing the separation of powers is as a bifurcated, rather than trifurcated, concept – in which, though independent, the judges should be seen as a part of the executive arm of Government.

30   Disappointingly, the Law Commission, in its recent report *Administrative Law:*

Judicial Review and Statutory Appeals (HC 669) (1994) – apart from noting that judicial review was available to vindicate the rule of law (para. 1.4) – did not consider the question of functions more directly. It defined its concerns more in terms of getting the balance right between allowing Government to get on with its jobs and allowing the aggrieved citizen to obtain remedies for a grievance.

31 The Regulations have been much amended. For up-to-date statements of the provisions see CPAG, note 2 above, or the *Encyclopaedia of Housing Law*, Volumes 3 and 4.

32 This is the amount the eligible rent is limited to where a restriction is imposed under Regulation 11 as amended by SI 1995, No. 1644 with effect from 2 January 1996.

33 (1992) 25 HLR 131 (CA).

34 (1995) 27 HLR 92 (Div. Court).

35 See for example *R* v *Secretary of State for Health and Social Services, ex parte City of Sheffield* (1986) 18 HLR 6; *R* v *Secretary of State for Social Services, ex parte AMA* (1993) 25 HLR 131.

36 (1995) 27 HLR 622 (CA).

37 (1990) 20 HLR 292 (QBD).

38 (1987) 19 HLR 254.

39 (1991) 23 HLR 534.

40 (1993) 25 HLR 487.

41 (1995) 25 HLR 41.

42 (1993) 25 HLR 566.

43 19 HLR 217.

44 (1990) 20 HLR 40.

45 For criticism of the limitations of the procedures for reviewing Housing Benefit decisions, see M. Partington and H. Bolderson, *Housing Benefits Review Procedures: A Preliminary Analysis*, Uxbridge: Department of Law, Brunel University (1984); R. Sainsbury and T. Eardley, *Housing Benefits Reviews: Final Report*, York: Social Policy Research Unit, University of York (1991).

46 National Audit Office, *Remote Control: The National Administration of Housing Benefit*, London: HMSO (1993), Table 2, cited in Rahilly, note 13 above, at 202.

9

Immigration and Judicial Review

PRAKASH SHAH AND WERNER MENSKI

INTRODUCTION

Immigration law has become a very specialized field of administrative law with its own legislative framework and unwritten rules.[1] There is now a growing number of specialist immigration solicitors and a specialist section of the Bar which concentrates on immigration work. Students are increasingly choosing (or even demanding) to study the subject either at the academic or at the professional stage of their education. The past decade or more has seen a growth in resort to judicial review in this area. Not only individuals but also non-governmental organizations, the Immigration Law Practitioners' Association and the Joint Council for the Welfare of Immigrants, have become involved in taking judicial review action in the High Court. On the other hand, it has been noticed that the standard and availability of legal assistance in immigration and asylum matters have not been adequate (Smith, 1993; Shah, 1995a). If legal services were fully available one might find an even greater level of litigation.

The response of judges has been determined by two main factors which will be considered in this chapter. The first factor is the statutory context which enables remedial action to be taken in quasi-judicial fora now administered under the Immigration Appellate Authority. The possibility of an appeal to this body will determine when or whether an application for judicial review may be entertained by the Divisional Court. Here we also take into account the changes introduced by the Asylum and Immigration Act 1996, the latest in a series of legislative changes which have affected this process. The second factor is the political context within which questions of immigration policy are constructed. The judiciary has not been immune to the dominant paradigms which have emerged as the state has sought to target specific streams of migration, and its response may be demonstrated by the emerging statistical evidence and the reasoning used by judges in particular cases. An allied reason for the judges' reaction has been their concern at the level of work now being dealt with at the Divisional Court.

THE STATUTORY CONTEXT

The appellate structure in immigration law generally derives from the Immigration Appeals Act 1969 but it only found a legislative basis in the Immigration Act 1971, Part II.[2] The Wilson Committee Report of 1967 recommended the institution of an appeals system in which the rule of law could be ensured by providing remedies against administrative decisions (by immigration officers, entry clearance officers and the Home Secretary) which would potentially affect a person's entire life (Juss, 1992: 368). The basic structure in the Immigration Act 1971 provides for an appeal to an adjudicator in the first instance and then to the Immigration Appeal Tribunal (IAT), with leave, if 'an arguable point of law' can be demonstrated (Bevan, 1986: 360). The statutory provisions are supplemented by the procedure rules made by statutory instrument. Where the IAT dismisses an appeal or refuses leave to appeal, the appropriate remedy was judicial review.

The primary aim of the appellate system was to uphold ideals of justice and fairness, to 'dispel beliefs', to provide assurance to immigrants and thereby to 'improve race relations' in Britain (Macdonald and Blake, 1995: 563). The paradigmatic assumption that firm controls were conducive to maintaining interethnic harmony, which lay behind the enforcement of restrictive immigration policies instituted since the 1960s, was thus also imported into the remedial sphere. In 1985 the Commission for Racial Equality concluded what has been described as 'the only empirical study of British immigration law which has been able to base its findings on current, internal communications from the Home Office and Foreign and Commonwealth Office' (Dummett, 1994: 347). Among the Commission's findings were that:

> ... the rules and the practices involved appear to protect the immigration authorities against disclosure of some of the very matters an appeals system should be able to attack. Adjudicators and the IAT have not generally attempted or been able to break down this protection. It would be a mistake to suppose that if an administrative system is seriously flawed, a system of appeals

against it will correct those defects. It will not. (Commission for Racial Equality, 1985: 123)[3]

It should be noted that certain types of administrative practice have been beyond the scope of the appellate system. This is partially due to the wide discretion which the 1971 Act leaves to the Secretary of State. That Act makes provision for the making of Immigration Rules by the Secretary of State, subject to a negative Parliamentary resolution. The appellate authorities can oversee whether decisions have been made in accordance with the rules or 'in accordance with the law' but they may not question the Secretary of State's refusal to depart from a provision of the rules. By ensuring that many areas of actual practice are not reflected in the rules, the immigration authorities can, on the one hand, reserve for themselves a great deal of discretion 'outside the rules', but may, on the other hand, opt to insist on the strict application of the rules (Vincenzi, 1992). This approach means that in many instances judicial review may be the only recourse that disappointed individuals have.

The case of British passport holders in East Africa is particularly interesting in this context. Prior to the Commonwealth Immigrants Act 1968, citizens of the UK and Colonies had a right of abode in the United Kingdom. When this was removed by the 1968 Act, the Government still acknowledged that it had an international responsibility to admit those who had nowhere to go and were compelled to leave their country of residence (Macdonald and Blake, 1995: 423). This condition was realized under tragic circumstances in Uganda (Shah, 1995b: 76-82). However, for many years the conditions under which individuals were to be admitted were kept secret, while a quota system was used to determine the numbers that could be let in. Refusal to issue a 'special voucher' could not be questioned in the appellate system, according to the House of Lords in *R v Entry Clearance Officer, ex parte Amin* [1983] 2 All ER 864. However, more recently the conditions under which individuals and family members may be admitted have come to light and may therefore permit an application for judicial review (Shah, 1992).

With the steady curtailment of substantive rights under immigration law (Bevan, 1986; Sachdeva, 1993: 13-41), a succession of changes also occurred in the remedial sphere. In May 1985, while announcing the imposition of a visa requirement for citizens of Sri Lanka, directly in response to the increase in asylum applications from Tamils fleeing the conflict in that country, the Home Secretary also announced a limitation in the right of MPs to make representations in Tamil cases.[4] Such limitations also followed the imposition of a visa requirement in 1986 upon nationals of Pakistan,

India, Bangladesh, Ghana and Nigeria in response to threatened industrial action by the Immigration Service Union (Joint Council for the Welfare of Immigrants, 1987; Drabu and Bowen, 1989). A drastic curtailment of protection from deportation was brought in by the Immigration Act 1988. It removed the power of an adjudicator and the IAT to consider the merits of certain decisions to deport. Where questions arise as to whether the decision was unfair or whether the individual exercising the power had the authority to make the decision, judicial review is the only remedy.[5]

More recently, ss. 10 and 11 of the Asylum and Immigration Appeals Act 1993 removed the right of appeal for an individual refused a visitor's visa, for an individual refused at a port of entry while not being in possession of such a visa, and for those carrying improper documentation. The judges in the House of Lords (legislative branch) spoke out against this change, fearing an increase in judicial review applications directly to the High Court (Shah, 1993).

The case of the Sri Lankan Tamils is instructive in more than one sense. Not only were they the first Commonwealth nationality to be subject to visa controls but it was the Government's desire to remove four such applicants expeditiously which prompted the enactment of the UK Immigration (Carriers' Liability) Act 1987 (Cruz, 1995: 36–7). Prior to the enactment of the 1993 Act, there existed no in-country right of appeal for asylum applicants who did not hold visas and who were refused leave to enter, nor for those treated as illegal entrants and who, thereby, became subject to summary administrative removal.[6]

Usually the possibility of applying for asylum without being present on UK territory does not exist,[7] and there is no visa category for refugees. Without some other sort of prior entry clearance for persons who require it for entry into the United Kingdom, checks by airlines make it virtually impossible to flee the country of origin (Cruz, 1995). Where the asylum seeker made it to the United Kingdom and was refused asylum, the only method of challenge in domestic law, in the absence of a substantive in-country right of appeal, was judicial review. However, even in asylum cases, the High Court could not go beyond reviewing the administrative decision of the Home Secretary on traditional judicial review grounds.[8] The matter came up for challenge, in the European Commission of Human Rights in Strasbourg, in *Vilvarajah and Others v UK* (1992) 14 EHRR 248, another case concerning Tamils, some of whom were tortured upon removal to Sri Lanka. The Commission found that there was a failure to provide an effective remedy under Article 13 of the European

Convention on Human Rights (ECHR) and that judicial review was an inadequate remedy (*ibid.*, at 280–284).[9]

Perhaps fearing the European Court's final ruling on the *Vilvarajah* case, the UK government introduced a Bill in Parliament[10] which, after a delay pending the general election of 1992, was reintroduced and passed as the Asylum and Immigration Appeals Act 1993. The new Act introduced for the first time an in-country right of appeal for all rejected asylum applicants (Gillespie, 1993). The European Court eventually rejected the Commission's interpretation of the requirements of Article 13 of the ECHR and stated that the remedy of judicial review was adequate to protect the rights of persons threatened with treatment contrary to Article 3 (torture, inhuman and degrading treatment or punishment) of the ECHR. It is questionable whether the European Court understood the relevance of judicial review then acknowledged by the judiciary. In a recent judgment, Sedley J noted that:

> According to the European Court of Human Rights, the UK government has asserted in that court that a rationality argument is available against the Home Secretary in relation to 'a challenged decision to send a fugitive to a country where it was established that there was a serious risk of inhuman and degrading treatment ...'. (*R v Secretary of State for the Home Department, ex parte McQuillan* [1995] 4 All ER 400, at 409F–G)

If not misleading, this submission to the European Court seems to suggest a rather ambitious view about the courts' willingness to question administrative decisions beyond traditional grounds, one which the Government has opposed in domestic proceedings.[11]

The new appeal rights were laced with restrictions and unrealistic time limits, the whole system being designed to process applications at a much faster pace than hitherto, without adequate regard for the rights of asylum seekers, and failing to address the underlying issue of the appropriateness of an administrative review procedure under the immigration appeals system for asylum seekers. In particular, the 1993 Act created a shorter appeals procedure for cases certified by the Home Secretary as being without foundation (mainly 'safe third country' cases). Only one appeal to a special adjudicator was made available.[12] For non-certified cases the further appeal to the IAT was retained (Macdonald and Blake, 1995: 414–18). Thus without-foundation cases could reach the judicial review stage after an appeal to the special adjudicator. For other cases judicial review was (and still is) an option after refusal of leave to appeal from the IAT. Where the appeal was decided by the IAT, either party could appeal further to the Court of Appeal (or the Court of Session, in Scotland) 'on any question of law'.[13] This measure was intended to take the pressure off the judicial review system but we are informed that immigration applications still constitute about 45 per cent of all applications.[14] We consider below the extent to which the High Court judges have stepped in to ensure the provision of an effective remedy for asylum seekers.

The Asylum and Immigration Act 1996 changed the 1993 system in that it shifted more categories of claim to the one-stop appeal procedure, including the so-called 'white list' cases, where individuals are certified on the basis that they arrive from countries considered to be safe.[15] The 'safe third country' cases are now treated in two ways. Where the case is certified as having involved a designated transit country, no in-country right of appeal exists.[16] This process applies to cases where an asylum seeker is deemed to have had an opportunity to claim asylum in a Member State of the European Union or another country designated by an order.[17] This marks a process of chipping away at the minimal guarantees provided by the appellate process, the government no doubt emboldened by the result in the *Vilvarajah* case. For other third-country cases the system of a one-stop appeal still applies.[18] Other changes in the 1996 Act have included the introduction of criminal sanctions for employers who recruit persons ineligible to work in the United Kingdom,[19] and the removal of social security benefits and access to housing for asylum seekers.[20] This last change was forced by the Court of Appeal's quashing of the Government's attempt to achieve the same result through secondary legislation.[21] In sum, this legislative measure marks a high point in Governmental attempts to remove asylum seekers quickly from the territory, to criminalize them and to ensure their impoverishment. It compromises the United Kingdom's international obligations further.

JUDICIAL REACTIONS

The response of the judiciary has been noticeably more conservative to immigration issues, especially when larger numbers have needed to resort to the courts (Legomsky, 1987: 242–6).[22] The functioning of the judicial review system has itself been politicized as the immigration caseload grew during the 1980s. Having continually increased from 1981, between 1984 and 1985 the number of judicial review applications in the immigration field doubled to 516 (59 per cent of the total civil caseload), while other civil law applications were actually declining (see Sunkin, 1987: 442–3). Proposals ranging from conducting a 'blitzkrieg' on cases to placing more responsibility upon the immigration appellate system have been suggested by (the then) Lord Justice Woolf (1992: 227).

Further research into the functioning of the judicial review system (conducted for the period 1987–89 and the first quarter of 1991) indicates that two-thirds of immigration cases were refused leave and, ultimately, only 11 per cent got past that stage (see Sunkin *et al.*, 1993a: 433 and 435). Immigration cases were the least likely to succeed at the leave stage, which is important, considering that the grant of leave itself is a significant factor in influencing settlement (see Sunkin *et al.*, 1993a: 435). Asylum applications, mainly by Tamils and later by Kurds, were particularly affected (Sunkin *et al.*, 1993b: 8–13).

Within the immigration-related caseload there seemed to be a high rate of judicial review challenges by applicants refused leave to enter as visitors by an immigration officer at a port of entry. Indeed, advisers were aware of this strategy to enable their clients to remain in the United Kingdom so that the purpose of the visit was not frustrated by immediate removal (Mole, 1987: 111; Macdonald, 1987: 165). In February 1986 the Court of Appeal reacted to this practice in the case of *Swati* [1986] Imm. AR 88 by insisting that these applicants should exhaust their alternative remedy under the Immigration Act by appealing to an adjudicator, albeit from outside the United Kingdom. The expected impact was realized as the caseload dropped dramatically; such 'genuine visitor' applications decreased from 183 in 1985 to 55 in 1986 (Sunkin, 1987: 447).[23]

The number of reported cases since the abolition of the visitor appeal rights in the 1993 Act remains low, probably because of practical obstacles and the lack of information about legal rights. In the one reported visitor case, *R v Secretary of State for the Home Department, ex parte Kaur and Lizzie* [1994] Imm. AR 180, the applicants were Kenyan nationals (at the time Kenya was not a visa country). They arrived in the United Kingdom without entry clearance and were refused leave to enter. As there was conflicting evidence, Schiemann J thought it was not the task of the court to resolve that conflict, but suggested, instead, that the applicants would have been better advised to obtain an entry clearance prior to arrival in the United Kingdom to avoid refusal at the port. Ironically, there would be no right to appeal a refusal of that by virtue of the 1993 Act.

In December 1993 a group of visitors from Jamaica was held at Heathrow and it seems that the officials were anxiously trying to prevent judicial review, the only remedy open (Harlow, 1994: 624). We have become aware of other practices in the processing of visit applications which could well lead to challenges in future. One interesting development has been the practice of entry clearance officers discouraging the making of an application by 'advising' individuals that they would not be successful. It has also come to our attention that, in other cases, applicants appear to be pre-screened by locally employed staff, with similar effect. A report by the National Association for Citizens Advice Bureaux notes that in a number of cases 'applicants wishing to apply for a visit are not allowed to give their application forms in, and are turned away at the front desk' (1996: 43).

Judicial impatience has also been noted in the case of marriages not deemed to merit a correlative right of residence for an overseas spouse. The rules have required that a spouse must show that the primary purpose of the marriage was not to secure entry into the United Kingdom, a requirement specifically aimed at controlling the influx of South Asians into the United Kingdom. The 'primary purpose rule' was tried and tested in the early 1980s by the immigration authorities (Sachdeva, 1993: 43–105). Eventually cases went through the system of immigration appeals and into the judicial review arena. The first major response of the High Court indicated that the primary purpose test imposed the burden of proof on the applicant and that that requirement was meant to apply regardless of whether a couple had satisfied the other requirement that the parties intended to live together.[24] That decision had a devastating effect on about 200 similar cases awaiting its outcome and gave *carte blanche* to entry clearance officers to place obstacles in the way of applicants (Sachdeva, 1993: 122–7). Posing the issue as a factual one also avoided questions of law arising and prevented cases being litigated at IAT or judicial review level (Mole, 1987: 31; Sachdeva, 1993: 126).[25]

Further clarification by the High Court and Court of Appeal of the manifold issues which the spouse rules have raised seemed to mitigate the harshest implications of the rule (see Sachdeva, 1993: 107–69). However, it was still claimed that entry clearance officers 'frequently continued [as they do today] to approach decision taking in a cynical and uninformed manner' (Scannell, 1992: 3; see also National Association of Citizens Advice Bureaux, 1996: 10–14). Juss (1993: 86) even suggests that entry clearance officers operate in an atmosphere of lawlessness and that even successful appellants are refused entry clearance (Juss, 1993: 90). More recent case law has been interpreted as 'growing evidence of judicial impatience and a sense of disappointment with the continuing flood of judicial review cases on primary purpose' (Sachdeva, 1993: 149).

An attempt to argue that the rule was *ultra vires* in *Rajput* v *Immigration Appeal Tribunal* [1989] Imm. AR 350 failed. Since that period, frustrated at the courts' unwillingness to make serious inroads into the primary purpose policy, advisers have chosen to litigate at the European level where some progress has been made,[26] but the results have been limited to securing rights for spouses of British citizens who may be able to demonstrate a European connection only. The Government has only responded with a concession outside the immigration rules allowing a spouse application where the marriage has subsisted for longer than five years or where there is a child of the marriage who has a right of abode in the United Kingdom.[27] This really is an admission that a quota system on spouses has been in operation all along (Sachdeva, 1993: 168).

The notion of procedural safeguards has been observed by a European commentator to be of primary importance to Anglo-American thinking (Schwarze, 1992: 147). In the Divisional Court it was recently argued that the courts had been under a duty to scrutinize claims for asylum with great care.[28] Sedley J declared that 'where, as is now the case, an entire appellate machinery has been interposed between the Secretary of State and the court regard has also to be had for the workings of that machinery. The eye of the court shifts to ensure that the appellate process has been lawfully and properly conducted.'[29] From the available evidence it is clear that in the sphere of asylum it may be no more than elegant rhetoric.

It has been claimed that cases have been rejected by the IAT despite manifest mistakes by adjudicators (Asylum Aid, 1995a: 36). Even judges have not been impressed by the quality of adjudicators' decisions (Woolf, 1992: 227). The requirement of leave to appeal to the IAT is important in this respect. It enables the IAT to have an important role in keeping a check on what issues are dealt with at higher judicial levels. A recurring question in judicial review proceedings is whether the IAT's practice of issuing relatively brief and unreasoned 'standard' refusals of leave to appeal is a proper course of conduct. Judges have upheld the propriety of this practice in a series of recent cases.[30] Their response may indicate that they do not wish to be overly concerned with details of the asylum appeals procedure and they thereby collude in the lack of transparency within the appellate structure.

There is clearly a deficiency in the provision of legal assistance to asylum seekers because of the political economy within the legal system (Shah, 1995a). The judicial branch has overridden this concern in order to accommodate the demands of administrative efficiency. It has already been confirmed by the House of Lords, in the immigration law context, that there is no breach of the principles of fairness in administrative law where, through the negligence of solicitors, an applicant is left unrepresented.[31] A strict approach is applied in the asylum context, where the procedures themselves have a way of letting the applicants down and appeals are regularly determined in their absence.[32]

The emphasis on time limits has further undermined the possibility that an applicant may confidently assert the right to be represented in what has become a complex area of law.[33] There is a marked reluctance to grant adjournments which may be required due to illness[34] or lack of representation.[35] Requests for adjournments are consistently contested by Home Office Presenting Officers.[36] Adjudicators themselves have cited the time limits in the 1993 Act as among their reasons for refusing adjournments (Asylum Rights Campaign, 1996: 50). A double standard appears to be in operation since adjournments requested by the Home Office Presenting Officers seem to be sympathetically granted.[37] The emphasis on time limits has been retained under the 1996 procedures.[38] Now that they are applied even more stringently, will advisers and representatives be able to prepare cases adequately? And will the judicial reaction to challenges on the basis of procedural fairness be favourable?

The formal institution of a notion of safe country of origin makes the quality of information available extremely important for sound decision-making. The standard of reasoning used by the Home Office to assess the situation in the state of origin has been analysed in detail and found to be severely deficient (Asylum Aid, 1995a; Asylum Aid, 1995b). The Secretary of State has privileged access to information both for and against an applicant's case but no source or date is given (Asylum Rights Campaign, 1996: 50). Where assertions are made that diplomatic sources have been used, there is a high level of judicial deference (see, for example, Shah, 1995c: 275–6).

The judiciary had already approved the safe third country principle before the enactment of the Asylum and Immigration Appeals Act 1993 (Shah, 1995c). Effectively this has meant pinballing asylum seekers from country to country, and potentially exposing them to *refoulement* (Amnesty International, 1993). The 1993 Act made a special provision in s. 2 which prohibited any practice, as laid down in the immigration rules, which would be contrary to the Geneva Convention on the Status of Refugees 1951. However, the third-country policy was endorsed by judges who thought that the 1993 Act did not heighten the United Kingdom's obligations under the 1951 Convention (*R* v *Secretary of State for the Home Department ex parte Mehari* [1994] 2 All ER 494). Neither could it be argued that:

> not least given the incorporation into English law of the 1951 Convention by the 1993 Act, removal of an asylum applicant to

a third country will only be lawful if the Secretary of State has received something in the nature of a positive guarantee that the applicant will be admitted to the third country's asylum procedures and his claim there properly dealt with under the 1951 Convention. (*ex parte Mehari*, at 506D–E).

Thus the Secretary of State could remove asylum seekers without an obligation to ascertain whether a proper solution could be found.

In *Abdi and Gawe* v. *Secretary of State for the Home Department* [1996] 1 All ER 641, the House of Lords maintained that a bare statement that the Secretary of State *believes* a country to be (a) safe (third country) is sufficient to show that a country is safe. As Lord Mustill (dissenting) put it, 'there is something unique in the position of the Secretary of State which translates a statement of belief into an item of evidence' (*ibid.*, at 644E–F). This is in the light of the fact, often ignored it seems, that the burden of proof is squarely on the Secretary of State to show that a safe third country certificate is good (*ibid.*, at 648C–D, *per* Lord Slynn).

A second issue which the House of Lords had to deal with in *Abdi and Gawe* was the extent of the duty on the Secretary of State to grant discovery of information which may be adverse to his case, so that an adjudicator may be sufficiently apprised of the facts to look at the decision afresh. Although the adjudicators do not have the power to order discovery,[39] they may request the production of documents.[40] An Amnesty International report surfaced in the High Court challenge.[41] This report showed that there were cases where Spain had returned applicants to the country of persecution. If such information were imputed to the Secretary of State should he or she reveal it? The firm answer by four of their Lordships was that there was no such obligation. Why is the common law of judicial review unable to step in to regulate a manifestly unfair procedure? Lord Lloyd thought that 'if the courts were to supplement the rules by imposing some such obligation on the Secretary of State, there would be a risk of frustrating the evident legislative purpose that "without foundation" appeals should be considered with all due speed' ([1996] 1 All ER 641, at 657J). Yet he could maintain that 'it would not, I think, be right to infer ... that justice is being sacrificed in the interests of speed' (*ibid.*, at 657C–D). The result of the case is to endorse a procedure in which the barest of assertions by the Secretary of State are accepted while the applicant, often hard pressed to obtain contradictory evidence, remains without an effective remedy. This situation will be even more hazardous if allowed to continue in the context of the safe country of origin appeals, where individuals are threatened with direct *refoulement*.

Extremely difficult issues are raised by the 1996 Act and there will no doubt be a large increase in the number of challenges in the High Court since there is no longer the possibility of applying to the IAT for safe country of origin and other certified cases.[42] The evidence on the new safe third country cases where there is no in-country right of appeal indicates that immigration officers have been prepared to concede cases relating to France and Belgium upon being threatened with judicial review. However, prior to the 1993 Act, when there was no in-country right of appeal in most cases, the judicial response indicated that no more than a cursory perusal of an application would be made (Shah, 1995c).

CONCLUSIONS

The judges have not shown themselves immune from the scare-mongering tactics of the executive, often raising the spectre of millions who will invade the United Kingdom. During the Ugandan Asians crisis Lord Denning had asked: 'Is it to be said that by international law every one of them has a right if expelled to come into these small islands? Surely not. This country would not have room for them. It is not as if it was only one or two coming. They come not in single files "but in battalions".'[43] The present Court of Appeal's views on current asylum issues also demonstrate the same hostility. Millett LJ stated recently that: 'Large numbers of persons in the Third World countries seek admission to the United Kingdom because of a desire to improve their conditions of life; and they falsely claim asylum because this gives them a means of admission.'[44] Simon Brown LJ[45] recently referred to a decision of Nolan J when attempting to arrive at an appropriate definition of the 1951 Convention's notion of persecution: 'considerations of policy may require a stringent test to be adopted if this country is not to be flooded with those claiming political asylum'.[46]

These policy dimensions can occlude a serious consideration of the level of administrative abuse which occurs in the immigration field, and may even lead to the conclusion that the judiciary participates in such abuse. Even though we may finally be on the eve of a judicial recognition of the importance of human rights jurisprudence in English law (see Laws, 1993 and 1994), the question which lingers is whether the recent history of inadequate supervision by the High Court in the immigration field will inevitably continue. What can one conclude about what the standards of procedural propriety, legality and rationality stand for after only a sample of judicial reaction has been analysed? And will it affect, in time, the entire law?

NOTES

1 The published immigration rules are rules of practice which are regarded as binding on the appellate authorities, but not regarded as strict rules of law. The latest rules are in HC 395 (1994-95) and Cm 3365 (1996). The Immigration Act 1971 does not exclude the operation of immigration law through administrative practice which may be at variance with the rules. Administrative practices are usually kept secret, putting individuals who may want to know what the rules are at a considerable disadvantage. There is an increasing body of case law both at the level of the Immigration Appeal Tribunal and in the courts. The *Immigration Appeal Reports*, the main set of law reports, contain many decisions at High Court level and above, and rather few of the decisions of the Immigration Appeal Tribunal. Knowledge of day-to-day practice therefore remains very important. A growing reliance is also placed on international conventions (see, generally, Macdonald and Blake, 1991: 29–37).

2 Dummett and Nicol (1990: 206) point out that while the 1969 Act was meant to provide a statutory basis for the appellate system, an extra-statutory system was operated until the coming into force of the 1971 Act.

3 Juss (1993: 85) notes, in particular, the failure by the authorities to provide full information in the explanatory statement or at the hearing.

4 *Race and Immigration*, No. 181 (July 1985), p. 2. The National Association of Citizens Advice Bureaux (1996: 54) has noted that: 'It has been a core element of Home Office policy to impose a visa regime on countries when they start to generate significant levels of asylum applications. Examples include Sri Lanka (made visa nationals in 1985), most of the former Yugoslavia (in 1992), and more recently, Sierra Leone and the Ivory Coast (both in 1994), Gambia (in 1995), and Tanzania and Kenya (both in 1996).' A list of visa countries has now been adopted at European Union level and includes Rwanda, Burundi, Nigeria, China, Sri Lanka and many other states where there are severe conflicts and risks of human rights violations. 5(5) *Statewatch* (September/October 1995); 234 OJ L, 3 October 1995: 1–3.

5 *R v Secretary of State for the Home Department, ex parte Mahli* [1990] 2 All ER 357 (CA); *Oladehinde and Alexander v Secretary of State for the Home Department* [1990] 3 All ER 393 (HL).

6 Immigration Act 1971, s. 13(3), s. 16(2); *Bugdaycay v Secretary of State for the Home Department and Related Appeals* [1987] 1 All ER 940. The lack of a substantive right of appeal in these cases was the subject of earlier criticism by advice agencies (Connelly, 1984: 14) and the House of Commons Home Affairs Select Committee, *Race and Immigration*, No. 180 (June 1985), p. 8.

7 *R v Secretary of State for the Home Department, ex parte Sritharan* [1992] Imm. AR 184.

8 *Bugdaycay* [1987] 1 All ER 940 at 955a, *per* Lord Templeman.

9 See further, Macdonald and Blake, 1995: 453–5.

10 *Campaign Against Racism and Fascism*, No. 4 (September/October 1991).

11 For example, Ralph Gibson LJ, in agreeing with the Government's submissions, noted, in *R v Secretary of State for the Home Department, ex parte Brind* [1990] 1 All ER 469, CA, at 484A–B: 'The court cannot, said counsel for the Secretary of State, decide whether an act of the minister, which is lawfully

within the power given by Parliament, is a breach of the obligation of the United Kingdom under the convention.'

12 Asylum and Immigration Appeal Act 1993, Schedule 2, para. 5.

13 Asylum and Immigration Appeals Act 1993, s. 9.

14 Remarks made by Tony Rawsthorne of the Immigration and Nationality Department's Asylum Division at a meeting, 'The future of asylum in Europe', organized by the Refugee Legal Centre and the United Nations High Commissioner for Refugees, London, 20 November 1996. At their peak in 1987, 45 per cent of all applications were on immigration issues although they declined to just over 20 per cent by the first quarter of 1991 (Sunkin *et al.*, 1993a: 443–4).

15 Asylum and Immigration Act 1996, section 1. See further Winterbourne *et al.*, 1996.

16 Asylum and Immigration Act 1996, s. 3(2).

17 Asylum and Immigration Act 1996, s. 2(3). The United States, Canada, Switzerland and Norway were considered to be possible early candidates for designation (Ghose, 1996: 49–50).

18 Asylum and Immigration Act 1996, s. 3(1)(a). It should be noted that an applicant may not raise a matter which is not connected with the third country certificate unless that certificate has first been set aside by an adjudicator. *Ibid.*, s. 3(1)(b).

19 Asylum and Immigration Act 1996, s. 8.

20 Asylum and Immigration Act 1996, ss. 9, 10 and 11.

21 *Re B and JCWI*, noted at 10(3) *Immigration and Nationality Law and Practice* 106 (1996).

22 While the discussion here is limited to more recent events, the reaction of the judiciary to the immigration issues of the late nineteenth and early twentieth centuries is instructive (for details, see Legomsky, 1987: 87–97 and Vincenzi, 1985).

23 S. Juss, [1986] *Cambridge Law Journal*: 372–4, at 374, in a comment on the *Swati* case, remarked that 'In the 1980s the number of applications for leave for judicial review has doubled. Governmental action on a whole range of issues has been challenged in the higher courts. Of this increase to about 1,000 applications per year, in the civil sphere, a high percentage of them (as much as 40%) has been in immigration. This will now change.'

24 *R v Immigration Appeal Tribunal, ex parte Vinod Bhatia* [1985] Imm. AR 39, approved by the Court of Appeal, at [1985] Imm. AR 50.

25 Forbes J, who decided *Bhatia* at the High Court, was at pains also to note that 'if there is no clear evidence either way ... or if the question ... seems evenly balanced, [the applicant] should no longer be given the benefit of the doubt' (cited by Bevan, 1986: 250 and Sachdeva, 1993: 126).

26 *R v IAT and Surinder Singh, ex parte Secretary of State for the Home Department* [1992] Imm. AR 565.

27 210 HC Official Reports (6th Series), cols 523–524.

28 In *Bugdaycay v Secretary of State for the Home Department* [1987] 1 AC 514, at 531 Lord Bridge stated that '[t]he most fundamental of all human rights is the individual's right to life and when an administrative decision under challenge is

said to be one which may put the applicant's life at risk, the basis of the decision must surely call for the most anxious scrutiny'.

29 R v. *Immigration Appeal Tribunal, ex parte Omar Mohammed Ali* [1995] Imm. AR 45, at 47.

30 *Sahota* v *Immigration Appeal Tribunal* [1995] Imm. AR 500 (CA); *R* v *Immigration Appeal Tribunal, ex parte Mehmet Yaziki* [1995] Imm. AR 98 (QBD); *R* v *Immigration Appeal Tribunal, ex parte Mohammed Rashid* [1995] Imm. AR 194 (QBD); *R* v *Immigration Appeal Tribunal, ex parte Rajendra Kumar* [1995] Imm. AR 385 (QBD); *R* v *Secretary of State, ex parte Beyazit* [1995] Imm. AR 534 (QBD) (*Yaziki* referred to and applied).

31 *R* v *Secretary of State for the Home Department, ex parte Al-Mehdawi* [1990] 1 AC 876 (HL).

32 In *R* v *Immigration Appeal Tribunal, ex parte Luis Pablo Flores* [1995] Imm. AR 85 (QBD), service of determination was made to the address of the solicitors, but receipt was made too late to appeal. The Divisional Court held that the IAT had no power to extend the time limit in which an application for leave to appeal had to be submitted. In *Kayanja* v *Secretary of State for the Home Department* [1995] Imm. AR 123 (CA), service of notice of hearing had been made by post office and not actually received. The appeal was determined in the absence of the applicant and his representative. The Court of Appeal held that the notice was deemed to have appropriately arrived.

33 Juss (1993: 83) notes the evidence of a Mr Langdon, head of the Immigration and Nationality Department, before the Home Affairs Select Committee, that 'the appeals system is probably of a more legalistic nature than was originally anticipated'.

34 In *Akinyemi* (11743), 30 December 1994 (unreported), IAT, the applicant's representative failed to appear due to illness and the adjudicator refused to grant an adjournment to the appellant who was present. In *Irobun* (11744), 19 December 1994 (unreported), IAT, despite a record of illness and consequent adjournments, a final adjournment was refused by the adjudicator.

35 In *Utobar* [1996] 3(1) ILPA Case Digest (12280), IAT, 12 June 1995, a client was 'dropped' for lack of means prior to his hearing before the adjudicator and was put in a position of having to ask for an adjournment, which was refused. There was an indication that the Refugee Legal Centre would take up his case although, prior to the IAT stage, they had not been able to give a firm commitment due to a full caseload. The Chief Adjudicator, sitting as President in the IAT, refused to overturn the adjudicator's refusal of an adjournment. The tone of the decision placed responsibility on the applicant himself for his dilemma. Significantly, the Chief Adjudicator has emphasized, extrajudicially, the need to process a large number of cases (Asylum Rights Campaign, 1996: 50). In *R* v *Secretary of State for the Home Department, ex parte Yeboah* [1995] Imm. AR 393, QBD, an adjournment was requested due to the representative's failure to appear before the adjudicator for a hearing of the adjournment issue. The adjudicator refused the application. Divisional Court held that the adjudicator's refusal was not reviewable.

36 Home Office Presenting Officers have stated that it is the policy of the Home Office to refuse adjournment requests (Winterbourne *et al.*, 1996: 126). If this

policy is proven then it may give rise to an additional ground for challenge in judicial review.

37 In *Bozkurt* (11783), 19 January 1995 [1996] 3(1) ILPA Case Digest, IAT, the Secretary of State appealed against the adjudicator's refusal to grant an adjournment on the basis that the Home Office Presenting Officer had been ill on the previous day and that it should have been possible to assign another officer to the case. The IAT held, applying *Walayat Begum* (10248) (unreported, IAT), that it was desirable to grant an adjournment particularly because oral evidence was to be called.

38 Procedure Rules 1996, Rule 5(1) and (2) and Rule 9(2).

39 *R v An adjudicator, Mr R. G. Care, ex parte Secretary of State for the Home Department* [1989] Imm. AR 423.

40 The Asylum Appeal (Procedure) Rules 1993, SI 1993/1661 (now repealed), provided an adjudicator with the power to *request* documents. Cf. Asylum Appeal (Procedure) Rules 1996, SI 1996/2070, Rule 28 (formerly Rule 27 of the 1993 Procedure Rules).

41 [1994] Imm. AR 402.

42 New para. 5(7) of Schedule 2 of the Asylum and Immigration Appeals Act 1993, inserted by s. 1 of the Asylum and Immigration Act 1996.

43 *R v Immigration Officer, ex parte Thakrar* [1974] 1 QB 684, at 702.

44 *Mbanza v Secretary of State for the Home Department* [1996] Imm. AR 136, at 143.

45 In *Sandralingam v Secretary of State for the Home Department* [1996] Imm. AR 97, at 107.

46 *R v Immigration Appeal Tribunal, ex parte Jonah* [1985] Imm. AR 7.

BIBLIOGRAPHY

Amnesty International (1993) *Passing the Buck: Deficient Home Office Practice in 'Safe Third Country' Asylum Cases*. July.

Asylum Aid (1995a) *No Reason at All: Home Office Decisions on Asylum Claims*. London.

Asylum Aid (1995b) *Adding Insult to Injury: Experiences of Zairean Refugees in the UK*. London.

Asylum Rights Campaign (1996) *'The Risks of Getting It Wrong': The Asylum and Immigration Bill Session 1996 and the Determinations of Special Adjudicators*. London.

Bevan, V. (1986) *The Development of British Immigration Law*. London: Croom Helm.

Commission for Racial Equality (1985) *Immigration Control Procedures: Report of a Formal Investigation*. London.

Connelly, M. (1984) 'Refugees and the United Kingdom', *Race and Immigration*, No. 168 (June): 8–16.

Cruz, A. (1995) *Shifting Responsibility: Carriers' Liability in the Member States of the European Union and North America*. Stoke on Trent: Trentham Books.

Drabu, K. and Bowen, S. (1989) *Mandatory Visas: Visiting the UK from Bangladesh, India, Pakistan, Ghana and Nigeria*. London: Commission for Racial Equality.

Dummett, A. (1994) 'Immigration and nationality' in McCrudden, C. and Chambers, G. (eds) *Individual Rights and the Law in Britain*, pp. 335–62. Oxford: Clarendon.

Dummett, A. and Nicol, A. (1990) *Subjects, Citizens, Aliens and Others: Immigration and Nationality Law*. London: Weidenfeld & Nicolson.

Dunstan, R. (1995) 'Home Office asylum policy: unfair and inefficient?', 9(4) *Immigration and Nationality Law and Practice*: 132–5.

Ghose, K. (1996) *The Asylum and Immigration Act 1996*. (A compilation of ministerial statements made on behalf of the Government during the Bill's Passage through Parliament.) London: Immigration Law Practitioners' Association.

Gillespie, Jim (1993): 'The Asylum and Immigration Appeals Bill: a review of the proposed asylum appeal rights', 7(2) *Immigration and Nationality Law and Practice*: 68–70.

Griffith, J. A. G. (1991) *The Politics of the Judiciary* (4th edn). London: Fontana.

Harlow, Carol (1994) 'Accidental loss of an asylum seeker', 57 *Modern Law Review*: 620–6.

Joint Council for the Welfare of Immigrants (1987) *Out of Sight: The New Visit Visa System Overseas*. London.

Juss, S. (1986) Comment on the *Swati* case, [1986] *Cambridge Law Journal*: 372–4.

Juss, S. S. (1992): 'Review and appeal in administrative law – what is happening to the right of appeal in immigration law?', 12 *Legal Studies*: 364–76.

Juss, S. S. (1993) *Immigration, Nationality and Citizenship*. London: Mansell.

Laws, J. (1993) 'Is the High Court the guardian of fundamental constitutional rights?', *Public Law*: 59–79.

Laws, J. (1994): 'Judicial remedies and the constitution', 57 *Modern Law Review*: 213–27.

Legomsky, S. H. (1987) *Immigration and the Judiciary: Law and Politics in Britain and America*. Oxford: Clarendon Press.

Macdonald, I. A. (1987) *Immigration Law and Practice in the United Kingdom*. London: Butterworths.

Macdonald, I. A. and Blake, N. J. (1991) *Immigration Law and Practice in the United Kingdom* (3rd edn). London: Butterworths.

Macdonald, I. A. and Blake, N. J. (1995) *Immigration Law and Practice in the United Kingdom* (4th edn). London: Butterworths.

Mole, N. (1987) *Immigration: Family Entry and Settlement*. Bristol: Jordans.

National Association of Citizens Advice Bureaux (1996) *A Right to Family Life: CAB Clients' Experience of Immigration and Asylum*. London.

Sachdeva, S. (1993) *The Primary Purpose Rule in British Immigration Law*. Stoke on Trent: Trentham Books.

Scannell, R. (1992) 'Primary purpose: the end of judicial sympathy?', 4(4) *Immigration and Nationality Law and Practice*: 3–6.

Schwarze, J. (1992) *European Administrative Law*. London: Sweet & Maxwell.

Shah, P. (1993) 'The erosion of remedies in visitor cases', 7(3) *Immigration and Nationality Law and Practice*: 93–5.

Shah, P. (1995a) 'Access to legal assistance for asylum seekers', 9(2) *Immigration and Nationality Law and Practice*: 55–8.

Shah, P. (1995b) 'British nationality and immigration laws and their effects on Hong Kong' in Werner Menski (ed.) *Coping with 1997: The Reaction of the Hong Kong People to the Transfer of Power*, pp. 57–119. Stoke on Trent: Trentham Books.

Shah, P. (1995c) 'Refugees and safe third countries: United Kingdom, European and international aspects', 1(2) *European Public Law*: 259–88.

Shah, R. K. D. (1992) 'Britain and Kenya: some immigration and nationality issues', 6(2) *Immigration and Nationality Law and Practice*: 35–9.

Smith, P. (1993) 'Reducing legal aid eligibility criteria: the impact for immigration law practitioners and their clients', *Civil Justice Quarterly*: 167–87.

Sunkin, M. (1987) 'What is happening to applications for judicial review?', 50 *Modern Law Review*: 432–67.

Sunkin, M., Bridges, L. and Meszaros, G. (1993a) 'Trends in judicial review', *Public Law*: 443–6.

Sunkin, M., Bridges, L. and Meszaros, G. (1993b) *Judicial Review in Perspective: An Investigation of Trends in the Use and Operation of the Judicial Review Procedure in England and Wales*. London: The Public Law Project.

Vincenzi, C. (1985) 'Aliens and the judicial review of immigration law', *Public Law*: 93–114.

Vincenzi, C. (1992) 'Extra-statutory ministerial discretion in immigration law', *Public Law*: 300–21.

Winterbourne, D., Doebbler, C. and Shah, P. (1996) 'Refugees and safe countries of origin: appeals, judicial review and human rights', 10(4) *Immigration and Nationality Law and Practice*: 123–35.

Woolf, H. (1992) 'Judicial review: a possible programme for reform', *Public Law*: 221–37.

10

Prisoners: Judicial Review and Social Welfare

SIMON CREIGHTON

Judicial review of prison matters has, in recent years, become a fertile area for academic study and legal practice. The classic view of judicial intervention into the realm of prison law is to characterize it as a steady process of progression which has allowed the Divisional Court to gradually extend its jurisdiction into all aspects of prison life. Indeed, the concept of prison law as a distinct area of practice and study has arisen largely from the interventionist approach of the courts. To a large extent, this interpretation is an understandable reaction to the proliferation of prisoner litigation in recent years, but on a more critical reading of the relevant judgments in their historical context, it is arguable that this simply represents a general societal move towards greater accountability. This in itself is a major development in opening up the closed world of prisons but should not be confused with the concepts of rights and welfare.

Historically, judicial review was not considered to be an appropriate remedy for the majority of issues affecting prisoners and the Divisional Court often took the view that it did not have the power to intervene in this area of law. In the rare cases where an application by a prisoner was made, the court was very reluctant to intervene. This classic summary of this approach was made by Lord Denning in 1972:

> If the courts were to entertain actions by disgruntled prisoners, the governor's life would be made intolerable. The discipline of the prison would be undermined. The Prison Rules are

regulatory directions only. Even if they are not observed, they do not give rise to a cause of action.[1]

In reaching this decision, Lord Denning was articulating two deep-seated traditions. First, that prisoners do not enjoy rights in the same manner as people at liberty and second, that once these rights have been removed, the authorities are the sole arbiters of fairness. This approach was first called into question with the decision of the Court of Appeal in 1979 that the disciplinary functions of the Boards of Visitors were susceptible to judicial review.[2] Then, in 1983, Lord Wilberforce articulated the view that prisoners retain all civil rights, save for those taken away expressly or impliedly through the fact of their imprisonment.[3] Since that judgment was delivered, a series of cases have extended the jurisdiction of the Divisional Court so that there are now very few decisions made about prisoners which are not amenable to judicial scrutiny.

One of the reasons why prison law has developed so largely through judgments of the Divisional Court is because the vast majority of decisions made about prisoners are firmly in the realm of public law.[4] The possibility of commencing private law claims is very limited and it is now clear that private law actions are only appropriate in cases where compensation is being sought as a result of negligence or the malicious actions of prison staff resulting in some form of damage or personal injury which can be compensated. The possibility of commencing private law actions against the authorities for breach of statutory duty simply does not exist for prisoners.[5]

While it is undeniable that judicial review has had a powerful policing effect on the administration of the prison estate, it is by necessity a remedy which can only operate within the rigid constraints of statute. Commentators on prison conditions have always seen a codified set of minimum standards as the key to establishing any genuine framework for progression. As Richardson stated when reviewing the first clutch of prison cases to be heard by the Divisional Court in the early 1980s: 'Prisoners should possess special rights vis-à-vis the prison authorities in a sufficiently detailed form to promote effective supervision by the courts.'[6] This represented one of the first attempts to critically assess the impact of judicial review and even at this early stage, it was apparent that there was a tension between what was open to review and what powers the court actually possessed to interfere with the decision made. In order to comprehend the pessimism that Richardson expresses, it is necessary to follow the history of prisoners' applications in some detail.

As well as examining the legal process, it is possible to identify a number of competing forces which have exerted pressure on the legal system to extend its jurisdiction into prison life. These forces include the jurisprudence of the European Court of Human Rights (ECHR), the role of non-Governmental pressure groups and the actions of prisoners themselves. In order to critically assess the impact of judicial review on prisoners' rights, the interrelation with the other forces for change and the validity of the criticisms advanced of judicial decisions, a brief examination of the legal structure and framework that governs the prison estate is essential.

The key piece of primary legislation which deals with the prison estate is the Prison Act 1952.[7] The Act is relatively brief and contains very little detail as to the day-to-day management of prisons. It has been described in the following terms: 'the Act is little more than a series of enabling and deeming provisions designed to give the Home Secretary maximum discretion in the organisation of the prison system'.[8] There are two crucial sections to the Act, s. 4 and s. 47, both of which require some explanation. Section 4 devolves maximum discretion of the Secretary of State in that it provides a general duty of superintendence for the maintenance of prisons and prisoners (s. 4(1)), requires him/her to ensure compliance with the Act and the Prison Rules (s. 4(2)) and requires him/her to exercise all powers conferred by statute, common law or charter (s. 4(3)). While the duty to both make and comply with the relevant law is established, there is no explanation of how this duty must be carried out. The point which is perhaps of most importance is that a clear onus of responsibility has been placed on this individual and it is this individual who can be brought to account for any failure to meet this duty. Interestingly, it was these powers that were invoked when seeking to defend actions brought by prisoners against prison governors on the grounds that it was only the Secretary of State who was charged with the duty. This 'ouster clause' was not completely abandoned until 1988 (see below).[9]

Perhaps the most important section of the Act is s. 47. This requires the Secretary of State to make Rules for the management of prisons and for the classification, treatment, employment, discipline and control of prisoners. These Rules are to be made by statutory instrument and must ensure that any person charged with an offence 'has an opportunity of presenting his case' (s. 47(2)).[10]

The Prison Rules 1964 are designed to fill in the missing detail of the Act and are subject to frequent amendment. Prison Rules were never designed to be justiciable in themselves.[11] The Rules contain a mixture of policy statements, discretionary powers and obligations to prisoners. They have been classified as dealing with a number of distinct matters, encompassing rules of specific individual protection, rules concerning administration, those dealing with policy matters and those relating to discretionary powers.[12] Although the Rules in themselves are not justiciable in that they do not confer individual rights which can be protected through private law actions, they are amenable to judicial review in the manner in which they are implemented.[13]

The missing piece of the formal legal structure of the prison estate may be found in a number of policy documents issued by the Prison Service, described as Standing Orders and Circular Instructions and, more recently, in Advice and Instructions to Governors. These contain detailed provisions to deal with minutiae of prison life, ranging from how prisoners should be classified, assessed for temporary release and disciplined, through to issues of staffing, gardening trophies and Christmas leave arrangements. There is no formal power attached to such policy documents, but they are the only practical explanation of how the multiplicity of statutory and discretionary powers are to be operated in practice.

It is true to say that all of these sources of authority are organic in that they are susceptible to change over the years and their present form has been shaped through legal action and through executive policy changes. For instance, Prison Rule 37A which protects the right to confidential legal correspondence was recently redrafted to specifically take account of decisions made by the High Court and European Court of Human Rights.[14] Conversely, Rule 27 which sets out the amount of daily exercise that prisoners may take was changed in August 1996 by the Home Secretary to make this a discretionary issue rather than a matter of rights. The change was presumably made to take account of future difficulties caused by overcrowding resulting from penal policies in force at that time. It is necessary to have a broad understanding of the scope and purpose of these powers in order to comprehend the framework within which judicial review has developed.

As can be seen from the explanation of the legal framework of the prison estate, prisoners are, by the very fact of their imprisonment, placed in a position where they are subject to a variety of decisions made by a public authority on a daily basis. These decisions can be quasi-judicial in that they relate to disciplinary functions and release from custody, or purely administrative which will often entail the exercise of discretion within the decision-making process. Perhaps unsurprisingly, it was the use of these quasi-judicial powers which first came under judicial scrutiny. It is instructive to look at judicial reviews of the exercise of formal disciplinary powers and decisions concerning release in order to appreciate the manner in which this area of the law has developed.

The disciplinary code within prisons derives from Prison Rule 47 which sets out a wide range of offences against prison discipline. The offences encompass aspects of the criminal law, such as a prohibition against assault (Rule 47(1)) through to those which only have application within the prison itself, such as refusing to work properly (Rule 47(18)) or offending in any way against good order and discipline (Rule 47(21)). Prisoners are automatically entitled to be released before their entire sentences have been served, a system described as remission. The sanction for being found guilty of any of these offences against prison discipline is the forfeiture of a portion of this remission.

The manner in which the disciplinary code is implemented has obvious parallels with the wider judicial process owing to the possibility for infringing on the liberty of the subject. It is arguable that it was only once the Divisional Court and Court of Appeal could be persuaded that this was the proper analysis of these powers that judicial review of prison issues became possible.

The disciplinary code remained relatively unchanged from its inception in 1899 to 1979 save for the decision to abolish corporal punishment in 1967.[15] The function of deciding upon guilt and innocence and awarding punishments could be carried out either by the prison governor or, in cases that were considered to be more serious and potentially warranting a severer penalty, by the Board of Visitors, a body created by the Prison Act 1952 (ss. 6–9). The first occasion on which the English courts considered the disciplinary code was in the case of *Fraser* v *Mudge*.[16] The case involved the right to legal representation at hearings and Lord Denning, in weighing up the conflicting principles of the need for a speedy hearing as against the rights of the accused opted for the former, said: 'If legal representation were allowed, it would involve considerable delay ... Those who hear cases must act fairly ... But that can be done and is done without the case being held up for legal representation.'

It is difficult to comprehend how the need for speed in the judicial process could outweigh what now appears to be the much wider principle of fairness within this process. It has been argued that the prison disciplinary system at the time was akin to the court martial procedure[17] but even in court martials, legal representation had been an entrenched principle for many years. However, within the framework of prisons, disciplinary hearings of this type were distinguishable from criminal charges on the basis that they were concerned with the loss of a privilege rather than the loss of liberty. The privilege in contention happened to be the possibility of leaving prison before a full sentence had been served.[18]

The courts were next required to examine the precise nature of the prison disciplinary hearing following the riots at Hull prison in 1976. Many prisoners were charged with serious disciplinary offences and were allocated to prisons around the country where disciplinary hearings were conducted by Boards of Visitors. The punishments handed out were severe and in several cases amounted to losses of over a year of remission. A Canadian prisoner, Ronald St Germain, applied for judicial review of the manner in which the hearings were conducted and the refusal of legal representation. At first instance, the Divisional Court held that although a judicial function was being carried out, the hearings were exempt from review as they were conducted in a closed institution.[19] The Court of Appeal overturned this judgment and accepted that the principles of natural justice prevailed in the exercise of judicial authority, even within such closed institutions.[20]

In reaching this judgment, the Court of Appeal made two crucial departures from previous perceptions. First, that such hearings did impinge on the liberty of the subject and that it was not possible to characterize the loss of remission as the mere forfeiture of a privilege. Second, in asserting the principle of natural justice as a basic requirement of fairness within these procedures, it paved the way for future judicial scrutiny of the precise procedures that would be followed.

The impact of this judgment became apparent with a series of judgments which examined the manner in which disciplinary hearings were conducted over the next five years. Adjudications were quashed by the Divisional Court for breaching the requirements of natural justice on a wide variety of issues. These included the failure to allow witnesses to be cross-examined,[21] a failure to explain the charges properly[22] and eventually, the right to legal representation was established.[23]

In exerting its authority in this manner, the court made it possible for the sources of authority within prisons to be examined in more detail. The *St Germain (No. 1)* case had resulted in the view that governors' disciplinary powers were administrative in nature as they derived from the authority vested in the Secretary of State from the Prison Act. This contrasted with the judicial nature of the powers exercised by the Boards of Visitors as an outside body. In the case of *King*,[24] the Court of Appeal upheld this approach in finding that the only remedy was against the Secretary of State personally. This required the prisoner to become involved in the cumbersome procedure of petitioning the Secretary of State and then applying to the court on completion of this process. The judgment was also a profound set-back to the attempts to promote the principles of natural justice in the disciplinary process. Griffiths LJ actually felt that

225

the governor's prior knowledge of the relevant parties was a distinct advantage that would enable a just decision to be reached. The contrast between this view and the stringent requirements of fairness in the criminal process could not be more stark.

The House of Lords finally accepted the absurdity of this view in *R v Deputy Governor of Parkhurst ex parte Leech*[25] and confirmed that the powers of a governor were directly challengeable as they were exercised under authority devolved from the Secretary of State. In his judgment, Shaw LJ explained why he felt that these were matters which the courts could now entertain:

> Now the rights of the citizen, however circumscribed by a penal sentence or otherwise, must always be the concern of the Courts unless their jurisdiction is excluded by some statutory provision ... It is irrelevant that the Home Secretary may afford redress where the rules have been infringed or their application has been irregular or unduly harsh. An essential characteristic of the right of a subject is that it carries with it a right of recourse to the Courts unless some statute decrees otherwise.[26]

The import of this decision is that it inverted the previously successful defences mounted to prisoners' applications for judicial review. Rather than looking to statute to see what rights were conferred on prisoners, the court felt empowered to look at any matters where their jurisdiction was not specifically excluded by statute. This can be seen as a logical extension of the construction of the law put forward by Lord Wilberforce in *Raymond v Honey*. The case is all the more remarkable for the fact that the specific point of law was originally spotted by the applicant Mark Leech, then a serving prisoner.[27]

The very fact that the case was conceived by a recipient of the system under challenge highlights the important role that prisoners have had in taking the initiative to promote and advance the rights of those in custody. The next changes to the disciplinary system were not to be made through the legal process but through another agency for change, the direct actions of prison inmates. The Woolf Report[28] was prepared following the serious disturbances at Strangeways prison.

One of the central platforms of the report, and one which was to be accepted by the Government, was a formalization of the disciplinary process. As a result, the Board of Visitors' unhappy role as adjudicators was removed and maximum punishments were established. A formal, internal review process was also put in place to be operated through the newly conceived request/complaints procedure. The willingness of the courts to impose the need for fairness in these procedures have ensured that this system has not remained static and more recent developments have included the publication of a *Prison Discipline Manual* in 1995 which sets out a detailed guide to the law and procedure to be followed and includes the right to free records of such hearings to enable appeals to be made. The *Manual* has to be kept in all prison libraries and must be made available to all prisoners facing disciplinary charges. During 1992, over 450 findings of guilt were overturned through the internal procedures.[29]

A continuing area of concern in the formal disciplinary process remains the role of governors as adjudicators. It is difficult to marry the managerial role which governors have to perform towards their staff with their acting as impartial arbiters of evidence at disciplinary hearings where they will often be called upon to weigh the veracity of evidence provided by officers against directly conflicting evidence of prisoners. This is not an issue which it is possible to reform through judicial review as it requires a change to statute rather than the interpretation of statutory provisions. The dissatisfaction with this system is shared by many members of the Prison Service as well as prisoners. A prison governor, in answer to a question concerning who should adjudicate at these cases, said: 'Essentially, it must be a person who stands aside from the day to day management of the prison.'[30] This again may be an area for which reform will come not from the intervention of the courts but from one of the other forces of change which were discussed at the start of this chapter.

The development of judicial review of the prison disciplinary system provides an important indicator of judicial attitudes to prisoners' rights. As this system is directly linked to the liberty of the subject, it directly addresses the extent to which prisoners are perceived to have rights as opposed to the enjoyment of privileges bestowed upon them. The other area which has been approached in this manner is parole which provides for the early release of prisoners from their sentences.

The Prison Rules 1952 envisaged that early release from prison could take place on the grounds of industry or good conduct (s. 25(1)). They did not envisage any formalized process of early release on licence, and in early challenges to exercise of discretion under these powers there was a familiar reluctance to accept that any jurisdiction actually existed: 'I would not think of interfering in any way whatsoever with the entirely unfettered power and discretion of the prison commissioners in this matter.'[31] Although this judgment clearly no longer has any legal weight, it does carry important themes for future challenges in the reluctance to closely scrutinize the exercise of discretion.

The Criminal Justice Act 1967 formalized the parole process: broadly speaking, it allowed all prisoners an automatic reduction of their sentence of one-third and made those prisoners serving longer sentences eligible for discretionary release between the one-third and two-thirds point of the sentence. Release between the two-thirds point and the expiry of a sentence could only be deferred if remission was lost through the disciplinary process. This formal recognition of early release arrangements and the separation of automatic release from discretionary release is an important distinction when assessing the challenges to the system that would come before the courts.

The very fact that all prisoners were to be allowed the same amount of remission, which would be lost rather than earned, contributed to the reform of the disciplinary process which has already been discussed. Once it had become established practice that release would fall on a certain date, the loss of remission was an actual deprivation of liberty rather than a privilege. This was drawn out by the ECHR in *Campbell and Fell* which observed:

> The Court, for its part, does not find that the distinction between a right and a privilege is of great assistance. What is important is that the practice of granting remission – whereby a prisoner will be set free on the estimated date of release given to him at the outset of his sentence – creates a legitimate expectation that he will recover his liberty before the end of his term of imprisonment.[32]

This was a view that was accepted by the domestic courts in the *Leech* case (above).

The corollary to this was that parole was clearly perceived to be a privilege which enabled prisoners to serve a part of their sentence in the community rather than in custody. The Criminal Justice Act 1967 provided for a tripartite structure for determining whether a prisoner was suitable for release on licence (ss. 59–60). This consisted of a Local Review Committee which would review prison reports and interview the prisoner and then send a recommendation to the Parole Board. The Parole Board would in turn consider the case and make their recommendation to the Secretary of State who would either make the decision personally or would delegate authority to junior ministers or civil servants.

The rights established pursuant to these procedures were hard to identify. The Local Review Committee Rules[33] allowed for the prisoner to be interviewed by a governor, to be afforded the opportunity to make representations to be considered by the Committee and to make written representations to the Committee. These rights did not extend to seeing any of the material that was considered at any stage of this process or to be informed of any reasons for the decision finally reached. This process was challenged by a prisoner sentenced to life who appeared to fit the criteria for release on licence but who had been consistently refused.[34] The applicant claimed that the interests of fairness in the administrative process required disclosure of reports and also of reasons for the decision. This was dismissed by the Court of Appeal with Lord Denning, then Master of the Rolls, commenting that:

> In the end I think the problem comes down to this: what does public policy as best demand be done? ... I think that in the interests of the man himself, as a human being facing indefinite detention, it would be better for him to be told the reasons. But, in the interests of society at large, including the administration of the parole system, it would be best not to give them.[35]

The decision is a strong indicator of the severe limitations that existed in seeking to promote change through judicial review. It should be remembered that at the time the Court of Appeal reached their decision, it had already been established that the procedure at disciplinary hearings fell within the jurisdiction of the court as it touched on the liberty of the subject. Although the Court of Appeal accepted that parole decisions were amenable to judicial review, by refusing to grant the opportunity to see the material on which the decision was based, any attempts to construct a challenge to this discretionary decision were rendered virtually impossible. As one commentator observed:

> The practical consequence of the decision in *Payne* is, it is submitted, to remove the deliberations of the Parole Board from the public domain, and to ensure that those deliberations and the decisions arising from them cannot be challenged.[36]

While the law in relation to parole, and in particular to prisoners sentenced to life, has progressed considerably since that time, this is a theme that continues to emerge in all aspects of prison litigation (see below).

The reference by Lord Denning to public policy also reveals a wider concern of the courts, and one which is often resolved only by the intervention of the ECHR. In defending actions seeking to impose wider duties on state institutions, it is common for an appeal to be made to the costs that would result in running a new system. In relation to the parole system, the ECHR was called upon to examine the procedures for recalling prisoners under a discretionary life sentence to prison. Discretionary life sentences are imposed for serious violent or sexual offences in cases where it is considered that the offender needs to be detained until s/he no longer poses a danger to the public.[37] The very nature of the sentence is such that it is accepted that the person receiving the sentence may be susceptible to change and that their detention is only warranted until they no longer pose a danger to others. It is not difficult to see why this should become the focal point for judicial reform of a secretive system.

The case of *Weeks* v *UK*[38] held that discretionary lifers who were recalled to prison after having been released on licence were entitled to see the reports which would be considered by the Parole Board and more importantly, that a 'paper' review of a case by the Parole Board did not satisfy the right to have detention reviewed by a 'court-like body', a right protected by Article 5(4) of the European Convention. The ECHR has two important advantages over the domestic courts. It is not bound by English legislation and it takes the view that certain human rights are fundamental and the state has a duty to organize its resources so as to accommodate those rights.

This decision was immediately followed by a series of cases before the domestic courts directly concerning discretionary lifers. In *R* v *SSHD ex parte Hanscomb*[39] the distinction between discretionary lifers, whose sentence is preventative as well as punitive, and mandatory lifers, whose sentences are fixed automatically by law, was recognized for the first time. This was then followed by the case of *Benson* in which the Divisional Court established the appropriate test to be applied when deciding upon release.[40] This case represents something of a watershed in judicial review of discretionary powers in that it was the first occasion that a prisoner sentenced to life was successful in challenging a decision of the Secretary of State on the issue of release from custody.[41]

The ECHR was also at the forefront of the next significant reform of the parole system. In an application brought by three prisoners with discretionary life sentences, the court re-examined the requirements of Article 5(4) when applied to the review procedures for release.[42] Once it had been accepted that the discretionary life sentence was a combination of the punitive and the protective, it was necessary for any decision on detention after the tariff period to be decided upon by a court-like body. The Parole Board could only fulfil this function if it allowed full disclosure of all reports, oral hearings, the right to legal representation and the ability to call and cross-examine witnesses.

This case brought about a profound change not only in domestic legislation with the introduction of the Criminal Justice Act 1991, but also in judicial attitudes to the very nature of the life sentences and the powers that could be exerted over the administration of the sentence. The following year, the Court of Appeal confirmed the right of disclosure of parole reports in advance of the new statutory arrangements for review.[43] In overturning previous authority, Lord Justice Taylor accepted that 'established views on prisoners' rights [in 1981] were very different from today'. A number of factors were identified as evidence of that change, including the decision of the ECHR in *Thynne, Wilson and Gunnell*.

Once it had been established that the administration of the discretionary life sentence fell within the jurisdiction of the court, it was inevitable that attempts would be made to extend these powers to the mandatory life sentence. This, however, has proven far more contentious due to the history and nature of the sentence. The life sentence for people convicted of murder was introduced as a mandatory sentence by the Murder (Abolition of Death Penalty) Act 1965. The problem for the judiciary lies in the very fact that the sentence is mandatory. Responsibility for setting the tariff and deciding on release has always been the sole prerogative of the executive. The tension arises as these are essentially judicial functions being concerned with length of sentence and fitness for release, undermining the element of discretion that the judiciary retain in nearly all other areas of the criminal justice system.

The mandatory life sentence is also interesting in that the ECHR has refused to directly exert its authority over either the sentencing or the release procedures.[44] While the jurisprudence of the ECHR does have an impact through the cross-fertilization of statements of principle on fundamental issues of human rights, there is an absence of any direct legal authority on this subject. This means that the views of the domestic courts are both the definitive statement of current law and an accurate reflection of how widely the court will draw its powers unfettered by outside influence.

The notion of a mandatory sentence has always caused concern amongst the judiciary. Lord Hailsham commented in 1987 that 'murder consists in a whole bundle of offences of vastly differing culpability ranging from [the] brutal to ... the mercy killing of a beloved partner'.[45] The House of Lords Select Committee on Murder and Life Imprisonment 1989[46] concluded that the sentence for murder should be at the court's discretion and a Committee which investigated the penalty for murder, constituted by the Prison Reform Trust and chaired by Lord Lane in 1993,[47] reached the same conclusion.

This argument for reform had always been fiercely contested by the Secretary of State on the grounds that murder is the most heinous crime for which the only punishment is the forfeiture of one's liberty to the state for the rest of one's life. Release from prison is essentially a privilege allowing that person to serve their sentence in the community but it will always be subject to a life licence permitting recall to prison for the remainder of the person's life. When the Criminal Justice Act 1991 was debated, Lord Lane tabled an amendment which was accepted by the House of Lords to abolish mandatory life sentences. This was rejected by the Commons with the (then) minister, Angela Rumbold, explaining the rationale for the sentence:

> According to the judicial process, the offender has committed a crime of such gravity that he forfeits his liberty to the state for the rest of his days – if necessary, he can be detained for life without the necessity for subsequent judicial intervention.[48]

It is possible to identify, in this statement, a theme which runs back to the original views expounded on the disciplinary process. The theory is that the prisoner has exhausted his/her judicial remedies in the criminal trial and, thereafter, all that remains is the exercise of purely discretionary administrative powers.

In *R v Secretary of State for the Home Department ex parte Doody*,[49] Lord Mustill approached the legal framework from precisely this position. He accepted, for the first time, that the mandatory life sentence is, in practice, comprised of two distinct parts, the punitive and the protective. The very fact that a tariff is set and that the majority of prisoners sentenced to life will be released made it fatuous to suggest otherwise – the comments of the ECHR in *Campbell and Fell* in which they identified the reality of practice as opposed to the wording of the relevant legislation are brought to mind. It is arguable that a number of competing views converged at the time, making the arguments for legal regulation of the life sentence system a possibility. These are the growing dissatisfaction with the mandatory imposition of the sentence, a general judicial trend towards 'openness' in the administrative process (as evidenced through decisions made in respect of the disciplinary system, the discretionary life sentence and the determinate parole procedures), and lastly, the increasing number of prisoners sentenced to life in prison. One of the inevitable effects of the abolition of the death penalty was to create a large group of prisoners serving indeterminate sentences – the numbers had grown from 1675 in 1981 to reach 3106 in July 1993, enough to fill five prisons.[50] This created not only a class of potential applicants who had an intimate knowledge of a previously closed world but also sufficient examples of the profound unfairness of a secretive system to make attitudes towards the applicants far more favourable.

In *Doody*, there were four applicants whose cases were joined for hearing at the House of Lords. The judgment is interesting in that it refused to make any findings as to the substantive merits of tariff-setting in the individual but, instead, made a number of findings as to the requirements of fairness. Lord Mustill commented that the previous right to make representations as to the length of tariff was meaningless without disclosure of material:

> It has frequently been stated that the right to make
> representations is of little value unless the maker has knowledge
> in advance of the considerations which, unless effectively
> challenged, will or may lead to an adverse decision.[51]

He went on to identify six elements of fairness that must be observed:[52]

(a) where an Act of Parliament confers an administrative power, there is a presumption that it will be exercised in a manner which is fair in all the circumstances;
(b) the standards of fairness are not immutable and may change with the passage of time, both in general and also in their application to decisions of a particular type;
(c) the principles of fairness are not identical in every situation and the context of the decision must be assessed;
(d) an essential feature of the context is the statute which creates the discretion, as regards both its language and the shape of the legal and administrative system within which the decision is taken;
(e) fairness will very often require that a person who may be adversely affected by a decision will have an opportunity to make representations on his own behalf either before the decision is taken with a view to producing a favourable result, or after it is taken with a view to procuring its modification, or both;
(f) since the person affected cannot usually make worthwhile representations without knowing what factors may weigh against his/her interests, fairness will very often require that he is informed of the gist of the case which he has to answer.

These principles of fairness can be regarded as the definitive statement of the extent to which judicial review can provide the protection of the law to prisoners. The comments of Lord Mustill in his judgment are instructive in this regard:

> I doubt the wisdom of discussing the problem in the
> contemporary vocabulary of 'prisoners' rights', given that as a
> result of his own act the position of the prisoner is so forcibly
> distanced from that of the ordinary citizen.

He concluded his arguments in favour of extending the principle of disclosure to the tariff-setting procedures with a familiar warning:

I wish to make it absolutely clear that ... this conclusion will not be a signal for a flood of successful applications for judicial review ... Only if it can be shown that the decision may have been arrived at through a faulty process, in one of the ways now so familiar to practitioners of judicial review, will they have any prospect of persuading the court to grant relief.

What then, has been achieved as a result of the *Doody* case in terms of judicial review? Immediately after the judgment was delivered, the Home Office agreed to introduce an 'open reporting' procedure for lifers' parole reviews. This change in policy was inevitable as the previous legal authority upholding the decision not to disclose parole papers was overturned in *Doody*.[53] Applications for judicial review since then, however, have tended to be successful only when restricted to procedural matters.

In December 1993, Rose LJ extended the open reporting policy to the review procedures for category A prisoners – those who are detained in the highest conditions of security.[54] He commented that as he was freed from previous authority by *Doody* he could approve his own views in an earlier case that

A prisoner's right to make representations is largely valueless unless he knows the case against him and secret, unchallengeable reports which may contain damaging inaccuracies are, or should be anathema in civilised, democratic society.[55]

It is important to note that Rose LJ felt able to approve these earlier comments not only because *Payne* had been overturned, but also because he considered that categorization was closely connected to liberty in that it has a direct bearing on parole prospects.

Successful applications for judicial review have been almost exclusively confined to this type of procedural question. When further challenges were made to the tariff-setting procedure, the Divisional Court agreed to quash a decision where insufficient disclosure of relevant material had been made,[56] but has refused to quash decisions made on the grounds that they are *Wednesbury* unreasonable.[57] The leading case on this topic – *R v SSHD ex parte Pierson* – has examined the extent to which the Secretary of State may depart from the judicial recommendations.[58] The Court of Appeal found that tariff-setting was distinct from normal sentencing practice and that in the absence of any policy statement or evidence of Parliamentary intent to curb the use of executive discretion, the Secretary of State may deviate from both the judicial view and the views of his predecessors. This case is due to be heard by the House of Lords in the near future (at the time of writing) and may clarify the extent to which the judiciary are prepared to draw parameters on the use of executive discretion.

One of the plainest illustrations of the limitations on judicial interference can be found in a challenge to a decision made by the Secretary of State not to authorize the release of a mandatory lifer, despite clear and positive recommendations in favour of release.[59] Steyn LJ set out the manifestly unfair system that is afforded to this class of prisoners and then conceded that there were no powers to place any meaningful restrictions upon it:

> A procedurally fair system is not afforded to mandatory life sentenced prisoners ... Given the essentially unfair system ... the courts must be aware that fundamental rights are at stake. But the courts can do no more than be extra vigilant in the exercise of their powers of judicial review.[60]

This analysis has, thus far, concentrated on the exercise of discretionary powers that are intimately connected to the liberty of the subject. It is not surprising that it is within these areas that judicial review has been such a powerful tool. The willingness of the courts to intervene, albeit on matters of procedure alone, contrasts sharply with challenges to pure policy decisions and the use of informal disciplinary powers. In this area, it is possible to discern the cutting edge of Lord Mustill's return to the view that prisoners are less eligible to enjoy 'rights' than other citizens.

In 1983, Leon Brittan, the Home Secretary, announced a change in policy for the manner in which parole would be considered.[61] In general terms, the policy changes were to restrict parole for certain categories of prisoner and it was apparent that no consultation had taken place with the Parole Board in advance of the changes. The challenge to this announcement was eventually heard by the House of Lords which dismissed the application without even hearing argument on behalf of the Home Secretary.[62] Lord Scarman opined that it was desirable for a policy to be adopted to discharge duties of this nature and that given the statutory power devolved upon the Home Secretary, it was entirely proper for him or her to set this policy as he or she saw fit.

It is possible to compare this attitude with a decision made in 1995 concerning changes in policy to home leaves, changes that were made after the 'new' standards of procedural fairness had been set down. In R v SSHD ex parte Briggs, Green and Hargeaves,[63] three prisoners sought to challenge a decision to alter eligibility for release on temporary licence, a decision seemingly made in the face of a media outcry over the leniency afforded to prisoners serving lengthy sentences for serious offences. The prisoners were particularly aggrieved that their expectations at the time of sentencing were no longer to be honoured. Although the court accepted that legitimate expectation can arise in the decision-making process,[64] as temporary release is a privilege they accepted the Secretary of State's contention that 'all the applicants could legitimately expect was to have their applications for home leave decided by reference to the criteria current at the time of the application'.[65] The logic of this judgment makes it very difficult for prisoners to ever succeed in pursuing a successful application based on this doctrine given that the majority of decisions made about them will be in connection with discretionary privileges rather than rights.

The following year, a challenge was made to the introduction of differentiated regimes in prison. The change replaced a long-standing practice of the dispensation of discretionary privileges and punishments in prison with a more austere and formal system. Leave was granted against a pilot scheme being run in Swaleside prison, but this had to be abandoned when the national guidelines were published. These guidelines reflected the policing aspect of judicial review in that they set out a formal practice for the giving of reasons for decisions made and an in-built appeals process. The duty to give reasons and to provide an internal appeals procedure was clearly designed to satisfy the *Doody* principles of administrative fairness. The effect of the safeguards built in to the new procedures was such that the application had to be withdrawn.

It is here that the central difficulty with judicial review as a mechanism for real change is apparent. The notion of administrative fairness is difficult to reconcile with a system which relies on the protection of information as an essential element of maintaining prison security and good order and discipline. A whole range of secret and undisclosable information is accumulated by the prison authorities, ranging from security reports prepared by outside police forces through to prison officers' subjective assessments and an actively encouraged prisoner informant system – a system which will inevitably create its own problems in terms of assessing the veracity of information obtained.[66] In addition to these problems, which are to a certain extent inherent in any informal disciplinary process, is the pure administrative impossibility in making effective disclosure of information on a day-to-day basis. Prison staff are required to exercise their discretion on a wide variety of matters each working day and have often relied on the difficulty that this can cause in providing information as a defence to procedural applications. How, then, have the courts viewed applications for judicial review on those issues that are not considered to be intimately connected to the liberty of the subject?

The pessimism expressed by Richardson, mentioned at the start of this chapter, arose from a finding of the court in relation to the transfer of a high security prisoner for security reasons.[67] The decision had first been hailed as a landmark as it accepted that transfers could be reviewed by the court. The decision was not found to be unreasonable, however, despite the fact that it seriously impeded preparations for a complex trial. The Secretary of State was deemed to have discharged his duty by having considered the problem caused to visits and preparation for trial, but was allowed to place security as paramount. How then has this area progressed since *McAvoy*?

Amongst the informal disciplinary powers available to prison governors are the power to segregate prisoners, either for their own protection or in the interests of good order and discipline (Prison Rule 43), and the power to transfer prisoners for short periods of time if that prisoner cannot be effectively segregated in their own prison. This practice, often referred to as 'ghosting', is widely resented by prisoners as it can lead to periods of many months being moved from one prison to another. The case of *Hague*[68] examined, *inter alia*, the manner in which this power was exercised pursuant to Circular Instruction 10/74, a directive issued to governors to ensure uniformity of treatment. This instruction was found to be unlawful in that it allowed prisoners to be automatically segregated on their arrival at a new prison and contained no need for the receiving governor to exercise his/her discretion as to the necessity for continued segregation. The instruction was found to be unlawful in that it bypassed the normal procedural safeguards that could be found in Rule 43, the actual authority to segregate a prisoner.

The result of the decision was that a new instruction was issued (Circular Instruction 37/90) which incorporated the required safeguards. This in turn was replaced by a newer version, issued in 1993, which extended the duty to the provision of reasons for the decision to transfer, presumably to meet the *Doody* criteria of fairness. A category A prisoner sought to challenge a decision to transfer him under these powers when the reasons given were that he was 'a disruptive prisoner who is doing his best to de-stabilise the wing'.[69] No specific incidents were referred to and the comments contrasted strongly with the excellent custodial reports the prisoner had been receiving elsewhere. The Court of Appeal dismissed the application for leave on the grounds that a governor was in the best position to make the assessment, that s/he was not required to give chapter and verse for the decision and that the governor was generally best placed to make an assessment as to whether a prisoner was disrupting the smooth running of a wing.

The finding of the Court of Appeal is strikingly similar to Lord Denning's often-voiced opinions on the autonomy that prison governors should have in making disciplinary decisions. It illustrates the gradual march to openness in the reporting procedure, from parole through to the formal disciplinary process and, eventually, the informal disciplinary powers. These advances are crucial in the regulation of power and in identifying those cases where the decision-making process has gone astray, for in the absence of relevant material it is impossible to identify decisions which may have been irrational or *Wednesbury* unreasonable. In parallel, the limitations to these advances can be found in the liberal discretion that statute bestows on the decision-makers, preventing substantive decisions from having any real prospect of success. It is arguable that the criticisms of judicial review as an agency for real change do still contain a great deal of validity. What is interesting, however, is the willingness of the courts to examine these issues in contrast to the long-standing 'hands off' approach.

Lord Ackner has identified three reasons for the willingness of the courts to intervene in public law matters, a willingness that has extended beyond the realm of prisons.[70] He identified the prime reason as the large mass of legislation that emerges from Parliament, some of which is 'ill thought out, ill phrased and ill digested', often devolving extensive powers to legislate by regulation. The second two factors were the gaps in legislation and, more contentiously, the greater public demand for the limitation of public powers. The first two factors are central to prison law, with the majority of prison rules and regulations being made by statutory instrument and the primary legislation often failing to recognize the complexities of the cases which it creates. The recent cases (at the time of writing) concerning the calculation of remand time in relation to custodial sentences, a problem which arose from the obliqueness of the relevant statute, provide a stark illustration of this contention.[71] It is probably less true to say that there is public opinion against the use of executive powers in dealing with prisoners and the former Home Secretary, Michael Howard, always proclaimed that he was more in tune with public opinion on penal matters than the judiciary, with some justification.

Before looking at the arguments for new legislation it is worth paying closer attention to the one issue that Lord Ackner did not touch upon – the lack of a written constitution and the impact of the ECHR on domestic law. This is a key area for study as many of the most fundamental challenges to the English prison system have stemmed from ECHR decisions. The precise status of the Convention and the rights which it preserves have always been the subject of much debate. The debate has proceeded from the bald view that: 'obligations in international law which are not enforceable as part of English law cannot ... be the subject of declaratory judgments or orders',[72] to the more sophisticated view adopted by the House of Lords in *Brind*.[73] The House held that there was no requirement for a minister to conform with the Convention when exercising discretionary powers as this would represent incorporation, a decision that can only be made by Parliament. The Convention, in their view, was no more than one of many competing considerations. Lord Bingham, in his opening address to the Lords as the new Lord Chief Justice, recognized that this is now a matter of major constitutional importance by seeking to provide the definitive exposition of the status of the Convention in English law. He argued that the Convention can now be called upon to resolve ambiguities and uncertainty in domestic law and to construe domestic statutes enacted to fulfil Convention obligations, such as the Criminal Justice Act 1991 which introduced discretionary lifer panels.

It is decisions made in the ECHR that appear to have the most profound impact on domestic prison litigation. In giving primacy to certain fundamental rights, the Convention makes it possible to circumvent defences based upon administrative inconvenience or the allocation of resources. This in turn allows the new rights which have been established to be scrutinized by the domestic courts once they are in operation. In the case of *AT* v *UK*,[74] the Committee of Ministers upheld a complaint by a discretionary lifer that the Government failed to implement the review procedures for mandatory lifers introduced by the Criminal Justice Act 1991 within a reasonable period of time. The Committee accepted the Commission's finding that the right to have one's detention reviewed by a court-like body was of such importance that the supervising State was obliged to organize its resources to meet this obligation. The initial finding of the Commission in this case was utilized by the Divisional Court when it found that discretionary lifer panels had to take place on the expiry of a prisoner's tariff rather than simply being referred for review at that time, a process which takes some six months.[75]

The *AT* v *UK* case also appears to have had an impact on the speedier procedures that have been implemented to allow for young prisoners serving sentences at Her Majesty's Pleasure (a sentence imposed upon young persons convicted of murder) to have oral reviews of their detention. The right was established by the European Court in February[76] and by July, the Home Secretary had announced interim arrangements for all such prisoners to have oral reviews in advance of new legislation being introduced. This was in stark contrast to the lengthy delays in arranging discretionary lifer panels following the *Thynne, Wilson and Gunnell* case of 1990.

It has been a long-held view that the domestic courts are only able to interfere 'at the margin rather than the centre of prison life'[77] and the development of judicial review in recent years has done nothing to dispel this critique. In 1989 Vivian Stern, the Director of NACRO, bemoaned the failure of the judiciary to impose any effective control over prisons as removing 'a lever for reform that has been very significant elsewhere', in particular the United States where whole institutions have been closed down on the order of federal courts.[78] Many of the transformations in legal practice and judicial intervention envisaged to be necessary at the time have in fact come to pass, but the same complaints continue to be made by prisoners concerning arbitrary decision-making, overcrowding and brutality. The central concern of the debates continues to be that social welfare and rights for prisoners can only be truly implemented through a reform of the legislative system, a concern that even the Prison Officers' Association took up when they posited the following:

> We propose in place of the scattered, partial and unenforceable
> obligations owed by the prison authorities to prisoners, a
> charter of minimum standards ... which would be enforceable
> by all those who occupy prison establishments.[79]

The experience of judicial review of prison law has, if it has achieved nothing else, highlighted the limits of this remedy for promoting genuine reform. Attempts have been made to promote new legislation to replace the Prison Act 1952 and the mass of statutory instrument and policy documents that it throws out. The Prison Reform Trust commissioned a Prison Bill which includes not only discretionary powers and privileges but also specific rights and standards with direct enforcement procedures as a model for such legislation.[80] It is fitting, perhaps, to leave the final words to Mark Leech, who has not only experienced prison life at first hand and has continued to promote awareness of prisoners rights since his release, but who has also tested the limits of the judicial review before the House of Lords. Despite the openness in all of the reporting procedures and the fact that all public law decisions made about prisoners are now amenable to judicial review, he remarked: 'The prison is still a silent world shrouded in darkness from the public who are forced to pay for it. It is a society in the midst of public society but closed to scrutiny and probing questions.'[81]

NOTES

1 *Becker* v *Home Office* [1972] 2 QB 407.
2 *R* v *Board of Visitors of Hull Prison ex parte St Germain* [1979] B 425.
3 *Raymond* v *Honey* [1983] 1 AC 1.
4 *O'Reilly* v *Mackman* [1983] 1 AC 237.
5 *R* v *Deputy Governor of HMP Parkhurst ex parte Hague* [1992] 1 AC 58.
6 G. Richardson, 'The case for Prisoners' Rights' in M. Maguire *et al.*, *Accountability in Prisons*, London: Tavistock (1985), p. 60.
7 The history of the Act and its predecessors is discussed in S. Livingstone and T. Owen, *Prison Law*, Oxford: Oxford University Press (1993), pp. 5–9.
8 *Ibid.*, pp. 9–10.
9 *R* v *Deputy Governor HMP Parkhurst ex parte Leech* [1988] AC 533.
10 For a fuller discussion of the Act see S. Creighton and V. King, *Prisoners and the Law*, London: Butterworths (1996), pp. 7–10.
11 Lord Denning in *Becker* v *Home Office*, note 1 above.
12 Livingstone and Owen, note 7 above, pp. 18–19 and N. Louchs and J. Plotnikoff, *Prison Rules – A Working Guide*, London: Prison Reform Trust (1993).
13 See *ex parte Hague*, note 5 above.
14 See e.g. *Silver* v *UK* [1983] 5 EHRR 347.
15 E. Fitzgerald in M. Maguire *et al.*, *Accountability in Prisons*, London: Tavistock (1985), pp. 29–31.
16 [1975] 3 All ER 78.
17 E. Fitzgerald, note 15 above, p. 32.
18 For an example of the wider context in which this decision was made, see *Kiss* v *UK* [1976] 7 DR 55.
19 *R* v *Board of Visitors of Hull Prison ex parte St Germain* [1978] 2 WLR 598.
20 *R* v *Board of Visitors of Hull Prison ex parte St Germain (No. 1)* [1979] 1 All ER 701.
21 *R* v *Board of Visitors Gartree Prison ex parte Mealy*, *The Times*, 14 November 1981.
22 *R* v *Board of Visitors Highpoint Prison ex parte McConkey*, *The Times*, 23 September 1982.
23 *R* v *SSHD ex parte Tarrant* [1984] 1 All ER 799.
24 [1984] 3 All ER 897.
25 Note 9 above.
26 *Ibid.*
27 For a fascinating account of the adjudication procedure and this case, see M. Leech, *A Product of the System*, London: Victor Gollancz (1992), pp. 97ff.
28 Cm 1456 (1991).
29 *Quinn* in M. Leech, *Prisoners' Handbook*, Oxford: Oxford University Press (1993), p. 324.
30 *Ibid.*, p. 325.
31 Winn J in *Hancock* v *Prison Commissioners* [1960] 1 QB 128.
32 [1984] 7 EHRR 165.
33 SI 1462 of 1967 issued pursuant to s. 59(6).
34 *Payne* v *Lord Harris of Greenwich* [1981] 1 WLR 754.
35 *Ibid.*, at 846.

36 G. G. Treverton-Jones, *The Legal Status and Rights of Prisoners*, London: Sweet & Maxwell (1989), pp. 156–7.
37 *R v Wilkinson* [1983] 5 Cr. App. Rep. S 105.
38 [1987] 10 EHRR 293.
39 [1988] Cr. App. Rep. 59.
40 *R v SSHD ex parte Benson*, *The Times*, 21 November 1988.
41 For a discussion of each of these cases see Livingstone and Owen, note 7 above, pp. 270–2.
42 *Thynne, Wilson and Gunnell* [1990] 13 EHRR 666.
43 *R v Parole Board & SSHD ex parte Wilson* [1991] 1 WLR 134.
44 For the most informative discussion of the ECHR's stance, see Wynne, *The Times*, 18 July 1994.
45 *R v Howe and Others* [1987] AC 417.
46 HL 78–1, London: HMSO (1989).
47 Committee on the Penalty for Homicide, Prison Reform Trust, 1993.
48 195 HC Official Report (6th Series), col. 309.
49 [1994] 1 AC 531.
50 Prison Reform Trust, note 47 above, p. 24.
51 At 563F–H: for a fuller discussion of the judgment, see S. Creighton, 'Inside tracks' [1994] *Law Society's Gazette*, 22 June: 20–3.
52 At 560D–G.
53 The case of *Payne v Lord Harris*, see note 34 above.
54 *R v SSHD ex parte Duggan* [1994] 3 All ER 277.
55 *R v SSHD ex parte Creamer and Scoley*, 21 October 1993, unreported.
56 *R v SSHD ex parte Raja and Riaz*, 16 December 1994, unreported.
57 *R v SSHD ex parte Causabson-Vincent*, 9 July 1996, unreported.
58 *The Times*, 8 December 1995.
59 *R v Parole Board and SSHD ex parte Pegg*, *Independent*, 9 September 1996.
60 *Ibid.*, at p. 15 of transcript.
61 49 HC Official Report (6th Series) Written Answers, col. 513.
62 *Re Findlay* [1984] AC 318.
63 Unreported, 25 July 1995.
64 See e.g. *R v SSHD ex parte US Tobacco International Inc.* [1992] 1 QB 353.
65 *Ex parte Briggs*, p. 13 of transcript.
66 See Creighton and King, note 10 above, pp. 101–2.
67 *R v SSHD ex parte McAvoy* [1984] 1 WLR 1408.
68 Note 5 above.
69 *R v Governor of HMP Long Lartin ex parte Ross*, *The Times*, 9 June 1994.
70 *Guardian*, 12 November 1996.
71 *R v SSHD ex parte Naughton*, *The Times*, 27 September 1996 and *R v Governor of HMP Brockhill ex parte Reid*, unreported at the time of writing.
72 *Uppal v Home Office*, *The Times*, 11 November 1978.
73 *R v SSHD ex parte Brind* [1991] 1 AC 696.
74 Case No. 20448/92, 29 November 1995.
75 *R v SSHD ex parte Norney*, *Independent*, 28 September 1995.
76 *Hussain v UK*, 22 February 1996.
77 Livingstone and Owen, note 7 above, p. 308.

78 V. Stern, *Imprisoned by Our Prisons*, London: Unwin (1989).
79 Prison Officers' Association, *Prisoners' Rights, Real or Imagined*, London (1985), para. 17.
80 Prison Bill 1996, published by the Prison Reform Trust, July 1996.
81 Leech, note 27 above, p. 11.

BIBLIOGRAPHY

Creighton, S. (1994) *Law Society's Gazette*, 22 June.
Creighton, S. and King, V. (1996) *Prisoners and the Law*. London: Butterworths.
Fitzgerald, E. (1985) in Maguire, M. *et al.* (eds) *Accountability in Prisons*. London: Tavistock.
Jameson, N. and Allison, E. (1995) *Strangeways 1990 – A Serious Disturbance*. London: Larkin Publications.
Leech, M. (1992) *A Product of the System*. London: Victor Gollancz.
Leech, M. (1992) *Prisoners' Handbook*. Oxford: Oxford University Press.
Livingstone, S. and Owen, T. (1993) *Prison Law*. Oxford: Oxford University Press.
Louks, N. and Plotnikoff, J. (1993) *Prison Rules – A Working Guide*. London: Prison Reform Trust.
Prison Officers' Association (1985) *Prisoners' Rights, Real or Imagined*. London.
Richardson, G. (1985) 'The case for Prisoners' Rights' in Maguire, M. *et al.* (eds) *Accountability in Prisons*. London: Tavistock.
Stern, V. (1989) *Imprisoned by Our Prisons*. London: Unwin.
Treverton-Jones, G. G. (1989) *The Legal Status and Rights of Prisoners*. London: Sweet & Maxwell.

11

Judicial Review and Gypsy Site Provision

DEREK OBADINA

The swift expansion in the last fifteen years of the activity of the courts of law in controlling the legality of administrative action is a success story which demonstrates that the common law has retained its vigour and, given the procedural tools, is able to adjust itself to the changing needs of society in a period which in retrospect, has been one of social upheaval.[1]

INTRODUCTION

The question of the extent to which judicial review is effective as a mechanism for controlling public authorities in the performance of their welfare and other functions has been the subject of intense speculation amongst lawyers in recent years.[2] The question can be investigated from two perspectives. First, the extent to which the intended beneficiaries of welfare legislation are able to secure effective judicial remedies where a public authority is in default of its duties under such legislation (retrospective control). Second, given that the courts view the relationship between themselves and public authorities as 'one of partnership based on a common aim, namely the maintenance of the highest standards of public administration',[3] the extent to which in exercising their functions under welfare legislation the generality of public authorities are guided by the norms generated in judicial review proceedings (prospective control).

This chapter examines these questions in the context of Part II of the Caravan Sites Act 1968, which until its repeal by Part II of the Public Order Act 1994 made provision for the establishment of caravan sites for the accommodation of gypsies. In so doing it draws on previously unpublished empirical data assembled by the author between 1986 and 1988 in the context of doctoral research.[4] The data concerned derived from information made available by legal and other officers in twenty local authorities in England and Wales, officials of the Gypsy Site Provision Unit of the Department of Environment, and representatives of national and local gypsy interest groups.

AN OVERVIEW

In the 1960s the long-standing associated problems of insufficient gypsy site provision and unauthorized gypsy encampments became the subject of official concern, prompting the Government to issue a series of circulars[5] urging local authorities to make use of their general powers under s. 24 of the Caravan Sites and Control Act 1960, to establish gypsy caravan sites.[6] It proved necessary for Parliament to enact Part II of the 1968 Act because 'nearly all local authorities ignored the advice of the Minister'.[7] The 1968 Act, which came into effect in April 1970, was based on a policy of 'give and take': s. 6 placed local authorities under a duty to provide adequate caravan site accommodation for gypsies; while s. 8 enabled the Minister to grant a designation order to any authority that discharged the duty, enabling the authority to exercise far-reaching eviction powers. To cater for possible recalcitrant authorities, s. 9 empowered the Minister to issue a direction against any authority compelling it to discharge the duty.

The hope of the Government that 'once the duty is laid on local authorities they will get on and do the job'[8] was not realized. In his report on the working of the 1968 Act, Sir John Cripps found that as of November 1978, six years after the 1968 Act took effect, local authorities had provided the prescribed accommodation for only one-quarter of the gypsy families in England and Wales.[9] In the light of the report and in order to boost the rate of gypsy site provision s. 70 of the Local Government, Planning and Land Act 1980 empowered the Secretary of State to give local authorities 100 per cent grant aid in respect of the capital cost of site provision, and strengthened the designation provisions. However, this failed to bring about a sustained increase in the rate of gypsy site provision.[10] Thus as at 1994, official statistics showed that during the period of the preceding thirteen years only 38 per cent of local authorities had obtained designation status; that 38 per cent of local authorities had made no provision for gypsy sites under the Act;[11] and that since 1979 £100m had been spent on grant aid for gypsy site provision.[12] The Conservative Government, stressing the need for 'value for money' in the provision of public services, argued that these figures demonstrated that the 1968 Act had failed and that the best way forward was for gypsies to help themselves by establishing their own sites or persuading the private sector to make such provision. Pursuant to that belief, the Government secured the enactment of Part II of the Public Order Act 1996 which repealed s. 6 of the 1968 Act, and removed the Secretary of State's power to grant aid site provision. Consequently local authorities no longer have a duty to provide caravan site accommodation for gypsies, but they may do so, if they wish, in the exercise of their general powers under s. 24 of the Caravan Sites and Control Development Act 1960.[13]

Judicial review had a chequered history in the context of the working of Part II of the Caravan Sites Act 1968. Initially, in *Kensington and Chelsea London Borough Council v Wells*,[14] decided in 1973, the Court of Appeal assumed a position of judicial restraint, holding that s. 6 was not susceptible to judicial enforcement at the behest of gypsies. However, ten years later, in *R v Secretary of State ex parte Ward*,[15] the Divisional Court established that gypsies had requisite standing to enforce s. 6 in the field of public law. This activist approach was carried forward in *R v Secretary of State ex parte Lee*[16] where the court, for the first time, adjudged an authority to be in breach of the s. 6 duty. The decision of the Court of Appeal in *West Glamorgan County Council v Rafferty*[17] represented the high point of judicial activism: there it was held that a decision by an authority to evict gypsies from an unauthorized encampment notwithstanding the authority was in breach of s. 6 was *Wednesbury* unreasonable.

This chapter is divided principally into three parts. In the first part we look briefly at the statutory scheme created by Part II of the Caravan Sites Act. The second part is divided into two sections and reflects the peculiar movement of judicial review in this area. The first section examines the decision in *Kensington and Chelsea v Wells* and then goes on to examine the extent to which respondent authorities were guided by relevant judicial norms in approaching their duties under s. 6 in the absence of judicial enforcement of that section. The second section examines the decisions rendered by the courts in the period of judicial activism, and then goes on to examine the impact of the ruling in *R v Secretary of State ex parte Lee*, on policy-making in local authorities. The third part of the chapter reflects on the lessons to be drawn from the empirical data with regard to the impact of judicial review on gypsy site provision under the 1968 Act in particular, and public administration in general. In a conclusion we examine the likely future impact of judicial review on gypsy site provision in the new statutory context brought into play by the Public Order Act 1994.

STATUTORY FRAMEWORK

The Section 6 Duty

Section 24 of the Caravan Sites and Control of Development Act 1960 empowers local authorities to provide and manage caravan sites, and 'to do anything appearing to them desirable' in connection with the provision of such sites. Building on this s. 6(1) of the Caravan Sites Act 1968 provided that:

> it shall be the duty of every local authority being the council of a county or a London borough to exercise their powers under section 24 of the Caravan Sites and Control of Development Act 1960 (provision of caravan sites) so far as may be necessary to provide adequate accommodation for gypsies residing or resorting to their area.

In county areas, the s. 6 duty was split between county and district authorities: the county council had the strategic function of 'determining what sites are to be provided and acquiring or appropriating the necessary land', while it was the duty of the council of a district in which any such site is located to equip and manage any site established by the county council.[18]

An authority proposing to establish gypsy sites pursuant to s. 6 might be obliged to undertake public consultation in three different contexts. First, under s. 8 of the 1968 Act all site-providing authorities had a duty to consult 'such authorities and persons as they consider appropriate'. Secondly, in a country area, the county council was under an additional duty to consult the council of the district in whose area the gypsy sites were proposed to be established. Thirdly, an authority, proposing to acquire land compulsorily for the purpose of gypsy site provision, was obliged to publicize the proposal and entertain objections to it and, in the event of any objections not being resolved, the authority was required to submit to a public inquiry procedure.

Ministerial Powers and Policies

The 1968 Act as originally enacted vested in the Minister powers designed to enable him both to dictate the level of gypsy site provision under s. 6 and to superintend the manner in which local

authorities approached their duties under that section. Thus s. 9(1) of
1968 Act obliged local authorities to give to the Minister notice,
describing the number and location of the sites which they proposed
to provide pursuant to s. 6. Second, under s. 6(2) it was open to the
Minister to exempt a London borough from the s. 6(1) duty where
he was satisfied that the authority had no land in its area suitable for
use as a gypsy 'accommodation', and to exempt a county authority
where he was satisfied that the number of gypsies resorting to its area
in the five-year period immediately preceding the enactment of the
Act was not such as to warrant the provision of caravan sites. Both
these powers, however, were repealed by s. 173 of the Local
Government, Planning and Land Act 1980.[19]

However, the Minister retained supervisory powers in three key
areas. First, where a district council objected to a proposal of the
county council to establish a site in the district, it was open to the
county to refer the dispute to the Minister. On such a reference the
Minister could direct the county council to abandon the proposal; to
proceed with it; or to refer it to him for determination.[20]

Second, under s. 12 of the Act the Minister was empowered to
make a designation order in favour of a local authority where it
appeared to him 'either that adequate accommodation has been made
therein for the accommodation of gypsies residing in or resorting to
the area, or that in all the circumstances it is not necessary or
expedient to make any such provision'. Such an order brought into
play s. 10 of the Act, which made it an offence for a gypsy to encamp
on an unauthorized site, and enabled a local authority to exercise
swingeing powers of eviction in respect of such sites, free of the
limitations and uncertainties that attended the eviction powers
otherwise available.

Third, the Minister retained a wide-ranging default power under
s. 9(1) of the 1968 Act which provided that:

The Minister may, if at any time it appears to him necessary to
do so, give directions to any such authority requiring them to
provide, pursuant to the said section 6, such sites or additional
sites, for the accommodation of such numbers of caravans, as
may be specified in the directions; and any such directions shall
be enforceable, on the application of the Minister, by
mandamus.

The attitude and policies of the Minister exercised a significant
influence on the way local authorities approached their duties under
the 1968 Act. On the vital issue of securing site provision by local
authorities under the terms of s. 6, the philosophy of the Department
of the Environment had, from the outset, always been distinctly

'non-interventionist'. Successive Ministers had taken the view that the provision of adequate accommodation for gypsies was best secured through 'co-operation and consultation with local authorities, rather than by coercion. Thus the Minister had always regarded the section 9 default power as "exceptional".'[21] The question of what circumstances might count as 'exceptional' was never spelt out by the Minister, but the writer was told by a senior civil servant that the Minister had always taken the view that it would not be right for him to intervene under s. 9 where an authority was encountering difficulty in discharging its duties under s. 6 as a result of financial problems or pressures of local public opposition, and that such intervention would be contemplated as a matter of course only where 'an authority refuses point blank to provide any caravan sites'.[22]

In his report on the working of the 1968 Act, Sir John Cripps was highly critical of the Minister's non-interventionist stance, identifying it as an 'important contributory factor' in the failure of local authorities to discharge their duties effectively.[23] This criticism inspired the Minister to adopt a more pro-active stance in the context of the operation of the designation provisions. Thus the Minister published Circular 8/81 setting out the 'designation criteria' local authorities were expected to meet before being granted designation status by the Minister. The general requirement was that authorities should provide sites that were 'sufficiently diverse and suitably designed to meet the accommodation needs of gypsies residing or resorting to a relevant part of its area'.[24] Pursuant to Circular 8/81 it became the practice for local authorities minded to provide gypsy sites pursuant to s. 6 to formulate time-related gypsy site provision programmes in the light of the designation criteria and submit them to the Department of the Environment for advance clearance. Where, in any such case, the Minister was satisfied that the plan met the designation criteria he would then give an assurance to the authority concerned that a designation order would be forthcoming upon completion of the programme.

INITIAL JUDICIAL REACTIONS

The decision in *Wells* must be seen against the background of prior jurisprudence, in particular the uncertainty in the law relating to the enforcement of statutory duties, and the role of the courts in proceedings concerned with their enforcement. Today there is a clear distinction between private and public law. In substance, public law is concerned with the enforcement of the proper performance by public authorities of the duties they owe to the public; whereas private law is concerned with the protection of the private rights of private individuals or the private rights of public bodies. The critical distinction is that in the former case, the public as a whole are the beneficiaries of what is protected by the law; whereas in the latter case, it is the individuals or bodies entitled to the rights who are the beneficiaries of the protection provided by the law.[25] However, prior to the decision in *Wells*, when called upon to examine the legality of administrative action, the courts tended to see their role as limited to the protection of individual legal rights, and this was especially so in the context of cases relating to the enforcement of statutory duties subject to Ministerial default powers.

This is illustrated by the decision of the House of Lords in *Pasmore v Oswaldwistle Urban District Council*.[26] There, in an action commenced by writ, the plaintiff alleged that the council was in breach of a statutory duty to provide such sewers as might be necessary for draining the district, and he sought an order of *mandamus* to enforce the duty. The court held that:

Where an Act creates an obligation and enforces the performance in a specified manner we take it to be a general rule that performance cannot be enforced in any other manner.

However, the court recognized that this 'general rule' – the *Pasmore* principle – was not a hard and fast one and that exceptions might be made to it where justified by 'considerations of policy and convenience'. In the event, the court refused to grant an order of *mandamus* on two grounds: first, the duty in question was of a general nature, more suitable for enforcement by the Minister than by individuals; second, granting the order would encourage a multi-plicity of claims against local authorities from aggrieved residents to the ultimate detriment of the rate fund. On the face of it the *Pasmore* principle applies to both ordinary actions and prerogative proceed-ings, but it is clear that in formulating that principle the court had the former category of action in contemplation, and even if it did not, under the doctrine of precedent the decision must be regarded as binding authority only for that category.

The matter is of some importance because there were a number of cases, both before[27] and after *Pasmore*,[28] where the courts appeared to acknowledge that prerogative proceedings were essentially con-cerned to vindicate the public interest in the proper performance of statutory duties by public authorities, and that consequently the existence of default power in the statutory scheme sought to be enforced should not preclude the availability of prerogative remedies. It was on this basis that the Court of Appeal in *Glossop v Heston and Isleworth Local Government Board* held that the court would be prepared to issue an order of *mandamus* against an authority shown to be in breach of a duty similar to that sought to be enforced in *Pasmore*, for the benefit of all the inhabitants of the local area affected by the default.

In *Kensington and Chelsea London Borough* v *Wells*[29] a number of gypsies had parked their caravans on land belonging to three local authorities without permission. Each of the authorities was awaiting a decision from the Minister on its application for an exemption order. In each case the authority sought possession of its land under R.S.C. Ord. 113. The defendant gypsies in each case, by writ, brought cross-actions against each of the plaintiffs, seeking an order of *mandamus*, requiring the authorities to provide a site for gypsies in their areas pursuant to their duties under s. 6 or, alternatively, a mandatory injunction restraining the plaintiffs from taking any steps to evict them until they had complied with their duties under the Act. The Court of Appeal unanimously granted the possession orders sought and rejected the cross-actions.

The plaintiffs, relying on the *Pasmore* principle, argued that the Minister's default power under s. 9 excluded judicial redress for the gypsies. But counsel for the gypsies argued that the *Pasmore* principle only applied where the statute sought to be enforced entitled an aggrieved party to make representations to the Minister with a view to getting him to exercise his default powers, but not where as in the case of the 1968 Act, an aggrieved party had no such right. The court rejected the distinction, holding that the *Pasmore* principle applied equally in both cases. Moreover, the court thought that the distinction sought be drawn did not 'really hold water' because in practice it was open to aggrieved gypsies to ask the Minister to exercise his default powers.

Roskill LJ, who delivered the leading judgment, considered that the case raised the question of 'whether there is any redress available in the courts at the hands of the individual gypsy'.[30] In answering that question he said that it was important to have regard to the nature of the duty sought to be enforced. He pointed out that under s. 6(1) the duty of a London borough was limited to the obligation to provide for fifteen caravans at a time. Even where an authority had provided the maximum number of pitches, there was no guarantee that any one particular gypsy would be allocated one of them. That consideration led him to conclude that s. 6(1) created a duty of a 'general kind', and did not create a duty in favour of each individual gypsy to have an individual caravan site, and that having regard to considerations of 'policy and convenience', Parliament could not have intended that every gypsy who was in need of accommodation should be able to sue the local authority for it.

Roskill LJ further held that the duty under s. 6(1) only arose if the Minister did not give an exempting direction under s. 6(2). Since, therefore, the local authorities had not received a decision from the Minister regarding their applications for exemption, it could not be said that they were in breach of the duty under s. 6. His Lordship also considered that, 'unless and until' the Minister activated his default powers under s. 9, the Councils could not be in breach of their duty under s. 6(1). His Lordship held that even on the assumption that the defendant authorities were in breach of their duties, it would be inconsistent with established principles for the court to grant the remedy of *mandamus* or mandatory injunction, since that would involve the court 'arrogating' to itself the right to dictate to a local authority the performance of a duty the control of the performance of which was, by s. 9, placed 'only' in the hands of the Minister.[31]

Roskill LJ appeared to express some limited sympathy with the plight of the gypsies. Nevertheless he considered that:

> Whatever grievance the gypsies may have their remedy does not lie in this court. It may lie in making representations to the Minister with a view to the Minister putting pressure upon the councils concerned and expediting a decision whether or not exemption should be granted where exemption has been applied for. Those are all matters outside the jurisdiction of this court.[32]

The decision of the Court of Appeal in *Wells* was unfortunate in two senses. First, the assumption made by the court that s. 9 provided an adequate remedy for aggrieved gypsies, and that therefore it was unnecessary for the courts to be concerned in the enforcement of s. 6, was erroneous, because as we have seen the Minister had always taken the view that those default powers were 'exceptional'. Second, by viewing the case only in terms of 'whether there is any redress available in the courts at the hands of the individual gypsy', the court failed to attend to the public interest dimension of the case (viz. whether or not the courts should play a role in the enforcement of s. 6 for the benefit of the generality of gypsies and the land owners liable to be adversely affected by unauthorized gypsy encampments), in a situation where the decision in *Glossop* afforded the court leeway to do so.

Applicable Administrative Law Norms in the Absence of Judicial Intervention

Ideally, from the point of view of prospective control, upon Part II of the 1968 Act taking effect, one would expect local authority lawyers to examine s. 6 in the light of administrative law jurisprudence with a view to determining what it required of their authorities, and to bring their conclusions on that point to bear in the policy-making processes of their authorities. The necessity for legal officers to do so survived the subsequent decision in *Wells*, for that case merely decided that s. 6 was unenforceable in judicial proceedings at the behest of gypsies, and it did not relieve local authorities of their duty to direct themselves properly in law in approaching the performance of the duty imposed by s. 6.

The fundamental question needing to be addressed by the hypothetical legal officer concerned the nature of the obligation imported by s. 6. Here it is relevant that in determining whether public authorities have complied with their statutory duties, both procedural and substantive, the courts have proceeded by asking whether Parliament intended to impose an absolute and qualified duty. An absolute duty imposes an unqualified obligation; the non-existence of the prescribed state of affairs constitutes breach of the duty, regardless of the state of knowledge of, or degree of effort made by the functionary. Where, on the other hand, a duty is classified as a qualified one the absence of the prescribed state of affairs will not mean that the authority is in breach if it can show that it has made reasonable efforts to comply with the duty. The wording of the statutory provision is an important determinant of classification. In particular where a duty is expressly qualified by words such as 'reasonably practicable', 'practicable' or the like, the courts are likely to say that it imports a qualified duty. In the absence of such words regard may be had to a number of considerations: the legislative background of the provision in question, the state of the law prior to its enactment and, against that background, its underlying purposes. In particular, where the underlying policy of the statutory scheme may be frustrated or impaired unless the duty is held to be unqualified, the courts may construe it as such.

In the light of these considerations, the hypothetical legal officer could reasonably be expected to reflect that a court was likely to view s. 6 as importing an absolute duty. This would be expected for two reasons. First, because the section was enacted precisely because local authorities had failed to heed Government advice that they establish gypsy sites. Second, because the duty imposed on local authorities under s. 6 had always been recognized as being unpopular amongst the generality of local authorities, and consequently, if it were to be construed as a qualified duty, local authorities might be reluctant to perform it effectively or give it due priority.

However, sometimes the courts will construe an apparently absolute obligation as a qualified one in the light of surrounding statutory provisions. This was the approach adopted in 1984 in *R v Secretary for Wales ex parte Price*,[33] where McCullough J held that having regard to the financial constraints faced by local authorities in implementing s. 6, and the elaborate processes of public consultation that local authorities were required by statue to submit to:

> There must be implied into section 6 a qualification that the duty of the County Council is to do that which is practicable or reasonably practicable or that it must use its best endeavours.

This approach ran counter to the well-established principle of statutory interpretation that the *prima facie* meaning or policy of a statute should be given effect unless there are clear indications to the contrary or if to do so would give rise to a gross anomaly. The financial and practical difficulties emphasized by McCullough J did not require him to gloss the *prima facie* unqualified duty imposed by s. 6 with a reasonable endeavours test as it was open to him to make allowances for them in the exercise of his remedial discretion. As we shall see below, it was for this reason that McCullough J's test was rejected in later cases.

Impact of Background Norms in the Absence of Judicial Intervention

In each of the local authorities investigated the council had established a committee specifically for the purpose of formulating policies and implementing them with regard to gypsy sites pursuant to s. 6 of the 1968 Act. In each case the composition of the body concerned was multi-disciplinary and included a representative from the legal department.

An examination of the maiden reports received by these committees and their minutes revealed that officers had briefed councillors on the provisions of the 1968 Act but that they had not received any explicit advice as to the juridical nature of s. 6. In the light of this, legal officers in seven local authorities who had been involved with gypsy site provision in the initial period were asked how s. 6 was viewed by legal officers, and the extent to which they or other officers had apprised councillors of relevant administrative law norms.

There was no case where officers were able to say that they had consciously reflected on the question of the juridical nature of s. 6 and the question of the likely judicial approach. In Cambridgeshire and Lincolnshire legal officers said that although they had not consciously reflected on the likely judicial approach, they had, in effect, advised the council on the basis that s. 6 imposed an absolute duty. In Jamestown County Council a senior legal officer said that 'we had always seen section 6 as imposing a mandatory duty, but one which is difficult to perform in practice'. He went on to say that councillors had not been specifically advised as to the nature of s. 6. That, he explained, was not unusual, since councillors would normally only ever be apprised of administrative law matters where legal officers wished to 'frighten' them away from adopting a course of action which might lead to legal challenge.

The Assistant County Secretary and Senior Legal Officer at Hertfordshire County Council, which authority would later be found to be in breach of s. 6 in the *Lee* case, said:

> I honestly don't think a great deal of thought was given to it [s. 6]. I doubt very much that it would have been viewed in administrative law terms as you are suggesting. The view of legal officers was that the authority should just get on and provide sites as and when circumstances permitted it to do so. I don't think anybody appreciated that section 6 gave rise to an absolute duty [and] Legal officers were not called upon to tender advice on the precise nature of the duty. If we had been asked at the time, we would probably have said something like, just get on with the task of providing sites as best you can.

A Senior Legal Officer in Oxfordshire County Council said that in the initial period:

> All legal officers realised that there was a statutory obligation on appropriate authorities to provide sites. It was certainly seen as a duty that was qualified by the practical difficulty in actually doing so. This probably led to a feeling that so long as an authority was using its best endeavours to provide sites the duty was not an enforceable one ... it was regarded as a general duty, which you could perform as and when you were able to, when you had the money to do it.

The Senior Legal Officer said that s. 6 first became the subject of close legal analysis in 1983 when the council was threatened with legal action by a firm of solicitors, acting for a group which the Council believed to be hippies who had argued that the Council would be in breach of s. 6 unless it provided them with a caravan site of their own. The response of legal officers was to seek advice from the Department of the Environment in the matter. In the event the 'hippies' left the county, and the matter was laid to rest.

At varying points in time each respondent authority had suffered at least one reversal in its attempts to make adequate gypsy site provision, arising from financial constraints, non-confirmation of compulsory purchase orders, or lack of district council support. In this situation one would expect that the hypothetical legal officer, being concerned to uphold relevant judicial norms, would be active in reminding the authority of its duties under s. 6 and seeking compliance therewith. In three of the authorities surveyed, it was apparent from decision-making documentation and responses of legal officers that such officers had undertaken an activist role. In other authorities, however, legal officers admitted that they had not always pursued the issue of gypsy site provision as vigorously as they might have. Officers gave various reasons for their inactivity including 'personal disillusionment', deriving from the failure of gypsy site initiatives; doubts as to whether the achievement of designation would solve the gypsy problem; and a perception on the part of legal officers that councillors were not interested in solving the problem of gypsy site provision.

In several of the respondent authorities it appeared that legal officers had been party to prolonged periods of 'non-decision-making'. No positive decisions were taken that the duty imposed by s. 6 would not be performed, but in practice the effect of decision-making was in the direction of avoiding the duty. In that connection local authorities would often rely on the practical problems inherent in making gypsy site provision as a basis for not performing s. 6 effectively. In Jameshire County Council for instance, from 1976 until 1981, the council had been under the control of a succession of Conservative majorities. In that time it had not formulated any clear gypsy site programme, and it had managed to provide only one official site. The authority's Deputy Solicitor linked the lack of progress made by the authority to the philosophy of the Conservative majority which had, he said, been 'laissez faire' and based on the 'belief that individuals should be self supporting and sites should not be provided for gypsies out of public monies'. He explained the position:

> When asked why we had not provided any caravan sites our official answer was that the Council was trying. In practice the authority was really just going through the motions. Officers kept things ticking over. But the authority could not bring itself to implement the Act because it lacked political will. What tended to happen was that we would consult and apply for planning permission, and then end up backing off each time an objector appeared ... the fact that District Councils kept objecting to gypsy site provision was a useful way of keeping the pot boiling.

In some cases, the Deputy Solicitor said, councillors had made formal decisions upon grounds which were not 'wholly admissible' in law. In such cases, he said, it was incumbent on him to ensure that the decision was recorded in an 'appropriate form'. He explained this in the following way:

> As a legal adviser and Secretary one is here to do the paper work, and fill in the gaps and details. It is part of our function to flesh things up in the appropriate form.

It became apparent from the responses of legal officers that the absence of Ministerial intervention under the s. 9 default power, and the absence of judicial intervention, had been significant factors in the failure of legal officers to assert relevant legal norms. Thus, the Deputy Solicitor of Wiltshire County Council explained:

> If one had been operating in an environment where all around one writs were being issued and local authorities were being done in the High Court, and being found wanting and ordered to do something, we would have been more conscious of our duties at all stages. It would have given strength to the arm of those who were trying to do something. It would have strengthened the arms of officers in saying to members: you ought to be trying harder. If you're the planning officer and you've been given the task of finding a site and you've got that on your desk and you've got other things on your desk and you know that your authority does not really want to provide sites anyway, and you know that there are certain other things they'd really like you to do, you're perfectly clear where your priority is.

Generally speaking, to the extent that local authorities actively pursued their duties under s. 6, the critical factor was not the role assumed by legal officers, or the extent to which administrative law norms were asserted by such officers, but rather the existence of the requisite political will among councillors in the political group that was in control of the council. This was illustrated in a dramatic way by the events that occurred in Cheshire and Haringey following the 1982 local government elections. In each case political control of the council switched to a new breed of radical Labour councillors who, pursuant to 'equal opportunity' policies, initiated and formally adopted gypsy site provision programmes. In Cheshire, for instance, during the stewardship of the Conservative Party the council had failed to formulate any policies directed towards the provision of gypsy sites in the county. In 1982 the new Labour administration formally adopted a county-wide gypsy site programme, envisaging the provision of 300 caravan pitches in the county. In Haringey prior to 1982 the council had failed to provide a single site under the 1968 Act. The Labour party had fought the election on the basis of an election manifesto that pledged 'Haringey Council is legally obliged to provide a site within the borough for Gypsies. We intend to provide a site within a year.' Within eighteen months of its election the Labour administration caused the council to establish a permanent caravan site for gypsies on vacant land at the rear of the borough's town hall.

Judicial Activism

In practice the question of whether judicial remedies are excluded by the existence of a default power has always depended on the view taken by the court as to the scope of its own jurisdiction, and its view as to the desirability or otherwise of judicial intervention in the area concerned.[34]

This was borne out by the dramatic shift in judicial policy on the enforcement of s. 6 brought about by the decisions in *R* v *Secretary of State ex parte Ward*;[35] *R* v *Secretary of State ex parte Lee*;[36] and *West Glamorgan County Council* v *Rafferty*.[37] These decisions did not involve judicial legislation; rather, courts subjected existing authorities to closer examination at a time when the courts were expanding the boundaries of judicial review, and the judicial climate, particularly at the level of the High Court, was more favourable to a range of minority interests hitherto regarded as outside the protection of administrative law.[38]

In *R* v *Secretary of State ex parte Ward* the London Borough of Hammersmith had in 1975 established a gypsy site (Westway) on land it had leased from the GLC on the basis of which it had obtained a designation order under the 1968 Act. In June 1983 Hammersmith resolved to hand the site back to the GLC in an uncleared state at the end of the lease on the ground that it was unable to comply with an abatement order made by a magistrate's court in respect of environmental pollution on the site. Shortly before the expiry of the lease, two residents of Westway sought judicial review of that decision.

Woolf J held that the applicant had sufficient interest in the matter within the meaning of Order 53, and s. 31 of the Supreme Court Act 1981, because as a resident of Westway he was 'personally and directly' affected by the decision of the Council. Here he distinguished *Wells* on the ground that that case was dealing with the question of whether or not an individual gypsy had a personal right which he could enforce in the courts, as opposed to the question of whether or not a gypsy could bring an action in the public law field under Order 53: in Order 53 proceedings s. 9 had the effect of limiting, and not excluding, the jurisdiction of the court in judicial review proceedings. Parliament intended that in normal circumstances the Minister should have the responsibility of overseeing whether local authorities were making adequate provision under s. 6, and that he should give effect to his views on those matters by making designation orders where appropriate and also by taking the existence of designation into account in deciding whether he should exercise his powers of direction under s. 9. In the light of these considerations and in order to avoid a conflict between the Minister's view of what was adequate and necessary and that of the court, the courts should refuse to intervene in judicial review proceedings in those cases where s. 9 provided the applicant with an adequate remedy. Woolf J ruled that as a matter of law s. 9 did not provide a remedy for the gypsy who was complaining about the manner in which an authority had made a decision under s. 6 and that consequently in that field the court retained full power to review the decision-making of the local authority.

In that connection Woolf J held that there was an obligation on Hammersmith to consider properly what sites they were going to provide and what sites they were proposing to cease to provide, and that the council were in breach of that obligation in that when making their decision they had failed both to realize that it would amount to an abdication of their duty under s. 6, and to appreciate the likely consequences of the decision. His Lordship granted an order quashing the decision of the council, but considered that it would not be appropriate to grant an order of *mandamus*, having regard to the powers of the Minister under s. 9. Finally, Woolf J examined the decision *R v Secretary of State for Wales ex parte Price*, and held that contrary to the view expressed by McCullough J, s. 6 should not be glossed with a reasonable endeavours test.

In *R v Secretary of State ex parte Lee*, gypsies alleged that Hertfordshire County Council was in breach of its duty under s. 6 and that the Secretary of State had misdirected himself in refusing to issue a s. 9 direction against the Council. The facts of the cases were essentially that in 1975 the county council formulated a gypsy site provision programme. However, owing to financial constraints, the refusal of the Minister of financial assistance, and difficulties in obtaining the co-operation of district councils, the council resolved to postpone implementation of the plan, pending an improvement in the financial position. In 1980 following the availability of grant aid under the Local Government and Planning Act, the Council adopted a new gypsy site programme, envisaging the provision of twenty-five additional pitches over the next four years. As at the date of the hearing in December 1981, the council had provided twenty-three additional pitches over and above the number of pitches in existence in 1975. In February 1982, the Minister had refused to intervene at the behest of a gypsy support group on the ground that since the council had and were endeavouring to implement a time-related programme of gypsy site provision, they were not in breach of their duty under s. 6.

Two preliminary matters were quickly disposed of by Mann J, viz. whether the applicants had sufficient interest in the matter and whether or not s. 9 precluded the applicants from seeking judicial review. Mann J followed the approach of Woolf J in *Ward* on both issues and determined them in favour of the applicants. The central question in *Lee* which did not arise directly in *Ward* was that of when an authority could be considered to be in breach of its s. 6 duty. Mann J expressly disapproved of the reasonable endeavours test propounded by McCullough J in *Price*, and held that the correct approach

> is to ask simply whether at the moment the question is to be answered, there is adequate accommodation for gypsies residing in or resorting to the area.

If the answer is no, then the authority would be in breach of the duty, but since public law remedies are discretionary, the court would not intervene 'if an authority is doing all that it sensibly can to meet an unqualified duty'.

Mann J said that 'so simple an approach' was

> appropriate, having regard to the language of the statute and to the consideration that the court is not dealing with a mere technicality but with the ability of people to have secure accommodation for their homes and with the removal of grossly injurious environmental impact upon the public and local residents of unauthorised gypsy encampments.

Applying this approach, Mann J found that the council was in breach of its duty under s. 6 since 'its assessment of what is an appropriate number of pitches has been above attainment, and far above it'. In considering what remedy to grant, Mann J considered the practical and financial difficulties faced by the council in implementing s. 6. He accepted that the latter must have been a decisive restraint before the availability of capital grant aid in 1979, but he noted that since that time the council had managed to provide only six additional pitches. His Lordship was critical of two policies set out in the Council's Policy Guide on gypsy site provision which indicated the unwillingness of the council to make use of compulsory purchase powers and to establish sites in the absence of agreement from the district council concerned, respectively. Both policies, his Lordship considered, 'manifest a failure to approach an unpopular statutory duty'. In the event, however, Mann J declined to grant an order of *mandamus*, taking the view that the default power under s. 9 'provides an adequate machine for achieving the performance of the County council's duty'. Instead he granted a declaration that 'Hertfordshire County Council is in breach of its statutory duty under section 6 of the Act of 1968'.

In *West Glamorgan County Council* v *Rafferty*, the council instituted proceedings under Order 113 for the repossession of certain land (Ferry Lane) owned by it that had been unlawfully occupied by gypsies in a situation where the council had not provided a single caravan site for gypsies in the county, in spite of the fact that the average number of gypsy caravans in the county over the period since 1970 had been 85, and where the council had not adopted any plan for the re-accommodation of the gypsies to be evicted.

In dealing with this case the Court of Appeal approved, in principle, of the test for breach of s. 6 laid down in *Lee*, but made clear that in considering whether an authority was in breach of the duty imposed by s. 6 the adequacy of accommodation provided fell to be tested by reference to the number of gypsies known to the council to be residing in or resorting to its area over a preceding period of reasonable length. Applying this test, the court found that the council was in breach of its duty and quashed the decision made by the council to seek repossession of Ferry Lane. In reaching this decision the court emphasized that the council was precluded from seeking repossession of Ferry Lane not simply because it was in breach of the duty under s. 6, but rather because weighing the council's legitimate interests as a landowner, and the various legal, social and humanitarian considerations, and the council's long and continued breach of duty, the decision of the council to seek eviction of the gypsies in the absence of any intention to provide or direct them to alternative accommodation was *Wednesbury* unreasonable, in the sense of being perverse.

Thus the three cases examined above – *Ward*, *Lee* and *Rafferty* – established the simple but profound principle, overlooked by the court in *Wells*: since local authorities are bound to abide by administrative law norms in approaching the exercise of their functions under s. 6, where they are shown to have failed to do so, the court ought to intervene at the behest of interested gypsies, the intended beneficiaries of the duty. The decision in *Lee* was particularly significant in that there judicial review performed an 'interest representation' role in the sense identified by Galligan[39] and others. Thus it is apparent that the court was aware of official statistics and other material showing that in the face of the various practical and financial difficulties besetting gypsies' site provision, the generality of local authorities had attached a low priority to the performance of the duty imposed by s. 6. The court had clearly taken the view that the political process was operating in a manner that ran counter to the objectives of the 1968 Act and the public interest in the efficient implementation of that Act. Consequently, the 'simple test' that Mann J propounded for detecting breach of s. 6 must have been intended as a corrective to the political process and to inspire a higher level of responsiveness from local authorities.

The Impact of *Lee*

With a view to gauging the impact of the new climate of judicial intervention on local policy-making, the responses of seventeen local authorities to *Lee* were examined. The operative assumptions were that legal officers in those authorities would, as a matter of course, reflect on the implications of the *Lee* case and consider whether it required the council to make any changes to policy or practice in gypsy site provision, and that having done so such officers would report to the council or relevant committee on the matter.

As would be expected, Hertfordshire responded to the *Lee* case by undertaking a major review of policy and practice. Pursuant to the advice of Counsel, the council amended its formal policy on gypsy site provision so as to meet the reservations expressed by Mann J in respect of the council's reluctance to establish sites in the absence of district council support, and its reluctance to make use of compulsory powers in aid of gypsy site provision. The council also adopted a new programme of gypsy site provision which envisaged the establishment of gypsy sites in each of its district areas.

Of the remaining sixteen local authorities which were surveyed, twelve had yet to achieve designation. On the test propounded in *Lee*, all of them were in breach of their duty under s. 6 of the 1968 Act. Consequently, in terms of the prospective control thesis, legal officers in these should have initiated a review of policy and practice.

This occurred in Kent. At the date of the judgment 24 per cent of the gypsy population in the county were without legal abode. As in the case of Hertfordshire, historically the county council had been reluctant to seek the establishment of gypsy caravan sites in the absence of relevant district council support. In the aftermath of *Lee* the Chief Executive of the council convened a meeting of his counterparts at district council level and 'warned' them that in the light of *Lee* the council would now have to go ahead and establish sites even where the district council was opposed to such provision. Subsequently, the Secretary of the county council submitted a report to the council in which he stated that in the light of *Lee* it was 'necessary to consider working practices to ensure that policy is being followed and whether any changes are necessary'. The Secretary identified 'two areas of possible concern', viz. the absence in several of the districts of a time-related and agreed programme for gypsy site provision, and, second, the reluctance of the county council to establish sites in the absence of district council support. In those areas where little progress had been made in agreeing sites with district councils, and illegal camping remained, the need to use compulsion is likely to have to be faced during the next year (at the time of writing). The council resolved to receive the Secretary's report and approved of the action taken earlier by the Chief Executive. Pursuant to this decision officers then moved to conclude time-related site provision programmes with relevant authorities.

Of the remaining eleven, non-designated authorities the *Lee* case did not lead to a re-evaluation of policy such as had occurred in Kent. Five of the authorities had substantially completed a programme of gypsy site provision previously agreed with the Department of the Environment, and therefore officers did not feel that *Lee* required their authorities to take any remedial action. In the remaining six authorities, the council was in the early stages of implementation of a gypsy site programme approved by the Department of the Environment. Consequently, officers submitted detailed reports to their councils as a means of strengthening the resolve of councillors in implementing the site provision programme.

In Hereford and Worcestershire, a non-designated area, however, the *Lee* case was a significant factor in a decision to give gypsy site provision a higher priority. In 1978 the county council had identified a need for approximately 460 gypsy caravan pitches. In the following eight years the council failed to provided any additional caravan accommodation and yet it closed down 96 roadside sites in the county. In 1982 against a background of growing pressure from HGSG, a local pressure group, the council began to formulate a county-wide programme of site provision. The most significant problem confronting the council in the past derived from district council opposition. County legal officers tendered written reports on the *Lee* case and its implications for the council to their own council and initiated discussion on it with legal officers at district level. In the light of this, five of the district councils that had previously opposed site provision in their areas now undertook to co-operate with the county council in the matter. By July 1985 the county council was in

the advanced stages of the formulation of a caravan site programme
but no additional caravan accommodation had been provided. The
HGSG relying on *Lee* asked the Minister to exercise his default
power against the council and renewed the application in 1986, but
on this occasion threatened to join the Department of the
Environment in judicial review proceedings against the council.
The Department of the Environment then brought pressure to bear
on the council, urging it to produce a time-related programme of site
provision. By April the council had done so and taken preliminary
steps in its implementation. In the light of this the Minister refused
to intervene. However, he said that he would 'keep the position
under review' and in this connection he directed the council to send
to him quarterly reports on the rate of progress made in meeting the
need for further caravan pitches in the county.

There were three undesignated authorities where there were
strong reasons for expecting *Lee* to evoke a reconsideration of policy
and practice in gypsy site provision but where legal officers did not
even bring *Lee* to the attention of councillors. In the first of them,
Mid-Glamorgan, the council had not formally adopted a programme
of gypsy site provision and official statistics showed that 52 per cent
of the gypsy caravans in the county were encamped on unauthorized
sites. Yet the County Solicitor did not consider it necessary to report
to councillors as to the implications of *Lee*. When asked why not, he
said that the authority was seeking to establish a site in one of its
districts; that the Secretary of State had not issued 'any warning or
guidance' following *Lee*; and that *Lee* 'was only a first instance
judgement'. In the second case, the council of a county in Wales had
taken a decision prior to *Lee* to defer implementation of a gypsy site
provision until 1986/87 because of lack of finance. When asked by
the author why he, like legal officers in other 'undesignated'
authorities, had not thought it expedient to report to councillors on
the implications of *Lee*, he said:

> Every local authority has its own culture, its own priorities and
> problems, and officers understand that culture and learn to read
> the minds of members, without it ever being articulated or set
> down and you learn to live within your culture and perform in
> accordance with that culture. We have our own culture, which
> I understand, and I have been with it since 1974 . . . If I lived in
> another one I might perform differently, but I know here what
> is important, what the priorities are, what direction they want
> followed. Today we have 25,000 unemployed people in the
> county, and the thrust of our policy is to get jobs for those
> people, and concern for gypsies is very far down the list of

things to be done ... I am only an instrument of the council's policies. I am not an independent, self-sufficient free-standing agent of the law, I am a straight-forward employee, here to do what they [members] want; if it's not their enthusiasm to do a particular thing, it's no job of ours to make them enthusiastic about it.

THE IMPACT OF JUDICIAL REVIEW, ON REFLECTION

It is apparent that in the face of a widespread failure of local authorities to discharge their duties under s. 6 of the 1968 Act in the way contemplated by Parliament judicial review failed to function effectively as a mechanism of retrospective control in the initial period. This was primarily due to the decision in *Kensington and Chelsea v Wells* where the court held, applying the decision of the House of Lords in *Pasmore*, that the existence of the Ministerial default power under s. 9 precluded judicial redress. There were precedents available at that time of, for example, *Wells* which illustrated that the existence of default powers did not necessarily exclude judicial intervention. It is difficult, therefore, to avoid the conclusion that the decision flowed from a lack of judicial sympathy with the clearly-stated objectives of the 1968 Act. However, the draughtsman must share some blame in the matter. It has always been clear that the courts will be disposed to interpret and apply public law legislation subject to administrative law jurisprudence,[40] in the absence of any expressed provision to the contrary. Consequently, the reaction of the court in *Wells* was clearly foreseeable at the time of the drafting of the 1968 Act. It seems not unlikely, therefore, that the default power was deliberately included in the 1968 Act so as to impede judicial redress. All this holds an important lesson for welfare groups operating in any field of legislative reform: the adequacy of draft legislation must always be tested against prevailing judicial attitudes and administrative law norms likely to be applicable to it in the event of its being enacted.

It is also apparent that the default power detracted from the efficacy of judicial review as a mechanism for prospective control during the initial period. Although the courts abdicated jurisdiction in favour of the Minister on the ground that in the light of the default power under s. 9 of the 1968 Act the Minister was the appropriate supervisory authority, the Minister himself had taken the view that it was inappropriate to exercise those powers on the ground that local authorities should enjoy autonomy in gypsy site provision. The absence of external intervention did not encourage legal officers to view s. 6 in terms of administrative law norms, nor encourage them to assert such norms. Most legal officers were seen to assert administrative norms relevant to the application of the section only after the court in *Lee* had specifically applied them to that context. Yet there were some legal officers who must have recognized that the *Lee* judgment raised legal implications vis-à-vis their authority's existing policy on gypsy site provision, and yet did not deem it to be appropriate to assert the judgment in the policy-making processes of their authorities. In some authorities, officers felt that it was unnecessary to report upon the *Lee* case in the absence of any indication from the supervising Minister. In other cases the role conception of legal officers was the important factor: legal officers saw themselves first and foremost as servants of the council and in the performance of that role they had sought to be supportive of the council's stance on gypsy site policy. Consequently they did not see it as appropriate to emphasize the *Lee* judgment in a situation where it ran counter to the perceived policy of the council.

The perception by legal officers of administrative law from a partisan perspective as a consequence of orientating towards a private as opposed to a public law role was not limited to gypsy site provision. I found it to be characteristic of legal and other officers in the context of the working of the homelessness legislation[41] and the exercise of discretionary powers;[42] and in his reports into the working of local government Sir David Widdicombe found it to be widely prevalent in local government. This trend must inevitably detract from the effectiveness of judicial review as a mechanism of prospective control, in that where judicial norms are perceived by officers as being antithetical to the policy or priorities of the council they may be prevented from reaching the policy-making process. To the extent that this occurs, the beneficiaries of judicial norms must themselves seek to assert and enforce those norms against public authorities that have failed to observe them as a matter of course. But the mechanism of self-enforcement cannot secure the effectiveness of judicial review where the beneficiaries are unaware that judicial norms have been established in their favour, or where they lack the wherewithal to engage in enforcement action. Section 5 of the Local Government and Housing Act 1989 seeks to ensure that local authorities have access to relevant legal advice by requiring them to appoint a 'monitoring officer' (who may but need not be a legal officer). It is the duty of that officer to prepare a report to the authority if at any time it appears to him or her that any proposal or omission by the authority or one of its officers constitutes or may constitute or give rise to a contravention of any enactment or rule of law. Further research could usefully be undertaken into the question of the extent to which s. 5 has affected the responsiveness of legal officers and their employing authorities to administrative law norms and underlying judicial expectations.

CONCLUSION: THE FUTURE ROLE OF JUDICIAL REVIEW IN GYPSY SITE PROVISION

The repeal of s. 6 of the 1968 Act by the Public Order Act 1994 now leaves gypsy site provision wholly within the discretion of local authorities: gypsies without abode must either persuade local authorities to exercise their site provision powers under s. 24 of the Caravan Sites and Development Act or else persuade them to grant planning permission in support of private sites. Furthermore, s. 77 of the 1994 Act enables a local authority to direct persons residing in vehicles on any land without the consent of the occupier to leave the land and remove their vehicles, and by virtue of s. 78, an authority may apply to the magistrate's court for an order authorizing it to remove any offending vehicle. In Circular 18/94[43] the Secretaries of State for England and Wales advise local authorities to use their powers to evict gypsies 'in a humane and compassionate fashion and primarily to reduce nuisance and to afford a higher level of protection to private owners of land', and to bear in mind their obligations under the social services, housing and education legislation when taking decisions about the future maintenance of authorized gypsy sites and the eviction of persons from unauthorized sites.[44]

Although the Government in securing the enactment of Part II of the Public Order 1994 disclaimed any intention to outlaw the gypsy way of life, there is a real danger that local authorities will, notwithstanding the advice proffered in Circular 18/94, exercise their eviction and planning powers in a manner that makes it difficult for gypsies to maintain their traditional way of life.[45] Not surprisingly, the sea change in official policy on gypsy site provision has led to a flurry of litigation by gypsies adversely affected by the operation of the new legal regime instituted by the 1994 Act. Consistently with settled jurisprudence the courts have held that in exercising the eviction powers under s. 70 of the 1980 Act[46] or enforcement powers under the planning legislation, or in dealing with applications for planning permission lodged by gypsies,[47] local authorities are bound to take into account all relevant considerations including the advice contained in Circular 18/94, and discount all irrelevant considerations. For a local authority determined to rid itself of gypsies, this minimalist application of *Wednesbury* principles is, by itself, unlikely to be experienced as much of a constraint since it does not seek to control substantive policy choices: it merely requires an

authority to ensure that it has before it at the time of making a
decision a formal report making reference to relevant but not
irrelevant considerations. While the courts have always disclaimed
jurisdiction to dictate policy to public authorities, the *Wednesbury* test
is sufficiently flexible enough to enable the courts to exercise a
measure of control over substantive policy choices made by local
authorities, if they so wish. Thus as effectively occurred in *R* v
Secretary of State ex parte Ward and *West Glamorgan County Council* v
Rafferty, the court could go behind formal decision-making
documentation to determine whether in arriving at its decision the
authority had properly directed itself on the basis of all material
considerations. The courts, however, have assumed a position of
judicial restraint in the new statutory context established by the
Public Order Act 1994, making it clear that they are not prepared to
go behind formal decision-making documentation to review the
manner in which a local authority has balanced relevant considerations, on the ground that they are 'not a court of appeal from the
decision of the local authority'.[48] Given these limitations, gypsies
without abode are likely to find that political rather than legal action
is the most profitable avenue for furthering their interests.

NOTES

1   Lord Diplock, 'Administrative law: judicial review reviewed', 33 *Cambridge Law Journal* (1974): 233.
2   C. Harlow and R. Rawlings, *Law and Administration*, London: Weidenfeld & Nicolson (1984), esp. ch. 5; G. Richardson and M. Sunkin, 'Judicial review: questions of impact', *Public Law* (1996): 79.
3   *R* v *Lancashire CC, ex parte Huddleston* [1986] 2 All ER 941, at 945.
4   D. A. Obadina, 'The impact of judicial review on local authority decision-making processes', University of Wales: unpublished doctoral thesis (1989).
5   Circular 6/62, Ministry of Housing and Local Government; Circular 26/66 *Gypsies*, Ministry of Housing and Local Government.
6   The best work on the background and evaluation of the Caravan Sites Act is B. Adams, J. M. Oakeley, D. Morgan and D. Smith, *Gypsies and Government Policy in England*, London: Heinemann Educational (1979).
7   HC Deb., vol. 759, 1 March 1968, cols 1927–1929.
8   Lord Avon, *ibid.*
9   *Accommodation for Gypsies* (1977).
10 See Third Report from the Environment Committee 1984–85: Department of the Environment Main Estimates 1985–86, HC 414.
11 Lord Irving of Lairg, HL Deb., vol. 555, col. 1145.
12 Department of the Environment, News Release 622, 3 November 1994.
13 For fuller accounts of the impact of the reforms introduced by Part II of the Criminal Justice and Public Order Act on gypsy site provision see: S.

Campbell, 'The criminalisation of a way of life', [1995] *Criminal Law Review*: 28; L. Clements and S. Campbell, 'Travellers rights', *Housing Adviser* (Nov./ Dec. 1994); D. Hawes, 'Gypsies, deprivation and the law', *Legal Action* (May 1958); R. Sandland, 'Travelling back to the future?', [1994] *New Law Journal*: 741; M. J. Allen and S. Cooper, 'Howard's Way – a farewell to freedom', 58 *Modern Law Review* (1995): 364; on the operation of new regime see S. Craig and R. Low-Beer, 'In defence of common humanity', 145 *New Law Journal* (1995): 1342.

14   (1974) 72 LGR 289.

15   [1984] 2 All ER 556.

16   54 P&CR 311.

17   [1987] 1 All ER 1005.

18   s. 7(1).

19   s. 173.

20   s. 8(3).

21   1978 HL Deb., col. 1083, Baroness Steadman.

22   Interview with a Senior Civil Servant in the Department of the Environment, Gypsy Sites Branch.

23   Note 9 above, para. 4.5.

24   Circular 8/81, Annex 2.

25   The Rt Hon. Sir Harry Woolf, 'Public law–private law: why the divide? A personal view', [1986] *Public Law*: 220.

26   1898 AC 387.

27   E.g. *Glossop* v *Heston and Isleworth Local Government Board* (1878) 12 Ch D 102; [1874–80] All ER Rep 836, CA.

28   *Reg. Leicester Guardians* (1899) 2 QB 632.

29   (1974) 72 LGR 289.

30   *Ibid.*, at 294.

31   *Ibid.*, at 299.

32   *Ibid.* His Lordship left open the question of whether 'if there were quite inordinate delay some redress in the courts might be open'.

33   (1984) JPEL 87.

34   J. Griffith, 'Restraint and activism in judicial review', *Cambridge Law Journal*; P. Cane, 'Ultra vires breach of statutory duty', [1980] *Public Law*: 11.

35   [1984] 2 All ER 556.

36   54 P&CR 311.

37   [1987] 1 All ER 1005.

38   For example, the courts established that contrary to a line of authorities laid down in the early part of the twentieth century, prisoners were entitled to protection under administrative law: *R* v *Board of Visitors of Hull Prison ex parte Germain* [1979] QB 425.

39   D. G. Galligan, *Discretionary Powers*, Oxford: Clarendon Press (1986), p. 275; P. Cane, *An Introduction to Administrative Law*, Oxford: Oxford University Press (1986), pp. 24–33.

40   F. R. Bennion, *Statutory Interpretation*, London: Butterworths (1984), pp. 725–31.

41   See D. A. Obadina, 'Homelessness and the law', 1 *Judicial Review* (1995): 244.

42 D. A. Obadina, note 4 above.

43 *Gypsy Sites Policy and Unauthorised Camping*, 23 November 1994.

44 Paras 10–13.

45 See articles cited at note 13 above.

46 *Regina* v *Wolverhampton Metropolitan Borough Council and Another, ex parte Dunne, Times Law Reports*, 2 January 1997.

47 *R* v *Lincolnshire County Council and Wealden District Council ex parte Atkinson, Wales and Stratford* [1997] JPL 65.

48 See especially *R* v *The Forest of Dean District Council ex parte Grenfil and Others*, QBD (unreported), 19 March 1996, CO/3973/95; *R* v *Kerrier District Council, ex parte Uzell Blythe and Sons* [1996] JPL 837.

12

Judicial Review in the Court of Session

CHRIS HIMSWORTH

INTRODUCTION

Along with the poor, the problems of judicial review are always with us. A century and a half ago, there was no doubting the poverty of Elspeth Pryde. When her husband, William Duncan, a weaver from Ceres in Fife, died in 1840, she was left in what the law report[1] described as a 'state of destitution'. She had a family of seven children (all under 14) and was pregnant with an eighth. The family income consisted of between two and three shillings a week earned by the eldest daughter as a weaver and between one shilling and one shilling and six pence earned by Mrs Pryde herself from the winding of bobbins. She applied to the local administrators of the poor law, the heritors and kirk-session of Ceres, for parochial relief and this was awarded in the sum of three shillings and six pence a week. 'Conceiving this allowance to be inadequate', Mrs Pryde sought to bring it under review in the Court of Session by the procedure then known as advocation.

In the Outer House, the Lord Ordinary refused relief. He viewed the question as one of great difficulty and delicacy. '[T]he Court, in any decision to be pronounced in this appeal, must take care not to sanction any principle, which, on the one hand, may enable those bound to afford adequate support to the poor, to evade their obligation, or which, on the other hand, may lead to an injudicious and improper interference with the peculiar duties and powers of kirk-sessions in the administration of the affairs of the poor.'[2] The Court had an undoubted power to review the proceedings of kirk-sessions but it should not 'rashly disturb the quantum of aliment awarded by those bodies, unless it shall appear that they have given an allowance so plainly elusory, as to amount in substance to a refusal to execute those statutes which devolve upon them the charge of the poor'.[3] He went on to observe that it was not only a matter of notoriety but of record (from reports to Parliament and the General Assembly) that the allowance to Mrs Pryde, small though it might appear, was in fact greatly above the average in the country, even in those parishes where the poor were most liberally provided for. If, therefore, relief were to be granted in this instance, the case would be followed by 'processes of the same description from every district in Scotland, and involve all concerned in the most interminable and ruinous litigation'.[4]

The Poor Law and the machinery for its administration may have passed away. Similarly the particular remedy of advocation in the Court of Session. But, in the operation of the modern supervisory jurisdiction of the court, so many of the difficulties raised by Mrs Pryde's action have a continuing significance. The court's overriding jurisdiction is asserted. If the statutes have not been executed, the court must intervene. But at what point does the court draw the line between an award which is 'palpably inadequate and elusory' and one which appears not to be so substantially flawed? When the Lord Ordinary cautioned against the adoption of an expanded view of the court's role bringing with it an unaccustomed broadening of its need to enquire into social conditions and a probable opening of the floodgates of judicial business, he was drawing on arguments with which we are familiar in our own time.[5]

The debate was carried forward in the First Division of the Inner House where the focus was upon three main questions and where, because of their seriousness, the Lord Justice-Clerk and a further seven judges were first consulted for their opinions. The questions were whether the heritors and kirk-session were subject to review if they refused to make any allowance at all; whether they might be reviewed on grounds of the inadequacy of an allowance; and, if so, whether the court should itself fix the rate of allowance or remit the issue to the heritors. From a court in which opinions were sharply divided, the eventual outcome was the decision that the Court of Session was competent to review the Poor Law decisions but that it should remit the decision on a substitute figure to the heritors. As Lord Jeffrey warned, the court was 'a most unfit tribunal to sit in judgment on such a question'.[6] What this decision did involve, however, was a rejection of the even more thorough-going reservations of Lord Cockburn, one of the consulted judges with whom, in large measure, Lords Cuninghame and Moncrieff agreed. Lord Cockburn described the point involved in the questions put to the court as one:

of the very deepest importance to the country. Whether deservedly or not, it is a fact, that for greatly more than a hundred years, the poor law of Scotland has been the subject of unanimous eulogy; and the particular part of it which has been most especially praised, has been that which practically subjects the whole poor to the discretion of the heritors and kirk-sessions; − the peculiar excellence of the combination of these two bodies being said to be, that any tendency to profusion in the one, is checked by an opposite tendency in the other, which has to pay.[7]

In Lord Cockburn's view, the correct approach for the court was certainly to intervene if the kirk-session was evading its duty but, if the complaint was addressed simply to the sufficiency of an allowance awarded, then review was incompetent. If an award was not claimed to be elusory then the court could not interfere with the exercise of, in the words of an Act of 1579, the 'gude discretions of the saids provosts, bailies, and judges in the parochins to landward'.[8] Rather, if there is a problem of the parochial boards being either too liberal or too shabby, the 'only just inference from this is, that it is a case for the interference of Parliament ... It is not Judges' work.'[9] A court does not have the local knowledge; there would be every chance of its being overwhelmed by litigation unbecoming it; that litigation would throw great burdens on parochial funds where it succeeded; and the correction of local errors in this way would be accompanied by the mischief of destroying the local respect and authority of the boards.[10]

It should be remembered that Lord Cockburn's more restrictive view of the judicial role did not prevail. The other judges were, for the most part, much more willing to scrutinize the actual level of the allowance made to Mrs Pryde and even to substitute a figure they preferred. It is valuable nevertheless to remind ourselves not only of the durability of problems of distribution of poverty and wealth but also of the similarly durable problems of judicial review of social policy. In criticizing the more intrusive approach adopted by his brethren as not 'judges' work', Lord Cockburn might as well be cautioning against what we would recognize a century and a half later as a broadening of the substantive grounds of judicial review. There can be little doubt of the dismissive view Lord Cockburn would have taken of proportionality as a ground of review. *Plus ça reste!*

But some things have, of course, changed. Poverty may not have gone away. Many of the other circumstances of the nineteenth century which led to applications to the supervisory jurisdiction of the Court of Session may have their late-twentieth-century counterparts. Most of the institutions of government, however, have changed beyond recognition, producing, in the field of social welfare law, systems of tribunals – both first-instance and appellate – which take their place between first-line decision-making and the reviewing jurisdiction. In the Court of Session itself the central debate on the proper role of reviewing judges has long been resolved in favour of the minority position represented by Lord Cockburn rather than the more expansive position represented by a majority of the court in *Pryde* v *Ceres*, some of whom would themselves have gone as far as substituting a new level of Poor Law allowance. In *West* v *Secretary of State for Scotland*[11] the court took the opportunity to restate the position in the modern law of Scotland:

(1) The Court of Session has power, in the exercise of its supervisory jurisdiction, to regulate the process by which decisions are taken by any person or body to whom a jurisdiction, power or authority has been delegated or entrusted by statute, agreement or any other instrument.
(2) The sole purpose for which the supervisory jurisdiction may be exercised is to ensure that the person or body does not exceed or abuse that jurisdiction, power or authority or fail to do what the jurisdiction, power or authority requires ...
(3) Judicial review is available, not to provide machinery for an appeal, but to ensure that the decision maker does not exceed or abuse his powers or fail to perform the duty which has been delegated or entrusted to him. It is not competent for the court to review the act or decision on its merits, nor may it substitute its own opinion for that of the person or body to whom the matter has been delegated or entrusted.[12]

In doing so, the court undertook a substantial survey of the historical emergence of its jurisdiction which, while probably understating the degree of judicial disagreement evident in cases such as *Pryde* v *Ceres*,[13] does make clear how well established has become the court's commitment to review on jurisdictional grounds.[14]

Another feature of the restatement in *West* was the opportunity taken by the Lord President to reaffirm that, as far as the *grounds* of review are concerned, 'there is no substantial difference between English law and Scots law ... So reference may be made to English cases ...'[15] There was no novelty in this as there had been a statement from Lord Fraser to the same effect in the House of Lords in *Brown* v *Hamilton District Council*[16] and both are well supported by a wealth of practical decision-making in the Court of Session in which both the general principles of *Wednesbury*[17] and *GCHQ*[18] and countless specific instances of English decisions are routinely acknowledged as being influential.

Given this asserted general similarity of the grounds of view in the two jurisdictions, the purpose of this chapter will be to focus rather upon the differences that nevertheless remain in the law and practice of judicial review, whether affecting the grounds of review themselves or otherwise. As an aside, however, it may be observed that the claimed similarity of grounds of review raises some interesting questions of inter-jurisdictional jurisprudence. It does appear that there are certain areas in which the Court of Session has maintained that its approach is different. The issue of non-jurisdictional error of law is the most prominent and will be returned to. In other areas questions may arise as to the authority to be attributed by the Scottish courts to English decisions. If there did appear to be a gap opening up between the approach being taken to a particular question in the two jurisdictions, is the better view that, on the strength of decisions of high authority in each system, the law is indeed different in each? Or should the view be taken instead that, in the light of the claimed overarching similarity of doctrine, any perceived difference is a temporary aberration awaiting definitive resolution – in favour of assimilation – by the Court of Session or House of Lords? It may, for instance, be pointed out that the Court of Session has not followed *R v Gough*[19] into a preference for a 'real danger' rather than 'real suspicion' test for bias as an aspect of breach of natural justice. Perhaps the different formulation of the test makes little enough difference in practice but, if there is a difference of substance between the two tests and it is the case that courts in the two jurisdictions are displaying different loyalties, is this to be interpreted as a real exception to the general principle that the same rules should apply in the two jurisdictions; or is it instead a temporary and superficial deviation which requires, and will receive, authoritative correction? The last word of the House of Lords, even though in an English case, should effectively, following *Brown* and *West*, be the law of Scotland – despite the absence so far of reconfirmation of the position in the Scottish courts. Arguably this is to overstate the impact of the remarks, which can in a formal sense be no more than *obiter dicta*, of the senior judges in *Brown* and *West*, but it may still be the preferred position. If so, since there has been no sign of reciprocal statements in the English courts of legal equivalence between the two jurisdictions, the Court of Session must be taken to have committed itself on issues affecting the grounds of review to a somewhat derivative (if not parasitic?) role.

This does not mean that the Court of Session will avoid taking the lead in the interpretation of statutory schemes common to both jurisdictions. Sometimes the conditions for challenge arise first in Scotland – an example was *Colas Roads Ltd* v *Lothian Regional Council*[20] on compulsory competitive tendering by local authorities. Sometimes those conditions are created by the use of judicial review in support of a political campaign launched initially in Scotland. The 'ghost trains' challenge to the threatened closure of the Fort William–London sleeper service is a recent example.[21] Nor does the declaration of substantive equivalence of the law between the jurisdictions preclude elegant restatements of the law, drawing on both Scottish and English authority, in the Court of Session. The case of the threatened termination of Lanark Blue cheese[22] was a good example of an opportunity taken by the First Division to contribute to the proper understanding of procedural fairness and natural justice.

The general approach of the Court of Session does, however, seem to imply that it is unlikely to push back the frontiers of judicial review. It is unlikely to be the forum for the generation, even if this were thought to be appropriate, of new grounds of review or of imaginative variants on existing grounds. In this respect, the Court of Session probably places itself in a position similar to that occupied by the courts in Northern Ireland.[23] Because of institutional restraint, it is not likely that the courts of either jurisdiction will adopt a cutting edge stance on, for instance, the development of new thinking on proportionality as a ground of review.

With these preliminary thoughts in mind, the remainder of this chapter will be devoted to the selective treatment of aspects of the Scottish law of judicial review, where differences between Scotland and England do occur. Rather than attempting also a full survey of the substantive areas of social welfare law covered by the other chapters, some illustrations from those areas will be incorporated into the analysis. The points of difference chosen for discussion are (1) the 'scope' of review where the Court of Session has (apparently) taken the step of departing from the public/private test relied upon so heavily by the English courts; (2) 'access' to review, where the Court of Session, in adhering to more narrowly defined principles of *locus standi*, is probably producing more restrictive rules, at least in relation to representative bodies, than in England; (3) despite the agreement on a general similarity of approach to the grounds of review, the different line taken by the Court of Session to 'non-jurisdictional' error of law; (4) the possible effects of a different approach adopted to the law of Crown privilege/public interest immunity and also to the vulnerability of ministers to interdict; (5) the consequences, at least in the area of immigration, of a more liberal use in Scotland of interim liberation (pending substantive decision; which in many instances is deferred indefinitely) and (6) certain distinctions deriving from wider institutional and constitutional differences – the appellate role of the sheriff in administrative matters and, more speculatively, the continuing impact of the 1707 Union and the prospect of devolution. The chapter will conclude with (7) consideration not of differences but of the hopes or fears of greater harmonization under pressure from the European Community and the European Convention on European Rights.

THE SCOPE OF REVIEW

If the Scots law of judicial review celebrates one main difference from English law, it must be in the definition of the supervisory jurisdiction itself. Whereas the English courts have tied themselves up in the intricacies of distinctions drawn between public and private law and permitted judicial review only in respect of issues with a sufficient public law element, the Court of Session has committed itself to a definition of its supervisory jurisdiction untrammelled by such distinctions. By the rules of court, a petition for judicial review must be used for an application to the supervisory jurisdiction of the court.[24] It is the Court of Session alone which can exercise powers of review[25] and attempts to bypass the Court's jurisdiction by raising an ordinary action in the sheriff court will be prevented.[26]

The limits of the supervisory jurisdiction are not, however, further defined. In the early years of the new review procedure introduced in 1985 there were contradictory indications of how the court should proceed. There were, on the one hand, signs that the English public/private test or something very like it should be adopted,[27] but, on the other hand, it was argued that the public/private distinction had no basis in Scots law and should be rejected. This view was most strongly expressed by Lord Clyde in *Watt* v *Strathclyde Regional Council*[28] and in his extra-judicial writing.[29] The arguments on both sides[30] eventually came to be rehearsed in *West* v *Secretary of State for Scotland*[31] when Lord President Hope and a unanimous First Division came down strongly on the side of a distinctively Scottish supervisory jurisdiction. In a judgment that ranged widely across the history of the Court of Session's powers of review, it was held that the defining characteristic of a decision susceptible to judicial review was a 'tripartite relationship' between the decision-maker, the body which conferred the power to decide, and the person (the applicant for review) affected by the decision. Since *West* there has been much uncertainty about quite what the court meant, both in early comments on the case[32] and in cases which have arisen since.[33] It still seems far from clear, for instance, which public employment decisions[34] and which non-public sector bodies[35] are reviewable.

West has almost certainly not squared the circle, although some English-based commentators have looked on it more optimistically than those in Scotland itself.[36] But it is a very difficult circle, for the same reasons as in England. Neither jurisdiction will easily redesign its legal architecture to accommodate the problems that inevitably arise at the boundaries of judicial review. There are, however, all the difficulties apart, two good reasons for not agonizing further over *West* and its aftermath in this particular account. One is that *West* and the differences of approach which it demands in Scotland do not reach into the relatively uncontroversial mainstream of judicial review. As we have seen, *West* was a case in which the court reaffirmed the applicability in Scotland of the same *grounds* of review as are relied on in England and the case in no way challenges the reviewability in Scotland of the main bodies with decision-making powers in the social welfare field. Second, there is a real possibility that the conceptual framework adopted in *West* may itself fall to be reviewed. *West* was the work of Lord President Hope and, on moving to the House of Lords, he was succeeded in October 1996 by Lord Rodger of Earlsferry. It could easily be that pressure for a clearer resolution of the uncertainties surrounding the scope of judicial review will again build up, as they did before *West*, and that, if the opportunity arises, a newly constituted First Division will re-engage with the problem and to different effect. This assumes, of course, that it remains a matter for a court to decide. There are good reasons for preferring that Parliament would play a stronger role in defining the appellate and reviewing jurisdiction of the Court of Session and thus in defining the ways in which the rights of citizens should be protected.

ACCESS TO REVIEW

In three main respects the rules in Scotland which govern access to judicial review differ from those in England. In the first place there is no specific period of time within which application to the court must be made. There is no three-month rule. On the other hand the court is prepared to consider a claim by a respondent that there has been undue delay – expressed as *mora*, taciturnity and acquiescence – in bringing the application. There has not been much recent authority on what will constitute *mora* in judicial review but it was, for instance, pled successfully in *Hanlon* v *Traffic*

Commissioner,[37] where it was made clear that the unreasonableness of delay will depend on the circumstances of the particular case, including the explanation for the delay and its impact on the respondent body.[38]

Second, there is no equivalent in the Scottish procedures to the requirement of leave to apply for judicial review. A leave requirement has never been a feature of application to the Court of Session's supervisory jurisdiction and there appears to be no pressure, whether on case-management grounds or otherwise, to introduce one now.[39]

Third, and of greatest potential significance, the rules on *locus standi* are different in the two jurisdictions. Instead of the 'sufficient interest' test of the English courts, the Court of Session requires a petitioner to establish 'title and interest' in relation to the case.[40] This formula, while attracting some technicality of interpretation, does not appear to have produced an effect noticeably different on the ground than the equivalent English rules.[41] An important exception, however, appears to be opening up in relation to access by representative bodies such as pressure groups, towards whom the Court of Session remains committed, it seems, to taking a much more restrictive approach than that recently adopted by the English courts. Whereas in England a new openness has developed[42] to replace an earlier less welcoming stance,[43] nothing has changed since the *Age Concern* case[44] in 1986. This was an important challenge to the validity of a circular issued to give guidance on the interpretation of supplementary benefit regulations governing extra payments for severe weather conditions and, instead of choosing a nominated 'old person' to rely, for standing, on his or her own vulnerability to cold,[45] Age Concern made the application in its own name. That body, said Lord Clyde, did have the necessary 'title' – a legal relationship to the new rules enjoyed apparently by any member of the public – but, because neither Age Concern nor its officers were potential claimants under the regulations, it did not have the necessary qualifying 'interest' in the proceedings. The option of the nominated personal applicant will often be available but, in those circumstances where there is no such person or the case is one in which it is a real public interest which calls out for representation through a pressure group organized for the purpose, Scotland lacks at present the necessary rules of standing to facilitate the process.[46]

NON-JURISDICTIONAL ERROR

One curiosity of the development of judicial review in Scotland, despite the reaffirmation of the general equivalence of the grounds of review to those in England and Wales, is the strand of argument which has kept alive the proposition that, when it comes to review on grounds of error of law, it is only errors of a jurisdictional character which should be struck down. There may be continuing good reason, therefore, to interpret more narrowly in Scotland 'illegality' as a ground of review.

The reason is that, in Scotland, the distinction drawn by the House of Lords in *Anisminic*[47] was taken seriously. In England the distinction between errors of law falling within the jurisdiction of the decision-maker and, therefore, unchallengeable in review proceedings and errors taking the decision-maker outwith its jurisdiction was conceptually drawn but then dropped as it came to be held that almost any error of law would be treated as jurisdictional and, therefore, challengeable.[48] This may have done some violence to the point of the distinction in *Anisminic* and it may have put another nail in the conceptual coffin of jurisdiction as a general basis for judicial review but it has eased the way towards the use of judicial review as the non-statutory equivalent of an appeal on grounds of law. Challenge of an authority's decision under the homelessness legislation does not, for instance, need to involve establishing jurisdictional error.

In Scotland it is not clear that the same position has been reached. For most practical purposes it is evident that the Court of Session does tend to keep in line with decisions of the English courts and, for instance, tracks English developments in the judicial review of homelessness decisions very closely.[49] From time to time, however, it is reasserted that the Inner House decision in *Watt* v *Lord Advocate*,[50] in which *Anisminic* reasoning was adopted, does require the jurisdictional/non-jurisdictional distinction to be treated seriously.[51] Some errors of law should still be treated as unreviewable.

On the other hand, this does seem to be an area ripe for reconsideration and there was an attempt to achieve this in *Cooper* v *City of Edinburgh District Licensing Board*.[52] The First Division, however, declined to take it on. It may be noted that in *Andrew* v *City of Glasgow District Council*[53] Lord Clyde held that, as a matter of statutory interpretation, the reasoning adopted by a Housing Benefit Review Board on entitlement to a higher pensioner premium was unsound in law and the decision should *prima facie* be reduced.[54] He observed, however, that '[n]o attempt was made to define the matter in terms of jurisdictional or non-jurisdictional error and I do not find recourse to that kind of analysis of any assistance here'.[55]

PROCEDURES AND REMEDIES

As we move on from the substantive grounds of review to procedural issues, the differences between the English and Scottish rules begin to multiply. We have already seen that procedures for access to judicial review are different in ways which can be important. Once under way, the proceedings are conducted according to the rules devised for the new application for judicial review in 1985 and revised and reissued in 1994.[56] These produce proceedings which are, in their detail, different from their English equivalent but which do not operate to substantially different effect.[57] Three differences of a procedural or remedial character should, however, be mentioned.

The first is a peculiarity which appears to have emerged in the area of what used to be called Crown privilege. Although success in judicial review will not often turn on matters of evidence, it will sometimes be important for an applicant to have access to documents held by the respondent public authority and, in Scotland, the general rules of recovery (discovery) enable this to happen. As in England, a claim of Crown privilege was available to protect from disclosure some documents or classes of document although, in the dark days prior to *Conway* v *Rimmer*,[58] the Court of Session had taken a different line from that of the English courts. The decision in *Duncan* v *Cammell Laird*[59] which required a court to accept without question a minister's certificate that disclosure of a document would be contrary to the national interest did not represent the law in Scotland.[60] There has been no *cause célèbre* in the Court of Session in recent years to prompt a substantial review of the law of Scotland such as has occurred in England,[61] but it may be assumed, with one exception, that developments of the law on both sides of the border have run broadly in parallel. The exception derives from *Parks* v *Tayside Regional Council*[62] in which it was held that, while the doctrine of Crown privilege as such applied to the Crown, Government departments and the Lord Advocate, it did not *eo nomine* protect a local authority. It has been argued that, in this respect, Scots law should remain different and that the terminology of 'Crown privilege' rather than public interest immunity should be adhered to.[63] If that position becomes established, it might perhaps produce quite sharp differences in the treatment of non-Crown bodies in judicial review and other proceedings although, as the *Parks* case itself also made clear, the liberal use of the doctrine of confidentiality – to protect from disclosure information which should, in the public interest, be kept private – may achieve the same effect in practice.

Linked by its connection with the handling of the Crown in judicial review is the question of remedies and, in particular, remedies against ministers. What has produced an apparent divergence here has been the differing responses to *Factortame*[64] and the insistence by the European Court of Justice in that case that the reluctance of English courts to provide injunctive relief against ministers must yield to the demands of EC law. Whereas in *M* v *Home Office*[65] the House of Lords took the view that the lessons of *Factortame* should have an application wider that the enforcement of EC law and that ministers should, in other situations too, become vulnerable to injunctive relief, the Court of Session has so far taken a narrower view in its insistence that the Crown Proceedings Act 1947 must continue to prevent interdicts against ministers.[66] It may be that, although the rules on public interest immunity and remedies against the Crown display an apparent difference between Scotland and England, these differences are not producing substantially different effects in the practice of judicial review.

There is no doubt, however, that, in one specific respect at least, a different approach to the award of remedies has had a significantly different impact.[67] This is the more generous approach adopted by the Court of Session in the grant of interim liberation at an early stage to those seeking judicial review of decisions to detain issued by immigration officers on the grounds that the applicant is an illegal immigrant to the United Kingdom. Whereas practice south of the border has been for the courts, on the urging of the Home Secretary, to order that applicants be held in detention pending a full hearing of their application, judges in the Court of Session have tended towards a more liberal approach at this point. An attempt to take advantage of the inter-jurisdictional difference by re-routing an application for review, more appropriately made to the English High Court, into the Court of Session has been resisted. The difference was not such that it could be said that a petitioner would not obtain justice in England – e.g. for ideological or political reasons.[68] It is, however, a difference which has in a small way been exploited to the advantage of imprisoned applicants in Scotland and has incidentally skewed the judicial review statistics as many applicants who have been successful in obtaining an early interim liberation have not thereafter pursued their case through to completion.[69]

It should be pointed out that choice of jurisdiction issues were initially raised in the quite different context of the judicial review in Scotland of the Social Fund Commissioner based in Birmingham.[70]

POINTS OF DIVERGENCE

It might be expected that Scottish differences would loom much larger than has been suggested in this account so far. It is well known that it has been in the Scottish courts and in Scottish constitutional writing that the impact of the Treaty and Acts of Union 1707 has been treated as having an enduring effect.[71] Quite what that effect continues to be is a matter of debate but, in its strongest form, a doctrine that places the terms of the Treaty in conflict with more orthodox ideas about the supremacy of Parliament might be expected to have a quite substantial impact upon judicial review, in a manner analogous to that of the EC Treaty.[72] If the EC Treaty demands that judicial review cases must now embrace the possibility of challenging the compatibility of UK statutes with EC law, then the same could be true of the 1707 Treaty if the case were successfully made for it to be accorded the same authority. The classic cases of *MacCormick* v *Lord Advocate*[73] and *Gibson* v *Lord Advocate*[74] would presumably be initiated today by application for judicial review. Neither of those cases established definitively the status of the 1707 Treaty although some of the appellate cases from the poll tax era[75] and latterly, interestingly enough, certain English cases[76] have kept the claims of the Treaty alive. It is one of those areas of Scots law which would benefit greatly from an authoritative reworking in a carefully targeted new application to the Court of Session.

There are, in the meantime, some inter-jurisdictional differences which, although at a lower level in the constitutional order, do have more of an impact on the everyday life of judicial review. It is, for instance, important at some points to take account of different appellate mechanisms in Scottish administration which have the effect of diverting some disputes away from judicial review. The best known of these is the extensive use of the sheriff not only to perform appellate tasks equivalent to those allocated to magistrates or to the county court south of the border but also to take appeals on limited grounds from district licensing boards and from education (parental choice) appeal committees.[77] In a similar way, the use of the Lands Tribunal for Scotland to handle most appeals under the right to buy legislation since 1980[78] pushed substantial business into a different appellate track from that used in England. The Scottish procedure for the investigation of sudden deaths by fatal accident inquiry conducted by the sheriff has attracted applications for judicial review[79] and it may be noted in passing that the peculiarities of a sheriff's tenure and procedure for dismissal under the Sheriff Courts (Scotland) Act 1971 have brought a rare instance of one former sheriff challenging (unsuccessfully) by judicial review his own dismissal.[80]

One type of business which, as in England, has never been removed from mainstream judicial review, despite its obvious claims to be so removed and despite some attempts over the years to create a new right of appeal to the sheriff, is challenges to local authority decisions on homelessness. Applications for judicial review of these decisions form a large part of the review business of the Court of Session and, as already mentioned, they have for the most part been a sector in which the Court has followed English developments closely because of the common origins of the two statutory codes in the Housing (Homeless Persons) Act 1977 and the continuing similarity of the statutory provisions.[81]

The devolution of legislative power to the Scottish Parliament may, of course, bring very much greater divergence between the two jurisdictions. It would be unwise to devote too much space to speculation about the prospects for the Parliament in Edinburgh and what it might do. Guessing at possible futures – the extent of legislative change in general or the fondness of new Scottish Governments for the sort of institutional reform which could produce quite different demands on judicial review or indeed its complete restructuring – is not likely to be very productive. What is much more clearly predictable is the scope that an additional legislature will bring for review based, in part at least, on the claim that the Scottish Parliament has acted outwith its powers. The Scotland Act will bring its own special procedures for the challenge of Scottish legislation but will be unable to prevent issues of legislative competence arising in ordinary review proceedings. The Court of Session will acquire new forms of business that will remain quite unknown in the Strand.

If devolution will bring with it a greater diversity between the two jurisdictions, it seems likely that this will develop under an umbrella – the European umbrella – of the increasing harmonization of administrative law. This is principally the harmonization developing under the EC Treaty, although the European Convention on Human Rights (ECHR) has recently made an important inroad into the Scottish legal system. For many years it has been a point of increasing divergence of approach that, while the English courts have made substantial progress in the direction of giving the ECHR recognition as an interpretative aid, the Court of Session did not. The decision of the Lord Justice Clerk, Lord Ross, and the Second Division in *Kaur* v *Lord Advocate*[82] cast a long shadow over the development of a sophisticated response in Scotland because it was in that case that he declared categorically that the ECHR formed no part of the law of Scotland and was not available as an aid to construction of a statute.[83] That approach was followed in a number of other cases[84] although attempts were made to escape its limitations.[85] One effect of *Kaur* was probably that judicial resistance to the incorporation of human rights standards by giving some recognition to the ECHR produced a wider resistance to the adoption of a rights-based approach to judicial review. There has been little sign in Scotland of the developments seen in England towards a stricter level of scrutiny of administrative action where 'fundamental rights' are involved.[86]

Suddenly, however, all this changed in July 1996 when Lord President Hope, in his last months in that office, took advantage of the case of *T, Petitioner*[87] to reverse the approach adopted in *Kaur* and to declare that the drawing of a distinction between the law of Scotland and that of the rest of the United Kingdom on the recognition to be given to the ECHR could no longer be justified.[88] Even before the introduction of the Human Rights Bill in 1997 it seemed likely that this decision would prompt much wider recourse to arguments based on the ECHR and enable the Court of Session's jurisprudence to develop in parallel with that of the English courts.

FUTURE CONVERGENCE?

This in turn reflects a wider imperative in the direction of greater harmonization of public law between Scotland and England in the interests of a broader European harmonization. We have seen that, in certain areas, the distinctiveness of Scots law has been reaffirmed – especially in defining the scope of the Court of Session's supervisory jurisdiction. We have also seen that in Scotland, the opportunity has not so far been taken to weave the implications of *Factortame* back into domestic law to provide broader possibilities of remedies against ministers, as was done in England in *M v Home Office*.[89] On the other hand, the landmark case of *Morgan Guaranty*[90] not only provided the opportunity to review and revise some core rules of Scots law on the effect of error of law but was also used quite explicitly to bring Scots law into line with English and, thereby, European rules in the area.[91]

In cases decided so far a chequered pattern has emerged but the challenge of increasing European harmonization has been thrown down and pressures in that direction must be expected to grow. It is a two-stage process. The first is the more obvious and entails the clear desirability and even necessity that, in cases where implementation of an EC rule is at issue, there be substantial common ground between the European jurisdictions – including, of course, between Scotland and England. If the European Court of Justice demands adherence to a common standard of proportionality or the availability of interim injunctive relief against the state, then that ought to be ensured by domestic courts. The second stage of harmonization is less obvious but occurs at those points where it is appreciated within domestic orders that, rather than have the emergence of systems split between those elements brought of necessity into line with EC law and the 'purely domestic' elements which are not so harmonized, it is preferable to carry the process of harmonization into the whole of public law. It is for this reason that the decision in *M* v *Home Office*[92] has been seen as a 'famous example' of internal harmonization[93] and it was this principle that underpinned Sedley J's insistence in *R* v *Ministry of Agriculture, Fisheries and Food, ex parte Hamble (Offshore) Fisheries Ltd*[94] that it would be better to avoid the parallel development of two doctrines of legitimate expectation – one European and one domestic. If this becomes the general pattern and EC harmonization does, as a result, penetrate deep into national systems, it is clear that its effect will far exceed any diversification which flows from existing differences between the Scottish and English jurisdictions or which may flow from the devolution of legislative power to the Scottish Parliament.

NOTES

1 *Pryde* v *Heritors and Kirk-Session of Ceres* (1843) 5 D, at 552.
2 *Ibid.*, at 553.
3 *Ibid.*
4 *Ibid.*
5 Perhaps the nearest parallels are to be seen in judicial resistance to the expansion of judicial review in *R* v *Hillingdon LBC, ex parte Puhlhofer* [1986] AC 484, at 518 (Lord Brightman) or the extension of the grounds of review to include proportionality in *R* v *Home Secretary, ex parte Brind* [1991] 1 AC 696, at 766–7 (Lord Lowry).
6 *Pryde* v *Heritors and Kirk-Session of Ceres*, at 577.
7 *Ibid.*, at 556.
8 *Ibid.*, at 558.
9 *Ibid.*, at 560.
10 *Ibid.*
11 1992 SC 385.
12 *Ibid.*, at 412–13.
13 For a brief critique of the historical material in *West*, see C. M. G. Himsworth, 'Public employment, the supervisory jurisdiction and points *West*', 1992 *Scots Law Times* (News) 257.
14 For the most substantial historical study as well as the fullest analysis of the modern law, see the title on 'Administrative Law' in Volume 1 of the *Stair Memorial Encyclopaedia of the Laws of Scotland* (by A. W. Bradley).

15 1992 SC 385, at 413.
16 1983 SC 1, at 42 (HL).
17 *Associated Provincial Picture Houses Ltd* v *Wednesbury Corporation* [1948] 1 KB 223.
18 *Council of Civil Service Unions* v *Minister for the Civil Service* [1985] AC 374.
19 [1993] AC 646. See also *R* v *Inner West London Coroner, ex parte Dallaglio* [1994] 4 All ER 139 and *R* v *Secretary of State for the Environment, ex parte Kirkstall Valley Campaign Ltd* [1996] 3 All ER 304.
20 1994 *Scots Law Times* 396.
21 See *Highland Regional Council* v *British Railways Board* 1996 *Scots Law Times* 274.
22 *Errington* v *Wilson* 1995 SC 550.
23 For the very close similarities to England maintained by the courts in Northern Ireland, see B. Hadfield, 'Judicial review in Northern Ireland: a primer', 42 (1991) *Northern Ireland Legal Quarterly* 332.
24 Rule 58.3, Act of Sederunt (Rules of the Court of Session 1994) 1994, SI 1994, No. 1443.
25 *Brown* v *Hamilton DC* 1983 SC 1 (HL).
26 See e.g. *McDonald* v *Secretary of State for Scotland (No. 2)* 1996 *Scots Law Times* 575 in which it was held that an action for damages in the sheriff court which depended upon the reduction of prison rules was incompetent.
27 See *Connor* v *Strathclyde Regional Council* 1986 *Scots Law Times* 530 and *Tehrani* v *Argyll and Clyde Health Board* 1989 SC 342.
28 1992 *Scots Law Times* 324.
29 See W. Finnie, 'The nature of the supervisory jurisdiction and the public/ private distinction in Scots administrative law' in W. Finnie, C. M. G. Himsworth and N. Walker (eds) *Edinburgh Essays in Public Law*, Edinburgh: Edinburgh University Press (1991).
30 For discussion of the position at that stage, see C. M. G. Himsworth, 'Judicial review in Scotland' in M. Supperstone and J. Goudie (eds) *Judicial Review*, London: Butterworths (2nd edn, 1997), pp. 19.4–19.14.
31 1992 SC 385.
32 See W. Finnie, 'Triangles as touchstones of review', 1993 *Scots Law Times* (News) 51; W. J. Wolffe, 'The scope of judicial review in Scots law', 1992 *Public Law* 625; and Himsworth, note 13 above.
33 See *Naik* v *University of Stirling* 1994 *Scots Law Times* 449, *Joobeen* v *University of Stirling* 1995 *Scots Law Times* 120 (Note) and *Blair* v *Lochaber District Council* 1995 *Scots Law Times* 407, on which cases see C. M. G. Himsworth, 'Judicial review in Scotland' in B. Hadfield (ed.) *Judicial Review: A Thematic Approach*, Dublin: Gill & Macmillan (1995) and C. M. G. Himsworth, 'Further *West*? More geometry of judicial review', 1995 *Scots Law Times* (News) 127.
34 See *Blair*, note 33 above.
35 See references in note 33 above. See also *Lennox* v *Scottish Branch of the British Show Jumping Association* 1996 *Scots Law Times* 105 which was an action of declarator and reduction rather that an application for judicial review. Cf. *Gunstone* v *Scottish Women's Amateur Athletic Association* 1987 *Scots Law Times* 611.
36 See, in particular, H. W. R. Wade and C. F. Forsyth, *Administrative Law* (7th edn, 1994), Oxford: Oxford University Press, at pp. vii, 667 and 682; and I. Cram and J. Bell, 'Towards a better public law?', 74 (1996) *Public Administration* 239, at 245.

37   1988 *Scots Law Times* 802.

38   See also *Bantop Ltd* v *City of Glasgow DLB* 1990 *Scots Law Times* 366.

39   See T. Mullen, K. Pick and T. Prosser, *Judicial Review in Scotland*, London: Wiley (1996), at p. 47.

40   For a full account, see A. W. Bradley, *Stair Memorial Encyclopaedia*, Vol. 1, paras 308–321.

41   But see *Simpson* v *Edinburgh Corporation* 1960 SC 313.

42   See especially *R* v *Inspectorate of Pollution, ex parte Greenpeace (No. 2)* [1994] 4 All ER 329 and *R* v *Secretary of State for Foreign and Commonwealth Affairs, ex parte World Development Movement* [1995] 1 All ER 611.

43   *R* v *Secretary of State for the Environment, ex parte Rose Theatre* [1990] 1 QB 504.

44   *Scottish Old People's Welfare Council, Petitioners* 1987 *Scots Law Times* 179.

45   Cf. Mrs McColl objecting to water fluoridation in *McColl* v *Strathclyde Regional Council* 1983 SC 225.

46   A situation commented on in the unreported English case of *R* v *Secretary of State for Scotland, ex parte Greenpeace* (Popplewell J, 24 May 1995). For comment on the Scottish rules, see C. R. Munro, 'Standing in judicial review', 1995 *Scots Law Times* (News) 279 and I. Cram, 'Towards good administration – the reform of standing in Scots public law', 1995 *Juridical Review* 332.

47   *Anisminic Ltd* v *Foreign Compensation Commission* [1969] 2 AC 147.

48   See S. A. De Smith, H. Woolf and J. Jowell, *Judicial Review of Administrative Action*, London: Sweet & Maxwell (5th edn, 1995), at pp. 244–56.

49   An interesting extra-judicial application of this was the attention given by both the Scottish Office and its consultees on a draft revised Code of Guidance on Homelessness to *Awua* v *Brent London Borough Council* [1995] 3 All ER 493. Consultees (e.g. the Chartered Institute of Housing in Scotland) claimed, on advice from Jonathan Mitchell QC, that the Government was misinterpreting the impact of the case but did not deny its authoritative status in Scotland.

50   1979 SC 120.

51   See especially *O'Neill* v *Scottish Joint Negotiating Committee for Teaching Staff* 1987 *Scots Law Times* 648; *Civil Aviation Authority* v *Argyll and Bute Valuation Appeal Committee* 1988 *Scots Law Times* 119; *Gordon* v *Kirkcaldy District Council* 1989 *Scots Law Times* 507.

52   1991 *Scots Law Times* 47.

53   1996 *Scots Law Times* 814.

54   Although, in fact, the application for review was rejected on the grounds that the result reached by the board (by the wrong route) was correct.

55   1996 *Scots Law Times* 814, at 816. Arguments based on *Watt* v *Lord Advocate* were pursued in *Murray* v *Social Fund Inspector* 1996 *Scots Law Times* 38.

56   See Act of Sederunt (Rules of the Court of Session 1994) 1994, SI 1994, No. 1443 replacing SI 1985, No. 500.

57   But for criticism of the impact of Social Fund cases in Scotland, including *Murray* v *Social Fund Inspector* 1996 *Scots Law Times* 38, see J. Gray and D. O'Carroll, 'Challenging the Social Fund', (1994) *SCOLAG* 102. See also the effect on Social Fund loans of sequestration proceedings revealed by *Mulvey* v *Secretary of State for Social Security* 1997 *Scots Law Times* 753; 1997 SCLR 348.

58   [1968] AC 910.

59   [1942] AC 624.

60   See e.g. *Glasgow Corporation* v *Central Land Board* 1956 SC 1 (HL).

61   For the more recent cases see *Air Canada* v *Secretary of State for Trade (No. 2)* [1983] 2 AC 394; *Makanjuola* v *Metropolitan Police Commissioner* [1992] 3 All ER 617; and *R* v *Chief Constable of West Midlands Police, ex parte Wiley* [1995] 1 AC 274.

62   1989 *Scots Law Times* 345.

63   *Ibid.*, following *Higgins* v *Burton* 1968 *Scots Law Times* (Notes) 52. For discussion see F. M. McShane, 'Crown privilege in Scotland: the demerits of disharmony', 1992 *Juridical Review* 256 and 1993 *Juridical Review* 41.

64   *R* v *Secretary of State for Transport, ex parte Factortame Ltd (No. 2)* [1991] 1 AC 603.

65   [1994] 1 AC 377.

66   *McDonald* v *Secretary of State for Scotland* 1994 *Scots Law Times* 692. But see also *Millar & Bryce Ltd* v *Keeper of the Registers of Scotland* 1997 *Scots Law Times* 1000.

67   There is a more general distinction between the jurisdictions in that the Court of Session is much less inclined to treat the question of whether to grant any remedy at all as a discretionary matter for the court. See e.g. references at Himsworth, note 30 above, p. 435. But see also Lord Clyde in *Andrew* v *City of Glasgow District Council* 1996 *Scots Law Times* 814, at 818 where, referring to the 'essentially equitable province of the supervisory jurisdiction' he declined a remedy where the right result had been reached for the wrong reasons.

68   See *Sokha* v *Secretary of State for the Home Department* 1992 *Scots Law Times* 1049, at 1054.

69   See Mullen, Pick and Prosser, note 39 above, p. 32. For another review see Sir William Gray, 'Judicial review in immigration cases in Scotland' in the proceedings of a Law Society of Scotland Seminar on Immigration Law (3 November 1995).

70   See T. Buck, *The Social Fund: Law and Practice*, London: Sweet & Maxwell (1996), pp. 211–14.

71   See e.g. D. N. MacCormick, 'Does the UK have a Constitution?', 29 (1978) *Northern Ireland Legal Quarterly* 1.

72   See below.

73   1953 SC 396.

74   1975 *Scots Law Times* 134.

75   For discussion see N. C. Walker and C. M. G. Himsworth, 'The Poll Tax and Fundamental Law', 1991 *Juridical Review* 45.

76   See *R* v *Secretary of State for Scotland, ex parte Greenpeace*, 24 May 1995, unreported, and *R* v *Commissioner of Police, ex parte Bennett* [1995] 3 All ER 248.

77   For discussion of the sheriff's powers see G. Little, 'Local administration in Scotland: the role of the sheriff' in W. Finnie, C. M. G. Himsworth and N. Walker (eds) *Edinburgh Essays in Public Law*, Edinburgh: Edinburgh University Press (1991).

78   See C. M. G. Himsworth, *Housing Law in Scotland* (4th edn, 1994), ch. 8. Recent reported cases include *Hamilton* v *City of Glasgow DC* 1996 *Scots Law Times* (Lands Tribunal) 14 and *McKay* v *City of Glasgow DC* 1996 *Scots Law Times* (Lands Tribunal) 9.

79 *Lothian RC* v *Lord Advocate* 1993 *Scots Law Times* 1132 (Note), *Smith* v *Lord Advocate* 1995 *Scots Law Times* 379 (Note).

80 *Stewart* v *Secretary of State for Scotland* 1996 *Scots Law Times* 1203.

81 For a recent example, see *McMillan* v *Kyle and Carrick DC* 1996 *Scots Law Times* 1149.

82 1980 SC 319.

83 *Ibid.*, at 329.

84 *Moore* v *Secretary of State for Scotland* 1985 *Scots Law Times* 38.

85 *Weeks* v *United Kingdom* 10 (1987) EHRR 293.

86 See e.g. *R* v *Secretary of State for the Home Department, ex parte McQuillan* [1995] 4 All ER 400 and *R* v *Ministry of Defence, ex parte Smith* [1995] 4 All ER 427.

87 1996 SCLR 897.

88 *Ibid.*, at 910–11.

89 [1994] 1 AC 377.

90 *Morgan Guaranty Trust Co. of New York* v *Lothian RC* 1995 SC 151.

91 See *Woolwich Equitable Building Society* v *IRC* [1993] AC 70 in which the House of Lords took a lead from *Amministrazione delle Finanze dello Stato* v *S.p.A. San Giorgio*, Case 199/82 [1983] ECR 3595. For a comment on this and other aspects of European integration, see M. G. Clarke, 'Scots or European lawyer – quid sum?', 1996 *Juridical Review* 361. See also C. M. G. Himsworth, 'Public law – in peril of neglect?' in H. L. MacQueen, *Scots Law into the 21st Century*, Edinburgh: W. Green/Sweet & Maxwell (1996).

92 [1994] 1 AC 377.

93 W. van Gerven, 'Bridging the unbridgeable: community and national tort laws after *Francovich* and *Brasserie*', 45 (1996) *International and Comparative Law Quarterly* 507, at 538.

94 [1995] 2 All ER 714. For a comment on the case, see C. M. G. Himsworth, 'Legitimately expecting proportionality', [1996] *Public Law* 46.

13

Judicial Review in Northern Ireland

JOHN FRANCIS LARKIN*

INTRODUCTION

In no UK jurisdiction is the nature and legitimacy of state authority so much a matter of contention as in Northern Ireland.[1] That fact and the violence generated directly and indirectly by such contention have necessarily had a shaping effect on the Northern Ireland legal system. A resulting apparatus of 'emergency' legislation including considerable powers of arrest, search and detention, and the use of judge-only courts for the trial of certain offences, have caused the legal system of Northern Ireland to differ markedly from that in England and Wales.[2] Although the procedural structure of judicial review in Northern Ireland is largely the same as in England and Wales,[3] the nature of many issues thrown up by Order 53 proceedings there makes it possible to discern the stamp of 'the troubles' throughout the public law jurisprudence of Northern Ireland. Even a cursory examination of the workload of the Crown Side of the Queen's Bench Division in Belfast shows that in 1995 of a total of 170 applications for leave 74 involved prison discipline,[4] suggesting strongly that Northern Ireland is not a 'normal' society. Further analysis of available figures over recent years strengthens that suggestion and throws up further symptoms of societal abnormality.[5]

It has been the boast of a former Lord Chief Justice of Northern Ireland that Irish lawyers have never required *R v Northumberland Compensation Appeal Tribunal ex parte Shaw*[6] to remind them of the

---

* I am grateful to Mr Justice Kerr for commenting on an earlier draft of this chapter. Any errors or inelegancies are mine.

proper reach of certiorari.[7] Certainly the Irish law reports of the nineteenth century teem with discussion about the availability of the prerogative writs, particularly in the context of challenges to the decisions of magistrates.[8] Whether the relative facility of Irish lawyers with the prerogative writs derived from the vexed relationship between Government and governed or from another source is unimportant for present purposes, it being sufficient to note the continued existence of that tradition. Notwithstanding its existence, however, it is a matter of some regret that Northern Ireland courts have not with few exceptions been responsible for substantive doctrinal development in judicial review, and it is largely from English courts that such development has been achieved. It might even be that the vaunted nineteenth-century tradition of public law has inhibited bolder recent development.[9]

In *Neill v North Antrim Magistrates Court*[10] a Divisional Court in Northern Ireland was faced with a challenge to committal proceedings where the accused had been denied a statutory right to cross-examine two witnesses. Their evidence was essential to three of the charges against the accused. The Magistrates Court admitted statements of the witnesses after receiving what amounted to double hearsay evidence about the reasons for the refusal to attend the committal hearing. The Divisional Court held that committal proceedings were immune from challenge on the basis of a previous decision of the Northern Ireland Court of Appeal, *R v Campbell*,[11] itself dependent on the earlier Irish authority of *R (Blakeney) v Roscommon JJ*.[12] On appeal the House of Lords[13] side-stepped the line of authority ending in *Campbell* and decided the case on natural justice grounds, with the failure to permit the statutory right to cross-examination resulting in the circumstances of that case in the return for trial being quashed on three of the four counts. While it was obviously open doctrinally to the Divisional Court to distinguish *Campbell* and *Blakeney* not least on the ground that natural justice or procedural fairness played no part in those decisions, the weight of the tradition against reviewing committal proceedings for insufficiency of evidence overcame any attractiveness of an argument grounded in procedural fairness. In this regard *Neill* may be seen as displaying the fault line between the 'old' judicial review and the new.

What follows is an examination of a number of issues, substantive and adjectival, where the approach and technique of the Northern Ireland courts on applications for judicial review may be discussed. Neither the enumeration of issues nor the discussion should be assumed to be (or to have pretended to be) comprehensive when all that is aimed at is some depiction, with analysis, of an aspect of public law in action in conditions of considerable social difficulty.[14]

PRISONERS

In prison discipline, noted above as the largest category of judicial review applications in Northern Ireland, the courts have been responsible for considerable substantive doctrinal development. No doubt both the volume of cases in this area and the platform for development thereby provided are due, in large measure, to the landmark decision of the Northern Ireland Court of Appeal in *Re McKernan's Application*[15] which opened the disciplinary adjudications of prison governors to judicial review. That step, possessing a force of logic that now appears irresistible, was followed by a series of decisions dealing with procedural fairness in adjudications, substantive defences and larger questions of legality in the context of prison rules.

On the issue of prisoners' witnesses in disciplinary adjudications, Carswell J (as he then was) in *Re Thomas McNeill Rowntree's Application*[16] concluded that 'a governor can refuse to allow a prisoner to have a particular witness called to give evidence only where it can reasonably be said that despite the omission of that witness the prisoner still has had a full opportunity to present his case'.[17] The learned judge disapproved of any suggestion in *Ex parte St Germain (No. 2)*[18] that the governor's discretion to call a witness was reviewable only on *Wednesbury* grounds: 'If the effect of the decision is to deprive the prisoner of a full opportunity of presenting his case, that is a breach of the Prison Rules, and a ground in itself for judicial review of the adjudication.'[19] Against a background of administrative convenience in prisons where the case for the prosecution in many contested disciplinary charges is made through agreed (or more often unobjected to) statements by prison officers, Carswell LJ (as he then was) observed in *Re Jason Barton's Application*[20] that: 'There may be cases when a governor ought, in the interests of fairness, to have a witness called even though no objection had been raised to admission of his statement.'[21] There is thus a two-tier approach to oral testimony in disciplinary adjudications: a presumptive duty to afford a prisoner the opportunity of adducing relevant evidence through witnesses; and a residual obligation on adjudicating governors to ensure the attendance of witnesses where fairness appears to require this. An unresolved complication, however, is the avowed powerlessness on the part of prison authorities to ensure the attendance of unwilling prisoner witnesses, a stance so far upheld by the courts.[22]

There has been in Northern Ireland a readiness to import the general defences of criminal law into prison discipline. In some instances, such as self-defence, the defence has been simplified in the process of transplantation to the prison adjudication. All that was required of an adjudicating governor, as Carswell J held in *Re Noel Campbell's Application*,[23] was that: 'Once the issue of self defence was raised, it was incumbent upon the governor to take into account that defence and any evidence which might be material to its validity. He had to be satisfied beyond reasonable doubt that the defence was ruled out before he could properly hold the offence proved.'[24] Recognizing duress as a defence has more far-reaching consequences for governors in the conduct of disciplinary adjudications, indeed sympathy was expressed by Carswell J in *Re William Jameson's Application*[25] at the problems it created for adjudicating governors. In that case there emerged a broad statement of a governor's duties which, although expressed in the context of duress, is capable of wider application. Where, it was held, the issue of duress is raised in any way at an adjudication whether or not the prisoner has pleaded not guilty the governor must take the issue into account and deal with it in his findings. Once the issue of a threat amounting to duress has been raised the governor must be satisfied beyond reasonable doubt that it has been ruled out before he or she may convict. Duress may be ruled out in either of two ways: (1) by a finding that no such threat was in fact made, 'if so, he [i.e. the governor] should spell this finding out in his decision'[26] or (2) by finding that if any threat was made, a reasonable person in the position of the prisoner would not have yielded to it. In the event of such a finding the governor:

> should specify that clearly in his decision, preferably with sufficient reasons for this court to see why he came to that conclusion. Such a finding needs to be based upon sufficient evidence, and the governor should make sufficient inquiry into the circumstances during the adjudication to find the facts necessary to found his conclusion. In some cases these may depend on his background knowledge of the running of the prison, and if so, he should preferably refer to them in the course of the hearing and give the prisoner an opportunity to deal with them.[27]

This approach offers, it is suggested, a general guidance for the conduct of adjudications and comes close to requiring the giving of an adequately reasoned conclusion as a condition of fairness or legality. For the most part it may be observed that on the issue of prison discipline the courts in Northern Ireland have developed a set of principles for the conduct of adjudications that can properly be called adjectivally generous.

Imposing limits on the extent of penalization contemplated by prison discipline has been much less enthusiastically endorsed by the courts. In *Re Samuel Henry's Application*[28] argument was advanced on behalf of the applicant that Rule 31(13) of the Prison Rules (Northern Ireland) 1982 which penalized the use by a prisoner of 'any abusive, insolent, threatening or other improper language' was *ultra vires* the rule-making power conferred by s. 13 of the Prison Act (Northern Ireland) 1953 by reason of its excessive interference with speech and its inherent vagueness suggesting potentially limitless application. While noting that the use of abusive, insolent or threatening language outside prison might not incur criminal liability, Kerr J did 'not think it could reasonably be suggested that one had a right recognised by a law to indulge in such behaviour much less a basic entitlement which required to be protected as a constitutional right'.[29] On the issue of vagueness:

> to allow abusive, insolent or threatening language to occur without sanction in a prison would inevitably involve a substantial threat to discipline and control of prisoners. I do not accept that these terms are vague. Of necessity they do not specify precisely the language that is forbidden but they are sufficiently clear to give prisoners fair notice of the type of language which is not permitted.[30]

The learned judge then read 'or other improper language' *eiusdem generis* the preceding words of Rule 31(14):

> it is clear that, in the context of the rule, the words, 'or other improper language' mean language of a like nature to that described as 'abusive, insolent or threatening'. Thus, for example, gratuitously offensive language falling short of abusive, or grossly lewd words which did not threaten would come within the class whereas imperfections of speech or lapses in grammar plainly would not.[31]

While the language attributed to the applicant in that case might well appear to raise no difficulties in its assignment to the categories of abusive and insulting,[32] the willingness of the court to uphold a scheme of penalization that could embrace a sexual joke or a verbal equivalent to the quizzically raised eyebrow suggests that on the larger questions of prison administration, as distinguished from the protection of individual rights at adjudications, there is a judicial reluctance to be seen to add to the burden of management in the substantive enforcement of discipline.

In any survey of the impact of judicial review on the life of prisoners the decision of the House of Lords in *R v Secretary of State for the Home Department, ex parte Doody*[33] must loom large. In Northern Ireland that decision was first cited in *Re Ronald McCartney's Application (No. 1)*[34] which concerned a challenge by a prisoner temporarily transferred to Northern Ireland from England under s. 27(1) of the Criminal Justice Act 1961 to a refusal by the Home Office of a period of temporary release for which the applicant had applied under a form furnished by the Northern Ireland prison authorities pursuant to the Northern Ireland home leave scheme for prisoners. At the time of making application for temporary release the applicant did not know that the Home Office would determine his application by reference to factors other than those appropriate to prisoners sentenced in Northern Ireland and detained there. The applicant did not appreciate, for example, that his English prison category would normally preclude any temporary release. In granting relief, Kerr J, having acknowledged the difference in subject-matter, described the decision in *Doody* as 'directly and usefully analogous to the present case'.[35]

Rather as Robert Penn Warren described the War Between the States as the South's 'great alibi'[36] so might *Doody* be characterized as the 'great analogy' of contemporary judicial review. Perhaps ironically for a passage which purports to be a restatement of extant principle, that part of Lord Mustill's speech beginning at page 560D has been granted the status of a new charter of procedural fairness for the entirety of administrative decision-making. The most recent concrete and novel application of *Doody* fairness may be seen in *Re Linda Quigley's Application*[37] where although a two-judge divisional court split on the precise basis for dismissing the application (Nicholson LJ on discretionary refusal of relief, Sheil J on a factual finding of no unfairness), the court held that, applying *Doody*, the Secretary of State for Northern Ireland must receive and consider any representations by or on behalf of a person arrested and detained under s. 14 of the Prevention of Terrorism (Temporary Provisions) Act 1989 before making an order under s. 14(5) extending the period of such detention.

Doody's elasticity is not without limit, however, and in the vexed area of removal from association[38] it has been held[39] that a governor is not required to give reasons to a prisoner or to receive representations from him before removing him from association under Rule 25 of the Prison Rules (Northern Ireland) 1982. Part of the conclusion appears to work backwards from a determination that because the giving of reasons is not to be required principally on security grounds the prisoner cannot therefore make effective representations 'and the procedure would be no better than a dialogue of the deaf'[40] so fairness cannot in such circumstances demand representations.

Curiously, given the precise subject-matter in *Doody*, its impact in Northern Ireland has not been so emphatic in the field of the procedural rights held by life sentence prisoners in relation to review and release. That may be in part because the system in Northern Ireland does not depend on the English two-fold division into tariff and risk elements, and relies upon an overall judgment about the appropriate length of sentence, taking into account a range of factors including comparable cases. Although by s. 1 of the Northern Ireland (Emergency Provisions) Act 1973 the release of any person sentenced to life imprisonment for murder is the decision of the Secretary of State for Northern Ireland, the executive decision-making process is funnelled through the Life Sentence Unit of the Northern Ireland Office and a Life Sentence Review Board. While arguments on behalf of the applicants in *Re Mark Wright and James Fisher's Applications*[41] were characterized by Girvan J as amounting 'to the proposition that the court should ensure that the applicants should be able to expect the same rights as those established for English mandatory life sentences by virtue of the House of Lords ruling in *R v Secretary of State for the Home Department ex parte Doody*',[42] and while the learned judge noted that 'the review procedure by the [Life Sentence Review] Board provides less than the full expectations that the principles of fairness might suggest were desirable (assuming *Re Whelan* [1990] NI still stands following the Doody decision)',[43] he preferred to determine the case without deciding whether *Doody* had imported procedural fairness into the Northern Ireland life sentence review and had accordingly overturned *Re Whelan*, the Northern Ireland equivalent of *Payne v Lord Harris of Greenwich*.[44] Although apparently shaken, the Northern Ireland system for reviewing life sentences remains standing – for the present.[45]

DISCRIMINATION IN LEGISLATION AND ADMINISTRATION

Also indicative of the peculiar problems of Northern Ireland is the prohibition by s. 19 of the Northern Ireland Constitution Act 1973 of discrimination by a range of public bodies including ministers of the Crown on the ground of religious belief or political opinion.[46] That provision has been resorted to as a basis of applications for judicial review as has s. 17 of the 1973 Act which provides that certain species of Northern Ireland legislation shall be void to the extent that they discriminate against any person or class of persons on the ground of religious belief or political opinion. These provisions have posed particular fact-finding difficulties for applicants for judicial review because the existence of discrimination unless inferred from conduct or result will often by its nature be concealed and almost certainly denied. In a number of instances private law actions for damages for s. 19 discrimination have been taken and it may be that private law procedure enjoys advantages over Order 53 proceedings in this sensitive area.[47]

It may appear paradoxical that an attempt by Government to provide for 'the education together at school of Protestant and Roman Catholic pupils' (Article 64(1) of the Education Reform (Northern Ireland) Order 1989) should give rise to a s. 17 challenge to the validity of Chapters I, II and III of Part VI of the Education Reform (Northern Ireland) Order 1989 making provision for integrated education. In *Re Most Reverend Cahal B. Daly's Application*[48] it was argued on behalf of the applicants, Catholic Bishops with dioceses in Northern Ireland, that those provisions designed to encourage the growth and development of integrated schools in Northern Ireland fell foul of s. 17 'in that their effect is or is likely to be disadvantageous to Catholics and in particular to Catholics who wish to have their children educated in schools with a Catholic character'.[49] Acknowledging the widening of that class during the course of argument, MacDermott LJ regarded the inquiry as starting 'with the question: "Who" is being less favourably treated than "whom"? The "whom" can be readily defined as those who favour integrated education. If that be right the "who" would be all who do not favour such education, which is a very wide class.'[50] Assuming that the 1989 Order did in fact favour integrated schools over non-integrated schools, the learned judge concluded that it could not be said that any damage suffered by the class contended for by the applicants had been 'caused by discrimination on grounds of religious belief because even if they had no such belief they would have suffered the same damage as all others'[51] who do not favour integrated education.

While factually it can be said, with respect, that this decision is unimpeachable, there is a disquieting dictum which appears to place certain aspects of state policy beyond the realm of the political. The political opinion limb of s. 17(1) played an incidental part in argument but in disposing of it the learned judge stated: 'For my part I do not consider that the Government's attitude towards integrated education is a matter of political opinion – it is founded in what I consider to be the non-political belief that as a matter of educational policy it is in the public interest to support integrated education.'[52] If the implications of this dictum were to be applied numerous and important matters of public policy, and state decisions about the 'public interest', would be withdrawn from the scope of s. 17 in a manner that cannot, it is suggested, have been contemplated by the legislature.

Such doctrinal development as has taken place in s. 19 judicial review has largely concerned the applicability of the *James* v *Eastleigh Borough Council*[53] 'but for' test for discrimination. In *Re Robert*

Lavery's Application[54] Kerr J was not persuaded that it was correct to import the 'but for' test to an interpretation of s. 19. The learned judge adduced two practical considerations (in the context of the political opinion limb of s. 19) against that test: first, given the wide diversity of opinion in contemporary society, '[t]o impose on the Minister the task of ensuring that no decision of his, however unwittingly, had the effect of according less favourable treatment to those holding a particular shade of political opinion would be to impose a burden quite incapable of practical fulfilment';[55] second, that because political opinion and religious belief unlike gender or race are voluntarily chosen or retained and while one should not be discriminated against on the ground of political or religious creed, 'it is at least arguable that a freely espoused belief does not require the degree or level of protection appropriate to an aspect of the human condition such as one's sex or ethnic origin over which no control or choice may be exercised'.[56] It is perhaps regrettable that, by reason of the applicant's success on another ground, this dissection of s. 19 was not explored fully on appeal, because when in *Re JF's Application*[57] in the context of the religious belief limb of s. 19 Kerr J again revisited the topic, he felt constrained by the decision of the Northern Ireland Court of Appeal in *Belfast Port Employers Association* v *Fair Employment Commission for Northern Ireland*[58] (a decision under fair employment legislation) to consider that it is not necessary 'to show that the less favourable treatment referred to in s. 19 of the 1973 Act must be intended for a breach of that provision to be established'.[59]

If one eschews what, it is suggested, is the impermissible approach of MacDermott LJ in *Re Most Reverend Cahal B. Daly's Application* of limiting the scope of 'political', it is suggested that one is faced with the intractable difficulty sketched by Kerr J in his first practical consideration against the adoption of the 'but for' test in *Lavery*. While the operation of the 'but for' test in relation to political opinion might present relatively little difficulty in the specialized sphere of employment, in the context of public administration generally (the sphere largely covered by s. 19) where decisions will frequently reflect policy choices that are ineluctably political and whose impact cannot be characterized as other than political, it promises absurdity or chaos unless checked in some other manner. One limitation on the scope of s. 19 was drawn in *Re John Joseph O'Neill's Application*[60] which involved a challenge to the Sunday closure (on sabbatarian grounds) of Cookstown District Council's leisure facilities. There, after observing that 'the fact that a decision coincides with the wishes of one group and is adverse to the interests of another does not, without more, establish that the deciding authority has treated one group more favourably',[61] Kerr J went on to conclude that 'for a breach of s. 19 to occur, the deciding authority must have the option to treat one group as favourably as it would another in the same circumstances and declines or fails to do so on the ground of religious belief or political opinion'.[62] With this emphasis on formal opportunity for discrimination the 'but for' test becomes a more measured tool for the application of s. 19. One may be permitted to wonder, however, if s. 19 thus restrained may be efficacious in countering discriminatory administrative action in the context of the practical evidential handicaps of judicial review.

Certainly in one area of considerable current controversy,[63] that of permitting and routing certain contentious parades, the need for s. 19 comparators has been problematic. Disorder created by Orange parades and opposition thereto has provided a problem for Irish administration since the early nineteenth century. While current public order legislation, the Public Order (Northern Ireland) Order 1987, establishes a regime of control for parades entrusting an enforcement and regulatory discretion to the police (Article 4) and the Secretary of State for Northern Ireland (Article 5), any challenge to the exercise of that discretion in any particular case can normally hope to succeed only on *Wednesbury* grounds. The exceptionally high burden imposed on applicants by that test in these circumstances is demonstrated by the leading case *Re Conor Murphy's Application*[64] and by the other challenges to police discretion that have followed it. In *Re Patricia White's Application*,[65] in addition to challenging the exercise of ministerial discretion, the applicant argued that in failing to exercise his powers under Article 5 of the 1987 Order to ban an unwelcome Orange procession on 12 July 1996 the Secretary of State for Northern Ireland was discriminating against the Catholic and Nationalist population of the Lower Ormeau Road area of Belfast by visiting on them the 'disorder, insult and affront'[66] associated with Orange parades in that area. This argument floundered in the absence of a suitable comparator, as Girvan J observed:

> The applicant has adduced no material to show that she has been treated less favourably by the Secretary of State than a Protestant in equivalent circumstances would have been treated if the circumstances were reversed and a Catholic procession was threatened through a Protestant area. The applicant can point to no comparable situation in which Protestants received different and more favourable treatment.[67]

While undoubtedly providing for the factual disposal of the application, it is possible that too much may be made of the absence of any exact comparator. A menacing procession of the Ku Klux

Klan permitted through a Black district in Mississippi would not have been counterpoised by any Black equivalent by which the conduct of state authorities might be weighed, yet the fact of the detriment and the more favourable treatment of the Klansmen over the Black community seems obvious.

STANDING

In line with what has been described above as the adjectival generosity of the Northern Ireland courts in judicial review, the standing of interest groups has not been seen as problematic. In 1988 applications for judicial review by the Equal Opportunities Commission for Northern Ireland of systemic disparity in marking between boys and girls at the 11-plus selection examination were entertained and granted,[68] and in 1995 an application by the National Graves Association Belfast Branch challenging a decision by the Secretary of State for Northern Ireland refusing to disinter and remove the remains of the last IRA member hanged in Northern Ireland from the grounds of HM Prison Belfast was also successful.[69] In the field of challenges to decisions of school admission appeal tribunals respondents have expressed concern at applications being brought for judicial review by children (with legal aid) despite parents being the proper parties before those tribunals. In *Re An Application by Danielle Kerr (A Minor)*[70] Girvan J, responding to an argument that an application for judicial review of a school admissions appeal tribunal decision not brought by appellant parents could not result in meaningful relief, left the issue open and observed that 'normally it is the party with the legal grievance who is the proper party to bring the appropriate proceedings to rectify the situation brought about by that grievance'.[71] This issue has not subsequently arisen for definitive determination but, it is submitted, the obvious interest of a child in attending a chosen school makes him or her a proper party entitled to all relevant relief.

ALTERNATIVE REMEDIES

Adjectival generosity is encountered also in the limited treatment that the issue of alternative remedies has received in Northern Ireland. Of particular relevance in the light of the hierarchy of appeals and review mechanisms established under social security legislation, the great danger of any extended alternative remedy doctrine is that it effectively removes issues about the quality of decisions affecting large numbers of citizens from the supervision of the Queen's Bench Division. In *Re Francis Jamison's Application*[72] an application challen-

ging, on *Wednesbury* and procedural fairness grounds, the refusal by a
Social Security Appeal Tribunal to adjourn the applicant's appeal
against refusal of invalidity benefit was met on the part of the
respondent by a submission that a suitable and effective alternative
remedy for the applicant lay by way of appeal to the Social Security
Commissioner. It was argued that the Commissioner had in fact
considered appeals raising issues similar to those raised by the
applicant. In rejecting the respondent's submissions, Kerr J drew on
the decision of the English Court of Appeal in *R v Panel on Takeovers
and Mergers ex parte Guinness plc*[73] with its distinction between
challenges grounded on procedural fairness and those based on other
grounds, with the former attracting less judicial reluctance in Order
53 intervention despite possible alternative remedies. Since the
challenge in that case was grounded on procedural impropriety, an
application for judicial review was considered proper and jurisdiction
was not declined, notwithstanding the possibility of an alternative
remedy.[74]

SUBSTANTIVE LEGITIMATE EXPECTATION

One of the warmest current debates in English public law is the
dispute between those who contend for the existence of substantive
legitimate expectation and those who refuse to extend the doctrine
beyond procedural rights. Until recently both positions were evenly
drawn, with lucid expositions from Sedley J in *R v Ministry of
Agriculture Fisheries and Food, ex parte Hamble (Offshore) Fisheries Ltd*[75]
(in support of substantive legitimate expectation) and Laws J in *R v
Secretary of State for Transport, ex parte Richmond upon Thames London
Borough Council*[76] (against). By its rejection of substantive legitimate
expectation (indeed, by appearing to characterize it as 'heresy'), the
English Court of Appeal in *R v Secretary of State for the Home
Department, ex parte Hargreaves*[77] has placed, at least temporarily, an
obstacle before the recognition of substantive legitimate expectation.

In Northern Ireland, *Re Archibald Harvey Croft's Application*[78] leaves
the development of substantive legitimate expectation tantalizingly
open. Although in delivering judgment the Lord Chief Justice
referred to his earlier rejection of substantive legitimate expectation
in *Re Police Association for Northern Ireland's Application*[79] and noted
that he was not to be understood to depart from it 'at present' he
went on to observe 'that on a head count of judicial dicta one may be
able to find a balance of support for substantive legitimate
expectation, and academic opinion seems to have adopted this as
the high ground. The resolution of the issue may be a matter of
judicial policy and choice and one may be fairly certain that the last

word has not yet been said on the subject.'[80] Although clearly *obiter*, certain remarks on the conditions giving rise to substantive legitimate expectation are helpful. If legitimate expectation can indeed extend to upholding substantive rights, 'there must be a clear and unambiguous representation or statement of policy to give rise to an expectation',[81] and on the question of whether there is a need for demonstration of reliance on representation and resultant detriment, the Lord Chief Justice found 'it difficult to suppose as a matter of principle that such a requirement could be dispensed with altogether'.[82]

PROPORTIONALITY

Notwithstanding the possible development of proportionality as a discrete ground of review hinted at by Lord Diplock in his classic speech in *Council of Civil Service Unions* v *Minister for the Civil Service*,[83] subsequent English decisions have evinced a reluctance to respond favourably. In *R* v *Secretary of State for the Home Department ex parte Brind*[84] although much was made of judicial lack of the administrative expertise necessary for the weighing exercise demanded by proportionality, the terms of rejection were cast in unrelievedly general terms. Lord Ackner declared that there is 'at present no basis upon which the proportionality doctrine applied by the European Court can be followed by the Courts of this Country'.[85] In *Re Robert Crawford's Application*[86] the revocation of an indeterminate sentence prisoner's release on licence by reason of his arrest and remand in custody on serious charges gave rise to a challenge partly founded on proportionality. It was argued on behalf of the applicant that his remand in custody combined with the unlikelihood of a grant of bail (a matter uniquely within the expertise of judges) made the proportionality of the revocation of licence without a prior hearing a matter which judges were entirely capable of weighing, thereby removing the traditional objection to this ground. Delivering the judgment of the Divisional Court, Kerr J noted that:

> While there have been judicial statements to the effect that the principle of proportionality would be difficult to apply in the field of domestic administrative law because in many areas of administrative decision judges are not equipped to balance the competing arguments, it should not be assumed that where an administrative decision involves matters with which a judge may be supposed to be familiar, application of the principle of proportionality is appropriate.[87]

The 'short answer'[88] to the applicant's argument was furnished by the single sentence of Lord Ackner partly quoted above.

Although *Crawford* constitutes a disappointingly firm barrier to any deliberate embrace of the concept of proportionality, so named, as a ground for review, that might not matter unduly in that the grounds for review appear to be in a state of overlap and flux. As Carswell LCJ suggested in *Archibald Harvey Croft's Application*, '[t]hese approaches, which tend to shade into each other, may in time coalesce, if the law is heading towards a generalized principle of the need for fairness in administration, which could supplant the several categories under which a decision may be set aside, just as in *Donoghue* v *Stevenson* Lord Atkin enunciated a generalized principle governing negligence'.[89] Although this outcome is described as no more than 'a future possibility',[90] the setting and source of the suggestion give rise to the anticipation of substantive development in Northern Ireland of the law of grounds for review.

At the time of writing there is good reason to suppose that the next great test for an emerging doctrine of substantive legitimate expectation or general fairness in Northern Ireland may be a response to the hint thrown out by Lord Lester in his recent tocsin 'International human rights law: a new year's legitimate expectation',[91] where on the strength of *Minister for Immigration and Ethnic Affairs* v *Teoh*,[92] he encouraged appropriate invocation of a substantive legitimate expectation of the rights enshrined in the European Convention on Human Rights and Fundamental Freedoms.[93] While the majority of judgments in *Teoh* appear to favour procedural rather than substantive legitimate expectation, there seems little doubt that the majority holding of the High Court of Australia combined with such authority as *R* v *Secretary of State for the Home Department, ex parte Ruddock*[94] offers a helpful platform for development.

APPENDIX: PRACTICE

In the judicial review practice of Northern Ireland may be discerned something approaching seasonal variation. In early summer there has been normally a series of challenges to police and central government decisions about controversial parades. At the same time but also stretching into early September are challenges to School Admission Appeal Tribunals concerning admission to post-primary schools. In December the prospect of Christmas gives rise to a number of challenges by prisoners to negative decisions on applications for temporary or compassionate release. To this seasonal variation may be added a more epochal fluctuation where certain bases of application once of great numerical and other importance have withered or disappeared or been transformed. An example here is the formerly significant number of applications challenging decisions of senior police officers under s. 45 of the Northern Ireland (Emergency Provisions) Act 1991 to defer the access of a person detained under s. 14 of the Prevention of Terrorism (Temporary Provisions) Act 1989 to his or her solicitor. The phenomenon is recorded in decisions such as *Re Patrick Duffy's Application* [95] and *Re McKenna's Application*[96] but the police practice appears to have changed, perhaps in the light of the European Court of Human Rights' decision in *John Murray* v *United Kingdom*.[97] Current attention in this area is now on securing for persons detained under s. 14 the right to be accompanied and advised by their solicitor during interviews. At present the Divisional Court in Northern Ireland has set itself firmly against such recognition.[98]

Order 53 procedure in Northern Ireland is characterized by flexibility and greater relative simplicity than pertains under the equivalent English rules. No doubt much of the easiness and efficiency possessed by the system is due particularly to the energy and skill of the Registrar but it is also due to the advantages that flow from the personal knowledge possible only in a small jurisdiction. At present there is an assigned judicial review judge, Kerr J, who has been responsible for considerable procedural innovation in the area.

In Northern Ireland the statement required by Order 53 Rule 3(2)(a) RSC (NI) consists of the three elements of: designation of applicant, relief sought, and supporting grounds, without the elaboration required by a Form 86A Notice,[99] and it is correspondingly shorter. Prior to Kerr J's appointment there was a tendency to plead grounds with some terseness. However, greater fullness in the setting out of grounds has been encouraged for some time.

As a matter of practice, cases raising issues of importance, particularly in the area of civil liberties, or cases appearing to the office to require urgent consideration are sent to the judge for consideration of leave. Much greater use is made in Northern Ireland of oral leave hearings where the proposed respondent is invited to attend. At such hearings leave itself is rarely at issue but the opportunity is taken for the judicial assessment of urgency, issuing directions including procedural timetables. At such hearings the opportunity is taken to clarify any opacity or deficiency in papers and to impose directions for amendment.

Skeleton arguments are not required by practice direction to be lodged save in respect of divisional court hearings. On occasion, however, following consideration of papers an indication will be sent in particular cases that a skeleton argument should be lodged.

In cases of objective urgency and particularly where there is any concern about the immediacy of an interim relief Kerr J has indicated that applications without supporting affidavit or statement will be considered. In several cases including a number involving challenges to the legality of detention under s. 14 of the Prevention of Terrorism Act 1989 the applicant's case has been presented in the conventional way via affidavit while by reason of constraint of time the factual basis of the respondent's case has been provided by oral evidence with full opportunity for cross-examination.[100]

POSTSCRIPT

The 1992 volume of the Northern Ireland Law Reports (published only in 1997) has thrown up an interesting example of substantive divergence in doctrine between Northern Ireland and England. If *R v Belfast Recorder ex parte McNally* [1992] NI 217 is followed in Northern Ireland, then the venerable distinction between jurisdictional and non-jurisdictional errors of law will have been restored there in respect of inferior courts, notwithstanding the decision of the House of Lords in *Page* v *Hull University Visitor* [1993] AC 682. In *McNally* a challenge to a sentence imposed on appeal by a county court judge based on the doctrine articulated in the line of authority beginning with *R* v *St Albans Crown Court ex part Cinnamond* [1981] QB 480 was rejected by Lord Lowry LCJ, who firmly characterized those cases as 'wrongly decided' [1992] NI 217 at 228j). It is suggested (and hoped) that the distinction thus sought to be restored will not long survive in the absence of doctrinal sustenance from the sister jurisdiction.

NOTES

1 The only published bibliography of 'the troubles' is R. Bell, *Northern Ireland Political Periodicals 1966–1992: A Bibliography of the Holdings of the Linenhall Library Belfast*, Belfast (1994). A valuable typescript handlist is 'A bibliography of 100 books in print on current Northern Ireland politics' produced by the staff of the Northern Ireland Political Collection at the Linenhall Library, 17 Donegall Square, North Belfast BT1 5GD. See also W. D. Flackes and S. Elliott, *Northern Ireland: A Political Directory 1968–1989*, Belfast (1993).

2 For a survey of the position *circa* 1984 see Sir George Baker's *Review of the Operation of the Northern Ireland (Emergency Provisions) Act 1978*, Cmnd 9222, London (1984). This may be updated by Lord Lloyd of Berwick's *Inquiry into Legislation against Terrorism*, Cm 3420, London (1996). For a critique of aspects of the Diplock system see D. P. J. Walsh, *The Use and Abuse of Emergency Legislation in Northern Ireland*, London (1983) and S. C. Greer and A. White, *Abolishing the Diplock Courts*, London (1986).

3 See P. Maguire, 'The procedure for judicial review in Northern Ireland' in Hadfield, B. (ed.) *Judicial Review: A Thematic Approach*, Dublin: Gill & Macmillan (1995). The standard guide to procedure is now ch. 19 of B. J. A. C. Valentine's definitive *Civil Proceedings: The Supreme Court*, Belfast (1997).

4 See the Northern Ireland Court Service, *1995 Judicial Statistics for Northern Ireland*, Belfast (1996), p. 56, Table B.16.

5 See the Northern Ireland Court Service, *1994 Judicial Statistics for Northern Ireland*, Belfast (1995) and the detailed analysis by B. Hadfield and E. Weaver, 'Judicial review in perspective: an investigation of trends in the use and operation of the judicial review procedure in Northern Ireland', [1995] 46 *Northern Ireland Legal Quarterly*: 113.

6 [1951] 1 KB 711.

7 Lord Lowry, ' Civil proceedings in a beleaguered society', [1987] *Denning Law Journal*: 109, at 124–5.

8 See, for example, the large number contained in the official collection *Judgements of the Superior Courts in Ireland in Cases under the Criminal Law and Procedure (Ireland) Act 1887 and Others*, Dublin (1890).

9 See Lord Lowry, note 7 above, at 126.

10 [1991] 7 NIJB 83.

11 [1985] NI 354.

12 [1894] 2 IR 158.

13 [1992] 4 All ER 846.

14 The student of judicial review in Northern Ireland will consult the useful articles by Professor Hadfield, 'Judicial review in Northern Ireland: a primer', [1991] 42 *Northern Ireland Legal Quarterly*: 332 and 'Introduction to JR in Northern Ireland', [1996] *Judicial Review*: 170–5. See also E. Graham, 'Judicial Review: the new procedure', [1980] 31 *Northern Ireland Legal Quarterly*: 317.

15 [1985] NI 385.

16 [1991] 11 NIJB 67.

17 *Ibid.*, at 73.

18 [1979] 3 All ER 545, at 550b.

19 [1991] 11 NIJB 67, at 74.

20 Unreported, QBD, 18 August 1995.

21 *Ibid.*, at 5–6.

22 See *Re Henry McKee's Application* (unreported, QBD, 6 September 1995), Kerr J at 6–7.

23 Unreported, QBD, 15 October 1993.

24 *Ibid.*, at 6.

25 Unreported, QBD, 23 July 1993.

26 *Ibid.*, at 4.

27 *Ibid.*, at 5.

28 Unreported, QBD, 1995.

29 *Ibid.*, at 9.

30 *Ibid.*, at 13.

31 *Ibid.*, at 14.

32 The curious should consult p. 3 of the judgment.

33 [1994] 1 AC 531.

34 Unreported, QBD, 6 September 1993.

35 *Ibid.*, at 9.

36 R. P. Warren, *The Legacy of the Civil War*, New York (1961), pp. 54–8.

37 [1997] NT 202.

38 See the discussion in S. Livingstone and T. Owen, *Prison Law*, Oxford (1993), pp. 216–27.

39 *Re Louis Maguire's Application*, unreported, QBD, 3 December 1993.

40 *Ibid.*, at 8.

41 Unreported, QBD, 20 December 1996.

42 *Ibid.*, at 6.

43 *Ibid.*, at 19.

44 [1981] 2 All ER 842.

45 At the time of writing (February 1997) two cases were listed which would probably require a full resolution of the impact of *Doody* on the life sentence review system in Northern Ireland; at page proof stage (January 1998) changes in the disclosure arrangements under that system resulted in the resolution of these cases.

46 For a discussion of the issues see the Second Report of the Standing Advisory Commission on Human Rights on *Religious and Political Discrimination and Equality of Opportunity in Northern Ireland*, Cm 1107, London (1990).

47 The first claim under s. 19 was a private law action, *Purvis v Magherafelt District Council* [1978] NI 26 commenced, however, before the present Order 53.

48 Unreported, QBD, 5 October 1990.

49 *Ibid.*, at 13.

50 *Ibid.*, at 14.

51 *Ibid.*, at 17.

52 *Ibid.*, at 15–16.

53 [1990] 2 AC 751.

54 Unreported, QBD, 13 May 1994.

55 *Ibid.*, at 12.

56 *Ibid.*

57 Unreported, QBD, 11 October 1996.

58 Unreported, CA, 29 June 1994.

59 Unreported, QBD, 11 October 1996, at 9.

60 Unreported, QBD, 20 March 1995

61 *Ibid.*, at 7.

62 *Ibid.*

63 On which see the *Report of the Independent Review of Parades and Marches*, Belfast (1997).

64 [1991] 5 NIJB 88.

65 Unreported, QBD, 11 July 1996.

66 *Ibid.*, at 3.

67 *Ibid.*, at 9.

68 [1988] 10 NIJB 44 and 88.

69 *Re Alphonsus Hannaway and others' Application*, unreported, QBD, 4 May 1995.

70 Unreported, QBD, 31 July 1997.

71 *Ibid.*, at 12.

72 Unreported, QBD, 14 October 1996.
73 [1990] 1 QB 146.
74 Unreported, QBD, 14 October 1996, at 11–12.
75 [1995] 2 All ER 714.
76 [1994] 1 All ER 577.
77 [1997] 1 All ER 397.
78 [1997] NI 1; but now see also the sober judgments of the Court of Appeal at [1997] NI 457.
79 [1990] NI 258.
80 [1997] NI 1, at 19a.
81 *Ibid.*, at 18e.
82 *Ibid.*, at 18g.
83 [1985] AC 374, at 410.
84 [1991] 1 AC 696.
85 *Ibid.*, at 763.
86 [1994] NIJB 83.
87 *Ibid.*, at 89d.
88 *Ibid.*, at 89e.
89 [1997] NI 1, at 14d.
90 *Ibid.*, at 14e.
91 [1996] *Public Law*: 187.
92 (1995) 128 ALR 353, see also R. Piotrowicz, 'Unincorporated treaties in Australian law', [1996] *Public Law*: 190.
93 A further helpful straw in the wind may be the decision of Girvan J in *Re Katherine Colgan and others' Applications* [1997] 1 CMLR 53, where at page 74 the learned judge notes that '[a] decision which results in unjustifiable inequality of treatment is open to challenge on the ground of unreasonableness since if there is no logical difference between two situations justifying a differential treatment, logic and fairness require equality of treatment'. It is to be noted, however, that as a member of the Court of Appeal in *Croft* (note 78 above) Girvan J sought to place these observations in a *Wednesbury* irrationality setting.
94 [1987] 2 All ER 518.
95 [1991] 7 NIJB 62.
96 [1992] 1 NIJB 1.
97 22 EHRR 29.
98 See *Re Charles Begley's Application*, [1996] NI 1 (QBD) and [1997] NI 275 (HL).
99 Helpfully reproduced in R. Gordon, *Judicial Review: Law and Procedure* (2nd edn), London (1996), pp. 346–8.
100 An example is *Re Linda Quigley's Application*, note 37 above.

14

Conclusion

TREVOR BUCK

'Social welfare' is a broad, generic category, as is evident from the range of topics covered in this collection. It includes, most obviously, a number of central and local government income maintenance schemes. There are also a range of services sometimes referred to collectively as the 'social wage', which can be thought of as income in kind; for example, health, education, personal social services, social housing. The way in which income maintenance schemes and income 'in kind' are delivered and the particular allocation of such resources have a wide-ranging impact on economic and social development, poverty and inequalities of income distribution.

Discourse on the shape and future of social welfare will always be a highly politicized area because ultimately in any democratic state the allocation of resources is a matter for political decision-making in a framework of accountability. As one might expect, the distribution of the 'social wage' favours those in lower income groups. Recent research suggests that the value of benefits in kind received by the poorest fifth of the population was about 70 per cent greater than for the richest fifth (Sefton, 1997). However, there are important differences in the distribution of particular services; housing and personal social services were found to be strongly 'pro-poor' but higher education for non-mature students was strongly biased in favour of the top income groups, whereas further and higher education for mature students have a small pro-poor bias (Sefton, 1997: Table 1). The research study also suggested that contrary to popular opinion, demographic changes appear to have reduced overall pressure on welfare services since 1979; the effect of a small child population more than offset the effects of an ageing population on health care and personal social security spending.

The size of the social wage has fallen as a proportion of final incomes (i.e. cash income plus social wage) from 14 per cent in 1979 to 13.1 per cent in 1993. Although the distribution of the social wage became slightly more pro-poor over the period, when one looks at income distribution generally, inequality has increased, even if the social wage is included in the measure of income. According to a common measure of inequality, the 'Gini coefficient', the increase in inequality since 1979 is smaller by around one-fifth, once the social wage is taken into account. Those expecting that welfare services would benefit mainly lower income groups may be surprised that the poorest half of the population are only receiving 60 per cent of the value of those services, or only 54 per cent once demographic effects are removed.

In general the research confirmed that welfare services have not been captured by the middle classes, but the widening gap in cash incomes has not been substantially offset by the growth in the social wage; a trickle-down effect, through this route, has been limited. Welfare spending has risen in line with the economy as a whole but only in the case of social housing has there been a clear shift in favour of the poorest.

The centre ground in British politics, well reflected by the Blair administration, is not ideologically committed to any formula of state, voluntary or private provision of welfare but rather to a pragmatic balancing of suitable providers across the range of welfare services. It would appear that the only remnant of ideology is the profound belief that different solutions can be found in the different areas of welfare provision. Previous forages into unorthodox 'unthinkable' solutions to perennial welfare issues (see Field and Owen, 1993) may yet become received wisdom under the New Labour administration. The symbolism of Frank Field's appointment as Minister for Welfare Reform cannot be underestimated.

However, there seems little doubt that the courts will continue to exercise a significant influence over social welfare matters. The views of academic commentators made thirty years ago would no longer have much currency. For example:

> the judges had been removed, had removed themselves or been restrained from entering large areas of competence in the modern state. The Welfare State seemed to have little room for the courts. (Abel-Smith *et al.*, 1967: 117)

However, one has to be reminded of the relative novelty of judicial review in the development of the law and administrative practice.

Indeed, a decade later, another commentator could suggest, presciently, that:

> [T]hose concerned with administrative law, with the proper role of the courts (whether or not with the adoption of an Administrative Division), with a consciousness that there has been historically an imbalance in their role leaning perhaps too heavily towards issues of property and less towards social and economic matters – indeed, those concerned like Lord Scarman with the universality of the common law – all of them will at least hope that the courts can contribute something valuable at a critical stage in the evolution of methods of social welfare in this country. (Williams, 1979: 113–14)

The concern of academics in the 1970s and 1980s with how discretionary powers, a characteristic feature of welfare legislative provisions, could be suitably regulated, remains an important constellation of debate. However, with some licence, one could say that the past twenty years of development in the jurisprudence of the substantive grounds of judicial review have produced a set of general administrative law principles which, in theory, can be applied to a wide range of discretionary powers in very different contexts. A distinguished academic commentator, for example, has stated that since Griffith's *The Politics of the Judiciary* appeared:

> [J]udicial review has undoubtedly taken giant steps forward. The charge of political bias would today be hard to sustain. At the doctrinal level, judicial review is more principled, one good effect of the exclusive administrative jurisdiction created by the reformed Order 53 procedure. Modern judgments are well reasoned and articulated. A flourishing and prestigious public law Bar has developed, to its credit very professional, concerned with standards and active in publication. As it should be, debate has been enriched by input from academics and based on empirical data they have provided. (Harlow, 1997: 252)

The focus now is more properly on the issue of how, when and in what manner such principles are to be implemented to provide appropriate accountability for those exercising such powers. The tools of administrative law have now been forged but we need to know more about the way in which the key players ought to organize themselves and apply these principles. Furthermore, little research has arisen which specifically concentrates upon the way in which judicial review is used in conjunction with other means of redress, e.g. the Parliamentary Commissioner for Administration, the local ombudsmen, challenge under the European Convention of

Human Rights (ECHR) and the media. Robson, for example, argues that judicial review has a distinct function in social security, in particular it enables the glare of publicity to politicize the impact of social security rules and in consequence achieve changes to those rules (Chapter 4).

A distinctive feature of welfare systems is ultimately the problem of how resources are allocated. Over time and across the various welfare services, different legal frameworks have adopted different solutions and approaches to these problems. The remedy of judicial review has penetrated these key areas but only to a limited extent. The House of Lords case of *R v Gloucestershire County Council ex parte Barry* [1997] 2 AER 1 illustrates the difficulties.

Mr Barry, aged 79, was severely disabled. He lived alone and had no family contact. He had been assessed in 1992 as requiring home help twice a week and meals-on-wheels four days a week. In 1994 he was informed by the local authority that help with his cleaning and laundry would be withdrawn due to the cut in funds allocated by Central Government. The Divisional Court refused to grant a declaration that the local authority was not entitled to take into account the resources available to it when his needs were reassessed in 1994. The Court of Appeal granted the declaration, stating that a local authority was so entitled. The House of Lords reversed that ruling. The majority judgment (Lord Lloyd of Berwick and Lord Steyn dissenting) was that a disabled person's 'needs' under s. 2 of the Chronically Sick and Disabled Persons Act 1970 should be assessed using eligibility criteria decided upon by the local authority as to whether the disability of a particular person dictated a need for assistance and, if so, at what level. Those criteria must be set, taking into account current acceptable standards of living, the nature and extent of the disability and the relative cost balanced against the relative benefit and the relative need for that benefit. In deciding the weight to be given to the cost factor, the authority must evaluate the impact of that cost on its resources. It followed therefore, in the opinion of the majority, that a disabled person's need for services could not sensibly be assessed without having some regard to the cost of provision. The person's need for services could not be decided in a vacuum from which all cost considerations were expelled.

The judicial disunity in this case reflected a wider disagreement about the capacity of such legislation to crystallize anything akin to a 'right' to welfare services. As is pointed out in both leading judgments, the duty owed by a local authority to disabled persons under the 1970 Act is unusual, precisely because it confers rights on individuals, at least at the latter stage of making arrangements under s. 2. However, at the earlier key stage which defines when that duty arises, the House of Lords held that the level of resources was a permissible factor for a local authority to consider. Lord Clyde states:

> The determination of eligibility for the purposes of the statutory provisions requires guidance not only on the assessment of the severity of the condition or the seriousness of the need but also on the level at which there is to be satisfaction of the necessity to make arrangements. In the framing of the criteria to be applied it seems to me that the severity of a condition may have to be matched against the availability of resources. Such an exercise indeed accords with everyday experience in relation to things which we do not have. If my resources are limited I have to need the thing very much before I am satisfied that it is necessary to purchase it. (At 16/17)

Even where it is decided in law that available resources are a factor to take into account this ought not to be an automatic signal for a judicial 'hands off' approach. As Lee points out (Chapter 2) many court judgments 'have profound economic consequences, and demand not only that funds be reallocated but that new funds be found'. The powerful policing effect that judicial review has had on the 'prison estate' referred to by Creighton is a good example of how judicial review can have such far-reaching consequences (Chapter 10).

Good standards of administrative justice must surely seek to advance fairness and equity in such decision-making. The development of practical principles in this crucial area is needed to provide a continuous force of accountability that is sometimes lacking through direct political means. Constitutional objections to the judiciary trespassing on executive territory are frequently too simplistic.

It has been argued that the overall implication of the advancement of judicial review as a check on public administration is that it adds a new layer to the recognized stages of policy formulation and delivery. Political scientists have recognized six stages: the emergence of a policy issue; its processing by the public authority (including consulting outside interests); decision; legitimation (e.g. approval by Parliament); implementation; and evaluation. However, it has been suggested that the intervention of the courts adds an additional stage to the policy-making process. This has been broadly described as 'adjudication' in which the court tests the policy when it is applied in practice (Hogwood, 1987). One commentator puts it explicitly:

> Today, any policy decision of any controversial nature is tested in the courts ... Judicial review has become an automatic resort of the disgruntled, and as such is a new and important stage in the public policy process. (James, 1996: 629)

In any one social welfare topic surveyed, it is often difficult to measure *precisely* the extent to which this 'adjudication' stage has had, and will have, an influence on future developments. Harris argues, for example (Chapter 1), that judicial review does not have the potential to reallocate power within an education system characterized by the inherent tension between individual and collective rights. However, he concedes it may, at the least, inhibit more serious potential excesses of power and authority.

In social welfare matters the process of policy design and implementation is inherently complex and in need of sophisticated fine-tuning. It will characteristically affect very large numbers of citizens and involve huge resources and, at any one time, several distinct social welfare areas will form a significant part of electoral concern, at both central and local government level. In some areas it might well be argued, however, that judicial review never reaches far enough into the policy-making process. Obadina argues that *Wednesbury* rationality is sufficiently flexible to enable the courts to exercise some control over policy choices made by local authorities, but in the context of Part II of the Public Order Act 1994, judicial restraint has prevented such development (Chapter 11). Others would disagree that *Wednesbury* review should be afforded a lower threshold on the traditional ground that it would import dangers of allowing the judiciary to make decisions on the merits of the case. In the view of one commentator (currently the Lord Chancellor), 'it is the constitutional imperative of judicial self-restraint which must inform judicial decision-making in public law' (Irvine, 1996). If, however, it is correct that the broad ethos of judicial review does constitute a distinct addition to public policy then there is now a compelling argument for administrators, politicians, lobbyists and welfare customers to review how this can be integrated into our public administrative systems. What might be required is a culture shift which does more than merely acknowledge the irksome nature of judicial review and the reluctant need to have greater numbers of officials capable of arranging administrative practice in order merely to avoid the embarrassment of judicial review challenge. Perhaps one contribution would be the investment of educational resources into training public bodies and their officials to recognize the positive contribution of judicial review. The ever-present prospect of judicial review supersedes many of the usual short-term political horizons which sometimes dominate the agendas of such bodies. Equally, it is possible that the bureaucratic temperament, to some extent, leans towards more long-term goals and in that sense there may be an unacknowledged commonality between judicial review and public organizational ends.

It is indeed ironic that while judicial review establishes standards of rationality for decision-making, there is often little rationality in the way in which judicial review may strike. The general experience in social welfare areas is probably an uneven pattern of litigation which can do nothing but harm the confidence which the principal players in such activity have in its ultimate value. The differential access allowed to petitioners has several causes, a principal one being, as Smith points out (Chapter 6), the unsatisfactory state of the legal aid system. However, it is suggested that a deepened integration of the principles guiding judicial review within public bodies may well result in a more rational management of judicial review challenge. The case study of the discretionary Social Fund (Chapter 5) demonstrates the potential for developing systems whereby there could be a negotiation between public bodies and representative interest groups of relevant and efficient 'targets' for judicial review treatment. It is not only welfare resources but also judicial resources which, in the real world, are in great demand. The efficient allocation of the latter must remain a continuing concern in the development of public law and administration.

Indeed, the potential impact of judicial review on our system of governance inevitably calls into question the ability of our judges to rise to the challenge. In some areas of activity, public confidence may be worryingly low. Shah and Menski (Chapter 9) conclude that in the field of immigration the judges have not shown themselves immune from the scaremongering tactics of the executive to the detriment of resolving a level of administrative abuse. The danger is that such inattention will tend to implicate the judiciary as participants in such abuse.

Judicial review at present is ultimately a 'last resort' remedy to be used when other statutory appeal systems have been exhausted. Given the wide range of such appeal mechanisms within the welfare arena its impact will remain an uneven one. As Pollard points out (Chapter 7), the high frequency of judicial review in relation to homelessness cases over the past twenty years has, in effect, converted the supervisory jurisdiction to an appellate one in that field. Equally, it is likely that judicial review will retain a role under the new legislative arrangements introduced by the Housing Act 1996 but, at the time of writing, that role remains uncertain. However, it is probable that its impact here will be marginal given the existence of a new statutory review procedure to be undertaken by housing authorities and the creation of a substantive right of appeal to a county court following an adverse review.

However, from the perspective of social action groups, Smith argues, there is a common discernible response by Government to the use of judicial review, the 'judicial review proofing' of administrative decision-making, and, if that does not prevent challenge, then the establishment of an appeal procedure, of which the homelessness case is one example (Chapter 6). Smith's prediction that the Housing Benefit scheme will soon be in need of legislative massaging to produce a statutory appeal procedure is also reflected by Partington (Chapter 8) though for different reasons. He argues that judicial review is simply not a sensible means of challenge in the context of a system of mass application. It is a remedy to be reserved to the unusual and difficult case and alternative remedies ought to be pursued mainly on cost grounds.

There are many social welfare areas where the impact of the European Convention on Human Rights (ECHR) will increasingly make its presence felt. This is already the case, as Fennell indicates (Chapter 3), in relation to challenges against the Mental Health Review Tribunals. The current moves to find a politically acceptable solution to the problem of incorporating the ECHR will no doubt yield greater opportunities for litigants. At the time of writing, the Human Rights Bill 1988 was completing its parliamentary progress. The traditional 'sovereignty' objections to the incorporation of the ECHR have been, it would appear, elegantly side-stepped by the new device enabling the judges to make a 'declaration of incompatibility'. However, there are clearly differing judicial views, not only on incorporation *per se*, but also on the future role of judicial review in such a context. During the second reading of Lord Lester's Private Member's Bill in 1996, Lord Donaldson suggested that Lord Woolf regarded that question 'with some equanimity' and indicated his own view that any future judicial review regime, where the ECHR was incorporated, would be likely to draw the judiciary further into the policy arena (House of Lords, *Hansard*, 5 March 1996, col. 1741). It will no doubt take some time before it is clear how the new arrangements will unfold. However, one can be confident that it *will* have a significant influence on the theory and practice of judicial review.

The future of judicial review is at the crossroads, not only in respect of the oncoming influence of the ECHR but also, as Himsworth suggests (Chapter 12), because of the challenges which devolution, particularly in Scotland, will bring. It will be fascinating to learn whether the possible diversity between the English and Scottish jurisdictions will indeed develop under a European umbrella of harmonization of administrative law principally through the EC Treaty. Equally, the theme of European influence is picked up in relation to the Northern Ireland jurisdiction (Chapter 13) by Larkin, who asks whether the principle of proportionality and the emerging doctrine of legitimate expectation will not have a greater role to play in the future.

General Bibliography

Abel-Smith, B. and Stevens, R. with assistance from Brooke, R. (1967) *Lawyers and the Courts*. London: Heinemann.

Adams, B., Oakeley, J. M., Morgan, D. and Smith, D. (1975) *Gypsies and Government Policy in England: A Study of the Travellers' Way of Life in Relation to the Policies and Practices of Central and Local Government*. London: Heinemann Educational.

Adler, M. and Asquith, A. (eds) (1981) *Discretion and Welfare*. London: Heinemann.

Adler, M. and Bradley, A. (eds) (1975) *Justice, Discretion and Poverty*. London: Professional Books.

Adler, M., Burns, E. and Johnson, R. (1975) 'The conduct of tribunal hearings' in Adler, M. and Bradley, A. (eds) *Justice, Discretion and Poverty*. London: Professional Books.

Adler, M., Petch, J. and Tweedie, J. (1989) *Parental Choice and Educational Policy*. Edinburgh: University of Edinburgh Press.

Alcock, P. and Harris, P. (1982) *Welfare Law and Order*. London: Macmillan.

Allen, M. J. and Cooper, S. (1995) 'Howard's Way – a farewell to freedom', 58 *Modern Law Review*: 364.

Amnesty International (1993) *Passing the Buck: Deficient Home Office Practice in Safe Third Country Asylum Cases*. July. London.

Annual Report by the Secretary of State for Social Security on the Social Fund, 1995/96 (1996). London: HMSO.

Annual Report of the Social Fund Commissioner for 1995–96 on the Standards of Reviews by Social Fund Inspectors (1996): London: HMSO.

Arden, A., Partington, M. and Hunter, C. (1994) *Arden and Partington on Housing Law* (2nd edn). London: Sweet & Maxwell.

Asylum Aid (1995a) *'No Reason at All': Home Office Decisions on Asylum Claims*. London.

Asylum Aid (1995b) *Adding Insult to Injury: Experiences of Zairean Refugees in the UK*. London.

Asylum Rights Campaign (1996) *'The Risks of Getting It Wrong': The Asylum and Immigration Bill Session 1996 and the Determinations of Special Adjudicators*. London.

Atkinson, A. B. and Micklewright, J. (1989) 'Turning the screw: benefits for the unemployed 1979–1988' in Atkinson, A. (ed.) *Poverty and Social Security*. Hemel Hempstead: Harvester Wheatsheaf.

Audit Commission (1996) *Trading Places: The Supply and Allocation of School Places*. London: The Stationery Office.

Avron, J. (1984) 'Benefit and cost analysis in geriatric care: turning age discrimination into health policy', 310 *New England Journal of Medicine*: 1294.

Bainham, A. and Cretney, S. (1993) *Children: The Modern Law*. Bristol: Jordans.

Baker, Sir George (1984) *Review of the Operation of the Northern Ireland (Emergency Provisions) Act 1978*. Cmnd 9222. London: HMSO.

Baldwin, N., Wideley, N. and Young, R. (1992) *Judging Social Security: The Adjudication of Claims for Benefit in Britain*, Oxford: Clarendon Press.

Beckett, F. (1994) 'Hobson's choice', *The Guardian* (Education), 20 September.

Bennion, F. R. (1990) *Statutory Interpretation: A Code* (2nd edn). London: Butterworths.

Bevan, V. (1986) *The Development of British Immigration Law*. London: Croom Helm.

Beveridge, W. (1942) *Social Insurance and Allied Services*. London: HMSO.

Birkenshaw, P., Harden, I. and Lewis, N. (1990) *Government by Moonlight: The Hybrid Parts of the State*. London: Allen & Unwin.

Bradley, A. (1975) 'National Assistance Appeal Tribunals and the Franks Report' in Adler, M. and Bradley, A. (eds) *Justice, Discretion and Poverty*. London: Professional Books.

Bradley, A. (1993) 'Social security tribunals and administrative legality', *Public Law*: 218–20.

Bradley, A. W. (1987) 'Administrative law' in Vol. 1 of *The Stair Memorial Encyclopaedia of the Laws of Scotland*. Edinburgh: The Law Society of Scotland.

Bradshaw, J. and Deacon, A. (1983) *Reserved for the Poor*. London: Routledge.

Brahams, D. (1985) 'When is discontinuation of dialysis justified?', *Lancet*, 19 January: 176.

Bridges, L. Meszaros, G. and Sunkin, M. (1995) *Judicial Review in Perspective* (2nd edn). London: Cavendish.

Brierley, W. (1935) *Means-Test Man*. Nottingham: Spokesman.

Buck, T. G. (1987) 'Unemployment benefit: the "full-extent normal rule"', *Journal of Social Welfare Law*: 23–36.

Buck, T. G. (1993) 'The Social Fund and judicial review', *Journal of Social Welfare and Family Law*: 159–73.

Buck, T. G. (1995) 'The duty to give reasons', *Independent Review Service Journal*: 10–11, 19.

Buck, T. G. (1996) *The Social Fund: Law and Practice*. London: Sweet & Maxwell.

Buck, T. G. (1997a) 'Defining the "family" and families under exceptional pressures' (unpublished paper).

Buck, T. G. (1997b) 'R v Social Fund Inspector, ex parte Harper (Casenote)', *Journal of Social Security Law* (forthcoming).

Buck, T. G. (1997c) 'Consistency in implementing a social welfare discretion' (forthcoming).

Calabresi, G. and Bobbitt, P. (1978) *Tragic Choices*. New York: Norton.

Calvert, H. (1978) *Social Security Law*. London: Sweet & Maxwell.

Campbell, S. (1995) 'The criminalisation of a way of life', *Criminal Law Review*: 28.

Cane, P. (1981) 'Ultra vires breach of statutory duty', *Public Law*: 11–17.

Cane, P. (1996) *An Introduction to Administrative Law* (3rd edn). Oxford: Oxford University Press.

Central Statistical Office (1996) *Social Trends*. London: HMSO.

Childress, J. F. (1970) 'Who shall live when not all can live?', *Soundings*: 339.

Clarke, M. G. (1996) 'Scots or European lawyer – quid sum?', *Juridical Review*: 361–73.

Clasen, J. (1994) *Paying the Jobless*. Aldershot: Avebury.

Clements, L. (1996) *Community Care and the Law*. London: Legal Action Group.

Clements, L. and Campbell, S. (1994) 'Travellers rights', *Housing Adviser*, Nov./Dec.

Commission for Local Administration in England (1997) *Local Government Ombudsman Annual Report 1996/97*. London: Commission for Local Administration in England.

Commission for Racial Equality (1985) *Immigration Control Procedures: Report of a Formal Investigation*. London.

Connelly, M. (1984) 'Refugees and the United Kingdom', 168 *Race and Immigration*: 8–16.

Council on Tribunals, Special Report (1986) *Social Security – Abolition of Independent Appeals Under the Proposed Social Fund*. Cmnd 9722. London: HMSO.

Council on Tribunals (1996) *Annual Report 1995–96*. London: HMSO.

Craig, S. and Low-Beer, R. (1995) 'In defence of common humanity', 145 *New Law Journal*: 1342–3.

Cram, I. (1995) 'Towards good administration – the reform of standing in Scots Public Law', *Juridical Review*: 332–44.

Cram, I. and Bell, J. (1996) 'Towards a better public law?', 74 *Public Administration*: 239.

Cranston, R. (1985) *Legal Foundations of the Welfare State*. London: Weidenfeld & Nicolson.

Creighton, S. (1994) *Law Society's Gazette*, 22 June.

Creighton, S. and King, V. (1996) *Prisoners and the Law*. London: Butterworths.

Cripps, J. (1977) *Accommodation for Gypsies* (report to Government).

Cruz, A. (1995) *Shifting Responsibility: Carriers' Liability in the Member States of the European Union and North America*. Stoke on Trent: Trentham Books.

Dalley, G. and Berthoud, R. (1992) *Challenging Discretion: The Social Fund Review Procedure*. London: Policy Studies Institute.

De Smith, S. A., Woolf, H. and Jowell, J. (1995) *Judicial Review of Administrative Action* (5th edn). London: Sweet & Maxwell.

Deacon, A. and Bradshaw, J. (1983) *Reserved for the Poor: The Means Test in British Social Policy*. Oxford: Blackwell.

Department of Health and Social Security (1970) *Supplementary Benefits Handbook*. London: HMSO.

Department of Health and Social Security and the Home Office (1978) *Interdepartmental Committee Report on Mental Health Review Tribunal Procedures*. London: HMSO.

Department of Social Security (1985) *The Reform of Social Security*. Cmnd 9691. London: HMSO.

Department of Social Security (1996) *Improving Decision-Making and Appeals in Social Security*. Cm 3326. London: HMSO.

Diamond, P. (1996) 'The end of discretionary awards', 8(1) *Education and the Law*: 61–8.

Diplock, Lord (1974) 'Administrative law: judicial review reviewed', 33 *Cambridge Law Journal*: 233–45.

Donnison, D. (1982) *The Politics of Poverty*. Oxford: Martin Robertson.

Doyal, L. (1981) *The Political Economy of Health* (2nd impression). London: Pluto Press.

Drabble, R. and Lynes, T. (1989) 'The Social Fund – discretion or control?', *Public Law*: 297–322.

Drabu, K. and Bowen, S. (1989) *Mandatory Visas: Visiting the UK from Bangladesh, India, Pakistan, Ghana and Nigeria*. London: Commission for Racial Equality.

Dummett, A. (1994): 'Immigration and nationality' in McCrudden, C. and Chambers, G. (eds) *Individual Rights and the Law in Britain*, pp. 335–62. Oxford: Clarendon Press.

Dummett, A. and Nicol, A. (1990) *Subjects, Citizens, Aliens and Others: Immigration and Nationality Law*. London: Weidenfeld & Nicolson.

Dunstan, R. (1995) 'Home Office asylum policy: unfair and inefficient?', 9(4) *Immigration and Nationality Law and Practice*: 132–5.

Editors of the Poor Law Officers' Journal (1927) *The Law Relating to the Relief of the Poor*. London: Law and Local Government Publications.

Edwards, T., Fitz, J. and Whitty, G. (1989) *The State and Private Education: An Evaluation of the Assisted Places Scheme*. London: Falmer.

Ensor, R. C. K. (1933) *Courts and Judges in France, Germany and England*. London: OUP.

Farrington, D. J. (1994) *Law of Higher Education*. London: Butterworths.

Farrington, D. J. (1996) 'Resolving complaints by students in higher education', 1(1) EPLI: 7–10.

Feintuck, M. (1994) *Accountability and Choice in Schooling*. Milton Keynes: Open University Press.

Fennell, P. (1988) 'Sexual suppressants and the Mental Health Act', *Criminal Law Review*: 660–76.

Fennell, P. (1996) 'Community care, community compulsion and the law' in Ritter, S. *et al.*, *Collaborative Community Mental Health Care*. London: Edward Arnold.

Fennell, P. (1996) 'Law and psychiatry' in Thomas, P. A. (ed.) *Legal Frontiers*. Aldershot: Dartmouth.

Field, F. (1982) *Poverty and Politics*. London: Heinemann.

Field, F. and Owen, M. (1993) *Private Pensions for All: Squaring the Circle*. Discussion Paper No. 16. London: Fabian Society.

Findlay, L., Poynter, R. and Ward, M. (1997) *CPAG's Housing Benefit and Council Tax Benefit Legislation* (10th edn). London: Child Poverty Action Group.

Finnie, W. (1991) 'The nature of the supervisory jurisdiction and the public/private distinction in Scots administrative law' in Finnie, W., Himsworth, C. M. G. and Walker, N. (eds) *Edinburgh Essays in Public Law*. Edinburgh: Edinburgh University Press.

Finnie, W. (1993) 'Triangles as touchstones of review', *Scots Law Times*: 51.

Fitzgerald, E. (1985) 'Prison discipline and the courts' in Maguire, M., Vagg, J. and

Morgan, R. (eds) *Accountability and Prisons: Opening Up a Closed World*, pp. 29–45. London: Tavistock.

Fox, D. (1986) *Health Policies, Health Politics: The British and American Experience 1911–1965*. Princeton, NJ: Princeton University Press.

Franks Committee (1957) *Administrative Tribunals and Enquiries*. Cmnd 218. London: HMSO.

Galligan, D. J. (1986) *Discretionary Powers: A Legal Study of Official Discretion*. Oxford: Clarendon Press.

Garner, J. F. (1974) 'Students – contract or status', 90 *Law Quarterly Review*: 6–7.

Ghose, K. (1996) *The Asylum and Immigration Act 1996*. (A compilation of ministerial statements made on behalf of the government during the Bill's passage through Parliament.) London: Immigration Law Practitioners' Association.

Gilbert, B. B. (1970) *British Social Policy 1914–1939*. London: Batsford.

Gillespie, J. (1993) 'The Asylum and Immigration Appeals Bill: a review of the proposed asylum appeal rights', 7(2) *Immigration and Nationality Law and Practice*: 68–70.

Gillian, R. and Lloyd, A. (eds) (1993) *Principles of Health Care Ethics*. London: Wiley.

Gordon, R. *Judicial Review: Law and Procedure* (2nd edn). London: Sweet & Maxwell.

Gostin, L. O. (1983) 'Perspectives on mental health reforms', 10 *Journal of Law and Society*: 47–70.

Gostin, L. O. and Fennell, P. (1992) *Mental Health: Tribunal Procedure* (2nd edn). London: Longman.

Graham, E. (1980) 'Judicial review: the new procedure', 31 *Northern Ireland Legal Quarterly*: 317–38.

Gray, J. and O'Carroll, D. (1994) 'Challenging the Social Fund', *Scottish Legal Action Group*: 102.

Greer, S. C. and White, A. (1986) *Abolishing the Diplock Courts: The Case for Restoring Jury Trial for Scheduled Offences in Northern Ireland*. London: Cobden Trust.

Griffith, J. (1979) 'Restraint and activism in judicial review', 38 *Cambridge Law Journal*: 228.

Griffith, J. A. G. (1985) *The Politics of the Judiciary* (3rd edn). London: Fontana.

Griffith, J. A. G. (1991) *The Politics of the Judiciary* (4th edn). London: Fontana.

Hadfield, B. (1991) 'Judicial review in Northern Ireland: a primer', 42 *Northern Ireland Legal Quarterly*: 332.

Hadfield, B. (ed.) (1995) *Judicial Review: A Thematic Approach*. Dublin: Gill & Macmillan.

Hadfield, B. (1996) 'Introduction to JR in Northern Ireland', 1 *Judicial Review*: 170–5.

Hadfield, B. and Weaver, E. (1994) 'Trends in judicial review in Northern Ireland', *Public Law*: 12–16.

Hadfield, B. and Weaver, E. (1995) 'Judicial review in perspective: an investigation of trends in the use and operation of the judicial review procedure in Northern Ireland', 46 *Northern Ireland Legal Quarterly*: 113.

Hall, C. and Ernsberger, R. (1993) 'Playing God in the hospital', *Newsweek*, 30 August: 4.

Halstead, J. (1994) *Parental Choice and Education*. London: Kogan Page.

Harden, I. (1992) *The Contracting State*. Buckingham: Open University Press.

Harlow, C. (1981) 'Administrative reaction to judicial review', *Public Law*: 116–32.

Harlow, C. (1994) 'Accidental loss of an asylum seeker', 57 *Modern Law Review*: 620–6.

Harlow, C. (1997) 'Back to basics: reinventing administrative law', *Public Law*: 245–61.

Harlow, C. and Rawlings, R. (1984) *Law and Administration*. London: Weidenfeld & Nicolson.

Harris, A., Smith, C. and Head, E. (1972) *Income and Entitlement to Supplementary Benefit of Impaired People in Great Britain*. London: HMSO.

Harris, J. (1985) *The Value of Life*. London: RKP.

Harris, N. (1992a) *Complaints About Schooling*. London: National Consumer Council.

Harris, N. (1992b) 'Educational choice in a multi-cultural society', *Public Law*: 522–33.

Harris, N. (1993) *Law and Education: Regulation, Consumerism and the Education System*. London: Sweet & Maxwell.

Harris, N. (1995a) *The Law Relating to Schools* (2nd edn). Croydon: Tolley.

Harris, N. (1995b) 'Quality control and accountability to the consumer' in Brighouse, T. and Moon, B. (eds) *School Inspection*, pp. 46–65. London: Pitman.

Harris, N. (1995c) 'Access to justice for parents and children in respect of schooling decisions: the role and reform of education tribunals', 7(2) *Child and Family Law Quarterly*: 81–94.

Harris, N. (1996a) 'Too bad? The closure of Hackney Downs School under section 225 of the Education Act 1993', 8(3) *Education and the Law*: 109–25.

Harris, N. (ed.) (1996b) *Children, Sex Education and the Law*. London: National Children's Bureau.

Harris, N. (1997) *Special Educational Needs and Access to Justice*. Bristol: Jordans.

Hawes, D. (1958) 'Gipsies, deprivation and the law', *Legal Action*: May.

Hill, M. (1969) 'The exercise of discretion in the National Assistance Board', 47 *Public Administration*: 75–90.

Himsworth, C. M. G. (1992) 'Judicial review in Scotland' in Supperstone, M. and Goudie, J. (eds) *Judicial Review*, pp. 401–39. London: Butterworths.

Himsworth, C. M. G. (1992) 'Public employment, the supervisory jurisdiction and points *West*', *Scots Law Times*: 257.

Himsworth, C. M. G. (1994) *Housing Law in Scotland* (4th edn). Edinburgh: Butterworths/The Planning Exchange.

Himsworth, C. M. G. (1995) 'Judicial review in Scotland' in Hadfield, B. (ed.) *Judicial Review: A Thematic Approach*. Dublin: Gill & Macmillan.

Himsworth, C. M. G. (1995) 'Further *West*? More geometry of judicial review', *Scots Law Times*: 127.

Himsworth, C. M. G. (1996) 'Public law – in peril of neglect?' in MacQueen, H. L. (ed.) *Scots Law into the 21st Century*. Edinburgh: W. Green/Sweet & Maxwell.

Himsworth, C. M. G. (1996) 'Legitimately expecting proportionality', *Public Law*: 46.

Hoath, D. (1982) *Council Housing* (2nd edn). London: Sweet & Maxwell.

Hogwood, B. (1987) *From Crisis to Complacency: Shaping Public Policy in Britain*. Oxford: Oxford University Press.

Housing Benefit Review Team (1985) *Review of Housing Benefit*. Cmnd 9520. London: HMSO.

Huby, M. and Walker, R. (1991) 'The social fund and territorial justice', 19 *Policy and Politics*: 87–98.

Huby, M. and Whyley, C. (1996) 'Take-up and the Social Fund: applying the concept of take-up to a discretionary benefit', 25 *Journal of Social Policy*: 1–18.

Irvine of Lairg, Lord (1996) 'Judges and decision-makers: the theory and practice of *Wednesbury* review', *Public Law*: 59–78.

Jacob, J. M. (1996) *The Republican Crown*. Aldershot: Dartmouth.

James, R. and Longley, D. (1995) 'Judicial review & tragic choices: ex parte B', *Public Law*: 367.

James, S. (1996) 'The politics and administrative consequences of judicial review', 74 *Public Administration*: 613–37.

Jameson, N. and Allison, E. (1995) *Strangeways 1990 – A Serious Disturbance*. London: Larkin Publications.

Jamieson, G. (1992) 'The Child Support Act 1991 and the Act of Union', 37 *Journal of Law and Society*: 484.

Jennings, B. (1991) 'Possibilities of consensus: towards democratic moral discourse', 16 *Journal of Medicine and Philosophy*: 447.

Johnson, H. and Riley, K. (1995) 'The impact of quangos and new government agencies on education', 48 *Parliamentary Affairs*: 284–96.

Joint Council for the Welfare of Immigrants (1987) *Out of Sight: The New Visit Visa System Overseas*. London.

Jones, B. L. and Thompson, K. (1996) *Garner's Administrative Law* (5th edn). London: Butterworths.

Juss, S. (1986) Comment on the *Swati* case, *Cambridge Law Journal*: 372–4.

Juss, S. (1992) 'Review and appeal in administrative law – what is happening to the right of appeal in immigration law?', 12 *Legal Studies*: 364–76.

Juss, S. (1993) *Immigration, Nationality and Citizenship*. London: Mansell.

Kennedy, I. (1983) *The Unmasking of Medicine* (2nd rev. edn). St Albans: Granada.

Kennedy, I. and Grubb, A. (1994) *Medical Law – Text with Materials*. London: Butterworths.

Kincaid, J. (1975) *Poverty and Equality in Britain*. Harmondsworth: Penguin.

Law Commission (1994) *Administrative Law: Judicial Review and Statutory Appeals* (HC 669). London: HMSO.

Laws, J. (1993) 'Is the Constitution the guardian of fundamental rights', *Public Law*: 59.

Laws, J. (1994) 'Judicial remedies and the Constitution', 57 *Modern Law Review*: 213–27.

Laws, J. (1995) 'Law and democracy', *Public Law*: 72.

Lee, R. (1986) 'Legal control of health care allocation' in Ockleton, M. (ed.) *Medicine Ethics and Law* (Proceedings of the 13th annual conference of the Association for Legal and Social Philosophy). Stuttgart: Steiner.

Lee, R. and Miller, F. H. (1990) 'The doctor's changing role in allocating US and British medical services', 18(1)(2) *Law Medicine and Health Care*: 69.

Leech, M. (1992) *A Product of the System*. London: Victor Gollancz.

Leech, M. (1993) *Prisoners' Handbook*. Oxford: Oxford University Press.

Legal Aid Board (1996) *Legal Aid Handbook 1996/97*. London: Sweet & Maxwell.

Legomsky, S. H. (1987) *Immigration and the Judiciary: Law and Politics in Britain and America*. Oxford: Clarendon Press.

Lewis, N. (1989) 'Regulating non-governmental bodies: privatisation, accountability and the public-private divide' in Jowell, J. and Oliver, D. (eds) *The Changing Constitution* (2nd edn), pp. 219–45. London: Macmillan.

Lister, R. (1975) 'SBATs – an urgent case for reform' in Adler, M. and Bradley, A. (eds) *Justice, Discretion and Poverty*, pp. 171–82. London: Professional Books.

Lister, R. and Lakhani, B. (1987) *A Great Retreat in Fairness: A Critique of the Draft Social Fund Manual*. London: Child Poverty Action Group.

Little, G. (1991) 'Local administration in Scotland: the role of the sheriff' in Finnie, W., Himsworth, C. M. G. and Walker, N. (eds) *Edinburgh Essays in Public Law*. Edinburgh: Edinburgh University Press.

Livingstone, S. and Owen, T. (1993) *Prison Law*. Oxford: Oxford University Press.

Lloyd, A. J. L. (1996) *Inquiry into Legislation Against Terrorism*. Cm 3420. London: Stationery Office.

Longley, D. (1990) 'Diagnostic dilemmas: accountability in the National Health Service', *Public Law*: 527.

Lord Chancellor's Department (1996a) *Striking the Balance: The Future of Legal Aid in England and Wales*. Cm 3305. London: HMSO.

Lord Chancellor's Department (1996b) *Judicial Statistics 1995*. Cm 3290. London: HMSO.

Lord Chancellor's Department (1997) *Rights Brought Home: The Human Rights Bill*. Cm 3782. London: The Stationery Office.

Louks, N. and Plotnikoff, J. (1993) *Prison Rules – A Working Guide*. London: Prison Reform Trust.

Loveland, I. (1988) 'Discretionary decision taking in the housing benefit scheme: a case study', 16 *Policy and Politics*: 99.

Lundy, L. (1996) 'Selection on ability: lessons from Northern Ireland', 8(1) *Education and the Law*: 25–38.

Lynes, T. (1972) *The Penguin Guide to Supplementary Benefits*. Harmondsworth: Penguin.

Lynes, T. (1975) 'Unemployment Assistance Tribunals in the 1930s' in Adler, M. and Bradley, A. (eds) *Justice, Discretion and Poverty*, pp. 5–31. London: Professional Books.

MacCormick, D. N. (1978) 'Does the UK have a Constitution?', 29 *Northern Ireland Legal Quarterly*: 1.

Macdonald, I. A. (1987) *Immigration Law and Practice in the United Kingdom*. London: Butterworths.

Macdonald, I. A. and Blake, N. J. (1991) *Immigration Law and Practice in the United Kingdom* (3rd edn). London: Butterworths.

Macdonald, I. A. and Blake, N. J. (1995) *Immigration Law and Practice in the United Kingdom* (4th edn). London: Butterworths.

MacGregor, S. (1981) *The Politics of Poverty*. London: Longman.

Mackay, T. (1904) *A History of the English Poor Law*. London: King.

McShane, F. M. (1992/93) 'Crown privilege in Scotland: the demerits of disharmony', [1992] *Juridical Review*: 256–73 (Part I) and [1993] *Juridical Review*: 41–51 (Part II).

Maguire, P. (1995) 'The procedure for judicial review in Northern Ireland' in Hadfield, B. (ed.) *Judicial Review: A Thematic Approach*. Dublin: Gill & Macmillan.

Martin, S. (1996) 'Suspension of benefit and judicial review', 237 *Scottish Legal Action Group*: 140–2.

May, T. (1993) *Social Research: Issues, Methods and Process*. Buckingham: Open University Press.

Meredith, P. (1992) *Government, Schools and the Law*. London: Routledge.

Meredith, P. (1995a) 'The future of local education authorities as strategic planners', *Public Law*: 234.

Meredith, P. (1995b) 'Judicial review and education' in Hadfield, B. (ed.) *Judicial Review: A Thematic Approach*, pp. 67–98. Dublin: Gill & Macmillan.

Miller, F. H. (1992) 'Competition law and anti-competitive professional behaviour affecting health care', 55 *Modern Law Review*: 453.

Mole, N. (1987) *Immigration: Family Entry and Settlement*. Bristol: Jordans.

Mooney, G. H. (1980) 'Cost benefit analysis and medical ethics', *Journal of Medical Ethics*: 177.

Morgan, D. (1995) 'Doctoring legal ethics: studies in irony' in Cranston, R. (ed.) *Legal Ethics and Professional Responsibility*. Oxford: Clarendon Press.

Mullen, T. (1993) 'The Social Fund – cash-limiting and social security', 56 *Modern Law Review*: 64–92.

Mullen, T., Pick, K. and Prosser, T. (1995) 'Trends in judicial review in Scotland', *Public Law*: 52–6.

Mullen, T., Pick, K. and Prosser, T. (1996) *Judicial Review in Scotland*. London: Wiley.

Munro, C. R. (1995) 'Standing in judicial review', *Scots Law Times*: 279.

National Association of Citizens Advice Bureaux (1996) *A Right to Family Life: CAB Clients' Experience of Immigration and Asylum*. London.

National Audit Office (1993) *Remote Control: The National Administration of Housing Benefit*. London: HMSO.

Newdick, C. (1995) *Who Should We Treat*. Oxford: Clarendon Press.

North, P. (chairman) (1997) *Report of the Independent Review of Parades and Marches*. Belfast: The Stationery Office.

Obadina, D. A. (1989) 'The impact of judicial review on local authority decision-making processes'. University of Wales: unpublished doctoral thesis.

Obadina, D. A. (1995) 'Homelessness and the law', 1 *Judicial Review*: 244.

O'Connor, M. (1994) *Giving Parents a Voice: Parental Involvement in Education Policy-Making*. London: Research and Information on State Education Trust.

Ogus, A., Barendt, E. and Wikeley, N. (1995) *The Law Relating to Social Security* (4th edn). London: Butterworths.

Oliver, S. and Austen, L. (1996) *Special Educational Needs and the Law*. Bristol: Jordans.

Parker, H. (1993) 'Citizen's Income' in Berghman, J. and Cantillon, B. (eds) *The European Face of Social Security*, pp. 181–98. Aldershot: Avebury.

Parkin, A. (1985) 'Public law and the provision of health care', *Urban Law and Policy*: 101.

Parliamentary Commissioner for Administration (PCA) (1994) *Annual Report for 1994* (HC 7). London: HMSO.

Partington, M. (1975) 'Supplementary benefits and the Parliamentary Commissioner' in Adler, M. and Bradley, A. (eds) *Justice, Discretion and Poverty*, pp. 155–82. London: Professional Books.

Partington, P. and Bolderson, H. (1984) *Housing Benefits Review Procedures: A Preliminary Analysis*. Uxbridge: Department of Law, Brunel University.

Pigou, A. (1928) *A Study in Public Finance*. London: Macmillan.

Piotrowicz, R. 'Unincorporated treaties in Australian law', *Public Law*: 190.

Piven, F. and Cloward, R. (1972) *Regulating the Poor*. New York: Vintage.

Prison Officers' Association (1985) *Prisoners' Rights, Real or Imagined*. London.

Pritt, D. N. (1971a) *Law, Class and Society: The Apparatus of the Law*. London: Lawrence & Wishart.

Pritt, D. N. (1971b) *Law, Class and Society: Law and Politics and the Law in the Colonies*. London: Lawrence & Wishart.

Pritt, D. N. (1972) *Law, Class and Society: The Substance of the Law*. London: Lawrence & Wishart.

Prosser, T. (1981) 'The politics of discretion: aspects of discretionary power in the supplementary benefits scheme' in Adler, M. and Asquith, S. (eds) *Discretion and Welfare*, pp. 148–70. London: Heinemann.

Prosser, T. (1983) *Test Cases for the Poor: Legal Techniques in the Politics of Social Welfare*. London: Child Poverty Action Group and originally in Lister, R. (ed.) (1974), *Justice for the Claimant*, p. 242. London: Child Poverty Action Group.

Public Law Project (1995) *The Applicant's Guide to Judicial Review*. London: Sweet & Maxwell.

Public Law Project (1996) *A Memorandum to Lord Woolf on the Question of Costs and Access to Justice in Judicial Review Cases*. London.

Rafferty, F. (1996) 'Bullying case may bring new claims', *Times Educational Supplement*, 22 November.

Rahilly, S. (1995) 'Housing Benefit: the impact of subsidies on decision-making', 2 *Journal of Social Security Law*: 196.

Rawls, J. (1972) *A Theory of Justice*. Oxford: Oxford University Press.

Richardson, G. (1985) 'The case for Prisoners' Rights' in Maguire, M., Vagg, J. and Morgan, R. (eds) *Accountability in Prisons*. London: Tavistock.

Richardson, G. and Sunkin, M. (1996) 'Judicial review: questions of impact', *Public Law*: 79–103.

Robson, P. (1979) *Housing and the Judiciary*. Glasgow: University of Strathclyde.

Robson, P. and Poustie, M. (1996) *Homeless People and the Law* (4th edn). London: Butterworths.

Robson, P. and Watchman, P. (eds) (1981) *Justice, Lord Denning and the Constitution*. Aldershot: Gower.

Sachdeva, S. (1993) *The Primary Purpose Rule in British Immigration Law*. Stoke on Trent: Trentham Books.

Sachs, A. and Wilson, J. (1978) *Sexism and the Law*. London: Martin Robertson.

Sainsbury, R. (1989) 'The Social Security Chief Adjudication Officer: the first four years', *Public Law*: 323–41.

Sainsbury, R. (1994) 'Internal reviews and the weakening of social security claimants' rights of appeals' in Richardson, R. and Genn, H. (eds) *Administrative Law and Government Action*. Oxford: Clarendon Press.

Sainsbury, R. and Eardley, T. (1991) *Housing Benefits Reviews: Final Report*. York: Social Policy Research Unit, University of York.

Saltman, R. and Van Otter, C. (eds) (1989) 'Public competition versus mixed markets: an analysis comparison', 11 *Health Policy* 43.

Sandland, R. (1994) 'Travelling back to the future?', *New Law Journal*: 741.

Scannell, R. (1992) 'Primary purpose: the end of judicial sympathy?', 4(4) *Immigration and Nationality Law and Practice*: 3–6.

Schwarze, J. (1992) *European Administrative Law*. London: Sweet & Maxwell.

Searle, C. (1994) 'The culture of exclusion' in Bourne, J. *et al.*, *Outcast England*, pp. 17–28. London: Institute of Race Relations.

Secretary of State for Education and Employment (1997) *Excellence in Schools*. Cm 3681. London: The Stationery Office.

Sefton, T. (1997) 'The changing distribution of the social wage', *STICERD Occasional Paper* 21. London: London School of Economics.

Shah, P. (1992) 'Britain and Kenya: some immigration and nationality issues', 6(2) *Immigration and Nationality Law and Practice*: 35–9.

Shah, P. (1993) 'The erosion of remedies in visitor cases', 7(3) *Immigration and Nationality Law and Practice*: 93–5.

Shah, P. (1995a) 'Access to legal assistance for asylum seekers', 9(2) *Immigration and Nationality Law and Practice*: 55–8.

Shah, P. (1995b) 'British nationality and immigration laws and their effects on Hong Kong' in Menski, W. (ed.) *Coping with 1997: The Reaction of the Hong Kong People to the Transfer of Power*, pp. 57–119. Stoke on Trent: Trentham Books.

Shah, P. (1995c) 'Refugees and safe third countries: United Kingdom, European and international aspects', 1(2) *European Public Law*: 259–88.

Shah, R. K. D. (1992) 'Britain and Kenya: some immigration and nationality issues', 6(2) *Immigration and Nationality Law and Practice*: 35–9.

Smith, P. (1993) 'Reducing legal aid eligibility criteria: the impact for immigration law practitioners and their clients', 12 *Civil Justice Quarterly*: 167–87.

Smith, R. (1986) 'How good are test cases' in Cooper, J. and Dhavan, R. (eds) *Public Interest Law*, pp. 271–85. Oxford: Basil Blackwell.

Smith, T. and Noble, M. (1996) *Education Divides: Poverty and Schooling in the 1990s*. London: Child Poverty Action Group.

Social Trends (1996). London: HMSO.

Standing Advisory Commission on Human Rights (1996) *Religious and Political Discrimination and Equality of Opportunity in Northern Ireland* (Second Report). Cm 1107. London: HMSO.

Stern, V. (1989) *Imprisoned by Our Prisons: A Programme of Reform*. London: Unwin.

Stevens, A. and Gabbay, J. (1991) 'Needs assessment needs assessment', *Health Trends*: 20.

Sunkin, M. (1987) 'What is happening to applications for judicial review?', 50 *Modern Law Review*: 432–67.

Sunkin, M., Bridges, L. and Meszaros, G. (1993a) 'Trends in judicial review', *Public Law*: 443–6.

Sunkin, M., Bridges, L. and Meszaros, G. (1993b) *Judicial Review in Perspective: An*

Investigation of Trends in the Use and Operation of the Judicial Review Procedure in England and Wales. London: The Public Law Project.

Swift, P., Grant, G. and McGrath, M. (1994) *Participation in the Social Security System*. Aldershot: Avebury.

Taylor-Gooby, P. (1993) 'The new educational settlement: National Curriculum and local management' in Taylor-Gooby, P. and Lawson, R. (eds) *Markets and Managers: New Issues in the Delivery of Welfare*. Buckingham: Open University Press.

Treasury Solicitors' Department and Cabinet Office (1994) *Judge Over Your Shoulder* (2nd edn). London: HMSO.

Treveton-Jones, G. G. (1989) *The Legal Status and Rights of Prisoners*. London: Sweet and Maxwell.

Tweedie, J. (1986) 'Rights in social programmes: the case of parental choice of school', *Public Law*: 407–36.

Unwin, L. (1989) 'Learning to live under water: the 1988 Education Reform Act and its implications for further and higher education' in Flude, M. and Hammer, M. (eds) *The Education Reform Act 1988: Its Origins and Implications*, pp. 241–55. London: Falmer.

Van Gerven, W. (1996) 'Bridging the unbridgeable: community and national tort laws after *Francovich* and *Brasserie*', 45 *International and Comparative Law Quarterly*: 507.

Van Otter, C. (1989) 'Public competition versus mixed markets: an analysis comparison', 11 *Health Policy*: 43.

Vincenzi, C. (1985) 'Aliens and the judicial review of immigration law', *Public Law*: 93–114.

Vincenzi, C. (1992) 'Extra-statutory ministerial discretion in immigration law', *Public Law*: 300–21.

Wade, H. W. R. (1969) 'Judicial control of universities', 85 *Law Quarterly Review*: 468.

Wade, H. W. R. (1993) 'Visitors and errors of law', 109 *Law Quarterly Review*: 155–9.

Wade, H. W. R. and Forsyth, C. F. (1994) *Administrative Law* (7th edn). Oxford: Oxford University Press.

Walford, G. (1991) 'Choice of school at the first city technology college', 17(1) *Educational Studies*: 65.

Walker, N. C. and Himsworth, C. M. G. (1991) 'The Poll Tax and fundamental law', *Juridical Review*: 45–78.

Walsh, D. P. J. (1983) *The Use and Abuse of Emergency Legislation in Northern Ireland*. London: Cobden Trust.

Ward, M. and Zebedee, J. (1997) *A Guide to Housing Benefit and Council Tax Benefit* (18th edn). London: Institute of Housing/Shelter.

Whincup, M. B. (1993) 'The exercise of university disciplinary powers', 5(1) *Education and the Law*: 19–31.

Whiteley, P. and Winyard, S. (1987) *Pressure for the Poor*. London and New York: Methuen.

Wikeley, N. and Young, R. (1992) 'The administration of benefits in Britain: Adjudication Officers and the influence of Social Security Appeal Tribunals', *Public Law*: 228–62.

Williams, D. G. T. (1979) 'Judicial restraint and judicial review: the role of the courts in welfare law' in Partington, M. and Jowell, J. (eds) *Welfare Law and Policy: Studies in Teaching, Practice and Research*. New York: Nichols Publishing.

Winterbourne, D., Doebbler, C. and Shah, P. (1996) 'Refugees and safe countries of origin: appeals, judicial review and human rights', 10(4) *Immigration and Nationality Law and Practice*: 123–35.

Wolfe, T. (1971) *Radical Chic and Mau-Mauing the Flakcatchers*. New York: Bantam.

Wolffe, W. J. (1992) 'The scope of judicial review in Scots law', *Public Law*: 625.

Woolf, H. (1986) 'Public law–private law: why the divide? a personal view', *Public Law*: 220–38.

Woolf, H. (1992) 'Judicial review: a possible programme for reform', *Public Law*: 221–37.

Index

(Note: cases indexed often appear under short forms of their titles)